MW00450552

# A HISTORY *of the* POPES

## VICARS OF CHRIST

CHARLES A. COULOMBE

MJF BOOKS
NEW YORK

Published by MJF Books
Fine Communications
322 Eighth Avenue
New York, NY 10001

*A History of the Popes*
LC Control Number 2005927571
ISBN-13: 978-1-56731-747-3
ISBN-10: 1-56731-747-2



This special edition is published by MJF Books in arrangement with Citadel Press, an imprint of Kensington Publishing Corp. Originally published under the title *Vicars of Christ: A History of the Popes*.

The publishers would like to thank Brother Andrew Papp of the Third Order of St. Francis Charities for granting permission to reprint the illustrations of the popes for this book.



Printed in the United States of America.



VB 10 9 8 7 6 5 4 3 2 1

To His Holiness
John Paul II,
Pope, Bishop of Rome, . . .
to
His Imperial and Royal Highness
Otto von Habsburg,
Archduke of Austria, Apostolic King of Hungary, . . .
inheritor of the Western Imperial tradition;
and to
His Royal Highness
Louis de Bourbon,
Duke of Anjou
*de jure* King Louis XX of France and Navarre
this book is respectfully dedicated, in memory of the past and hope for the future

# *Publisher's Note*

Charles A. Coulombe's *Vicars of Christ: A History of the Popes* was originally published in 2003, when John Paul II was pope of the Roman Catholic Church. John Paul II's long pontificate ended with his death on April 2, 2005. After a brief conclave, German-born Cardinal Joseph Ratzinger, John Paul II's trusted confidant and chief adviser on doctrine, was elected to the papacy on April 19, 2005. He took the name Benedict XVI. A well-respected theologian, Ratzinger vowed to follow the lead of the personally popular John Paul II, promising to maintain the Vatican's adherence to fixed, traditional values and the strict letter of Catholic law. The present edition preserves the integrity of Coulombe's history as it was written, including references to John Paul II as the current pope.

# Contents

# Acknowledgments

First and foremost, thanks to my agent, Jake Elwell, and my editor, Richard Ember, for making this book a reality; to my nephew, Philip Coulombe, for saving the manuscript when it looked as if the computer was going to eat it; to the late James Francis Cardinal McIntyre; the late Father Feodor Wilcock, S.J.; the late Father Mark Falvey, S.J.; and Archimandrite Boniface Luykx for showing me what Catholic clergy can be, when they really believe; and to a host of friends for making my life bearable.

I would also like to thank such disparate groups as the Institute of Christ the King-Sovereign Priest; the Miles Jesu; the Houston Catholic Worker House; the Poor Clares of Santa Barbara; the Dominican Nuns of Hollywood; and the Carmel of Des Plaines, Illinois, to name a very few out of many, for keeping the Faith.

# A History of the Popes

## Vicars of Christ

# INTRODUCTION

THE "POPE OF ROME" is the best known and most influential moral and religious leader in the world. Pick up the paper, turn on the TV, and there he is. Every government in the world has to deal with him somehow. Love him or hate him, there is no denying his importance. It's this way today, and it's been this way since Emperor Constantine legalized Christianity in the fourth century.

In all that time, there have been wonder-working saints, lecherous murderers, and many mediocrities on the papal throne—every kind of human being imaginable. Most books about the popes have tried to either whitewash every sin any pope has committed, or make them all out to be anti-Christs. Writers seem to have left very little middle ground on this emotional topic.

The truth is there have been obviously good and obviously evil popes, controversial popes, and forgotten popes. In this book, they all have their day in court. One by one, each pope will be profiled, and their rich history, with all its pageantry, intrigue, holiness, and crime, will be unveiled.

Formosus was so hated by his successor, the corrupt Stephen VII, that his rotting corpse was disinterred and subjected to a court trial. St. Leo the Great frightened Attila the Hun into sparing Rome, while St. Gregory the Great banished the plague from the Eternal City by holding a procession. St. Leo III crowned Charlemagne emperor by surprise on Christmas Day, but John XII (himself the son of a pope) was killed by his mistress's lover, and died in her arms. John Paul II raised the popularity of the papacy to incredible heights, played a huge role in bringing down communism—and exorcised the devil from a girl during a public audience.

The history of the popes is the history of Christianity, still the dominant religion in Europe and the Americas. Understanding the papacy in its historical setting is important for understanding the modern world.

Unfortunately, this is a difficult task for the modern English speaker. A major problem is cultural. In Great Britain, as in much of northern Europe, the secular authorities threw off papal control of their churches during the Protestant revolt of the sixteenth century. Hatred of the papacy and of still-Catholic nations became a part of the British national religion, and from England this hatred was exported to and became part of the foundation of the United States, Anglo-Canada, Australia, and New Zealand. In the English-speaking world, Catholicism was worse than an enemy: it was a defeated enemy. On the one hand, this attitude produced the much-written-of "Black Legend" school of history, wherein anything the Spanish ever did was evil. On the other, it produced in popular histories an ingrained view of the papacy that veered from suspicion and contempt to pure loathing.

In the United States, this was further aggravated by the perception of Catholics as "foreigners." The following elegant quatrain was coined by a Klansman in 1920s Michigan (as told to me by his son):

*I'd rather be a Klansman, in robes of snowy white,*
*than be a Roman Catholic, in robes as black as night.*
*For a Klansman is an American, and America is his home,*
*But a Catholic owes allegiance to the Dago Pope of Rome.*

In a word, *Catholicism,* since the Reformation, has been, to a greater or lesser degree, the enemy in English-speaking lands, despite the great numbers of Catholics who have made their homes in such places since the nineteenth century. Thus anti-Catholicism becomes the one form of bigotry still acceptable in polite society.

In the sphere of history writing, this means that it is often as hard to find a fair portrayal of things Catholic in American books written today as it was to find even-handed treatment of capitalism in Soviet-era Russian histories. Thus we have the "popes can do no good" school of history.

A second genre of writing about popes is that of people—priests or lay—who, although of Catholic origins, echo slavishly the wildest charges of anti-Catholics. These people are able to claim some extra knowledge of the topic because of their supposed faith.

On a purely ideological level, moreover, the papacy is out of step with the deepest belief of the past two centuries: the cult of change. "Change is good," we repeat as a mantra. But the role of the pope from the beginning has been that of conservator or preservationist. The Coronation Oath of the pope administered since the Renaissance, declares that the new pontiff vows "To change nothing of the received tradition, and nothing thereof, I have found before me guarded by my God-pleasing predecessors, to encroach, to alter, or to permit any innovation therein; To the contrary: with glowing affection as their truly faithful student and successor, to reverently safeguard the passed-

on good, with my whole strength and utmost effort. . . ." This shows a mentality entirely different from that of most of us. (See Appendix for full text of Oath.)

The reason for this mind-set is to be found in the very notion of Catholic tradition. The Church teaches that Divine Revelation, that body of knowledge necessary to be believed if one is to be saved (such doctrines as the Trinity, the Incarnation, Transubstantiation, and so forth) ceased with the death of St. John the Evangelist, about A.D. 104. These teachings are considered to be factual things, as true of themselves as the laws of science—or more so. The pope's primary mission is to safeguard this deposit of faith from change, which would be error, so when doctrinal disputes arise he must determine what the Church has always taught on the matter. Although many are under the impression that "papal infallibility" and "defining dogma" mean that the pope can alter or originate doctrines as he pleases, the reality is just the opposite. These terms actually mean that when the pope speaks at the highest level of his authority, the Holy Spirit will prevent him from defining untruths. Thus, before the Immaculate Conception or the Assumption of the Virgin Mary could be defined, the pope of the day had to be satisfied that, despite later denials by prominent theologians (including, in the case of the Immaculate Conception, St. Thomas Aquinas), the teachings had been held by the earliest Christians.

It is this wildly different concept of truth that has most often led modern popes into conflict with the news media and governments of present day. As guardians rather than owners of the Church's doctrines, the popes are simply unable to alter the Church's stand on such topics as abortion, contraception, divorce, or women's ordination. This inability to change doctrine has not merely brought them conflict—where many modern women demand the right to abort their children—in times past certain monarchs and noblemen similarly wished barren wives killed or put aside in favor of fertile ones. New queens were easy to obtain, not so princes. Many a pope ran into conflict over this question.

Another important part of the papal conservatorship is that of safeguarding the Sacraments—in the Catholic view as necessary to salvation as right belief—and the various liturgies that embody them. J. R. R. Tolkien, for one, understood this very clearly. As he informs his son on p. 339 of his *Collected Letters* (Houghton Mifflin Co., New York, 1981):

> I myself am convinced by the Petrine [papal] claims, nor looking around the world does there seem much doubt which (if Christianity is true) is the True Church, the temple of the Spirit dying but living, corrupt but holy, self-reforming and re-arising. But for me that Church of which the Pope is the acknowledged head on earth has as chief claim that it is the one that has (and still does)

> ever defended the Blessed Sacrament, and given it most honor, and put it (as Christ plainly intended) in the prime place. "Feed my sheep" was His last charge to St. Peter; and since His words are always first to be understood literally, I suppose them to refer primarily to the Bread of Life. It was against this that the W. European revolt (or Reformation) was really launched—"the blasphemous fable of the Mass"—and faith/works a mere red herring.

Tolkien's historical conception of the papacy was reflected, oddly enough, in his *Lord of the Rings* by the figure of Gandalf, the great wizard. He belongs to no one of the nations of Middle Earth, and in a very real sense he is leader of all the free and faithful. This is so because his power is magical rather than temporal, just as the pope's is sacramental. To one character's statement "There is no purpose higher in the world as it now stands than the good of Gondor," Gandalf replies, "The rule of no realm is mine, neither Gondor nor any other, great or small. But all worthy things that are in peril as the world now stands, those are my care . . . for I also am a steward." Thus might Boniface VIII have spoken to French king Philip the fair, or Gregory VII to Emperor Henry IV, or Innocent III to King John. Gandalf also reminds one of the Fisher-King in the Grail legends, who himself is a symbol of Peter-in-the-boat, one of the earliest logos of the papacy.

Of course, this ideal view certainly did not and does not apply to all popes, by any means. As stewards or vicars of Christ, they have often failed. Infallibility does not, in Catholic teaching, protect most papal statements, or any papal actions (except beatification and canonization of saints). It will prevent a pope from defining heresy as dogma. But beyond that, the pope is prisoner of his personality, his upbringing, and his circumstances, as are we all. It is interesting to note that before Vatican II, each night before retiring the reigning pontiff went to confession and signed a renunciation of any liturgical mistakes he might have made during the day's numerous ceremonies. This last was essential if any of his clerical flock were not to seize on such an error as a precedent for his own masses.

Because the pope's flock lives in the world, and since the most pressing outside influence on any individual is that of his government, from the time of Constantine, popes have been concerned with politics. Of course, before Catholicism became legal, there were such questions as whether the faithful could serve in the imperial legions. But for the most part, papal concern with civil rule was primarily in terms of being martyred under it.

With legalization, however, came responsibility. In a period when land meant power, property and then temporal sovereignty were seen as essential if the papacy was to pursue an independent course in dealing with the great ones of this world. But these things had also the effect of sometimes diverting the popes from or even blinding them to their spiritual duties. Yet, at least as

often, temporal power has allowed them to exercise their spiritual interests freely in the face of powerful and unfriendly potentates.

All of this background is essential for a fair evaluation of the popes we are going to meet. It is manifestly unfair to judge any religious leader by one's own spiritual views or lack thereof. If the Dalai Lama does not impose Jewish or Muslim dietary laws on his flock, we cannot blame him; for that matter, we ought not to be upset with the Islamic caliphs for permitting polygamy, enjoined in the Koran. Indeed, if either had done differently, we would have to say he was a poor Buddhist or they poor Muslims. Unless we are willing to claim that our own religion is right and that of the leaders under discussion wrong (as unmodern a view as one could have), we can only judge others according to how well they safeguard their own faith, however odd it might appear to us.

So it is with the popes. If we are to be fair with them, the only evaluation we can make of each of them is whether they did well by the Church's own lights. If, in pursuit of this, many have done things that outrage our sensibilities, it should be borne in mind that our society allows many things that would have done the same for them.

A tremendous paradox is at work in the papacy. In it we see flawed human beings who attempt to exercise a position that Catholics believe partakes of and demands spiritual perfection. This creates an unending internal conflict. As Bela Lugosi observed of people at large in *Glen or Glenda?*, "One does wrong because he is right, another does right because he is wrong." Some of the holiest popes have made horrible decisions; some of the worst have, often unwittingly, done wonderful things.

This paradox continues to our own day. As noted earlier, the current pope (as of this writing), John Paul II, is an internationally known figure. Owing to his trips, his role in the fall of communism, and the activities of Vatican delegations, the Holy See has never loomed so large in foreign affairs since the end of World War II.

Within the Church, however, the papacy has probably never wielded so little control since the French Revolution. As exemplified by Archbishop Weakland of Milwaukee's rejection of Roman attempts to preserve his cathedral from radical interior alteration, and by Cardinal Mahony of Los Angeles's discounting of Vatican regulations limiting the use of lay distributors of Communion, many bishops today are "titularists"; they accept papal authority in theory, they deny it in practice.

There are, of course, historical reasons for this. One is the auto-demolition of Vatican control over dioceses initiated by Paul VI and continued by John Paul II; however, there is another. Just as in medieval Europe, similar situations developed when bishops who were wealthy feudal lords—reflecting the civil power structure of the day—had the power to snap their fingers at the pope. Today, reflecting the patterns of control in contemporary society, bish-

ops of larger dioceses are in effect CEOs of major corporations. Such cities as Chicago and Los Angeles are, in disposable income, much bigger operations than the Vatican. Add to this the widespread disbelief of Catholicism among the clergy and the corresponding ignorance of it among the laity, and it would be hard to see how things can be other than they are.

Whether this is a good or bad thing depends largely upon one's point of view. But it is important to remember, as we shall see in the lives of the popes, that the Church has known such times before, and doubtless will again. By the same token she will doubtless know further periods of revival and strength. At her heart lies what she considers to be a mystery: the changing of bread and wine into the Body and Blood of Christ. It must surprise no one that the Church's cyclical history, with themes of death and resurrection, is likewise a mystery.

The famed 1950s–60s television psychic Criswell, as un-papal a man as one is ever likely to meet, said, "We are all lighted candles in a darkened room, weary travelers on the road of life." It is the contention of the Catholic Church that she and her popes continue the work of Christ, that she is the Mystical Body of Christ; through this body alone, she maintains, can such travelers find the way to salvation. To Catholics, she is "the light that shineth in darkness," although the darkness does not comprehend it. To her enemies she is the most successful means of enslaving the mind of humanity that there has ever been. Whichever the reader believes, we will show the popes as they were and are: wielders of great power on the one hand, and weary fellow travelers of us all on the other.

## A Note On Oral Tradition and Miracles

Prior to the liberation of the Church by Constantine in 312, Church records are very sketchy. The reasons for this are not hard to figure out—the ongoing persecutions by Roman imperial authorities led to both intense secrecy on the part of Christians and destruction of many written records. Thus, unwritten tradition is an important witness to the history of the earliest popes.

Such tradition is often disregarded by modern historians, owing in no small part to their own biases. For example, let's examine St. Dionysius the Areopagite. Traditionally, this Athenian disciple of St. Paul was regarded as both the author of a number of theological treatises, such as *The Divine Hierarchies*, and the first bishop, successively, of Athens and Paris. From the time of Martin Luther, however, both his authorship and his episcopate have been challenged. So universal among scholars has this challenge become, that *DH*'s author is invariably referred to as the "Pseudo-Areopagite." It is taken for granted that the writings attached to the name "must" have been written in the second century because of their "theological complexity."

The problem with this view is that it presumes a number of "facts not in evidence" (as Perry Mason would say). The major presumption here is that Christian doctrine was not in fact taught by Christ and the Apostles, but rather, as according to H. G. Wells, it was a simple ethical notion to which a religion later accreted. But we know from the writings of such as Philo of Alexandria that the Jews of the Roman world held quite a complex theology indeed, which is to a degree reflected in the Gospel of St. John. So the argument against St. Dionysius having been unable to write complex theological tracts purely because he was a contemporary of Christ is a bit specious. Moreover, when the writings bearing his name first appear in records, they are already attributed to him. The idea that people would accept such an attribution without some kind of evidence is hard to believe. In any case, since the folk of the second century lived so much closer to the events of the apostolic era than we do, we might as well accept their version of the facts, unless we are provided with substantial evidence to the contrary. At this late date, such evidence, if it exists, is highly unlikely to surface.

In this study, therefore, we accept the given account at face value. Not only are there no really compelling arguments to the contrary (except, perhaps, our own opinions), but succeeding generations took them as truth, and these in turn affected their own behavior. If we are to understand the various characters we examine, we must follow their example.

So too with accounts of the miraculous. The standard approach is to look at a saint or a relic's supposed wonder-working capabilities and then declare that "since such things *can't* happen, the event *must* have been otherwise." But this sort of reverse reasoning is extremely unhelpful to our understanding. On the one hand, acceptance of the miraculous, and of apparitions of Christ, the Virgin, and the saints, certainly *were* accepted by the vast majority of Christians and so affected the conduct of history. On the other hand, as the work of Joan Carroll Cruz and others shows, such events have been recorded down to our own time, and many are impossible to disprove. Here, too, for both reasons, we take the accepted accounts as given. Hence, there will be no "traditionally," "supposedly," or any of the other adjectives with which writers on these topics surround them. Accept or reject them, but on the same basis that you might any historical account—and remember that they have indeed had an objective measurable effect on generations who followed.

## CHRIST AND THE CHURCH

Subjectively speaking, there are many Christs: the noble ethical teacher of H. G. Wells's imagination, earlier referred to; the seventh incarnation of the god Vishnu, beloved of Westernizing Hindus; the blasphemer of Talmudic fable; the non-material Christ Principle of the Christian Scientists; the great,

non-sacramentalizing Jesus of the Protestants; and the Christ of the Catholics.

It is the latter with whom we deal in this book. Today, many Catholic scholars enjoy pitting against each other "the Christ of Faith" and the "Jesus of history." Pleasurable for them as this pastime may be, it does not aid us in our present goal because, as we shall see, it is not the conception of Christ that has informed the papacy. Even as one may not understand the Caliphate without understanding how the caliphs saw Mohammed, so too with Christ and the popes. One may deny the divine inspiration of the Koran, but such a denial does not help in comprehending Islam.

The discovery of a fragment of the Gospel of St. Mark among the Dead Sea Scrolls helps shore up the historicity of the Gospel accounts of Jesus. Because the library at Qumran where these scrolls were taken was sealed in A.D. 70, it means that this gospel at least was in wide circulation throughout Palestine during the lifetime of Christ's contemporaries. (Since the Essenes who ran Qumran as a secluded monastery were not among the most up-to-date of their contemporaries, the presence of a gospel in their midst is worth noting, for all that they were certainly not Christians.) More important, the Gospel of St. Mark was abroad when there were still many who could refute it, if its historical accuracy was dubious. Among other things, this fact calls into question the conclusions of the whole biblical criticism industry which has grown up since the nineteenth century.

The significance of the popes to their followers is that they are *Vicars of Christ*, *visible* heads of the Church on Earth. A vicar is a representative, or a viceroy. Just as the governor-general of Canada is a stand-in for that country's queen, Elizabeth II, so, too, is the pope seen to be merely a stand-in, a steward, for Jesus Christ, held to be the *invisible* head of the Church. So who, in the Catholic conception, is He?

For starters, Jesus is the Second Person of the Holy Trinity. Obviously, much ink has been spent trying to explain what this means. In a nutshell, God is seen as a triune being, made up of three separate persons; Father, Son, and Holy Spirit. The Father eternally begets the Son, and the Holy Spirit eternally proceeds from the Father and the Son. None are subordinate to the others, and are one God, not three: indivisible, and yet distinct Persons. For God, all things are *now*, hence Christ's comment in the Gospel that "before Abraham was, I *am*." (John 8:58) This in turn hearkens back to God's self-description in the Old Testament that "I am Who am." (Exodus 3:14) Notice of the triune nature of God is seen as far back as Genesis, wherein God says "let *Us* make man in *our* image." (Genesis 1:26)

Catholics believe that the Second Person of the Holy Trinity entered time (and so, history) by incarnating in the womb of a virgin, which act was accomplished by said virgin's being "overshadowed" by the Holy Spirit. This was done to repair the damage done by the fall of Adam and Eve. Said fall

darkened human nature, made Man incapable of entering heaven, weakened his will, and darkened his intellect. In order to serve as a worthy vessel for the God-Man's appearance in our world, Mary, the Virgin chosen for this role by God "from all eternity," was conceived without Original Sin, the quality that prevented human union with God after death. This occurrence is called "the Immaculate Conception of the Virgin Mary." It is indicated in the Gospel of St. Luke, wherein the Archangel Gabriel hails Mary as "full of grace," a salutation that could not be given to any other human of the time, carrying, as they all did, the sin of Adam on their souls.

In His Incarnation, Christ acquired human nature and became a man "like us in all things save sin." The link between His Divine and human natures is called the "hypostatic union." Though He possessed two wills corresponding to each of His natures, Christ nevertheless was and is one Person.

After His birth, accompanied by various signs and wonders, Jesus' mother and foster father took Him into Egypt to avoid Herod's executioners. Returning with His parents when He was three years old, Jesus' early life was spent in obscurity, save for the incident at the Temple in Jerusalem, where He demonstrated His perfect knowledge of the Scriptures and the Law to the priests, doctors, and scribes. He reappears at the age of thirty, shortly after the death of St. Joseph, His foster father. This chronological gap, often called "the Lost Years," is unaccounted for by the canonical Scriptures, except for the cryptic comment, "He grew in wisdom among God and men." (Luke 7:52) Many writers have tried to fill in this gap with more or less fanciful explanations that Jesus spent His time among the Essenes, in Egypt, India, or Tibet, or even (among the more advanced schools) with various extra-terrestrials aboard a spacecraft or on some other planet. The likelihood, however, is that He spent this time alongside His foster father, working as a carpenter and studying the Old Testament.

Christ's ministry over the next three years is the main subject of the Gospels. In the course of it He gathered about Him a band of Twelve Apostles, who became the first bishops, and seventy disciples, who were the first lay-folk. At the Last Supper Christ ordained His apostles, giving them the power to change wine into His blood, and bread into His flesh. Ever since, this has been the central rite of His Church, of which He said, "Unless a man eat my body and drink my blood, he shall not have life in him." (John 6:54)

The next day Jesus was crucified by the Roman governor Pontius Pilate at the behest of the Jewish high priest, Caiaphas. On the Cross, Jesus offered expiation for all the sins of mankind by His own Divine death, His sacrifice of Himself; this act was united with the changing of bread and wine into His flesh and blood. Thus the description of the Mass as a sacrifice.

When He died, Jesus descended into the "Limbo of the Just," wherein were all those virtuous who had died under the Old Law; bringing Himself directly to them, He liberated them from their intermediate state. On Easter

Sunday Christ rose again, bringing the Just of the Old Testament with Him. Jesus spent the following forty days with His disciples, organizing and counseling the infant Church, and bestowing on her the seven Sacraments. Having chosen St. Peter to lead the apostles before His Crucifixion, He made him the first pope. The forty days concluded, He ascended into heaven, after first commissioning His apostles to baptize, to absolve sins, and to "make disciples of all nations." With Him went the liberated souls of the Old Law. He promised that He would be with the Church always, even to the end of time. Not least of the ways He would do this would be through the Sacraments, particularly through the Eucharist. Further, the Comforter would be sent to them. A few days later, in accord with Christ's promise, the Holy Spirit descended upon the apostles and disciples, and gave them the grace and power they would need to spread the Church, the Mystical Body of Christ, throughout the world. St. Peter and his successors in the papacy would direct the Church's efforts until the end of time, when Christ would return and take up the Church's leadership directly.

Whether one believes all of this or not, this is the view of Christ held by the Catholic Church. This is the Invisible Head of the Church Whom the popes and their subjects have tried to follow and emulate. Their success or lack thereof is the body of this book. Until the legalization of the Church almost three centuries after her Founder's death, every pope would be martyred and so honored as a saint. The same could not be said of all of their successors.

# The Apostolic Age

## St. Peter

### (32–67)

Called the "Prince of the Apostles," and originally named Simon, Peter was born in Bethsaida, a town on the northern end of Lake Genesareth. His father was named Jona, and his brother was the apostle St. Andrew. St. Philip, another apostle, came from the same town. At the beginning of Christ's ministry, Simon Bar-Jona was living with his wife and mother-in-law at his home in Capharnaum. He owned his own boat and pursued the comfortable career of lake fisherman and may be considered to have been middle class. A fisherman of the time required a certain amount of capital to own his own boat, and given the general poverty among the Palestinians of this period, such relative prosperity would stand out.

His bourgeois existence was disturbed initially by meeting St. John the Baptist, who was preaching repentance and the imminent coming of the Messiah. Together with his brother Andrew he joined the ranks of St. John's disciples, going with them to Bethania on the eastern side of the Jordan River. Accosted by messengers of the Sanhedrin, who demanded to know who this Messiah was, St. John pointed to Jesus of Nazareth, his first cousin, who was passing by. "Behold the Lamb of God," (John 1:36) he said. Andrew and another of John's band went to interview Jesus that day.

Upon his return, Andrew informed Simon that Jesus was indeed the Messiah and took Simon to Him. They traveled with Jesus, following him to Galilee for the marriage feasts at Cana, on to Jerusalem and Judea, back through Samaria, returning at last to Galilee. There Simon and Andrew returned to their fishing.

But the adventure was far from over. Working the nets with James and John, the sons of Zebedee, the two brothers were accosted again by Jesus, who said, "Come ye after me, and I will make ye to be fishers of men." (Luke 5:10) From then on, these four apostles stayed with their Master. He soon after preached the Sermon on the Mount, cured the son of the centurion at Capharnaum, then did the same for Simon's mother-in-law. Shortly after this, the college of twelve was filled, and Christ began His ministry in earnest. In a sense, our story now gets underway.

* * *

In the four Gospel accounts, Simon is shown to be headstrong and fiery, but with a streak of cowardice. Although he was not Jesus' favorite (that would be John, son of Zebedee), nor given charge of the money (that office was reserved to Judas Iscariot), Simon soon emerged as the leader of the twelve. He often spoke to Jesus on behalf of them, and in turn was given instructions for all of them by Jesus.

Finally, when Jesus and the apostles were encamped by Caesarea Philippi, His ministry reached a sort of crisis point. All sorts of expectations had been raised, and there are as many different views of who Jesus was as there were groups in Palestine. To the Sadducees, who had abandoned most Jewish doctrines but nevertheless provided most of the Temple priesthood and leadership, he was a rebel and a rival for power. To the Pharisees, who retained all points of the Jewish faith, but added to it their own notions, he was a critic with whom they nevertheless had something in common (He ate with them—a Near Eastern recognition of unity—but not with the Sadducees). To the Zealots and others He was believed to be a leader who will eject the Romans from Palestine and retake the throne of His ancestor David from the Herodian usurpers. Some believed He was a prophet, in true Old Testament style. Still others held him to be a blasphemer and Sabbath breaker. On this particular occasion, Jesus demanded of the apostles, "Whom do men say that the Son of man is?" (Matthew 16:13)

The apostles answered, "Some John the Baptist, and other some Elias, and others Jeremias, or one of the Prophets." Jesus replied, "But whom do you say that I am?" As had become customary, Simon answered on behalf of all the twelve. "Thou art Christ, the Son of the living God." Jesus then said, "Blessed art thou, Simon Bar-Jona: because flesh and blood have not revealed it to thee, but my Father who is in heaven. And I say to thee: That Thou are Peter [*Kipha*, a rock]; and upon this rock [*Kipha*] I will build my church, and the gates of hell shall not prevail against it. And I will give to thee the keys of the kingdom of heaven. And whatsoever thou shalt bind on earth, it shall be bound in heaven: and whatsoever thou shalt loose on earth, it shall be loosed also in heaven." (Matthew 16:13–20; Mark, 8:27–30; Luke 9:18–21).

This passage from the Gospel is really the charter of the papacy. As far as Catholics and some others are concerned, this is where the story really begins. For Jesus made Peter the head of His Church, and Peter's successors will rule it until the end of time. Non-Catholics often claim that Jesus' remarks cannot refer either to Jesus Himself or to Peter's declaration of faith, but that the name change means clearly that it is Peter himself upon whom the Church is to be built. They point out that the talk about keys and binding (that is, commanding) and loosing were Hebrew legal terms referring to the passing of jurisdiction from a lord to his steward. Any number of non-Catholic critics have devised ingenious alternative explanations for this episode and its wording.

But the Catholic view has at least simplicity on its side. In any case, it is their understanding which has shaped the papal office.

Peter's actions immediately following his elevation were not particularly inspiring. At the Last Supper, he assured Jesus that he will follow Him unto death; Jesus answered that Peter will deny Him before the cock crows thrice—a prophecy fulfilled. In the garden Peter fell asleep with the others while Jesus endured His agony there. After letting his anger have full rein by cutting off the High Priest's servant's ear, he then fled with the other apostles. While Jesus was questioned and tortured, Peter warmed himself by the fire and indeed made the promised threefold betrayal, for which he mourned the rest of his life. (In so doing, he shows how far subsequent popes will be able to fall from their high calling.)

Peter rapidly recovered from his fall (a recovery not always to be shared by his successors). When the women discovered the empty tomb, the angel they encountered sent a special message to Peter. Jesus appeared to Peter before the other apostles the first day following His resurrection, and then at Lake Genesareth gave him a special commission to defend and feed His flock. After Christ's Ascension into heaven, Peter was left in charge of the others.

After he came down from Mt. Olivet following the Ascension with the other apostles and disciples, Peter immediately acted as leader. He organized the elevation of Matthias in Judas's place, and after the descent of the Holy Spirit at Pentecost, he gave the first sermon to the multitude. His preaching on the life, death, and resurrection of Christ brought about the conversion of many. He took the lead in miraculous activities as well, going with John and curing a lame man at the Beautiful Gate. Preaching at the Temple's Porch of Solomon, he attracted still more converts.

Dragged before the Sanhedrin, Peter masterfully defended the Christians against all charges, and himself judged Ananias and Sapphira. The sick were brought near him so that his shadow might fall upon and heal them.

Peter's activity soon went beyond Jerusalem, as he preached throughout Judea and Galilee. After Philip the Deacon converted a large number of Samaritans, Peter and John went there to organize and bestow the Holy Spirit on them. Shortly after, he judged Simon Magus, who attempted to buy the spiritual powers of the Church for himself (although Simon himself died in an attempt to fly, many others throughout history have likewise tried to bribe the hierarchy—some with success; hence the word *simony* to describe this particular sin).

Though persecution of the Christians had continued all this time, it subsided after the chief enforcer, Saul of Tarsus, left to persecute the Christian community that had sprung up in Damascus, Syria.

Freed by Saul's departure from immediate worry, Peter evangelized the Palestinian coastal plain. In Lydda (Lod), he cured a man of palsy; in Joppa

(Yafo), he raised a girl from the dead; and in Caesarea, he converted the Roman centurion Cornelius, the first named gentile convert, and his family. Fresh from this experience, he returned to Jerusalem to find the Jewish Christians demanding to know why he had entered the house of gentiles and eaten their food. Peter replied with an account of the vision he had had at Joppa, wherein he was told to accept the gentiles. Both the apostles and people at Jerusalem accepted his defense.

Three years after his conversion experience on the road to Damascus, Paul of Tarsus returned to Jerusalem to confer with Peter, thus acknowledging his need for approval from the head of the apostles.

But this period of tranquility was not to last. In A.D. 42, Herod Agrippa I assumed the Judean throne and immediately began persecuting the Christians. The new king had James the Great, visiting from his apostolate in Spain, beheaded. He then imprisoned Peter and intended to execute him. But Peter, freed from his chains by an angel, fled to the house of the mother of a disciple, John Mark. A number of Christians were praying there. Peter told them to tell James the Less (cousin of Jesus and first bishop of Jerusalem) what had happened, and then he escaped the city.

He next set up his headquarters in Antioch, capital of Syria and third largest city of the empire. It is for this reason that he is considered founder of the Patriarchate of Antioch (a title today claimed by five prelates of as many rites—Melkite Catholic, Greek Orthodox, Syrian Catholic, Syrian Orthodox, and Maronite). From there Peter made many missionary journeys and interacted with Paul.

While Peter, James, and John worked with Jews, Paul worked with gentiles. The question of whether or not gentiles must first be converted to Judaism and accept circumcision and the dietary laws became a burning issue. A council was held of the remaining apostles and other bishops, and these gathered about A.D. 51 at Jerusalem, in what is the first Council of the Church. Peter, who at first had favored freeing gentile converts of Jewish customs, was persuaded to reimpose the Jewish ways on newcomers. Paul, whose work was primarily with gentiles, opposed him. Knowing the necessity of winning Peter to his position, Paul at length persuaded Peter to return to his own original teaching. Thus the Council of Jerusalem liberated gentile converts from circumcision and other traditions, which led the Church well on its way to a complete break from Judaism.

Some time after the Council, Peter left for Rome, capital of the empire. From this time onward, the headship of the universal Church has been bound up with the bishops of Rome. With him was his disciple Mark. Peter was Mark's primary source for his Gospel; in time, he would be sent by his teacher to Alexandria, Egypt, second city of the empire. Thus the three churchmen who claim the title of Patriarch of Alexandria (Greek Orthodox, Coptic

Orthodox, and Coptic Catholic) are all called "Successor of St. Mark," as the pope is called "Successor of St. Peter."

During his time in Rome, Peter wrote his two Epistles, worked among the converts of the city, and reunited with Paul. During the twenty-five years he spent in the city, Peter converted many among the older families of the Roman nobility. In the catacomb of St. Priscilla, located under a villa garden of the patrician Acilii Gabriliones's family on the Salarian Way, Peter instructed neophytes in the Faith. Another friendly noble, Pudens, opened his house (on the site of which is today a church dedicated to St. Pudentiana, his daughter) for worship to the Christians.

But, as always, persecution dogged the infant Church. At a time when divorce was common, the Church forbade it; open sexuality of all kinds was more or less encouraged by the authorities, and the Church insisted that it belonged solely within marriage. Infanticide was widespread, and the Church condemned it. The state declared that all gods were more or less true, and the Christians said that there was but One who might be worshiped. The emperor claimed divine honors, but the Christians refused to give them. Worse, the central act of the Christian religion, the consumption of bread and wine transformed into the Body and Blood of Christ, was kept strictly secret—this was the famed *disciplina arcani* ("discipline of the sacred mystery"). But garbled accounts of what went on during the secret ceremonies emerged, and imperial officials, angered by the other dissenting elements of the Christian lifestyle, seized upon them happily. For were the Christians not cannibals?

Under this pretext, the emperor Nero, seeking a scapegoat for his own mismanagement, made Christianity illegal throughout the empire. Thus began the first general persecution.

When the order came down, Peter decided to flee the city. As he made his way out of Rome, he encountered Christ Himself on His way in. "Where are you going, Lord?" he asked in surprise, "*Quo vadis, Domine?*" "To Rome, Peter," came the reply, "to be crucified again." Mindful of his cowardice in Jerusalem, the first pope sadly returned to the city.

As he feared, Peter was among the first wave of arrests, as was Paul. They were held in the Mamertine prison. (The chains that held Peter, along with those which bound him in Jerusalem, are venerated in a church at that location today.) The two were ordered executed. As a Roman citizen, Paul was beheaded. But Peter was merely a Judean, and so was to be crucified. Feeling himself unworthy of dying in precisely the same manner as the Lord he had denied, he asked to be crucified upside down. His request was granted, and Peter died in Nero's gardens on the Vatican Hill.

Interred in a nearby catacomb on the same small mount, his tomb soon became a place of pilgrimage. At first semisecret, it was marked by Emperor Constantine with a huge basilica, itself replaced in the sixteenth century with

the masterpiece we see today. From the time of the basilica's construction, the popes have said their major Masses over their first predecessor's tomb.

Paul, buried outside the walls of the city, on the Ostia Way, similarly had a basilica erected over his tomb. Early on, the skull of Peter was placed there as well. During the early twentieth century, when Peter's headless skeleton was brought out of his tomb, the skull from St. Paul's fitted it perfectly.

As the first pope, St. Peter established the pattern for all his successors. Like many of them, he had sinned through omission and cowardice, and occasionally through his hot-headedness. Despite Divine favor, he remained all too human. But this first and best of popes overcame all that, sustained his flock around the known world, and at the end, died for it. In his first Epistle, he laid down the basic foundation of the Church's social teaching, which has come down through the centuries:

> Be ye subject to every human creature for God's sake: whether it be the king as excelling;
>
> Or to governors as sent by him the punishment of evildoers, and for the praise of the good:
>
> For so is the will of God, that by doing well you may put to silence the ignorance of foolish men:
>
> As free, and not as making liberty a cloak for malice, but as the servants of God.
>
> Honor all men. Love the brotherhood. Fear God. Honor the king.
>
> (Peter 2:13-17)

Despite the hatred of the emperors and their civil servants for the Christians, this remained their program, as evidenced by the prayers for the emperor in the earliest liturgies, and by the service of Christians in the army and civil service. When ordered to burn incense to the emperor or his gods, they refused, and often paid with their lives. But in the end (as we shall see) they had the victory.

In the Latin Catholic calendar, Sts. Peter and Paul are honored on June 29, a Holy Day of Obligation in many countries. Until 1970, the same calendar boasted three other feasts for St. Peter: his chains were honored on August 1, his chair at Rome on January 18, and his chair at Antioch on February 22. The Byzantine and Syrian rites honor him on January 16, the Armenians on the Fifth Sunday after Pentecost.

# St. Linus

(67–76)

Linus came from Volterra, in Tuscany. Son of Herculanus, his father ordered him to Rome. There he heard Peter preach the Gospel and became a fervent Christian. His virtues, knowledge, and zeal induced Peter to consecrate him bishop and choose him as a companion for his apostolic travels. When Peter went to Jerusalem to preside at first council, he left Linus in Rome as his vicar. Linus was one of those in Rome mentioned by St. Paul in 2 Timothy 4:21: "Make haste to come before winter. Eubulus and Pudens, and *Linus* and Claudia, and all the brethren, salute thee" (emphasis mine). Returning to Rome, Peter entrusted to Linus an important mission in Gaul, centering around Besancon. There the bishop made numerous converts by virtue of his eloquent preaching.

A short time after the persecution of Nero broke out, Linus returned to Rome in order to help Peter and Paul. When they were imprisoned, he replaced them in governing the Church and was chosen by Peter as his successor (the only pope to be so selected). Linus accompanied St. Peter to his martyrdom, and afterward was helped by Marcellus and some of the other faithful to bury him.

During his reign many important events occurred, among them the death of Nero, the destruction of Jerusalem (with its Temple, thus severing the Church's last connection with Judaism), and the dispersion of the Jews, many of whom converted to the Christian faith. He wrote the Acts of Peter, particularly with regards to Peter's dealing with Simon Magus. As pope, Linus decreed, in keeping with the teaching of Sts. Peter and Paul, that women should cover their heads at worship, a tradition maintained until the 1960s. St. Linus performed many miracles; apart from raising a dead person to life, he was expert at casting out devils. On one occasion, he expelled the demon from a possessed girl who was the daughter of an ex-consul named Saturninus. Angered at his child's subsequent conversion, the angry father had St. Linus imprisoned and then beheaded. He was buried near St. Peter on the Vatican Hill.

In Volterra, San Lino, a simple convent church with a single nave, was built at the request of Raffaello Maffei on the sight where Linus's residence once stood. The high altar is surmounted by a wood panel of the Virgin and saints by Francesco Curradi and the nave displays *The Birth of the Virgin* by Cesare Dandini (first half of the seventeenth century) and *The Visitation of Elizabeth* by Cosimo Daddi 1619. The presbytery houses the funeral monu-

ment of Raffaello Maffei, which was executed by an artist from Fiesole, Silvio Cosini, in 1522.

Mentioned in the Roman Canon of the Mass, his feast in the Western Church is September 23, and in the Coptic rite July 1.

## St. Cletus
(76–88)

Cletus was the son of Emilianus, born a Roman patrician. Reigning under the emperors Vespasian and Titus, he was a disciple of Peter. As such, he accompanied his master on the latter's apostolic trips around southern Italy. Commissioned by St. Peter to do so, he established the first Christian community at Ruvo, in Apulia. Today, the underground grotto where he met with his flock is preserved as the Crypt of San Cleto, underneath the Church of Purgatory in Ruvo, where his traditional feast, April 26, is still honored.

The crypt of the church was a Roman-era spring and reservoir. In it is a small altar in front of a pillar, in which is a statue of St. Cletus; on either side are two small pools where he baptized the Ruvians in secret. His experience in shepherding and protecting this small community stood him in good stead when he was recalled to Rome after the martyrdom of St. Linus.

Cletus divided Rome into twenty-five parishes and began the custom, continued ever since, of beginning papal letters with the words "Health and Apostolic Benediction." St. Cletus chose a particular place on the Vatican Hill for the interment of the popes beside the tomb of St. Peter, and he erected a chapel on the site. This small church was the first incarnation of the great basilica of St. Peter we see today. Martyred under Emperor Domitian, he too was buried on the Vatican Hill.

There has long been confusion as to whether or not St. Cletus and St. Anacletus, who followed St. Clement I, were actually the same person. As in all of these scholarly disputes so many centuries after the event, there is an element of unreality to revisionist claims. Nevertheless, we will leave the last word in this matter to Alban Butler, author of *The Lives of the Saints:*

> Certain French critics think Cletus and Anacletus to have been one and the same person; but Orsi (t1., l. 2, n. 29, p. 282) shows them to have been distinct popes. Eusebius indeed confounds them, as he did Novatus and Novatian, and the popes Marcellus and Mar-

> cellinus; mistakes to which, from the likeness of names, the Greeks were most liable, as they wrote at so great a distance. But the Latins, who had authentic records by them, could not be so mistaken; especially the author of the first part of the Liberian Calendar, which appears, in most particulars, to be copied from the public registers of the Roman church: which authorities make it clear that Cletus sat the third, and Anacletus the fifth bishop of Rome. (Butler, *The Lives of the Saints*, vol. II p. 113)

(Given that the learned Dom Prosper Gueranger and any number of other real authorities endorsed Butler's opinion, we do so as well.) St. Cletus is mentioned in the Roman Canon of the Mass.

## St. Clement I
(88–97)

St. Clement, on the basis of his writings, is considered the earliest of the Church Fathers, those Christian writers of the first few centuries whose works are invaluable for finding the beliefs of the early Church (even today, in the Catholic Church, their unanimous agreement on any point of faith is considered infallible). He is identified with Clement of Philippians 4:3 and was a descendant of the imperial family of the Flavii. His cousin was the celebrated consul Tiberius Flavius Clemens. Born in Velletri, Latium, his memory is still treasured in that city—the cathedral there bears his name.

Son of Faustinus, a Roman senator, Clement was elected to govern the Church after the martyrdom of St. Cletus. He instituted the notaries public (*scrivani*), which were given the task of carefully recording the facts of the martyrdoms and all that the persecuted Catholics said in front of their judges and the emperors. Although a similar office had existed under the pagan authorities, modern-day notaries public owe their origins to this action. After Theodosius the Great made Catholicism the religion of the empire in the late fourth century, all civil notaries throughout the Roman dominions had likewise to be authorized by the pope. At various times during the Middle Ages, successive popes deputized this power to the leading bishop—the "Primate"—in each European country. In England this was the Archbishop of Canterbury (after the Reformation, the Protestant cleric bearing that title continued to exercise this right, and does so today. In colonial America, this

power, as with so many others, was in turn deputed to the royal governor of each colony, who then consigned it to the colony's secretary. This continued after the Revolution, which is why every American notary public is given this office under the jurisdiction of the secretary of state in his or her state of residence).

In A.D. 96, a schism occurred in Corinth, for reasons unclear. A group in that city revolted and drove away their bishop. He in turn appealed to Clement to solve the situation, since all sides would accept the pope's judgment. What makes this appeal particularly interesting historically is that St. John the Evangelist (last remaining of the Twelve Apostles and author of the Gospel and Epistles bearing his name, as well as the Apocalypse) was still alive at this point. Whether dwelling at Patmos or Ephesus, he was much closer to the scene than Clement in Rome was. Yet it was to Clement that the Corinthians turned.

In any case, the result was Clement's famous letter to the Church in Corinth. Apart from commanding the Corinthians to maintain unity with each other and all Christians, to be loyal to their bishop, and to end their schism, this letter is important for a number of other reasons. Among other things, it sets forth the doctrine of the Apostolic Succession—that is, that the Apostles laid hands on their successors, who were the bishops, priests, and deacons.

So revered was this letter that for many centuries afterward, the Corinthians read it every Sunday at the Liturgy. By some it was considered a part of the New Testament, as it still is in the Ethiopian Orthodox Church.

Clement probably compiled and composed part of the *Apostolic Constitutions*, a collection of laws and liturgy, which some modern scholars claim only date from 380. What is most likely is that their last revision took place around that time. With their analysis of then-contemporary liturgy, law, and doctrine, they offer a fascinating insight into the practices and beliefs of the early Church—a Church, which in all essentials, was identical to present-day Catholicism.

But Clement would not be allowed to rule the infant Church in peace. The emperor Trajan began the third persecution of the Christians. St. Clement, owing to his patrician heritage, was encouraged to give up his position in return for great promised rewards. He refused and was condemned to exile and hard labor in the mines of the Tauric Chersonese (Crimea), where criminals were routinely deported. There the pope found about two thousand exiled Christians. Clement immediately began to guide them, and he miraculously found a spring to relieve their lack of water. Due to his preaching and example, many of the pagan exiles converted as well. So displeased was the imperial court by this event that the pope was ordered bound to an anchor and drowned in the sea.

In 860, Sts. Cyril and Methodius, on their way back from the Khazars,

found St. Clement's relics in Crimea and brought them back to Rome. A church had been built on the site of the town house of the Flavii, and there the relics of St. Flavius Clemens, the martyred consul, had been enshrined. The body of St. Clement was placed under the altar next to his kinsman, and there, in the crypt of the Basilica of San Clemente, they remain today, watched over by Irish Dominicans.

In 988 an embassy from Rome to Prince Vladimir the Great (Christianizer of Russia and Ukraine) carried some relics of St. Clement and his disciple—St. Titus—as a gift. These relics were placed in the Church of Our Lady (Desiatynna) in Kiev, which was set up by Prince Vladimir who further dedicated his royal chapel to St. Clement.

In the eleventh century, Prince Yaroslav the Wise was proud to show St. Clement's relics to French ambassadors who had come to ask his daughter Anna to marry their king Henry I. He further ordered the painting of the pope's icon, which remains in the Cathedral of St. Sophia to this day.

In 1147, the bishop of Chernihiv—Onuphry—thanks to St. Clement's relics, claimed the right of the Church of Kiev to elect a metropolitan regardless of the wishes of the patriarch of Constantinople: "We have St. Clement's head, just as Greeks ordain (metropolitans) by the hand of St. John."

In Kievan Rus, the cult of St. Clement expanded and churches were built in his honor. Byzantine priests tried to counteract the expanding of the cult of the convict pope, as they now called him. Clement was a powerful symbol of the former unity of Rome and Constantinople despite the ever-growing schism between those two patriarchates. Certainly he may be invoked by those seeking the reunion so deeply wished for by the present-day holders of those offices. The fate of St. Clement's relics in Kiev after the Mongol invasion of 1240 and the destruction of the Church of Our Lady remains unknown.

Meanwhile, the church that had housed the relics and the anchor of St. Clement in Crimea was soon submerged under the Black Sea. But the waters receded yearly around the Feast of St. Clement so that people could go into the church to serve liturgies and honor his memory.

So, today, the Russian Catholics and Orthodox, and the Ukrainian Catholics and Orthodox, all claim St. Clement as their founder, since all four declare themselves the successors of the church in Kievan Rus. In 1963, Pope John XXIII founded the Ukrainian Catholic University of Pope Clement in Rome.

Because of this devotion in both East and West, he is honored liturgically throughout Christendom. In the Latin Calendar, his feast is November 23; he is the patron of the dioceses of Velletri (being a native of the place) and Seville, Spain (liberated from the Moors on his feast day). The Byzantine and Syrian churches honor him on November 24, and the Russians the next day.

His named is invoked daily in the Roman Canon of the Mass, and in the Syrian and Coptic liturgies as well.

St. Clement is patron of mariners (due to his drowning), stonecutters and marble-workers (because of his work in the mines). Blacksmiths and bakers claim him as well. Venerated in Scandinavia after the Vikings converted (in token of their seagoing interests), his name was given to the church Danish sailors frequented in medieval London—St. Clement Danes. Even after the Reformation, blacksmiths continued to celebrate his feast by electing one of their own to impersonate him and preside over their revels. In the English countryside, English schoolchildren used, until the end of the nineteenth century, to go from door to door asking for apples (beloved of blacksmiths, perhaps for their utility in quieting horses) in St. Clement's name—the custom may survive in a few places yet. Thus, one of the earliest witnesses to papal primacy has continued to be honored in England and Russia—two countries notable for denying obedience to his successors.

## St. Anacletus

**(c.97)**

Just as St. Clement was the last of St. Peter's successors to be consecrated a bishop by him, Anacletus was the last of them to be ordained a priest. He served as St. Clement's vicar for three years while his predecessor was in exile. Born in Athens, he ordered, while pope, that a bishop should be consecrated by no less than three other bishops (which custom, as a rule, is retained today); that clerics should be ordained by their own bishops; and that all should receive communion after the consecration at Mass. He was reigning when St. John the Evangelist was brought to Rome to be boiled in oil (unsuccessfully) before the Latin Gate. Anacletus further decorated the chapel by the tomb of St. Peter. At last, after a pontificate of nine years, he was executed.

## St. Evaristus
(97–105)

Evaristus was a Hellenized Jew of Antioch, Syria; his father was a native Jew of Bethlehem. It was during his pontificate that St. Ignatius of Antioch, a Church Father whose letters are particularly important for the light they shed on the beliefs and practices of the early Church, was brought to Rome to be martyred.

Evaristus further developed the work of St. Cletus in dividing Rome into parishes; he decreed that seven deacons were to stand beside the bishop when the bishop proclaimed the Gospel. Considering the role of the clergy in Rome in selecting popes, this organization was not only important at the time, but was the beginning of the College of Cardinals. (Even today, every cardinal-priest, even when archbishop of a large foreign city, is also pastor of one of these Roman parishes.) Moreover, Evaristus ordered that Christian marriage vows must be pronounced in front of and the union blessed by a priest.

Inspired by the ceremonies around the opening of Solomon's Temple as described in the Old Testament, Evaristus regulated the ceremonies to be observed in the consecration of churches—small and unobtrusive as they had to be at that time. He was martyred by order of the emperor Hadrian. His feast is October 26 in the Roman calendar.

## St. Alexander I
(105–115)

Roman by birth, Alexander became pope after having preached in Rome and converted many pagans. Among his most notable converts was a prefect of Rome, Hermetus, with his family and more than a thousand of his slaves.

As pope, Alexander ordered the mixing of wine and water at Mass, as well as the blessing and use of holy water (combined with salt, itself symbolic of eternity and purity).

His interrogation by Aurelianus, an emissary of Emperor Hadrian, and the

torments Alexander endured are described in the still extant nearly contemporaneous history of his martyrdom. He was beheaded with the priest Eventius and the deacon Theodulus on the Via Nomentana. In 834, some of his relics were sent to the diocese of Freising, Germany. Most remain under the high altar of the Dominican church of Santa Sabina in Rome, where both Sts. Dominic and Thomas Aquinas lived at various times. St. Alexander's feast in the Latin Church is May 3.

## St. Sixtus (Xystus) I

(115–125)

A Roman patrician born, Sixtus's father, a scion of the Elpidia family, was named Pastor. Unfortunately, like most of the pre-Constantinian, we are not aware of the exact circumstances of his election, owing to the destruction of records. As pope, Sixtus made three decrees of importance: that none but those in holy orders should touch the sacred vessels (a decree followed until the 1960s); that bishops who had been summoned to see the pope would not be received back by their diocese without papal authorization; and that after the Preface at Mass the Sanctus (which symbolizes the praise of God by the angels in heaven, and which had been said by the priest alone) would be recited by priest and people together. He too was martyred, with a feast day of April 6 in the Roman calendar. The Italian town of Alatri celebrates the feast of the transport of his relics on January 11.

Buried near the other popes on the Vatican Hill, St. Sixtus I's body remained there until 1132. In that year the reigning pope permitted its transportation from Rome to Alife, a small town in the province of Caserta, where a terrible plague was raging; the locals believed that Sixtus's relics would work a miracle against the plague.

Near Alatri the mule transporting the reliquary stopped and refused to continue. The bishop of Alatri intervened and ordered the stubborn animal brought to his cathedral, where it halted. It was then decided to give a finger of the saint to carry to Alife, while the remainder of the body remained in Alatri. Hidden during the invasion of the Saracens, for four centuries the remains were lost until the Wednesday after Easter of 1584, when they were discovered by Bishop Donato. For this reason, St. Sixtus was named patron of the city. Ever since, January 11 has been the great festival of Alatri, with a solemn Mass and procession.

## St. Telesphorus
### (125–136)

Born to Greek parents in Thurio, Calabria (part of Magna Graecia, and whose parish church is dedicated to her most famous son today), St. Telesphorus preached very fervently in Rome and converted many pagans. Prior to his elevation to the papacy, he spent time on Mount Carmel, in Palestine, with the hermits there, and so is claimed as one of their own by the Carmelites. He introduced the Midnight Mass of Christmas, made fasting during Lent obligatory, and placed the *Gloria in Excelsis* (a prayer of praise to Christ as God) in its current location in the Roman Mass. In Telesphorus's time, the Gnostic heretics Cerdo and Valentinus first came to Rome. Martyred under Emperor Antoninus Pius, St. Telesphorus's feast is January 5 in the Roman, February 3 in the Carmelite, and February 22 in the Byzantine calendars.

## St. Hyginus
### (136–140)

Born in Athens, Greece, after Hyginus was elected pope he organized the degrees of the clergy. At the time of his accession, Antoninus Pius had altered his policy regarding the Christians. Persecutions continued in various places in the empire, but the emperor himself ordered his governors to leave them alone.

Trouble of another sort awaited Hyginus. He was forced to anathematize and excommunicate the heretic Cerdo. Cerdo taught that there were two Gods. One was the difficult and annoying Yahweh of the Old Testament; the other was the nice fellow of the New Testament, who sent his son to earth to rescue humanity from the tyranny of Yahweh. This was Jesus Christ, who was not really incarnate or crucified, but only appeared to be. In essence, this was dualistic Gnosticism, and it would crop up from time to time throughout the history of the Church. Some of its more extreme adherents held that, since Yahweh was evil, all the heroes of the Old Testament were also evil, and their opponents good. These notions arose from the old idea that matter (and hence,

its creator) was evil and a trap for the souls of mankind. The good god was the creator of spirit alone.

The Egyptian Platonic philosopher, Valentinus had come to Rome with Cerdo. His was a more refined and elegant teaching, although at root equally dualistic. He maintained that from the real God and creator of the universe had proceeded thirty successive aeons or emanations, each progressively more physical and less perfect. The last of these was the master of this world, and Jesus had been sent from the True God to save humankind from this master. Hyginus, a very mild man, who condemned only when he felt it absolutely necessary, refrained from excommunicating—that is, banning from reception of the Sacraments—Valentinus. (Interestingly enough, although many authorities claim that the Church only fixed the number of Sacraments at seven during the Middle Ages, the *Gospel of Philip*, a text composed by Valentinus's followers about this time, actually enumerated the same seven Sacraments we have today.)

A word about "Gnosticism" is important at this point, because it is a word that recurs throughout Church history to the present. It comes from the Greek word *gnosis,* which in this context meant "saving knowledge"—that which the individual needs to know to be saved. In later times, Gnosis would come to mean almost exclusively the kind of dualist beliefs just seen. But at this time, it was a word like "democracy" today. Everyone claimed to have it, orthodox and heretic alike. For many, it was indeed the secret understanding that matter was a trap from which the soul must escape (rather like today's Christian Science and New Thought). But for others, such as St. Clement of Alexandria (d.c. 217), true Gnosis was simply Christian orthodoxy. For St. Clement, the real Gnostic was the informed Catholic. Thus we see the danger of assigning modern definitions to historical use of words.

St. Hyginus was martyred after four years in the papacy, despite the emperor's policy. His feast at Rome is January 11, and at Athens, January 19.

## St. Pius I

**(140–155)**

Born in Aquileia, the son of Rufinus, Pius I faced the same doctrinal problems that had begun in Hyginus's reign. In addition to Cerdo and Valentinus (whom he finally excommunicated, despite his predecessor's reluctance), Pius had to deal with yet another teacher of similar doctrines from Pontus, Marcion. He, too, Pius excommunicated.

Pius's brother, Hermas, is the author of *The Shepherd*, a book that was held by many of the Church Fathers, such as Sts. Irenaeus, Jerome, and Athanasius, to be second only to Holy Scripture itself as a source of teaching—in many churches it was read at Mass. In addition to moral and doctrinal teachings, Hermas gives guidance for Christians under persecution.

The relative peace of the past few pontificates continued and allowed Pius to regulate internal affairs of the Church more closely. He made several decrees, most notably one ordering forty days of penance for priests who allowed any drops of the Precious Blood to reach the ground during Mass. Pius ordered that these drops must be taken up by the priest's lips, the dust gathered and burned, and the ashes thrown into consecrated ground. Similar regulations prevailed until after Vatican II, although little reverence is shown such spillage (or dropped Eucharistic hosts) today. He also ordered that Easter must always be celebrated on a Sunday.

Pius turned the houses of Pudens and Praxedes into churches (on their sites today are the churches of Santa Pudentiana and Santa Prassedes, filled with ancient mosaics) and often officiated there himself. He also welcomed the famous apologist and Church Father St. Justin Martyr, a former pagan philosopher who turned his skills to the Church's use (and later was martyred). Pius was martyred in his turn, and his feast in the Roman Calendar is July 11.

# St. Anicetus

(155–166)

Anicetus was born in Emesa (modern Homs), Syria. Most notable of his decrees was the one forbidding clerics to take too much care of their hair, which was considered a form of vanity in the consecrated.

St. Polycarp, student of St. John the Evangelist and bishop of Smyrna (modern Izmir, Turkey) visited Rome in Anicetus's time to participate in a conference on one of the longest-lasting controversies in Christendom—figuring the date of Easter. In Asia Minor, Easter was observed on the day of Passover itself, whatever day of the week it might fall on. But in Rome (and most of the universal Church followed this decision) Christ's rising from the dead was celebrated on the Sunday following Passover.

Although the conflict, which placed Polycarp and Anicetus on opposite sides, was unresolved (as it remains), "the bonds of charity were unbroken" (an example, perhaps, for later Catholics and Orthodox). Anicetus allowed Polycarp to celebrate Easter in Rome on the date he was accustomed to in Smyrna. Moreover, during his stay, Polycarp helped the pope combat heresy and convert pagans.

There was another joy to Anicetus's pontificate. Marcion, a bishop who had taught his own variety of dualistic Gnosticism, was reconciled to the Church on the proviso that he try to convert his followers. This he was trying to do when he died.

Anicetus was also martyred. Buried in the cemetery of St. Callistus in 1604, his relics were given by Pope Clement to the prince of Hohenems, who put them in the chapel of his palace in Rome. St. Anicetus's feast is April 17.

## St. Soter
### (166–175)

St. Soter was born in Fondi, Campania, Italy. He wrote a letter to the Church at Corinth reprimanding its members for their sexual behavior and their easy readmittance of public sinners to communion. The bishop, Dionysius, replied that the Corinthians would obey the letter and would read it at every liturgy.

Soter sent aid to the Christians condemned to the mines in Asia and fought the heresy of the Montanists in Africa (these were sort of like Pentecostals, claiming to speak in tongues, and so on, and converted Tertullian, a noted Christian writer). He also decreed that consecrated virgins (nuns) were not to touch altar cloths or offer incense in church, in order to maintain the sanctuary as a preserve for those in holy orders alone. Another of his decrees ordered all save the gravest of sinners should receive communion on Maundy Thursday in remembrance of the Last Supper. St. Soter was martyred during the renewed persecution ordered by the new emperor, Marcus Aurelius, and his feast day is April 22.

## St. Eleutherius
### (175–189)

Eleutherius was either a Greek or an Albanian (both nations claim him), born in Nicopolis (modern Prevesa), Epirus (on the Greek side of the current Graeco-Albanian border), and had served as deacon to St. Anicetus. At the beginning of his pontificate, St. Ireneus, bishop of Lyons and disciple of St. Polycarp, brought a letter from his flock, appealing to the pope to give peace to the Church in their city by condemning the Montanist heretics there. He also reported the martyrdom of forty-eight Christians there.

During the reign of Eleutherius there appeared two new heretics: Blastus, who taught that God had created evil, and Florinus, who held that the West should accept Asia Minor's date for Easter, against whose teachings the pope and St. Ireneus fought. Ireneus, bishop of Lyons and a native of Smyrna, had

been a student of St. Polycarp, who himself had been taught the Faith by St. John the Evangelist and wrote at this time his famous book *Against the Heresies*, which is still renowned. St. Eleutherius renewed his predecessors' condemnations of the teachings of Marcion, Valentinus, and Cerdo, as well as continuing the struggle against the Montanists. These last were becoming extremely powerful because they were helped by the able pen of Tertullian, a North African writer who is considered a Church Father, despite having embraced a heresy.

A minor king of the Britons, Lucius, visited Eleutherius as well. It is unknown precisely where Lucius's territory lay, though various writers have identified it with various places—some pointing to Gloucestershire, others to Wiltshire, and still others elsewhere. But about the year 182, Lucius appealed to Pope St. Eleutherius for instruction in the Faith. The pontiff responded by sending him two missionaries: Faganus and Deruvianus. They baptized Lucius, making him, as eighteenth-century English author of the *Lives of the Saints,* Alban Butler, happily remarks, "the first Christian King in Europe." Lucius founded the church of St. Peter-upon-Cornhill in the city of London; Thean, pioneer bishop of the city, constructed the first building on this site with the help of Lucius's butler, Ciran. Meanwhile, Faganus and Deruvianus baptized more Britons and organized a hierarchy.

Eventually, Lucius gave up his throne and left to preach the Faith on the continent. First in Noricum, around Augsburg, and then in Rhaetia, centering at Chur, he evangelized the locals. Persecution in the latter place forced him to take refuge on a hill called to this day *Sankt Lucius Steig*—the "Hill of St. Lucius." Finally, he was caught and martyred. His relics are at the Cathedral of Chur, of which diocese St. Lucius is patron.

St. Eleutherius himself was martyred as well, during the confusion shortly after the death of Marcus Aurelius's more pacific (toward the Christians, that is—he liked to fight in the Colosseum as a gladiator) son Commodus. His feast day is May 26.

## St. Victor I
(189–199)

This pope, born in North Africa of Latin parents, was renowned for his energy. He convened synods in various parts of the Church to settle the Easter controversy. At a Roman synod, he finally excommunicated the churches of Asia Minor for insisting on keeping Easter on Passover, although St. Ireneus begged him not to. Victor also renewed the condemnations of the Montanists and excommunicated the Roman priest Florentinus, another Gnostic, and Theodotus of Byzantium, a Monarchian. This last group taught that Jesus was simply a regular man in whom the Holy Spirit had taken up residence after His baptism in the Jordan River. Victor further decreed that baptism might be administered with any natural water, rather than just holy water.

He also received control of a cemetery on the Appian Way, donated by the noble maiden, St. Cecilia. Known today as the patroness of music, she would later be martyred for her refusal to embrace paganism and for converting her husband to the Faith. It was her family burial place; although it passed out of the hands of the aristocratic clan called the "Caeciliaii," their greatest daughter would indeed be buried there, in time. This place would play a large role in Church history. Martyred under Septimius Severus, St. Victor's tomb is in St. Peter's, and his feast is July 28.

# Stability and Persecution

## St. Zephyrinus
(199–217)

The pontificate of St. Zephyrinus was troubled by the persecution of Septimius Severus. This pope consolidated the pontifical supremacy over the bishops and fought against the heresies of the Montanists and the Encraitites, yet another dualist sect who taught that marriage and fornication alike are evil, and that only virgins may be saved.

Zephyrinus renewed the discipline of the Church toward adultery and immorality. Tertullian, as mentioned, now a Montanist, opposed this decision in his treatise *On Chastity*, for which Zephyrinus excommunicated him. The reproach of avarice and other sins levied against him by St. Hippolytus, who felt that Zephyrinus's moral judgments were too lax, seems not to have been deserved.

A well-trained administrator, if not a theologian, Zephyrinus summoned to his side Callixtus, a very holy man who had lived outside Rome, at Antium (modern Anzio). The pope ordained Callixtus deacon, and placed him in charge over the cemetery given by St. Cecilia, which ever since has been known as that "of St. Callixtus." The subterranean nature of this and the other cemeteries that came into Christian hands led them to be called "catacombs."

The catacombs are important witnesses to the beliefs of the early Church—almost as much as the writings of the Church Fathers. Although we think of them as secret, they were not. The authorities knew of them, and despite the fact that the pagan Romans generally cremated their dead, the imperial authorities did not molest the tombs (although they sometimes seized them during persecutions). Masses were said on top of the tombs; thus arose the custom, prevalent until the 1960s, of having relics of the saints laid into each altar.

At this time, the arguments over the exact relationship between the human and the divine natures of Jesus that had been brewing reached a fever pitch. Theodotus and his disciples organized a church of their own and persuaded Natalis, a priest who had been tortured for the Faith, to act as their pope. But after a while, Natalis began to suffer torments in dreams, which he believed were God's punishment on him. Putting on sackcloth and ashes, he threw

himself at the feet of the pope in tears and begged to be reconciled. This Zephyrinus did gladly.

But a second difficulty would be much worse. In Rome there was a great theologian, Hippolytus. He initially taught that the Divine *Logos* (the Word) became man in Christ, that He differs from God the Father in every particular, and that Christ is the intermediary between God and Creation. What this meant, in fact, was that Christ was not God—a denial of the Trinity. As might be expected, a school arose in opposition to Hippolytus's teachings. These "Modalists," as they were called, held that it was not the Logos but the Father who had become incarnate in Christ, and that it was the Father rather than the Son who had died on the Cross. This was another denial of the Trinity, albeit from the opposite angle. In either case, the Divine nature of Christ was downgraded, which led to various other heresies being condemned; without the Divinity of Christ, the whole doctrinal structure of the Faith would collapse, and His sacrifice become meaningless at best, absurd at worst.

Asked to mediate, Zephyrinus declared that he worshiped only one God, Jesus Christ, but that it was the Son and not the Father who had been crucified. He refused to condemn either side as heretical.

This simply made Hippolytus angry. Above all, he blamed Callixtus, as Zephyrinus's closest counselor and expert theologian. The die was cast for the Church's first formal schism.

St. Zephyrinus's relics are in the church of San Silvestro in Capite, Rome. His feast is August 28.

## St. Callixtus (Callistus) I

(217–222)

Callixtus's election to the papacy caused Hippolytus to withdraw from communion with him. His own adherents declared Hippolytus Bishop of Rome, thus making Hippolytus the first of a number of anti-popes.

But what sort of man was Callixtus? He was born a slave, and at adulthood was owned by Carpophorus, a Christian. For his own faith he was sent to the mines of Sardinia, but he was able to return during the tolerant reign of Emperor Commodus when, as mentioned previously, he settled at Anzio. Because of his reputation as one who had suffered for the Faith, he was called to Rome by St. Zephyrinus.

The Church that Callixtus headed had grown considerably since the days

of St. Peter. Not only were large numbers of Christians to be found throughout all the cities of the empire, in Rome itself they lived at the imperial court. Also in Rome, Christianity appealed especially to the highest and the lowest of classes—the ancient nobility that predated the reign of the emperors, and the slaves. The nobles, who had watched as their city fell from the supposed austere virtue of its (and their families') youth and became corrupted in every manner saw in the new religion salvation not only for themselves as individuals but for Rome. To the slaves, whose lives were a never-ending hardship and considered worthless by society, Christianity offered personal hope and dignity. This fellowship that transcended class was a scandal to Roman society, dominated as it was by the "new classes," who owed their positions to the very corruption and hardship which nobles and slaves loathed. So too were the rigid marriage customs of the Christians, who permitted no divorce. However repugnant Christianity might be to contemporary mores, it was growing. Some emperors tried to suppress it, others to ignore it. But nothing, not even the growth of heresies, seemed able to stop it.

Such rapid growth meant, too, that Christian discipline needed to be adaptable. What served for a small band of fiery apostles could not do likewise for a supranational body that encompassed every sort of individual. The challenge facing Callixtus was to make this adaptation without sacrificing what was essential.

Heretofore, it had been the custom to rigidly exclude from the Sacraments any Christian who had committed adultery and fornication. Because of this, many catechumens—those who, convinced of the truth of Catholicism, were studying it in preparation for becoming Church members—postponed their baptisms until they were quite old, or in danger of death. Since Christ had taught that none might gain heaven unless they were baptized with "water and the Holy Spirit," this meant that many souls were in grave danger.

To remedy this situation, Callixtus decreed that those guilty of sexual crimes might return to the Sacraments after due penance. He ruled that early baptism was preferable, and, moreover, that the committing of a mortal sin was not, by itself, to be considered sufficient to depose a bishop. He attributed his power to alter custom in these regards to the power of loosing and binding given St. Peter and his successors. As Christ had given them complete power to forgive sins, Callixtus declared that these changes were thereby within his authority. He made it quite clear that within the Church there was to be no distinction between slave and free, low or great. In violation of the civil law, Callixtus declared that noble ladies might marry slaves or commoners. Further, he declared that the laws of the Church regarding marriage, having been laid down by Christ, took precedence for the Catholic over those of the state.

Though no one who claimed to be Christian dared disagree with the last named declaration, some could and did dispute the rest of his program.

Tertullian, who was smarting over being condemned as a heretic, and Hippolytus, who so far as he and his followers were concerned *was* pope, disagreed violently. In the latter case, the anti-pope, free-born himself, could not tolerate the notion that there could be any kind of spiritual equality between those whom God had caused to be born in different social classes, or that the ignorant could be considered the same with the educated in the eyes of God. Nothing could redeem Callixtus in Hippolytus's eyes—not even the pope's condemnation of the Modalist heretics, the lack of which condemnation by St. Zephyrinus Hippolytus had blamed on Callixtus.

Nevertheless, Callixtus paid his critics no heed, during the period of peace secured by the reign of Emperor Alexander Severus (indeed, it was he who established the quarterly fasts called the "Ember Days," observed in the Latin Church until Paul VI abolished them in 1966). Although the emperor's father, Septimius, had persecuted the Christians fiercely, he had taken one to wife—doubtless due to their reputation for marital fidelity. Alexander, while he would not embrace his mother's religion, nevertheless would not persecute it.

Callixtus would meet his end neither from official persecution nor from the acts of his enemies among the Christians, but rather from a Roman mob. Across the Tiber in what is now called the Trastevere quarter, there was an old tavern—*Taberna Meritoria*. During the reign of Caesar Augustus, a spring of oil had emerged in the tavern's floor and flowed for a whole day before vanishing. Though the local pagans made no claim as to what the significance of this event was, they considered it miraculous. Because it occurred at the time of Christ's birth, the Christians maintained that it had been a sign for them. During Callixtus's pontificate, the tavern came into the hands of Christians, who turned it over to the Church. Taking advantage of the peace given Catholics by Alexander Severus, Callixtus turned the place into a chapel. Although it was owned by the Christians who worshiped there, the local tavern keepers' guild disputed their rights to it. The question was brought before the emperor, who ruled in favor of the Christians, saying that "it was better that God should be worshiped there, in whatever fashion, than that it should be given over to revelry."

This did not sit well with the local mob. They grabbed Callixtus after he had said Mass in the chapel one day and threw him into a nearby well, where he drowned. Afraid of what they might do to his body, the Christians did not bury him in the catacomb that bears his name, but in another, on the Via Ardeantina.

Nevertheless, the Christians retained control of the tavern-chapel. Eventually, on its site was built the great basilica of Santa Maria in Trastevere. Under its high altar is the final resting place of the relics of St. Callistus, and nearby is the small chapel of San Callisto, which contains the well in which the pope was drowned. His feast is October 14.

## *St. Hippolytus*

*Anti-Pope (d. c.236)*

Hippolytus was the first of the anti-popes; we have already seen how he attained that distinction. Probably, he was an Alexandrian Greek, who came to Rome early in life, became a disciple of St. Irenaeus, and was ordained a priest. He certainly was one of the greatest scholars and writers of his day. Although most of his works have been lost, one that survives in its entirety is his chilling *Antichrist*, a vision of the Apocalypse. A strenuous opponent of the Christological heresies of his day, he went so far as to condemn both Sts. Zephyrinus and Callixtus I for not condemning the Modalists. By the time the latter did so, Hippolytus was in full swing, and not inclined to relent—the more so because St. Callixtus's lenience and egalitarianism offended Hippolytus's rigorist tastes.

Hippolytus's few supporters continued to recognize him as pope during the pontificates of SS. Urban I and Pontian. During the latter's reign, Hippolytus wrote a scathing (and libelous) biography of St. Callixtus I, the *Philosophumena*, which served both to degrade that pope and justify Hippolytus's position.

Among his surviving works is one he wrote in 215, before the schism. Entitled *The Apostolic Tradition*, it is an extremely valuable exposition of the liturgy of that time. Of interest to modern readers is the widespread notion (popularized at the time of its introduction in 1970) that the newly written Eucharistic Prayer II of the Catholic New Mass was taken from St. Hippolytus. In reality, as Michael Davies observes in his *Pope Paul's New Mass* (Angelus Press, 1992):

> Thus we do not know to what extent the text we have corresponds to what Hippolytus actually wrote. All the scholars who have studied it agree that during its history it has suffered additions and modifications with each successive edition. Such scholars as Ratcliff and Dix have taken a very critical attitude to its textual integrity. The most controversial section of the entire text is the Eucharistic Prayer, where considerable modification of the original has been suspected—there are important differences in the various editions. Finally, Hippolytus made no claim that his Eucharistic Prayer was one actually used in the third-century Rome. He makes it plain that the prayers in the Apostolic Tradition are no more than models of the kind of prayer he considers desirable.

That said, the work remains an important testimony to liturgical thought in the third century. Moreover, his works became very popular in the East;

not merely amongst the Byzantines, but with the Copts, Ethiopians, Armenians, and Syrians.

Internal disputes among Christians went unnoticed by pagan authorities. After Alexander Severus's overthrow, Maximinus, his successor, once more ordered persecution. Both St. Pontian and Hippolytus were banished to the mines in Sardinia. There the two were reconciled and the schism came to an end. They died together, and their bodies were brought back to Rome on the same day, August 13, 236. Pope Pontian was interred in the papal tomb in the catacomb of St. Callixtus, and St. Hippolytus at a spot on the Via Tiburtina.

Since their return, the pair was equally honored by the Roman Church as martyrs. The schism was speedily forgotten, and St. Hippolytus remains as the only canonized anti-pope. The date of his remains' return is kept as his feast on the Roman calendar.

St. Hippolytus retains his popularity in the East. In the Byzantine Rite, both among Catholics and Orthodox, his feast is January 30. It is worthwhile, in the light of the later schism between Rome and Constantinople, to quote the entry on St. Hippolytus in the Synaxarion still used by both Byzantine Catholics and Eastern Orthodox:

> A priest of Rome under Pope Saint Zephyrinus' episcopate (199–217), Hippolytus composed numerous treatises in Greek against all the heresies concerning the unity of God in the Holy Trinity and the divine Monarchy. He clearly commented upon a good number of Holy Books, fixed the date of Easter, composed a universal history, and fixed the Apostolic Tradition by means of canonical laws. During his doctrinal controversies, he went to blameworthy excess and unjustly accused Archdeacon Callistus of heresy. Upon Pope Zephyrinus' death when Callistus became Bishop of Rome in 217, Hippolytus unfortunately separated himself from the Catholic Church and set himself up as an anti-pope, fighting Callistus and his successors: Urban (222–230) and Pontian (230–235). Exiled from Pontian to Sardinia under Emperor Maximin of Thrace (235), he retracted and suffered martyrdom at the same time as Pope Saint Pontian. Upon Maximin's death in 238, under Pope Saint Fabian (236–250), the second successor of Pontian after Pope Saint Anterus (235–236), his remains were brought back to Rome and honorably laid in a grotto on the Tiburtina Way in the cemetery which bears his name.

If anything, he is even more popular among the Copts and Ethiopians. Here is the entry in the Coptic calendar for him on Amshir 6, our February 13:

On this day the church celebrates the appearance of the body of St. Apolidus (Hippolytus), Pope of Rome. He was a virtuous and a perfect man in his generation. He was chosen to the Roman See after Father Augius. This was in the first year of the enthronement of Abba Cladianus, 9th Pope of Alexandria. Pope Apolidus was always teaching his people and guarding them from the pagan influences, confirming them in the faith of the Lord Christ.

When reports of St. Apolidus reached the infidel Emperor Claudius Caesar, he arrested him and tortured him severely. The emperor then tied his feet with a heavy stone, and cast him in the sea on the 5th day of Amshir.

On the following day, one of the faithful found the body of the saint floating above the water, and the stone was bound to his feet. The man took it to his home and shrouded the body. The news spread in the City of Rome and in all the neighboring cities, and it reached Caesar, who asked for the body, but the man hid it.

This father left a great wealth of teachings about the Incarnation and several sermons about Christian teaching. He also established thirty-eight by- laws.

*His prayers be with us all. Amen.*

What this account may lack in historical accuracy, it perhaps makes up in fervor. In addition, it shows that as far as the Copts are concerned, St. Hippolytus *was* the pope.

# St. Urban I

(222–230)

Urban, a Roman by birth, was elected while the schism of St. Hippolytus continued. Because the watchful peace of Alexander Severus continued for most of his pontificate, Urban was able to continue the peaceful organization of the Church begun by his predecessor. Important to this was his decree that properties once given the Church could never be alienated: "Things that have been offered to the Lord by the faithful should not be put to any other use than such as is for the benefit of the Church, the Brethren in the Christian faith, or the poor: because they are the offering of the faithful, the return made for sin, and the patrimony of the poor." It was Urban who ordered that the chalices and patens in which the transformation of the wine and bread into the blood and body of Christ would take place were to be of gold and silver—a rule maintained rigorously until the 1960s.

Unfortunately, the emperor's rule was tottering. The many converts made under Urban I, to say nothing of the noble folk already members of the Church, aroused the anger of the mob. Alexander Severus began to permit a resumption of persecution, in a limited way, to quiet popular dissatisfaction with his governance. St. Cecilia, friend of the pope, had married a pagan nobleman named Valerian. She converted not only him, but also his brother Tiburtius. Soon the two brothers were beheaded, and the wife was martyred soon after. Her body remained incorrupt, however, during the intervals between her exhumations (most recently in 1599), and doubtless still is incorrupt in her present tomb in the Roman church of Santa Cecilia.

Urban took shelter in the catacombs, where the Christians began to gather for the Liturgy, forsaking their chapels above ground. Even during the persecution, he succeeded in making many proselytes. Finally, he was found and taken from a catacomb a little after the martyrdom of his friend St. Cecilia. He was beheaded with many other Christians on May 25, which is now his feast day.

Buried at first in the catacombs, his relics are now also enshrined in the Church of St. Cecilia; the friends remain as close in death as they were in life.

## St. Pontian
(230–235)

Son of Calapurnius, Pontian was a Roman-born. In his time the schism of Hippolytus continued. During the peaceful reign of Alexander Severus, he continued the quiet progress of the Church. News came to Rome of the condemnation by the Church in Alexandria of teachings attributed to the great Church Father, Origen; among them the notion that all men will eventually be saved, and that the devil himself will one day also be reconciled to God. A synod called by Pontian in Rome approved the Alexandrian condemnations; but how much of what is called "Origenism" was actually taught by Origen is debatable. Certainly, he was a strenuous defender of the doctrine of "no salvation outside the Church," a teaching hard to reconcile with universal salvation, given that most men and women (to say nothing of devils!) live and die outside the Church. Universal salvation would void the necessity of Church membership and reception of the Sacraments that give the Church her ability to save souls. (Even so, it is an idea popular among such modern priest-theologians as Karl Rahner and Hans Urs von Balthazar, who presumably did not realize that such teachings would put them out of a job.)

As related earlier, when Alexander was overthrown by Maximinus, both he and St. Hippolytus were rounded up and sent to Sardinia, reconciling and dying there together. Pontian abdicated upon his exile so that the Church in Rome would have a resident shepherd.

As mentioned, his relics were interred at the catacomb of St. Callixtus. Some have found their way to Troia, in Apulia. St. Pontian's feast day is November 19.

## St. Anterus
### (235–236)

Elected pope to replace St. Pontian on his abdication, the Greek Anterus served for only forty-two days; he was beheaded at the order of Maximinus. Despite his short reign (or perhaps because he suspected it would be short) Anterus wrote a great many Epistles that tended toward tightening hierarchical relationships within the Church in the face of growing persecution.

But the biggest effort of Anterus's short pontificate was the fight against the Manicheans, another dualist group, which was of Persian origin. Originating under the influence of Mani, a third-century teacher who had been expelled by the Zoroastrians of Persia for his teachings against marriage and government, they soon became extremely numerous, being both better organized and more coherent doctrinally than most such groups. In response to Anterus's opposition, they and others denounced the pope to Maximinus.

Anterus was taken captive by the Praetorian prefect, Vitalian, and the prefect of the city, Sabinus. During his imprisonment, Anterus was tortured and then beheaded. His relics are in San Silvestro and his feast is January 3. The Aegean island of Naxos as well as Calabria claim him as a native; both honor his memory.

## St. Fabian
### (January 10, 236–January 20, 250)

When the Roman clergy gathered to elect a new pope, they were much surprised to see a dove land on the unknown Fabian's head. Taking this as a sign of the Holy Spirit's favor, they duly chose him for the office.

St. Fabian was fortunate in the personality of the two emperors who ruled for most of his time as pope. Gordian III (224–244) was tolerant of Christians, and Philip the Arabian (244–249) was himself baptized a Christian with his son by Fabian. It was with imperial approval that he brought back to Rome the bodies of Pope Pontian (d. 235) and the anti-

pope Hippolytus (d. 236) from Sardinia, and had them properly buried in Rome.

St. Fabian reorganized the local clergy, dividing the Roman diocese into seven districts or "diaconates" for the administration of social welfare (as opposed to priestly parishes, which division had already been accomplished, as already reported), each headed by a deacon assisted by a subdeacon. He was praised for his skill as an administrator by St. Cyprian of Carthage (d. 258), the noted Church Father. He was also responsible for founding several churches in Gaul—Tours, Toulouse, Narbonne, Clermont, and Limoges. Fabian also originated the consecration of holy oils on Maundy Thursday.

Unfortunately, this tranquil period was not to last. In 249, Philip the Arabian died and was replaced by the virulent anti-Christian, Decius, who unleashed a new persecution. St. Fabian was among the first to be rounded up and thrown into prison, where he died—probably of mistreatment—shortly thereafter. He was buried in the papal crypt in the cemetery of St. Callistus on the Appian Way. His body was later removed to the church of St. Sebastian in Rome, where his tomb remains. The feast day of St. Fabian is January 20, along with St. Sebastian. Among the Byzantines—Catholic and Orthodox—he is honored on August 5. The Egyptian Copts observe his day on February 5 (Amshir 11, in their calendar). The official account of his life in their Synaxarion is very interesting, indeed:

> On this day, St. Fabianus, Pope of Rome, was martyred. This father was a righteous scholar. He was ordained Pope for the city of Rome, so he taught his people and guided them in the way of Christian perfection.
>
> Decius, the head of the army, killed Emperor Philip, and replaced him as emperor. Decius incited a severe persecution against the Christians, and many were martyred. This infidel built a huge temple in the middle of the city of Ephesus, and erected in it idols, where he offered sacrifices to them. He then ordered to behead everyone who refused to sacrifice to these gods.
>
> When Decius knew that St. Fabianus was against the worship of idols and that he was teaching the faithful to be steadfast in their faith, he brought him to Ephesus. Decius commanded St. Fabianus to sacrifice to the idols. St. Fabianus did not yield to him and ridiculed his idols. The Emperor punished him with many tortures for a long time and at the end, he beheaded him with the sword. St. Fabianus thus received the crown of martyrdom.
>
> This pope stayed on the throne for twelve years, the major part of which was tranquil and peaceful.
>
> *His prayers be with us and Glory be to our God forever. Amen.*

His relics are kept at one of the oldest churches in Rome, San Martino ai Monti, originally a house church and seat of one of the seven diaconates St. Fabian set up.

## St. Cornelius
(251–253)

The fierce persecution of Decius made it impossible to elect a new pope for sixteen months after St. Fabian died. During this period of vacancy (*sede vacante*), Novatian, a Roman priest, formed a party in order to ensure his own election to the papacy. It was not until Decius had been killed and the no less Christian-hating but rather busy Gallus (who had all sorts of insurrections and foreign incursions on the borders to deal with) took the throne, that the election could take place.

The priest Cornelius was elected, but Novatian managed to have himself consecrated a bishop. Novatian's followers elected him as he wished, and so he is counted as the second anti-pope. To support his position, Novatian introduced a heresy, denying to the Church the power to pardon sins through priests after baptism, and established relations with Novatus, a Carthaginian heretic.

Cornelius came from a noble Roman clan, the Cornelii. Despite his high birth, however, he was extremely humble. He had administered the affairs of the Church during the horrible months after St. Fabian's death, so Cornelius was the obvious choice to everyone but Novatian and himself. But the larger part of the clergy and laity of Rome elected him, an act sanctioned by sixteen visiting bishops (two of whom were African) then in the city.

Despite both the persecution and Novatian's activities, Cornelius did manage to accomplish a number of things. With a lady named Lucina, he brought the bodies of Sts. Peter and Paul out of the catacombs, returning St. Peter to his former place on Vatican Hill, while enshrining St. Paul at Lucina's estate on the Via Ostia, on the site of what is now the great basilica of St. Paul Outside the Walls.

During the persecutions, a number of Christians had saved their own lives by offering incense to the gods or the emperor, as required by law. But many of these *lapsi*, as they were called, regained their courage and wished to return to the Church despite the ongoing danger. In 252, Cornelius convened a synod of sixty bishops at Rome to decide the proper course of action. The

synod decreed that the Lapsi could rejoin the Church after a severe penance; however, Lapsi priests and bishops would lose their faculties forever. Novatian, who had been invited as a gesture of reconciliation, refused to accept this finding or to receive communion alongside the penitent Lapsi. He was duly excommunicated.

Cornelius was then exiled to Civitavecchia by Gallus because of his activities concerning Sts. Peter and Paul, as well as his ever-growing conversions. From there he continued to act as the leader of those who did not join Novatian. While in exile, Cornelius continued to correspond with St. Cyprian, bishop of Carthage, who had been a great help to him throughout the few years of his pontificate.

Cornelius was eventually recalled and imprisoned by the emperor, who blamed him for the disorders provoked by Novatian and feared his correspondence with St. Cyprian. But Cornelius could not be stopped by prison. After converting his jailer and many of the prison guards, he was executed. His feast is September 16, and most of his relics are in Santa Maria in Trastevere.

The greatest center that is devoted to St. Cornelius and remaining in the world today is Kornelimunster in Germany. This latter abbey was founded by Louis the Pious, son of Charlemagne, in 814, as the Abbey of Inda. Just a few miles south of Aachen, Louis built the monastery for St. Benedict of Aniane, who served as first abbot. Highly favored by the emperor, Kornelimunster was made an imperial abbey. It received a large estate—all the surrounding country for an hour in each direction—the so-called *Muensterlaendchen*—and precious relics from the treasury of Charlemagne. One of these was the *Salvator heiligtuemer*, one of the outer burial cloths of Christ (the inner one is kept at Turin). These are exposed every seven years.

In 875, half of the grave cloth was exchanged by Charles the Bald (son of Louis the Pious) with Pope John VIII for relics of St. Cornelius and St. Cyprian. Charles initially enshrined them in the collegiate church of Saint Mary he had founded at Compiegne, France. From the relics, it soon took the name of the Abbey of St. Corneille. Until the Revolution, pilgrims came from all over Europe to venerate the relics. Several kings of France were crowned there: Louis II the Stammerer (877), Eude (888), Louis V (979), and Hugh II (1017). Some had their tombs there: Louis II the Stammerer (879), Louis V (987), and Hugh II (1025), later renovated by St. Louis IX. The Benedictines replaced the canons in 1150 and the abbey, which depended directly on the pope, thrived. Vast rebuilding in the Gothic style began, but was left unfinished in the sixteenth century because of the religious wars that beggared France. After the destruction caused by the Revolution, all that remains today is the fourteenth-century cloister as well as parts of the bell tower and the nave.

Fortunately, the monks had sent part of St. Cornelius's skull to Inda. This

relic brought many visitors to the abbey during the Middle Ages because of St. Cornelius's relics' record for curing epilepsy. After a time, the monastery was renamed *Monasterium Sancti Cornelii ad Indam*—Kornelimunster. Since the thirteenth century, large numbers of pilgrims have come each year to the Korneliusoktav (the week after September 16), during which a fair is held.

In addition to his fame in Germany, St. Cornelius is named every day in the Roman Canon of the Mass. Because of his posthumous role in France and Germany, St. Cornelius might well be considered a minor patron for all of Western Europe.

## *Novation*

*Anti-Pope (251–c. 258)*

Novatian had been a Stoic philosopher and was renowned for his eloquence. He joined the Church as a catechumen and, when taken very ill, was baptized by sprinkling rather than immersion. Because he was recovering, he did not receive the Sacrament of Confirmation. In those days, those who waited until danger of death to be baptized (as well as those not confirmed) were considered ineligible for the priesthood, because it was thought that they did not have the courage or strength necessary for ordination.

Nevertheless, he was ordained. Soon after, the persecution of Decius began, and Novatian at first shut himself up in his house, declaring to all who came to him asking for help that he would no longer work for the Church; he had another philosophy.

He soon emerged, however, and declared that he would have nothing to do with the Lapsi. This made Novatian popular among a number of the persecuted, and so he soon acquired many followers. At this time a correspondent of his, the priest Novatus, arrived in Rome from Carthage. While there Novatus had raised a schism against St. Cyprian, declaring his treatment of the Lapsi too rough. But when he arrived in Rome, Novatus turned about completely, in order to encourage his friend Novatian in his ambitions.

Soon, Novatian added heresy to schism by claiming that the Church had no power to forgive the sin of apostasy, the act of a Church member leaving the Church. After his death, his disciples would expand this to say that the Church could not absolve murder or fornication, and that the second marriages of widows and widowers were invalid as well.

When Cornelius was elected pope, Novatian prevailed on his followers not to receive Communion from Cornelius's priests. When giving them the Body and Blood, he would insist that they swore an oath to that effect. He then

convinced three bishops from remote corners of Italy to consecrate him bishop. One of these later repented and asked Cornelius to forgive him, which that pope did. Cornelius deposed the other two bishops and sent replacements to their dioceses.

Following the synod that condemned him, Novatian set about organizing a parallel church. Consecrating bishops and sending them throughout the empire, the Church he created lasted for a number of centuries. At the time, however, St. Cyprian of Carthage and St. Dionysius, Patriarch of Alexandria, rallied to St. Cornelius's side, thus limiting the growth of the schism somewhat. But within a few years there were some in every province of the empire. The Novatianist Church would linger on until about 600.

## St. Lucius I
### (253–254)

A Roman, Lucius's pontificate was extremely short. Soon after his election, he was exiled. Following his return, he was imprisoned and beheaded. Nevertheless, he declared those who stole the assets of the Church excommunicated—an excommunication later confirmed by other popes and the Council of Trent. He also continued the policies of St. Cornelius toward both the Lapsi and Novatianists.

Lucius's feast day is March 2. In the Middle Ages, a pope sent his head to Copenhagen, Denmark, where he became patron. Until the Reformation, the feast of the Translation of his Head on (August 25) was a Holy Day of Obligation in that city, complete with an Octave—an eight day period of celebration following major feasts.

## St. Stephen I
### (May 12, 254–August 2, 257)

Another Roman noble, this time of the Julii family, Stephen faced problems early on. St. Cyprian had been approached by various Catholics in Gaul for relief from Marcian, the bishop of Arles, who had joined the Novatianists. Marcian and those of his priests who followed him were refusing communion and absolution even to the dying. Unable to do more than encourage the Gauls who appealed to him, St. Cyprian wrote the pope, asking him to depose Marcian. Stephen did speedily. Unfortunately, the two were not always to remain in such agreement.

The main event of the pontificate of Stephen was the "dispute of the rebaptized." In the light of the ongoing struggles with the Montanists, Manicheans, and now the Novatianists, St. Cyprian and St. Firmilian, bishop of Caesarea, along with many of their partisans, espoused the notion that heretics had to be rebaptized to enter the Church. Stephen opposed them, asserting the traditional doctrine of the Roman Church, which was that any baptism, done with water in the name of the Father, Son, and Holy Spirit, was valid. Thus, if they met that criterion, baptisms administered by heretical priests were accepted when those who had been thus baptized sought admission to the Church.

This pope further ordered that vestments used at Mass could not be worn as everyday wear.

St. Stephen was martyred under Emperor Valerian, who had replaced Gallus. He was beheaded while sitting in his chair in the catacombs, from which he had been officiating at Mass.

His relics have had a long and strange history. Initially interred in the catacomb of St. Callixtus, they were brought to San Silvestro in Capite in 761. In 1160, however, they were stolen and enshrined at the cathedral in Trani. Finally, in 1682 they were brought to Pisa Cathedral, where his head had been since 1047.

St. Stephen's feast day is August 2 in the Latin Church, and November 3 among the Armenians. He is patron of Modigliano in Tuscany, Lesina in Croatia, and minor patron (that is, one of the lesser saints who have patronage of a place—opposed to major patron, who is usually the saint who first brought the Faith to a given spot) of Speyer, Germany. He is also patron of the chivalric Order of St. Stephen, founded by Grand Duke Cosimo I of Tuscany in 1561, and still presided over by Archduke Sigismund, grand duke

of Tuscany; their chapter meetings are held in the national church of San Stefano dei Cavaliere in Pisa.

## St. Sixtus II
### (August 31, 257-August 6, 258)

Successor to St. Stephen I was Sixtus II, an Athenian; he held the pontificate for only eleven months. St. Dionysius of Alexandria consulted with him in three letters about certain difficulties in Egypt. He further counseled the pope to exercise forbearance with those who insisted on rebaptizing heretics, although he himself held the Roman position. Sixtus did.

A new persecution arose at this time, however. Emperor Valerian forbade the Christians not only to preach but even to gather in the catacombs. Knowing that it would result in his death, Sixtus II violated this law. He was arrested at the catacomb of Praextatus during the Liturgy and was beheaded at the entrance to that of St. Callixtus. With him at the end was his Spanish deacon, St. Lawrence.

Seeing Sixtus led to execution, Lawrence cried out, "Father, where are you going without your son? Whither are you going, O holy priest, without your deacon?" The pope replied, "I do not leave you, my son; but a greater trial and a more glorious victory are reserved for you, who are stout and in the vigor of youth. You shall follow me in three days." He then ordered Lawrence to distribute all the remaining treasure of the Church among the poor, for fear they would be deprived of them by imperial confiscation.

Lawrence did, even selling the sacred Mass-vessels to do so. When news of this came to the prefect of the city, the prefect demanded that Lawrence bring him all the Church's treasures. The deacon did—three days later he gathered all the poor, cripples, orphans, and widows the Church supported. He then brought the prefect to see them and said, "Behold the treasures of the Church!" The deacon then began to lecture the prefect, which that official did not appreciate. He had Lawrence roasted on a gridiron: at last the deacon said, "You may turn me now, this side is done." He then prayed and died.

St. Sixtus II is commemorated in the Roman Canon of the Mass. His feast is August 6 in the Latin Church; August 7 at Pisa; August 9 at Rome, Tortona, and Athens; August 10 in the Byzantine calendar; and March 26 among the Copts.

The Byzantine Rite commemorates Sts. Sixtus II and Lawrence on the same day. Their Synaxarion says:

> Saint Laurence was archdeacon of the Roman Church. He guarded the church's vessels and distributed its goods to the poor. At the time of Emperor Valerian's terrible persecution, the Bishop of Rome, Saint Sixtus II, was beheaded in Callistus' cemetery. According to the witness of Pope Saint Damasus I (366–384) who extolled and rendered the martyrs' memory illustrious by his poetical inscriptions, Saint Laurence was also seized and cruelly beaten. His fingernails were pulled out. He was delivered over to the fire and was submitted to many other tortures. Thrown into prison, he triumphed over all by his faith and ended his martyrdom in 258.

## St. Dionysius
### (July 22, 259–December 27, 268)

Dionysius was of Greek descent, from southern Italy—Magna Graecia, as the region was called. For almost a year after St. Sixtus II's death, the papacy remained vacant while Valerian's persecution raged. But after his death, the new emperor, Gallienus, issued an edict of toleration, which gave the Church legal existence. The churches and cemeteries were restored to Catholic ownership.

Once Dionysius was elected pope, he reordered the parishes of Rome that had been disrupted during the persecution of Valerian. Dionysius ordained many priests to replace those martyred and sent money to redeem Christian prisoners from Cappadocia (they had been taken from Caesarea when that province was devastated by Gothic barbarians). He was illustrious for virtue and doctrine, as testified by St. Dionysius of Alexandria. He wrote important letters, of which there remains a fragment brought back by St. Athanasius of Alexandria. The Carmelites maintain that he, too, had spent time following the rule of Mt. Carmel. In the Roman calendar he is commemorated on December 30, and by the Carmelites on January 19.

## St. Felix I

### (January, 269–December 30, 274)

After being elected pope, Felix ordered that Masses should be celebrated on the tombs of the martyrs, a custom already in existence, but mandatory from this time until the 1960s.

Felix received a letter from the clergy of Antioch, Syria, asking him to solve a dissension that had wracked that patriarchate. The bishop of Antioch, Paul of Samosata, taught that Christ was merely a man, but had acted as the "Temple of the Holy Spirit," in whom the Divine Word dwelt through its "operation." The clergy of the place had held two councils to depose him, both of which he had managed to survive. But the third, held in 269, condemned him for heresy, avarice, pride, and other crimes, and deposed him. A man named Domnus was chosen in his stead; however, Paul refused to vacate his house and appealed to the new emperor, Aurelian.

Aurelian's reply was that the house should go to whomever the bishops of Rome and Italy assigned it. Felix ruled in favor of Domnus and wrote a letter to St. Maximus, bishop of Alexandria, explaining the Catholic dogma of the Incarnation. This letter has been prized ever since by the Church in Egypt.

Nevertheless, Aurelian soon found persecution a useful safety valve for the population, and had Felix executed. In the West, his feast is May 30. He is still revered by the Copts, as the following quote from their Synaxarion shows.

> The Departure of St. Felix, Pope of Rome, Hatour 6 (November 2)
>
> On this day, the holy father St. Felix, Pope of Rome, departed. He was born of Christian parents in Rome in the year 210 A.D. They raised him with high principles and he gradually advanced in the clerical ranks. Astasius, Pope of Rome, ordained him a deacon. Pope Justus, seeing his righteousness and virtues, ordained him a priest.
>
> When Abba Dionysius, Pope of Rome (who was contemporary of St. Thaouna, Pope of Alexandria) departed, this father was chosen for the Roman See. He shepherded the flock of Christ with the best of care. When Aurelianus Caesar reigned, he incited persecution against the believers of the Lord Christ. He tortured them using very painful methods, and many of them were martyred by his hands. Since great tribulation befell St. Felix from the Emperor, he entreated God to take these tribulations away from His people.

Because of his prayers, the Emperor died in the second year of his reign.

When Diocletian reigned, he also persecuted the Christians and started torturing them. Pope Felix prayed to the Lord to spare him from witnessing the torture of the Christians. So, he departed in the first year of the reign of Diocletian, after he had sat upon the Apostolic throne for five years. He left many sayings and discourses, some of which were useful teachings and others were about the doctrines.

## St. Eutychian
### (January 4, 275–December 7, 283)

Little is known of the life of this pope, except that during his pontificate Manichaeanism spread throughout the empire, becoming very powerful and arousing great concern among churchmen. Eutychian did begin the custom of blessing the fields. He was a martyr and his feast day is December 9.

## St. Caius
### (December 17, 283–April 21, 296)

By the reign of Dioceletian, Christianity had infiltrated even the imperial family itself. Caius, a native of Salona in Dalmatia and grandson of the emperor, was called by his relative to Rome, where he converted to Christianity. He was elected pope in 283. In his pontificate the persecution of Diocletian broke out—the bloodiest yet. The pope's efforts to save the Christians through his family links were in vain. After living for some years in the house of Gabinius, his brother, Caius too had to withdraw to the catacombs: Diocletian, much as he wished the destruction of all the Christians, long hesitated to also condemn the pope, his grandson. Finally, in a burst of fury, he condemned him, and St. Caius was martyred.

During his pontificate, St. Caius ordered that all bishops must pass through the several degrees of the clergy: Ostiarius (Porter), Lector, Exorcist, Acolyte (the minor orders); then Sub-Deacon, Deacon, and Priest (the major orders). This decree remained in force until Paul VI's changes in the 1960s.

Caius's relics were found in the cemetery of St. Callistus in 1622, at which time they were transferred to the Roman church of San Caio, which had originally been his house. That church was destroyed in 1876, by order of the new Italian government, and St. Caius's relics were re-enshrined in the church of Santa Susanna. It had been the house of Caius's niece Susanna, who had been martyred by Dioceletian with her brother Gabinus over her refusal to accept the marriage her imperial great-great uncle ordered with his pagan adopted son, Maximianus Galerus. St. Caius's feast is April 22 (the date of his interment) in the Roman calendar, and August 11 in the Byzantine.

## St. Marcellinus

### (June 30, 296–October 25, 304)

Born in Rome, the son of Projectus, Marcellinus was lenient toward the Lapsi, which much annoyed the Donatists, a rigorist anti-Lapsi sect (similar to the Novatianists on this point) who sprang up in North Africa. Apparently he was weak in some way during the persecutions, but gathered his strength, facing and receiving martyrdom. Since by this time the cemetery of St. Callistus had once again been confiscated, Marcellinus was buried in that of St. Priscilla, which he himself had either bought or enlarged. His feast is April 26 in the Roman calendar, and June 7 among the Greeks and Russians.

## St. Marcellus I

(June 27, 308–309)

Following the death of Marcellinus, the persecution was so great that an opportunity for the clergy and people of Rome to gather and elect a new pope did not occur for four years. Finally, another Roman was elected—Marcellus—who was very strict against those Christians who had been guilty of weakness and idolatry during the persecution. The new emperor, Maxentius (Dioceletian having retired), enraged by this very strictness, imprisoned Marcellus and threatened the pope with death if he would not renounce his office and adore the idols. After refusing, Marcellus was condemned to serve in the imperial stables. He continued to spread the Faith among the city population. He was freed by the faithful, but then recaptured by the soldiers of Maxentius and left to die of starvation in prison. He too was buried in the cemetery of St. Priscilla. His relics are now in the Church of San Marcello al Corso in Rome, the site of a house belonging to a Roman lady named Lucina, where Marcellus had lived as pope. It was turned by Maxentius into municipal stables, and this is where Marcellus acted as horse-groom. Some of his relics were sent to Haumont and Maricolles in Belgium and to the great French Abbey of Cluny. His feast is January 16 in the Latin Church, June 7 in the Byzantine.

## St. Eusebius

### (April 18, 310–September 26, 310)

The history of this pope long remained unknown; some information was learned in the nineteenth century when De Rossi discovered in the cemetery of St. Callixtus the epitaph that Pope St. Damasus composed in his honor. A Greek by birth, Eusebius fought the Rigorists, who refused to admit to penance the people who had lapsed during the persecutions; and against Heraclius, who demanded that they be readmitted to the Sacraments without any penance at all. Both were exiled by Maxentius to Sicily, where Eusebius died. In October 210, his body was brought back to Rome and laid in the cemetery of St. Callixtus, which Maxentius had returned to the church. St. Eusebius's feast is September 26.

# FREEDOM AND HERESY

# St. Miltiades, or Melchiades

## (July 2, 311–January 10, 314)

Born in Africa, Miltiades had already shown ability in dealing with the secular authorities as deacon of Rome by obtaining from Maxentius the restitution of the confiscated assets of the Church. This was a talent that he would greatly need in this pontificate.

Emperor Maxentius had, under the system established by Diocletian (wherein there would be two halves of the empire, each under an emperor and a caesar), as his caesar, one Constantine. Constantine's father, Constantius Chlorus, was commander of the legions in Britain and married to a British Christian princess, Helen. After his father became caesar in the West at Diocletian's command, Constantine was sent to be raised at the imperial court. After completing his education, Constantine rejoined his parents in Britain.

Constantius died on July 25, 306, and Constantine was proclaimed emperor by the legions at York on March 1, 307. After a few years of uneasy coexistence with Maxentius, he led his troops across the channel and made for Rome.

On his way to fight Maxentius at the Milvian bridge near Rome, Constantine, who—like his father—had not persecuted his mother's people, had a vision. He saw in the sky a cross with the words *In Hoc Signo Vinces*—"In this Sign, Conquer." He ordered the cross painted on all of his soldiers' shields, and, sure enough, on October 28, 312, he defeated Maxentius at the bridge, then occupied Rome. Today, the site of this victory is occupied by the church of Santa Croce al Flaminio, itself the headquarters of the Constantinian Order of St. George, an ancient order of knighthood headed by the heir to the throne of Naples.

Constantine immediately allowed liberty to the Christians and the freedom of church building. Because this upset some of his pagan subjects, in 313 he enacted the Edict of Milan, which allowed toleration for all religions in the empire. In short order Constantine exempted Christian clergy from civil offices and ordered all his soldiers on Sunday to say an official prayer to the One God, which might be said by Christian and pagan alike. Thanks to the easygoing mores of contemporary Romans, marriage as well as birthrates had

dwindled alarmingly; with the prevalence of abortion, homosexuality, widespread divorce, contraception, and the like, child rearing was seen as an annoying inconvenience. The result—a diminished workforce and depleted legions—ever more created the need for foreign slaves and mercenaries to keep the state going. To combat these evils, Constantine ordered new marriage laws based on those of the Christians. In addition, he made many gifts of land and buildings to the Church.

Among other gifts given the papacy by Constantine was the Lateran Palace, formerly a home of Constantine's in-laws, the Laterani. From that time on, this palace would be the residence of the popes, up until the beginning of the fourteenth century when the popes left for Avignon. (Today, it houses the administrative offices of the Diocese of Rome.)

In 313, the emperor requested that Miltiades hold a synod to examine the Donatist problem. As previously mentioned, they were a group centered primarily in North Africa, who taught that those who had deserted the Church during the persecutions could never be readmitted. Meeting October 2 to 4, the synod of the Lateran duly condemned them as heretics.

St. Miltiades died on January 10, 314, and was buried in the cemetery of St. Calixtus. His head is at the Gesu, the Jesuit Church in Rome, and most of the rest of his relics are at San Silvestro in Capite. His feast is December 10.

## St. Sylvester I

### (January 31, 314–December 31, 335)

Sylvester was a Roman, the son of Rufinus and Justa. As the second pope after Constantine's legalization, St. Sylvester saw the Church benefit tremendously from the emperor's patronage. In addition to the Lateran Palace, given to his predecessor, St. Sylvester witnessed the imperial donation and building of the original basilicas of St. Peter and St. John Lateran in Rome, the Holy Sepulchre in Jerusalem, and the Nativity in Bethlehem, to name a few. In addition, he helped Constantine in his continuing education in Christianity.

In August 314, Constantine convened a council of 130 bishops of Gaul in the town of Arles to deal with the Donatists. Having condemned them and passed resolutions on other matters, the Council sent its decisions to St. Sylvester, acknowledged his supremacy, and asked him to circulate their decisions to other regions of the Church.

More serious than the Donatist heresy was that of the Arians, who taught that Christ was not God. Though they believed Him to be the highest of God's creatures, they held that He was no more than that. St. Sylvester and Constantine jointly convened the First Ecumenical Council at Nicaea, the imperial summer home, to deal with the issue. St. Sylvester sent Bishop Hosius of Cordova to preside over the 250 bishops of the Council in his name. Among other highlights, the Council Fathers condemned Arianism and composed the Nicene Creed used at Mass today, which affirms Christ's status as second Person of the Holy Trinity. Between dramatic events, Arius, the priest who began Arianism, was slapped across the face by St. Nicholas of Myra, the American Santa Claus.

St. Sylvester I was buried at the cemetery of St. Priscilla on the Via Salaria, but in 762 he was removed by Pope Paul I to the church of San Silvestro in Capite. His feast day on the Latin Calendar is December 31, which is why, in German-speaking lands, New Year's Eve is called "Sylvester." Among the Byzantines, his feast is January 2. The Armenians celebrate his day on the Saturday before Epiphany. For the Copts it is January 15 (Tubah 7):

> The Departure of St. Sylvester, Pope of Rome:
>
> On this day in the year 335 A.D., St. Sylvester (Sylvester), Pope of Rome, departed. He was born in Rome. For his virtues, his ascetic life and his knowledge, he was chosen for the pontificate of Rome in 314 A.D., after the departure of his predecessor St. Miltiades. That was in the eleventh year of Emperor Constantine's reign and less than a year after the issuing of the edict of Milan, which granted freedom to Christianity.
>
> He baptized Emperor Constantine, for he was not yet baptized. He was occupied with wars, demolishing pagan temples and building churches.
>
> The life of this father was a bright and shining life. He continued to teach the people, and remove all doubts from them. He explained to them that which was difficult to understand. He frequently debated with the heretics and converted many of them to believe in the Lord Christ, and baptized them.
>
> He composed several discourses and he wrote several books about the knowledge of God and the mystery of Incarnation.
>
> During the seventh year of his papacy, the Ecumenical Council of Nicea convened, and he excommunicated Arius and all who supported him. When he completed his good course, he departed in peace. He occupied the Roman chair for 11 years.

A further note on Constantine: As reflected in the Coptic account of St. Sylvester, it was long held by most Christians that the pope had baptized Constantine—many also maintained that he had cured the emperor of leprosy. An alternative view, believed by most writers today on the authority of the historian Eusebius, a semi-Arian, was that Constantine was baptized on his deathbed by an Arian bishop. The alternative view has, certainly, antiquity on its side.

Moreover, it is bound up with the story of the "Donation of Constantine." This was a document that purported to be a conferral upon the popes of all temporal and spiritual control of Italy. Beginning in the fifteenth century, it was claimed that this was in fact an eighth-century forgery. Nevertheless, papal claims do not rest on this document, because both the pope's claim and his use of supreme power in the Church predate the 700s.

In any case, Constantine's dealing with the Church is seen by many as a corruption of Christianity, by tying it to the state. Some (such as the Jehovah's Witnesses) even point to the emperor as the founder of the Catholic Church. Although he did set an example for Catholic (and Orthodox) rulers that would be followed down to present time, it is the memory of his and his mother's sanctity which held the imagination of Christians closer to him in time. His mother, St. Helen, went to the Holy Land to find the True Cross and other relics of the Passion of Christ. It was she who spearheaded his building program. While she alone is venerated liturgically in the Latin Church (on August 18), all of the Eastern Rites venerate them both. Constantine is daily invoked in the Armenian Mass, and Maronites and Melkites all have feasts for him. In the Byzantine rite, both Catholic and Orthodox, he and his mother are commemorated on May 21. The Byzantine Synaxarion says of them:

> The holy and great Emperor Constantine was the son of Constantius Chlorus, Caesar of the Western provinces of the Roman empire. He was born around 280 in Naissus, near the Dardanelles. Upon his father's death in 306, he was proclaimed Caesar and his successor on the throne. Learning that Maxentius and Maximin had formed a league against him, he invaded Italy in 312. It is there that, advancing to the head of his troops one afternoon, he saw in the sky a luminous column in the form of a cross beneath the sun with this inscription: "By this you will conquer." He engaged in battle on October 29, near Pons Milvius. Maxentius was conquered and, when pursued, crowned himself in the Tiber River. The next day, Constantine triumphantly entered Rome. The Senate proclaimed him Augustus and Emperor of the West, whereas Licinius remained master of the East. In 313, an edict was promulgated

at Milan by the two Emperors allowing full liberty to everyone to render worship to God as he wished. Jealous, Licinius again persecuted the Christians. Constantine, having defeated him on two occasions, had him killed in 324. Thus he was left the sole Emperor of East and West. All persecutions against the Church stopped, and Christianity triumphed. It is at this time that he lay the foundations of Constantinople, the city named after him. It was surnamed "New Rome" because the imperial seat was transferred there from "Old Rome." Desiring to exactly know the true faith, Constantine gathered all the bishops in the land of Nicaea in 325. They confirmed the Orthodox faith and proclaimed the Son consubstantial with the Father, anathematizing Arius, his followers, and their blasphemy. The Council was presided over by Osius, the Bishop of Cordova, Spain, and by Vitus and Vincentius, priests of the Roman Church and legates of Pope Sylvester. Saint Constantine sent his mother to Jerusalem in 326 to find the sacred wood upon which Christ our God according to the Flesh was crucified. Helen discovered it in 327. She returned to Constantinople and then went to Rome to die in 329. Constantine fell sick in Nicomedia. He asked for and received holy Baptism and died on May 22, 337. Transported back to Constantinople, his remains were deposited in the Church of the Holy Apostles which he himself had built.

Saint Helen died an octogenarian in 329. She was buried in a porphyry sarcophagus in a round church in Rome, on the so-called Lavicana Way. This sarcophagus is now preserved in the Vatican Palace.

Even more enthusiastic for the emperor is the Coptic Liturgy, which has two feasts for him. Here are their liturgical descriptions:

The Departure of the righteous Emperor Constantine the Great.
28 Baramhat (April 6)

On this day of the year 53 A.M. (337 A.D.) the righteous Emperor Constantine the great departed. His father's name was Constantius I Chlorus which means (Green), and his mother's name was Helena. Constantius reigned over Byzantium, Maximianus reigned over Rome, and Diocletian reigned over Antioch and Egypt. Constantius was pagan, but he was honorable, loved to do good, compassionate and merciful. He went to the city of El-Ruha (Urfa—Gr. Edessa) and there he saw Helena, liked her and he married her. She was a Christian, and she conceived Constantine. Constantius left

her in El-Ruha and returned to Byzantium. She brought forth Constantine and raised him up very piously, taught him every kind of learning, sowed in his heart mercy and compassion for the Christians, but she did not dare to have him baptized.

Constantine grew up, and he was a bold and skilful horseman. He went to his father who rejoiced in him when he saw that he was full of wisdom, knowledge, and he was a skilful horseman. After his father's death he received the kingdom and he reigned with justice and integrity, and stopped all unfair practices. All the people were subject to him and they loved him and his righteous judgement spread throughout the Empire. The nobles of Rome sent asking him to come and save them from the injustice of Maximianus. Constantine marched with his army toward Rome to save them. During the war he saw in the heaven, in the middle of the day, a Cross made of stars, and on it was written in Greek words which being interpreted as "With this you shall conquer." The light of the Cross was more shinning than the sun, and he showed it to his ministers and the nobles of his kingdom. They read what was written, marveled and they did not know for what reason that cross had appeared. That night the angel of the Lord appeared to him in a vision and told him: "Make a sign for yourself like that sign which you had seen, and with it you shall conquer your enemies." The next morning, he prepared a large flag with the sign of the cross on it, and made the sign of the cross on all the armaments. He engaged with Maximianus in a battle and fought. Constantine overcame Maximianus who withdrew with his army, and while crossing the bridge over the Tiber river, the bridge broke and he and most of his men perished. Constantine entered Rome and its people welcomed him with joy and gladness, and its learned men praised the Honorable Cross and called it the Savior of their city. Then they celebrated for the Cross seven days and Constantine became the Emperor of the East and the West.

When Constantine established himself in Rome, he and most of his soldiers were baptized by the Pope of Rome, in the eleventh year of his reign, which is the fourth year after the appearance of the Honorable Cross. He sent throughout the kingdom and commanded to set free all those who were imprisoned for the sake of faith, and that they should not work during the Passion week as the Apostles commanded.

Then he sent his mother Helena to Jerusalem where she discovered the Holy Cross of Our Lord Christ. In the seventeenth year of his reign the Holy Council of the Three Hundred and Eighteen

bishops assembled at Nicea in the year 325 A.D. which arranged the affairs of the Christians and put down the cannons of the church. He rebuilt the city of Byzantium and called it after his name "Constantinia" and he brought to it many of the bodies of the apostles and holy martyrs. He departed in the city of Nicomedia, they laid him in a gold sarcophagus, carried him and brought him to Constantinia. The Patriarch, bishops, priests, and all the people received him with prayers, psalms, and spiritual hymns, and laid him in the sanctuary of the holy apostles. All the days of his life were seventy five years.

*To our God is the glory, might, and dominion and may His mercy and grace be upon us forever. Amen.*

The Reign of the Righteous Emperor Constantine, the Great.
Misra 12 (August 18)

On this day also, is the commemoration of the enthronement of the Righteous Emperor Constantine the Great, over the city of Rome. When he reigned over Byzantium, succeeding his father Constantius Chlorus in the year 306 A.D., he abolished the injustice throughout the kingdom. His fairness and fame spread throughout the Empire. The nobles of Rome asked him to come and save them from the injustice of Maximianus. He sorrowed for their misfortune, and he pondered in what way he could deliver them. The sign of the cross appeared to him, to which he adhered. Constantine went and fought against Maximianus and defeated him. While Maximianus was retreating, crossing the bridge over the Tiber River, the bridge broke and he perished, drowning along with his soldiers. That was in the seventh year of the reign of Emperor Constantine. When Emperor Constantine entered Rome, all its nobles and people welcomed him in a grand festival, and with great joy. They celebrated his victory for seven successive days. The poets of Rome and its orators praised the Honorable Cross, describing it as the savior of their city and the supporter of their Emperor.

The account of the appearance of the Cross to Emperor Constantine and his victory over Maximianus is written under the commemoration of the departure of this righteous Emperor, which is on the 28th day of Baramhat.

*Glory be to our God forever. Amen.*

## St. Marcus I

### (January 18–October 7, 336)

Born a Roman, Marcus accomplished a lot in his short pontificate. To the Bishops of Ostia he gave the use of the pallium (a circular band of white wool, originally worn around the shoulder by only the popes, denoting their authority) and the right to consecrate the pope, which privileges the See of Ostia guards to this day. He also built the Roman churches of San Marco and Santa Balbina (formerly the house of Balbina, daughter of the jailer of the Mamertine prison, who had saved St. Peter's chains). St. Mark's relics are in the former church, where they were transferred from the cemetery of Balbina, which he himself opened. His feast is October 7 in the Roman calendar. Like most of the immediately post-Constantinian popes, St. Marcus was venerated as a Confessor of the Faith, and the healings at his tomb confirmed his sainthood in the eyes of the faithful.

## St. Julius I

### (February 6, 337–April 12, 352)

A native of Rome, Julius protected St. Athanasius and other orthodox bishops persecuted by the Arians after they fled to Rome in 339. The next year, with fifty other bishops, Julius held a synod that condemned the Arians; these decrees were then sent to the synod of eastern bishops then meeting at Antioch. In 342, he received permission from the co-emperors Constantius and Constans, to hold another council at Sardica. This council reaffirmed the decrees of Nicaea against the Arians, forbade the translation of bishops from one See to another, and allowed any bishop deposed from his diocese to appeal his cause to the pope.

Julius built the churches of Santi Apostoli and Santa Maria in Trastevere, and was himself interred in the catacomb of Calepodius. Within two years he was hailed as a saint. His feast is April 12. He is mentioned daily in the Syriac Liturgy and has his own anaphora. His feast is January 28 in the Coptic rite.

## Liberius
### (May 17, 352–September 23, 366)

Liberius was the first pope not to be canonized in the Western Church, although, as reported later, the Easterners have a very different view of him. One of his major early accomplishments was the building of a basilica in honor of the Virgin—Santa Maria Maggiore—on the Esquiline Hill. The site was signified to him by an apparition of the Virgin and confirmed by a miraculous fall of snow on the lot in the middle of August.

During his pontificate, the Arian heresy was at its height, having at one point the allegiance of the emperor, Constantius II, and all but five of the bishops. Despite the rulings of Nicaea and Sardica, the Arian party continued to grow in strength; orthodox bishops, like St. Athanasius, patriarch of Alexandria, were driven from their dioceses. At a Roman synod, Liberius sided with Athanasius and tried to persuade Constantius to hold a council at Aquileia. The emperor refused and held a synod of his own at Arles. In response, Liberius convened a gathering of bishops at Milan. Neither synod resulted in much, but Liberius continued to defend St. Athanasius.

Arianism, with its denial of the mystery of the Trinity, appealed to the intellectually proud because it was easily accessible to human reason. (Thus, many of the same sorts of educated folk who sixteen centuries later would respond to Unitarianism heeded the Arian call.) At the same time, it appealed to Jews and the more literate pagans (such as the followers of the Neoplatonists Proclus, Iamblichus, and Plotius) with its simple monotheism. Above all, Arianism's de-divinizing of Christ snipped the tension-filled bridge between heaven and earth. In political terms, denial of the Incarnation put God safely away in His heaven and allowed Caesar to reign peacefully on earth. This latter notion may have had some appeal to Constantine; his immediate successors would embrace it fully.

The emperor, hell-bent on promoting Arianism, exiled Liberius to Beroea (modern Stara-Zagora, Bulgaria) in 355. Constantius then appointed the anti-pope, Felix II, to rule in Liberius's stead. The emperor next convened what appeared to be an ecumenical council at Sirmium—although not convened by the pope, the emperor's role and the participation of so many bishops lent the gathering a seeming authority. This conclave approved several semi-Arian creeds, whose ambiguous language could be interpreted in either an orthodox or a heretical fashion. At last, after great pressure, Liberius gave in and signed them, in return for being allowed to return to Rome in 358. Similar pressure led him to excommunicate St. Athanasius for a time.

In 363, Liberius offered pardon to the bishops who had accepted Arianism at the 358 synod of Rimini, if they would renounce the heresy. This led many steadfast orthodox to oppose him. He died in Rome.

Because of his weakness, the folk of his own patriarchate, the West, have ever since refused to honor him as a saint. But the Easterners do. Among the Greeks, his feast is August 27. The Copts, who might be supposed to have little use for one who excommunicated one of the leading saints and fathers of the Egyptian Church, are very laudatory of him in their Synaxarion:

> The Departure of St. Leparius, Bishop of Rome.
> Nasi 4 (September 9)
>
> On this day, St. Leparius (Liberius), Bishop of Rome, departed. He was ordained during the reign of Emperor Constance, the son of Constantine. When Athanasius, Pope of Alexandria, and Paul, Patriarch of Constantinople, were exiled, they came to him. St. Liberius took them to Emperor Constance, who wrote to his brother, and they were allowed to return.
>
> After Constance was killed in Rome, Constantius sent to St. Liberius asking him to accept the followers of Arius, and to accept the exile of Athanasius, but he refused this petition. Constantius exiled St. Liberius, then came to Rome where he killed the killers of his brother. The heads of the monasteries and the priests met him and asked him to release their father Liberius. The emperor returned him from his exile, and he continued to teach and preach to his flock. He resisted the followers of Arius, until he departed in peace. He sat on the Episcopal throne for fifteen years.
>
> *May his prayers be with us. Amen.*

# *Felix II*

*Anti-Pope (355–358)*

As previously mentioned, as part of his campaign to replace orthodox bishops with Arian ones, the emperor Constantius in 355 exiled Pope Liberius to Beroea for his refusal to give up the Nicene Creed and condemn St. Athanasius. At that time, the clergy of Rome took an oath to accept none other than Liberius as Bishop of Rome, so long as he lived.

Felix was archdeacon of Rome at the time. The emperor, then in residence at Milan, invited Felix to see him. There he persuaded the archdeacon to become pope, and Felix was consecrated by three Arian bishops. Despite their oath, the Roman clergy accepted Felix as pope, but the lay folk refused to have anything to do with him.

In May of 356, Constantius visited the Eternal City. The Romans demanded the return of their pope from him, which soon came about due to Liberius's signing the semi-Arian creed at Sirmium. The bishops there wrote to Felix and the Roman clergy, asking them to accept Liberius again as pope; they recommended that Felix and Liberius co-govern Rome. But on Liberius's arrival, the people rose up against Felix, who holed up with his supporters in the church of Santa Maria in Trastevere. The unanimous vote of the senate and people of Rome banished Felix from the city forever, although Liberius allowed those of Felix's appointees who recognized him to keep their positions. Felix retired to Porto, where he lived until his death.

Since, however, it is mostly clerics who wrote the histories of those times, in some works Felix was considered the true pope. He himself did refuse to accept Arianism, and so his feast has been kept in the past on July 29.

# St. Damasus I
## (October 366–December 10, 383)

A native of Spain, Damasus served as archdeacon to Liberius after his return from exile. Although a majority voted for him, a small minority declared the deacon Ursicinus the winner, and raised a tumult until the new (and orthodox) emperor, Valentinian III, banished him to Cologne.

Although the tide had turned against the Arians, Damasus continued to struggle against them. New heresies arose and in their turn were condemned. At a synod in Rome held in 368, he condemned the teaching of Apollinaris, the new patriarch of Alexandria, who held that Christ had no human intellect, and that His flesh was united with his Godhood, having been brought from heaven for the purpose of being crucified. For the Apollinarists, Christ was really neither God nor man. The next year, it was the Macedonians' turn.

At this time, there were three Patriarchates in existence: Alexandria, which encompassed Egypt, Nubia, Ethiopia, and Cyrenaica; Antioch, including Syria, Palestine, Cyprus, Sinai, Armenia, Mesopotamia, Asia Minor, Thrace (modern Bulgaria and Turkey-in-Europe), Persia, and all points East; and Rome, which comprised Spain, Gaul, Britain, North Africa, Italy, and Illyricum. This last was a region covering most of modern Greece, Albania, Macedonia, Serbia, Montenegro, and Croatia.

After the division of the empire into East and West, Illyricum was generally under the political sway of the Eastern emperors, although remaining within the patriarchate of the West. This gave rise to many administrative difficulties. Damasus solved these by appointing St. Aescholius, archbishop of Thessalonica, as papal vicar for Illyricum.

A great pain for the pope was the defeat and death of the emperor Valens at the hands of the Visigoths at Adrianople in 378. Although an Arian and a furious enemy of the orthodox, Valens's death signified the beginning of the end for the Roman empire. This was concealed at the time, however, by the accession of Emperor Theodosius I, who took control of both halves of the empire.

Where Constantine had simply tolerated and patronized the Faith, Theodosius made it the official religion of the empire. He granted official Roman citizenship to all the baptized. From this time on, Church and empire would be considered temporal and spiritual sides of the same thing—Christendom. St. Ambrose, archbishop of Milan and Theodosius's major spiritual adviser, elaborated what would come to be, until the Treaty of Westphalia in 1648, the theory of Church/state relationship held by almost all Christians in varying degree.

In keeping with his role as protector of the Church, Theodosius called, with Pope Damasus's approval, the first Ecumenical Council of Constantinople. This gathering finalized the version of the Nicene Creed as recited today and placed the empire firmly on the side of orthodoxy, where it would remain until it dissolved.

Theodosius himself is venerated as a saint by the Armenians on January 17 (who also name him daily in their Liturgy), and by the Copts, who observe two feasts in his honor in common with the other Fathers of Constantinople I on January 18 and November 3.

In 379, Damasus convened a synod that defined the Canon of Scripture; three years later he approved and sent delegates to the Ecumenical Council of Constantinople.

His administrative skills were put to use in beautifying churches (his own house was transformed into the church of San Lorenzo in Damaso) and transforming the catacombs into shrines. Not only did he open them up, but also his poems in honor of various martyrs were set in mosaic on their tombs. In later centuries, these fragments of his poetry became extremely useful identifying these saints' resting places.

Nor were his literary triumphs confined to poetry. He revised the Roman Liturgy, giving it the form that it would basically hold until 1970. Moreover, in keeping with his love of Scripture, he commissioned St. Jerome to make a new translation of the Bible into Latin. The resulting work, the *Vulgate*, remained the normative Catholic version of the Bible until the 1960s. His relics are at his own church of San Lorenzo in Damaso, and his feast is December 11.

## *Ursicinus*

*Anti-Pope (366–?)*

A deacon of Rome, Ursicinus was the favored candidate at Liberius's death by those who considered themselves the most loyal of the late pope's adherents. Despite the bloodshed they caused at the election, Damasus won. Refusing to recognize this action, they declared Ursicinus the winner anyway.

Terrorizing the new pope's adherents, they were brought to heel by Valentinian III, who exiled Ursicinus to Cologne in 367. Eventually, he was allowed to go to Milan, but never Rome. Still considering himself pope, Ursicinus eventually converted to Arianism. Eventually, those of Ursicinus's adherents who remained in Rome submitted to Damasus.

## St. Siricius

### (December 17, 384–November 26, 399)

Born at Rome in 334, he was a conscientious wielder of the Roman primacy. Siricius issued many decrees "for all the churches." His letter to Bishop Himerius of Tarragona, Spain (February 10, 385) is important because it is the earliest actual papal decree still existing. What we know of prior legislation comes from various histories and lists. In this letter, Siricius forbids repeating Arian baptism as well as baptizing on the feasts of Easter and Pentecost; the eves of these great days were given over to this Sacrament. Siricius further relaxed penances, set a minimum age for ordination, enforced celibacy, and punished violators of monastic chastity.

Siricius further set down, in a series of decrees at a synod held at Rome in 386, the necessity of papal permission for consecration of bishops in the Western patriarchate; he quickly informed the North African bishops of this decision.

In 390, Siricius dedicated the basilica of St. Paul Outside the Walls. Buried in the cemetery of St. Priscilla, his relics are now at Santa Prassede. His feast is November 26.

## St. Anastasius I

### (399–December 14, 401)

Roman-born and friend of the great saints Paulinus of Nola and Jerome, Anastasius condemned both the Origenists (who claimed the authority of the Church Father Origen for their teachings, although this is, as reported, debatable), who believed in universal salvation, and the Donatists, who held, as also reported, that the Lapsi could not be forgiven. In North Africa, these last had begun to raise armed bands of thugs, called the *Circumcellions,* who harried and terrorized the orthodox.

But Anastasius further declared that those who received Donatist baptism could be ordained priest and those of their clergy who converted might retain their churches. Anastasius's relics are in Santa Prassedes, and his feast day is April 27.

## St. Innocent I
### (December 22, 401–March 12, 417)

Born in Albano, outside Rome, Innocent came to the pontificate at a time when the empire was tottering. Theodosius the Great, last emperor to rule both halves of the empire, died, leaving his weak sons—Honorius in the West, and Arcadius in the East—to deal with the ever greater threat from the Germanic barbarians. In the face of this threat, it was necessary for the new pope to consolidate papal supervision of the Church.

Innocent issued new decrees promoting celibacy and combating adultery; moreover, he prevailed upon Honorius to proclaim laws against the Donatists, which led many of them to return to the Church.

He stood up for St. John Chrysostom—the exiled bishop of Constantinople—one of the leading Greek Church Fathers, who had fallen afoul of the emperor Arcadius for denouncing imperial immorality. St. John also prepared the version of the Liturgy in greatest use in the Byzantine Rite today.

When Alaric—king of the Visigoths—entered Italy, Emperor Honorius fled to Ravenna, where he was secure from attack within its impenetrable marshes. Never again would Rome be the seat of empire. Despite Innocent's attempts to mediate between emperor and king, Alaric conquered and sacked Rome in 410; in deference to the pope, he left the churches and monasteries in peace.

The fall of Rome fell upon the rest of the empire like the proverbial thunderclap. Remaining pagans claimed that the Eternal City had fallen because the Romans had abandoned worship of the old gods. St. Augustine, bishop of Hippo, North Africa, wrote his brilliant *City of God* to refute this idea.

In internal discipline, Innocent ordered that none of the dying who offered repentance could be refused final absolution. He also decreed that only bishops should, as a rule, give the Sacrament of Confirmation. Innocent further ruled that both its prayers and those of the Eucharist should never be spoken in front of infidels.

Another heresy emerged in this pontificate, that of Pelagianism. Named after Pelagius, the British priest who originated it, Pelagianism denied both Original Sin and Divine Grace, holding that the personal will was all, and that the individual could, through his own good intentions and works alone—regardless of belief or Sacraments—win salvation on his own. Pelagius moved to North Africa, where he soon ran afoul of St. Augustine. Two synods of North African bishops were convened against the Pelagian heresy in 416. One of

Innocent's last acts before his death was to confirm and approve the synods' decisions. His feast day is July 28.

## St. Zosimus

### (March 18, 417–December 26, 418)

A native of Mesuraca in Greece, Zosimus accomplished a good deal in his short reign. He gave to the bishop of Arles in Gaul the privilege of consecrating the bishops of Narbonne and Vienne.

Not so happily, Pelagius sought refuge in Rome from the condemnations he had suffered in North Africa. At first, he was successful in convincing Zosimus that he was wrongly persecuted. But when the pope explored his theology a little more closely, he reconfirmed the condemnations.

Zosimus was buried in the cemetery of St. Ciriaco; his feast among the Latins is December 30, and with the Italo-Greeks, January 29.

## St. Boniface I

### (December 29, 418–September 4, 422)

When St. Zosimus died, a group of the electors—mostly deacons—selected the archdeacon Eulalius as pope; the next day, the priests met and elected Boniface. On appeal to the emperor, Honorius at first found in favor of Eulalius; however after two synods were held at Ravenna to thrash the whole question out in detail, he changed his mind. Moreover, he issued an imperial decree that after a doubtful election, another should be held.

Boniface continued the fight against Pelagianism and solved a dispute that had broken out in southern Gaul as to which of the dioceses there should have the primacy over all the bishops of the region, confirming Vienne and Narbonne in their independence.

The emperor's nephew Theodosius II had succeeded Arcadius on the Eastern throne and had given Illyricum to the nascent patriarchate of Constantinople's control. But Boniface was able to prevail upon him to give it back.

In addition, Boniface enforced the law forbidding slaves to become priests. He was buried in the cemetery of Maximus on the Salarian Way, and his feast day is October 25.

## St. Celestine I
### (September 22, 422–July 27, 432)

Archdeacon to St. Boniface I, Celestine was born in Campania. In his time, Nestorius, the archbishop of Constantinople, taught that there were two persons in Christ—one human, one Divine. Because of this, he held that the Virgin Mary could not be called "Mother of God," but only "Mother of Christ." When he first announced this notion, his flock arose and threw him out of his cathedral. Nevertheless, he soon gathered many allies in Syria and the East.

Nestorianism was condemned at a Roman synod in 430 and the next year at the Ecumenical Council of Ephesus, to which Celestine sent three legates to preside—and which he approved. It was perhaps particularly fitting that this council, which did so much to define the place of Mary in the Church, was held in the city where the Virgin had lived with St. John until shortly before her death. Knowledge of this sojourn, which was a result of Jesus' placing His Mother in St. John's care at the Crucifixion (which guardianship continued after John became bishop of Ephesus) had been retained as a tradition of the place from its occurrence.

The condemnation of the Council carried with it the force of law, because Church laws were now civil as well. For the most part, the Nestorians fled beyond the eastern frontier into the Persian frontier. That empire—the long-term enemy of Rome—saw an opportunity in Nestorianism. Because Christianity was linked with Rome, Persian authorities had subjected the local faithful to terrible persecutions. When the Nestorians arrived, they were given control of the churches of Persia. An aggressive missionary program led to the establishment of Nestorian dioceses throughout Central Asia, leading by the thirteenth century to a chain extending from Persia to China. But the Mongol depredations led to the ruin of most of these, and by the seventeenth century, the Assyrians (as Nestorians were now called) were only to be found in remote parts of eastern Iraq and western Persia.

All that, however, lay far in the future. In 429, Celestine sent St. Germanus

of Auxerre to Britain, to combat Pelagianism there. (As a by-product, he also organized British resistance to the Anglo-Saxon invaders.) Three years later, the pope sent St. Palladius to evangelize Ireland; in 432, he sent St. Patrick. The latter's advice to his flock, "As ye would be Christians, be ye Romans," reflects the origin of his mission.

Celestine was buried in the cemetery of St. Priscilla, but in 820 relocated to Santa Prassedes with so many other catacomb popes. From there, his relics were transferred to Mantua, where they rest in the cathedral named in his honor. There his feast is kept on April 6, but in the rest of the Latin world, on the following day. The Syriac Orthodox celebrate his day on March 3 (and he is mentioned daily in some of their Liturgies), while the Byzantines do so on April 8. Copts venerate St. Celestine on June 25, and Ethiopians on June 27.

In the Coptic Synaxarion, the following account, while not strictly accurate, reflects the devotion of the Copts to him:

> The Departure of St. Celestine, Pope of Rome.
>
> On this day also, the great Pope Celestine, bishop of the city of Rome, departed (July 27th, 432 A.D.). This saint was the disciple of St. Boniface, bishop of Rome. At the time of his death, he commended that father Celestine would succeed him, and then he cautioned him saying, "Take heed O my son for there would be ravening wolves in the city of Rome." This father was a righteous and well learned monk. When Pope Boniface departed on September 4th, 422 A.D., they ordained Celestine in his place on September 10th, 422 A.D., during the reign of Emperor Honorius. This Emperor died in the city of Raffeen in France in the year 423 A.D. One of the Emperors (Julian the Infidel) wanted to appoint Nestorius a patriarch for Rome and expel Celestine the saintly Pope. The people rose up and expelled Nestorius which made Emperor Julian enraged against him. This Saint fled to one of the monasteries nearby Pentapolis (Five cities) and dwelt there. God wrought many signs and miracles by his hands.
>
> Then, the angel Raphael appeared to him in a dream saying: "Rise up and go to the city of Antioch to its patriarch St. Demetrius, and abide with him for the Emperor had decided in his heart to kill you upon his return from the war." When he woke up, he went forth from that monastery along with two brothers and came to the city of Antioch. He found its Patriarch ill, told him what had happened to him, and stayed in one of the monasteries of Antioch. Sts. Ignatius and Boniface along with a third venerable person appeared to the Emperor in a dream and said to him, "Why have you left the city of the saints without a bishop. Behold, God will remove your

soul from you, and you shall die by the hands of your enemies." The Emperor asked, "What shall I do?" They replied, "Do you believe in the Son of God?" He answered saying, "I do believe." They said to him, "Send and bring our son bishop Celestine with honor, and restore him to his throne." When the Emperor awoke from his dream, he wrote to the patriarch of Antioch, Demetrius, asking him to inform his envoys of the whereabouts of Celestine, and return him to his See. They found him and returned him to his Chair with great honor, and the people received him with joy and happiness. The peace and the affairs of the church were established by his presence.

When Nestorius blasphemed and the Council assembled for him, Celestine was unable to attend the Council, because of his illness, so he sent two priests with a letter excommunicating Nestorius in it. The Emperor believed in what Nestorius said; nevertheless he yielded to the decisions of the Council and exiled Nestorius to Egypt.

When the Lord willed for Celestine to depart from this world, St. Boniface, his predecessor, and St. Athanasius, the Apostolic, appeared to him and told him, "Affirm your people in the faith, for Christ is calling you." When he woke up he commanded his people saying, "Take heed to yourselves, for behold ravening wolves shall come into this city." Having said this he added, "I am leaving, for the saints are calling for me." When he said that, he departed in peace.

*May his prayers be with us, and Glory be to God forever. Amen.*

## St. Sixtus III
### (July 31, 432–March 28, 440)

A Roman by birth, Sixtus was of a very trusting disposition. Although he warned Nestorius to give up his heresy, he was very lenient toward the Nestorians and Pelagians, leading some to claim that he favored them. While this was not true, it does show the importance of impressions. At the same time, he was called upon through the efforts of Proclus, archbishop of Constantinople, to once again detach Illyricum from the West.

When the Roman nobleman Bassus began to slander the pope, he was

condemned by a synod of bishops and ordered imprisoned by the emperor. But Sixtus visited him in prison when he was dying, gave him the Last Rites, and buried him with his own hands.

Sixtus was very much a builder. He rebuilt Santa Maria Maggiore, the great basilica (in commemoration of the Council of Ephesus's reaffirmation of Mary's divine motherhood) and restored the baptistery of St. John Lateran—whose general interior appearance has remained more or less unchanged since then. In addition, he built the churches of Santa Sabina and San Lorenzo Outside the Walls. Buried in the cemetery of St. Cyriaca, his feast day is March 28 in the Roman Calendar, and February 14 among the Syrians.

## St. Leo I (the Great)

### (September 29, 440–November 10, 461)

While still a deacon, on a diplomatic mission to Gaul on the emperor's behalf, Leo was elected pope. As soon as he returned to Rome, he was ordained as priest, consecrated as bishop, and enthroned as pontiff. Against the background of crumbling imperial authority and barbarian invasion, St. Leo took a firm hand in Church affairs. In Northern Italy as well as in Africa, he corrected abuses and ended disputes. He gave the Spanish bishops, at the time in conflict with Priscillianism (a heresy that declared the human body to be evil), a concrete plan of action. In Gaul, he ordered Bishop Hilary of Arles (who wanted the primacy of southern Gaul for his own diocese) not to interfere with elections in other Gaulish dioceses.

St. Leo's greatest spiritual challenges, however, came in the East. Eutyches, a monk who taught that Christ had only a single nature (His Divine Nature having absorbed His human one), had convinced many to agree with him. These *Monophysites*, as they came to be known, were particularly strong in Syria and Egypt and had the ear of the emperor at Constantinople, Theodosius II.

In June of 449, St. Leo sent Bishop Flavian of Constantinople a letter wherein he condemned Monophysitism. Two months later, the emperor convened a council illegally at Ephesus, which condemned Flavian and rehabilitated Eutyches. St. Leo came to Flavian's aid, however, and persuaded Theodosius to quash his own gathering. In 452, St. Leo called for another council to be held at Chalcedon, near Constantinople. Although Bishop Flavian

said that no council was necessary since the pope had already spoken, St. Leo proceeded with the affair. Saying that "Peter had spoken through Leo," the bishops endorsed the condemnation of Monophysitism. Unfortunately, through misinterpretation of the Council, many of the Syrians, Egyptian Copts, Armenians, and Ethiopians separated from the main body of the Church. Those in the East who did not were called *Melkites*—"Royalists"—because they held to the Faith of the emperor.

Whether or not religious peace was restored in the East, in the West the empire was collapsing. In 452, Attila the Hun came south into Italy, ravaging the area around Milan. St. Leo met him near Mantua and persuaded him to leave. Sources differ as to what happened; some say simply that the pope's bearing overawed the barbarian chieftain, others that Attila saw St. Peter himself hovering over the pope's shoulder, prepared to strike the Hun down. Whatever the case the city was spared. Three years later, Gaiseric, king of the Vandals, came by sea from North Africa, likewise with plundering on his mind. Although St. Leo was unable to make him leave, he did convince him to spare the city of Rome.

Initially buried in the porch of St. Peter's, in 688 the body of St. Leo was moved into the interior. Made a Doctor of the Church in 1754, his feast is November 10 on the Latin calendar, and February 18 on the Byzantine. Following is their Synaxarion's account of him:

> Memory of our Father among the Saints Leo, Pope of Rome (✝461)
>
> Born in Tyrrhenia (Tuscany) around the end of the Fourth century, Saint Leo at first was an archdeacon of the Roman Church. After Pope Saint Sixtus III's death, he was elected to succeed him in 440 by reason of his eminent qualities and the purity and integrity of his life. In 451 when the Fourth Ecumenical Council was gathered in Chalcedon, Saint Leo, inspired by the Holy Spirit, wrote on the then debated questions, clearly professing a double energy and a double will in Christ. He sent a letter on this subject in 449. When the Fathers received it, they saw it as a pillar of faith and an inspired writing from the very mouth of God. In common they cried out in agreement: "This is the faith of the Fathers, this is the faith of the Apostles. We all believe likewise. Anathema to anyone who does not believe this. Peter has spoken through Leo." Saint Leo composed numerous works in Latin. He died on November 10, 461, and was buried in the Church of Saint Peter. His holy body was rediscovered in 1607.

# St. Hilarius

## (November 19, 461–February 28, 468)

Born in Sardinia, Hilary had been archdeacon to St. Leo I. He served as his papal legate to the "Robber Synod" of Ephesus (so-called because the conferees were terrorized by imperial troops into making rulings desired by the emperor), where, with St. Flavian, he was abused and imprisoned. He made his escape back to Rome.

Hilarius settled some disciplinary disputes in Gaul and Spain and ordered that annual synods be held in southern Gaul, where the various dioceses were constantly arguing about precedence. His synod in Rome, held on November 9, 465, is the first Roman synod of which the complete acts have survived.

This pope was buried in the cemetery of St. Cyriaca, and his feast is September 10.

# After the Fall

## St. Simplicius
### (March 3, 468–March 10, 483)

Born at Tivoli, Simplicius reigned over a Church ever-more threatened by internal and external enemies. During his pontificate, Romulus Augustulus, last of the Western Roman emperors, was deposed by the head of his Germanic Guards, Odoacer. This is often seen as "the fall of the Roman Empire." But it was not, at least in the minds of contemporaries. Although the Arian Vandals ruled North Africa (and persecuted the Catholics), Spain and southern Gaul received similar treatment from the also-Arian Visigoths, and Northern Gaul was being absorbed by the still-pagan Franks; all these peoples considered themselves in some sense subject to the emperor. When Odoacer put Romulus out to pasture and made himself king of Italy, he also sent back the imperial diadem to Constantinople, saying that the empire henceforth needed only one ruler. So it was considered as the empire continued, but with one head, rather than two. This concentration of the imperial dignity had far-reaching effects.

For one thing, the archbishops of Constantinople, given their role as imperial quasi-chaplains, wished to have second place in the Church, after Rome but before Alexandria and Antioch. This development was resisted by Simplicius, although it had been enacted by later (but non-Papally approved) sessions of Chalcedon. Since the two older eastern patriarchates were in a virtual state of civil war (eventually resulting in two separate lines of patriarchs for the two Sees), Constantinople's ambitions were that much more enhanced.

The struggle against the Monophysites was severe. Three emperors in succession favored them over the orthodox and used the question of Constantinople's standing as a weapon. The last of the three, Zeno, published a confession of faith, the *Henoticon*, which hoped to bring peace by accepting Nicaea but ignoring Chalcedon—in this he had the aid of Constantinople's patriarch, Acacius. Even so, Simplicius was able to secure the deposition of two Monophysite patriarchs of Alexandria. From this time dates the Coptic Orthodox Church, which originally was anti-Chalcedonian, and which has maintained its own line of patriarchs of Alexandria. This development was paralleled by the Syriac Orthodox Church, which has its own patriarch of Antioch. The

split developed along national lines, with the orthodox Melkites oriented ever more toward Greek Constantinople, and the Copts, Syriacs, Ethiopians, Nubians, and Armenians retreating more into themselves.

Because the emperors of the East and the kings of Ethiopia, Nubia, and Armenia were Monophysite, and because the Germanic kings were Arian or pagan, for the first time since Constantine there was not a single Catholic king on earth. In the face of this, Simplicius strove to bring the far-flung portions of the Church ever closer in unity with Rome. To that end, he appointed Zeno of Seville papal vicar in Spain, a very necessary step to rally the faithful there under their Visigothic overlords.

St. Simplicius's feast is March 2.

## St. Felix II (III)

### (March 13, 483–March 1, 492)

A Roman by birth and a widower (one of his grandsons was Pope St. Gregory I), Felix's great problem was the ongoing struggle with Monophysitism. The year after his accession, he condemned the Emperor Zeno's *Henoticon.* This led to a break with both the emperor and the patriarch of Constantinople. After the latter's name, this is called by historians the Acacian Schism. Though it lasted only until 518, it paved the way for a number of later schisms.

Felix further decreed strict regulations for the readmission to the Church of those who accepted Arianism during the persecution of the Vandals in North Africa. His feast day is February 25.

## St. Gelasius I
### (March 1, 492–November 21, 496)

Gelasius was born in Rome to North African parents. He continued the fight against the Acacian Schism, winning the patriarch Euphemius himself over; the emperor Zeno continued on his way, however. Euphemius was banished to Ancyra (modern Ankara, Turkey), where he died in 515.

Both Pelagianism and Manichaeanism continued as well; against the latter, Gelasius ordered the laity to receive from the cup, thus contradicting the Manichaean claim that wine was a creation of the devil. He also ended the pagan festival of the Lupercalia. This had occurred on February 15 from the earliest days of the city of Rome; honoring the wolf who suckled Romulus and Remus, it featured sacrifices of goats and (among other things) the striking of passersby by young men clad only in thongs made from the hide of these sacrifices. Gelasius ordered priestly ordinations to take place during the Saturdays of the Ember Weeks, those quarterly penitential observances (abolished by Paul VI in 1969) that had served since Apostolic times to consecrate the four seasons to God.

Gelasius was a great liturgist. He produced the Gelasian Sacramentary—the forerunner of the Roman Missal—containing many ceremonies either still in use today, or abolished only in 1970. Furthermore, he was an inexhaustible writer of letters and treatises. St. Gelasius's feast is November 26.

## Anastasius II
### (November 24, 496–November 16, 498)

Born in Rome, Anastasius sent a letter of congratulations to Clovis, king of the Franks, on his baptism by St. Remigius at Rheims, Christmas Day, 496. This event, the conversion of the first of the barbarian kings to Catholicism, is considered the birthday of France. Because Clovis was the first, the king of France ever after was called the "Eldest Son," and his realm the "Eldest Daughter," of the Church. The descent of the Holy Spirit in the form of a dove bearing the Sacred Ampulla filled with chrism to crown Clovis with, is the ori-

gin of the sacred character attributed to the French monarchy by its subjects and its loyalists since the revolution.

Anastasius continued the fight against the Acacian Schism, but maintained that sacraments given by its adherents were valid. He also condemned Traducianism, the heresy that teaches that human souls are in some way handed down to children by their parents, rather than new creations by God at the moment of conception, the orthodox belief.

## St. Symmachus

### (November 22, 498–July 19, 514)

Born in Sardinia, Symmachus was a convert from paganism and arose to be archdeacon of Rome under Anastasius I. Although the majority of the clergy voted for him, a minority favoring lenience in ending the Acacian Schism elected the archpriest Laurentius. Both candidates were consecrated the same day by their adherents, who appealed to Theodoric—Arian king of the Ostrogoths—for a settlement.

He found in favor of Symmachus; however, in 501, Laurentius renewed his claim to the papacy. This time Theodoric refused to judge, but managed to get both factions to agree to a synod. At the first session, the mob attacked and beat Symmachus and his supporters. As a result, he refused to attend any more meetings. The priests of the synod then declared that they could not judge the pope and that all the churches should be given back to him. Theodoric, however, favored Laurentius, and so all the churches remained in the latter's hands—except Symmachus's refuge of St. Peter's—until the Laurentian party dissolved in 506.

Once firmly ensconced, Symmachus gave much money to the poor and supported those persecuted by the Arians. He gave refuge to many North African bishops driven to Sardinia by the Vandals. In mind of his own experiences, he issued regulations regarding papal elections—among these was the proviso that if anyone promised his vote to another, or deliberated on the topic in an assembly while the pope yet lived, that person would be excommunicated. Symmachus also ordered that the Gloria was to be sung at all Sunday Masses and martyrs' feasts. His own feast day is July 19.

## *Laurentius*

*Anti-Pope (498–506)*

Archpriest of Rome under Anastasius, Laurentius was the leader of that minority among the clergy who had urged the pope to accept the *Henoticon*. Once Anastasius had died, the disputed election took place and the minority hailed Laurentius as pope. After Theodoric found in favor of Symmachus, Laurentius acknowledged him as pope and became bishop of Nocera. But in 501 he came back to renew his claim. As mentioned, despite the synod's finding in Symmachus's favor, Theodoric gave control of all but one of Rome's churches to Laurentius, over which he presided until his death in 506. After which his followers turned to Symmachus.

## St. Hormisdas

(July 20, 514–August 6, 523)

A native of Frosinone, in the Campania, Hormisdas had served as archdeacon to St. Symmachus. A widower, before he went into major orders he had a son—Silverius—who himself would one day be pope.

In contrast to the difficulties of the last few pontificates, Hormisdas had a very happy reign. The last of the Laurentians were reconciled, and the death of Emperor Anastasius I allowed his successor—Justin I—to join Hormisdas in healing the Acacian Schism at long last. On March 28, 519, Patriarch John of Constantinople and 250 Eastern bishops signed a formula of union, in which they accepted the Council of Chalcedon and the authority of Rome in matters of Faith.

Hormisdas was also able to get along with King Theodoric, who ceased to persecute the orthodox; his co-religionist, King Thrasamund of the Vandals, died as well and persecution in North Africa also ceased. St. Hormisdas was buried at St. Peter's, and his feast is August 11.

# St. John I

(August 13, 523–May 27, 526)

A native of Populonia in Tuscany, John inherited a church at peace. This would not last long. The emperor Justin I, happy at having ended the Acacian Schism and wishing to impose orthodoxy throughout his empire, turned over the Arian churches to the Catholics and ordered all the Arian Goths in his dominions to convert.

Theodoric, king of the Ostrogoths in Italy, was quite concerned about the well-being of his coreligionists and fellow Goths. He asked John to go to Constantinople and prevail upon Justin to return their churches to the Arians and allow those who had converted to return to their former religion. The pope was quite willing to do this, but all he could do was ask the emperor to be tolerant toward the Arians; he could not, as head of the Church, actually ask him to favor heresy.

Justin was overjoyed at John's arrival. He received him magnificently and asked the pope to crown him. On Easter Sunday, April 19, 526, John celebrated the Latin Rite Mass in the great cathedral of Hagia Sophia. It was a high point in Western–Eastern relations.

But this embassy did not achieve what Theodoric had wanted; not only was the relief that he sought for the Arians not achieved, but the papacy and the empire were now closely aligned. Upon Hormisdas's return to Italy, Theodoric had the Pope thrown into prison, where he died a few days later. St. John I's feast is May 27, the day of his burial at St. Peter's.

## St. Felix III (IV)
### (July 12, 526–September 17, 530)

Born at Fimbri, near Benevento, Felix's election represented a desire to please King Theodoric, who had proved through his imprisonment of St. John I and his execution during the pope's absence of the latter's friend Boethius (author of the *Consolations of Philosophy*, written in prison while awaiting death) that the safety of the Church depended on his whim. However, Theodoric died that same year, proving that the king's own life was also dependent on factors beyond his control.

In any case, Felix was thus freed to pursue his policies in peace. While Pelagianism had been defeated, a moderated form (semi-Pelagianism) had become popular in southern Gaul. This, too, the pope condemned in 529, and that same year he approved the teachings of the local Council of Orange in southern Gaul, which explained Original Sin and condemned Pelagianism.

Not only did Felix deal successfully with Theodoric's successors, he also built the church of Santos Cosma e Damiano, restored San Saturnino, and finished decorating San Stefano Rotondo (now owned by the German College). His feast is February 13.

In 527, St. Felix was notified of the death of the emperor Justin. Replacing him on the imperial throne was his nephew, Justinian I. Like Theodosius before him, Justinian aspired to be both the restorer of the Roman Empire and the paladin of the Church. Upon his accession, active imperial rule encompassed only the old Eastern provinces—modern Turkey, Bulgaria, Greece, Serbia, Albania, Montenegro, Cyprus, Syria, Jordan, Palestine, Israel, and Egypt. His ambition was to reconquer the West from the barbarians, and much of his energy was set to that purpose. The next several pontificates would be deeply affected—for good and for ill—by this desire.

How did he regard the papacy? His behavior toward individual popes, his revision of Roman Law, the *Codex Justinianus* (which has served as the basis of most code law in the Christian world and even influences today the common law of English-speaking countries) is extremely clear: "We will that all peoples under our sway hold the faith delivered to the Romans by the Apostle Peter which he still preserves there."

But the emperor's political needs—often unknown to him—tended to compete with his religious aspirations. He expected, in view of the latter, successive popes' unswerving support in his pursuit of the former. Owing to the papacy's interest in doctrinal orthodoxy regardless of political result, and con-

cern for Catholics outside the empire, conflict was perhaps inevitable. As the empress Theodora was herself at first a Monophysite, and because the imperial unity required for the march west made her co-religionists' support in Egypt, Asia Minor, and Syria essential, Justinian at times favored compromises that successive popes found intolerable.

How well did Justinian's program of renovation succeed? In some ways, not well. Although imperial armies would reach, eventually, as far as southern Spain, this expansion would not last a century. The East was becoming ever more removed culturally and psychologically from the West; Justinian's was the last reign in which Latin could be heard commonly in Constantinople.

But in other ways, his influence endures to present day. Apart from the Code of Law referred to earlier, many of the great churches he built survive today, such as Hagia Sophia (now a mosque in Turkish Istanbul). Until the classical revival of the nineteenth century taught the Greeks to refer to themselves once again as "Hellenes," their common name for their nationality was *Romanoi* ("Romans"). Such still-Christian establishments he founded as the Monastery of St. Catherine atop Mt. Sinai continue to remember him and fly the golden double-eagle flag as testimony of their allegiance to his long-vanished empire. Even today, Muslim Bedouins around Mt. Sinai continue to defend it, in token of their ancestors'—Dacian soldiers settled there for protection—allegiance to Justinian. He and his wife are revered as saints by the Eastern Orthodox Churches, as this selection from the Russian Orthodox Synaxarion shows:

> November 14—The Holy Right-Believing Emperor Justinian and Empress Theodora: Saint Justinian, a major figure in the history of the Byzantine state, was also a great champion of Orthodoxy, a builder of churches and a Church writer, and he was of Slavic descent—born in Bulgaria. During his reign (527–565) Byzantium won glory with military victories in Persia, Africa, Italy—as a result of which paganism was decisively routed amongst the Germanic Vandal and West-Goth tribes. By command of the emperor Justinian the pagan schools in Athens were closed. With the aim of spreading Christianity through the regions of Asia Minor, Justinian sent there the bishop of Ephesus John, who baptized more than 70 thousand pagans. The emperor gave orders to build 90 churches for the newly-converted, and he generously supported church construction within the empire. His finest structures of the time are considered to be the monastery at Sinai, and the church of Hagia Sophia at Constantinople. Under Saint Justinian many a church was built in the name of our Most Holy Lady Mother of God. Being a man of quite diverse an education, Saint Justinian assidu-

ously concerned himself over the education of clergy and monks, ordering them to be instructed in rhetoric, in philosophy and in theology.

The right-believing sovereign devoted much attention and effort into the struggle with the Origenists of his time, who then were reviving the Nestorian heresy. Against their heretical speculations was composed the Church-hymn "Only-Begotten Son and Immortal Word of God, Who for our salvation . . ." and he commanded its singing as obligatory in the churches. From that time through the present day this hymn is sung in the Divine Liturgy before the Small Entrance [i.e., 2nd Antiphon]. At the command of the sovereign, in the year 553 was convened the Fifth Ecumenical Council, censuring the teachings of Origen and affirming the definitions of the Fourth Ecumenical Council at Chalcedon. The Holy Emperor Justinian brought about orderly rule and law within the realm. Under his guidance and supervision was compiled a complete compendium of Roman laws, which has come down to us as a codex of law known as "the Justinian Codex." The "Novellae" [i.e., "Church-laws"] of Justinian find inclusion in all the variants of the Russian Church-law NomoKanon Books.

In his personal life, Saint Justinian was strictly pious, and he zealously fasted quite often. The Holy Emperor Justinian died in the year 565.

Together with the emperor was enumerated to the ranks of the Saints his like-minded spouse, the Empress Theodora, who died in the year 548. She was at first a notorious sinner, and an adherent to the Monophysite heresy, but then she repented and led a virtuous life, keeping purity of both soul and body.

Although opinion of him in the West is far more mixed (the usually placid Fr. Alban Butler offers a scathing attack on him in *Lives of the Saints,* volume III, page 507), it is notable that Dante put Justinian into the *Paradiso* (canto VI).

# Boniface II
## (September 17, 530–October 532)

The old Roman families who had produced so many of the popes were clearly in decline—the clergy of the City were divided into "Byzantine" and "Gothic" factions. To avoid an open split between the factions, and avoid outside interference in an election, St. Felix III appointed as his successor his archdeacon, Boniface, the son of Sigisbald. Thus the stage was set for the first pope of Germanic descent. When St. Felix felt death approaching, he gathered his clergy and a number of Roman senators and patricians. Before them he bestowed his pallium on Boniface and excommunicated anyone who would dispute his succession to the throne of Peter.

When St. Felix died, Boniface automatically assumed the papacy. But the majority of the Roman clergy refused to accept him, and they elected Dioscurus instead. Both were consecrated on September 22—Dioscurus at the Lateran Basilica, and Boniface in the hall of the Lateran Palace. It seemed that the Church would have another schism, but Dioscurus died on October 14.

The clergy accepted Boniface at this point, and a synod was held at which Dioscurus was posthumously excommunicated. His supporters officially asked for forgiveness, which Boniface gave them.

The next year the pope convened another synod at which he presented a constitution officially allowing popes to nominate their successors. This was ratified by the clergy, who also accepted Boniface's choice of the deacon Vigilius as the next pope. But the faithful at large resented this move, and the emperor Justinian disapproved. Later that year Boniface held a third synod in which he burned the constitution he had promulgated.

His interventions elsewhere, however, were more successful. He approved the acts of the Second Council of Orange in southern Gaul, thus condemning the last traces of semi-Pelagianism there. At the request of the bishops of North Africa, he decreed the official recognition of the archbishop of Carthage as primate of Africa. When the patriarch of Constantinople, eager as ever to attach Illyricum to himself, disallowed the election of the bishop of Larisa in Thessaly, the new prelate appealed to Boniface who countermanded the patriarch's order.

In 532, the vandal king Hilderic was deposed by a usurper, Gilimer. Justinian, anxious to begin the restoration of the empire, in response broke the alliance with the vandals that Emperor Zeno had concluded, and prepared for war. Despite this, Boniface's two-year pontificate ended as peacefully as it had tumultuously begun.

## Dioscurus

*Anti-Pope (September 17–October 14, 530)*

As previously noted, Dioscurus was a Roman deacon whose anti-pontificate lasted twenty-two days. Originally an Alexandrian Greek cleric, he was adopted by the Roman diocese. Under St. Symmachus, he represented the pope at Theodoric's court of Ravenna; St. Hormisdas used him similarly at Constantinople. During the reign of St. Felix III, Dioscurus was the leader of the Byzantine party at Rome, which led directly to his illegal election as pope in opposition to Boniface.

## John II

**(January 2, 533–May 8, 535)**

The death of Boniface opened up precisely the problems he had sought to avoid by appointing a successor. Not only were promises of votes sold back and forth, but so were sacred vessels—and practically anything else a profit could be found for. At last, the senate of Rome and King Athalaric (son of Theodoric) outlawed simony, and the election took place. The winner was a Roman-born priest, Mercurius, son of Projectus, assigned to the basilica of San Clemente. Not wishing to be pope with a pagan god's name, he decided to be called John—the first pope to change his name.

In contrast to the disorder that had raged for the preceding period, his election was greeted with joy. Emperor Justinian sent his profession of faith and a number of valuable gifts. Athalaric, although an Arian, was overjoyed at the prospect of peace in his largest city.

Justinian's support was quickly rewarded. At the time, another dispute over the Trinity had broken out in the East. The emperor (who attempted to find an ambiguous formula that might please both sides) was opposed by the *Acoemetae*, or "Sleepless Monks" who prayed in shifts around the clock (rather like the modern cloistered orders who practice Perpetual Adoration of the Blessed Sacrament). John ruled in favor of the emperor. He also solved some jurisdictional problems in southern Gaul.

The most dramatic event in John's pontificate, however, was Justinian's invasion of Africa. The imperial general Belisarius quickly defeated the Vandals. The old imperial administration was restored, and the Church in Africa was

freed from persecution. This event, however, required a great deal of reorganization in the Church as well.

The African bishops in synod asked John for a decision as to whether bishops who had become Arians under Vandal persecution and wished to return to the Church could be reinstated in their old jobs. However, the letter arrived after John's death; his successor would deal with the question.

## St. Agapetus I
### (May 13, 535–April 22, 536)

Born in Rome, the son of the priest Gordianus, Agapetus was archpriest of the basilica of San Giovanni e Paolo at the time of his election. Immediately he was faced with the question of the lapsed Arian bishops in Africa. His reply to the question posed to his predecessor was that those bishops who had become Arian should be satisfied with being readmitted to the Church, without attempting to regain their former clerical status.

Athalaric, king of the Ostrogoths and friend of the papacy, died and was replaced with Theodahat. The new king, worried by the defeat of the Vandals and aware that Emperor Justinian's long-threatened project of reconquering Italy for the empire was about to be launched, sent Agapetus to Constantinople to ask the emperor to desist.

Once in the city, Agapetus had no more luck with Justinian than St. John I had with Justin I in forwarding a gothic king's cause at the imperial court. But as with St. John, the trip was a personal triumph. Justinian presented the pope with a Catholic declaration of Faith, and, at Agapetus's urging, deposed Anthimus, the semi-Monophysite patriarch of Constantinople. Unhappily, the pope died in the imperial city. His body arrived at Rome on September 20, 536, and was buried in St. Peter's. His feast day on the Latin calendar is September 25, and on the Byzantine, April 18.

## St. Silverius

### (June 8, 536–June 20, 537)

Born at Frosinone in Campania, Silverius was the son of Pope St. Hormisdas, coming into the world while his father was still one of the lower clergy (who at that time could marry). He was appointed pope while still a subdeacon by King Theudahat of the Ostrogoths (the Roman clergy later ratified Silverius's accession); the Gothic ruler hoped to secure his shaky position by having a loyal pope in Rome.

This hope was shattered by Justinian's general, Belisarius, who, as long expected, led the imperial armies in conquest of Italy. Rome was speedily liberated and once again an emperor had direct control of the birthplace of the empire. Even so, although the major cities of the peninsula were swiftly occupied, Byzantine troops would face Ostrogothic guerrillas until 552.

Pleased as the Romans were by this event, the immediate results were not too pleasant. The empress Theodora pursued her goal of making Monophysitism the religion of Church and empire and made a deal with the rather ambitious deacon Vigilius, who had been Boniface II's choice as successor in that pope's abortive attempt to alter the method of choosing pontiffs. If she could arrange for him to be pope, he would revoke St. Agapetus's condemnation of Anthimus. This would pave the way for that prelate's restoration as patriarch of Constantinople—paving the way for an eventual rejection of the Council of Chalcedon.

The Ostrogoths were able to rally enough troops to besiege Rome. Although they were driven off, it was alleged that the pope had corresponded with them during the siege. Silverius was duly accused of high treason against the empire (an easy charge to make, given his appointment by the Gothic king). He was deposed and exiled to Patara, in Lycia, Asia Minor (modern Finike, Turkey), birthplace of St. Nicholas. Vigilius was appointed pope in his place by the emperor on March 19, 537.

Once ensconced in his place of exile, rather than fretting, Silverius began assisting the local clergy and their bishop in their routine work. Soon, the bishop of the place, now knowing Silverius very well, informed the emperor that his "guest" was in fact completely innocent of all charges. Justinian ordered him set free and returned to Rome for a new trial. But General Belisarius ordered his henchmen to waylay Silverius and deposit him on the island of Palmaria (Ponza), off Anzio. There St. Silverius died of hunger and cold. His relics remain on the island, and his feast is June 20.

Although he met his death there, the people of Ponza embraced St. Silverius as their patron, attributing to his intercession with God their great success at fishing. Not only is St. Silverius's feast day a huge celebration on the island itself, drawing back hundreds of expatriate Ponzesi every year, their descendants around the world continue to honor him.

St. Silverius is revered in the United States, in Dover Plains, New York (rural Dutchess County), where Ponzesi have dedicated a sanctuary to him. The late Ercito Mazzella (d. January 1997) organized a committee and purchased eighty-one acres of wooded land in this small town, creating the "San Silverio Shrine of Dover Plains, New York." This shrine serves as the location for the annual feast and other events to honor St. Silverius. Since the property was purchased, membership in the society has grown and today it is one of the largest Italian organizations in the United States.

Bahia Blanca, in the Argentine province of Buenos Aires, received a large number of Ponzesi immigrants at the beginning of the twentieth century. Every year, the last Saturday of November, the town witnesses a procession of St. Silverius. It wends its way through the streets to the docks, where the fishing boat crews render tribute to him on board.

Ponzesi have brought the St. Silverius devotion to Sardinia, where there is a chapel dedicated to him on the beach at Vignola. In the 1920s, fishermen of Ponza went to catch lobster off Sardinia from March to September and sell them in the ports of Marseilles and Barcelona. The lobster zone was above all off the north coast of Sardinia; at the beach of Vignola was a large open air camp of boats and men. The landowner determined to build a shelter for these poor fishermen. This they turned into a chapel to their patron Saint—today it doubles as both place of prayer and of rest.

Completely unconnected to the far-ranging sons of Ponza is the small village of St. Sylvere off route 20N near Drummondville, Quebec. Founded in 1887, the village's French Canadian inhabitants keep St. Silverius's feast as their annual celebration.

Nor is the saint forgotten in his birthplace of Frosinone in Latium, where he and his father, St. Hormisdas, are co-patrons. In his honor a series of celebrations occur in June: in addition to High Mass and a procession, there is a music festival, sports events, dog shows, and various exhibitions. The festivities continue for some days after June 20.

# Vigilius
## (March 29, 537–June 7, 555)

Son of Johannes, who had been appointed consul of Rome by the emperor, Vigilius came from a distinguished Roman family. Ordained a deacon by Boniface II in 531, later that year (due doubtless to his impressive social standing as well as political acumen), he was appointed by the pope to be the pope's successor. As previously noted, this proce-dure, unpopular as it was among most Catholics throughout the known world, was rescinded the next year.

St. Agapetus I, equally impressed with Vigilius's abilities, appointed him papal legate (*Apocrisarius*) to the emperor at Constantinople. Empress Theodora, anxious to win control of the Church for the Monophysites, sought to make an ally out of him. She promised him the papacy and seven hundred pounds in gold if he would help her. When news came of the pope's death, he returned to Rome armed with imperial letters of favor and a large amount of money.

By the time Vigilius arrived, however, the Gothic king had appointed St. Silverius as pope. Shortly after, Belisarius occupied Rome. Vigilius gave the letters recommending him as pope to the general; after the siege began and St. Silverius was condemned and exiled, the way was clear. Vigilius was consecrated and enthroned on March 29, 537. The majority of the Roman clergy and people, however, refused to recognize him until the news came of St. Silverius's death, then they accepted him as Pope.

The three following years of routinely wielding papal authority—administering his See and solving disciplinary problems in Portugal and ever-excitable southern Gaul—brought Vigilius to an understanding of his proper role. In 540, he sent letters to Justinian and St. Mennas, patriarch of Constantinople, in which he reiterated his approval of the teachings of Ephesus and Chalcedon and of the condemnation of Anthimus.

But four years later, new doctrinal quarrels in the East demanded his attention. Justinian issued a decree renewing imperial condemnations of Origenism. To lure imperial attentions elsewhere, Bishop Theodore Askidas of Caesarea in Cappadocia (modern Kayseri, Turkey) pointed out that condemnation of the school of theology in Antioch, which had been friendly to Nestorianism (the opposite heresy to Monophysitism) would please the Monophysites. Justinian, keen to reconcile the Monophysites—co-religionists of his empress, a strong party in the capital, and perhaps a majority of the

populations of Syria and Egypt—without accepting their heresy, was glad to do so.

Three Antiochene theologians had written as many documents condemning Ephesus and upholding Nestorianism, in part. These were the famous "Three Chapters," which would hold a large place in history for the next two centuries. In 544, Justinian condemned them, which condemnation was signed by the Eastern patriarchs and bishops. But in western Europe, many prelates, although recognizing the heretical elements of the Three Chapters, felt that it was inexpedient to condemn them, because any such condemnation might weaken the authority of Chalcedon. Vigilius refused to endorse the condemnation and was called to Constantinople by the emperor to settle the question with a synod.

It was literally an offer Vigilius could not refuse. On November 22, 545, while the city was again under siege by the Goths, he celebrated the feast of St. Cecilia in the basilica of Santa Cecilia in Trastevere. Before the Mass had finished, the imperial prefect entered the church, seized the pope, and hustled him off to a ship waiting in the Tiber. Thinking he was fleeing the encircled and starving city, the mob gathered on the bank, throwing stones and cursing him.

Vigilius was then conveyed to Sicily, where he stopped for some time, during the course of which he dispatched grain ships to relieve the starving Romans. These, however, were captured by the Ostrogoths when they entered the Tiber. The pope finally reached Constantinople in December 546 or January 547.

Once before the emperor, Vigilius attempted to convince him of the need to send troops to relieve Rome. But Justinian was far more concerned with condemning the Three Chapters—a particularly bad judgment, as the city would fall to the Goths in 546. Vigilius was reluctant to do this, not because they were orthodox, but because he feared the practical result in the West. In response, Justinian refused to let the pope return to Rome until he did so. In 548, Vigilius did issue a decree condemning the Three Chapters while reaffirming Chalcedon; however, on reflection as to the probable result in the West, he withdrew it. In 553, the emperor at last convened a council in Constantinople, to which most of the Eastern and a few of the Western bishops came.

This assemblage duly condemned the Three Chapters and then dispersed. Faced with great pressure, on December 8, 553, Vigilius approved the synod's judgments. Thus it became, in retrospect the fifth Ecumenical Council, Constantinople II. Because of its irregular circumstances, however, and the pressure brought to bear on Vigilius (including having certain of his supporters in the city imprisoned) to confirm it, it was long before it was universally recognized as such. Writing a half century later, Pope St. Gregory I, called "the Great," wrote (in his *Dialogues*) that "the *four* Councils are like the four

Gospels." On February 26, 554, Vigilius wrote a Constitution setting forth his condemnation of the Three Chapters in detail.

The result was as bad as Vigilius had feared. A number of bishops in the West formed a schism. Illyricum, which had oscillated between Rome and Constantinople for over a hundred years, split with both. This rift would not be healed until 700, by which time the Illyrian metropolitan See of Aquileia had declared itself a patriarchate (which title was retained after Aquileia was reconciled; when that city was ravaged in war, the title was transferred to Venice—the archbishop of that city is still today called "Patriarch of Venice").

But whatever the results in the long term might be, Vigilius was free to return to his own city—and did so equipped with Justinian's "Pragmatic Sanction," a document conceding to the popes certain aspects of the civil administration in Italy, which his successors would use in their attempts to rebuild the ravished country. He began the trip as soon as he could, in the spring of 555. Worn out by the events of the past five years, however, he died at Syracuse, Sicily, on the journey home. His body was returned to Rome and interred at San Silvestro in Capite.

## Pelagius I
### (April 16, 556–March 3, 561)

Pelagius was born into a noble Roman family, to John, imperial vicar over half of Italy. Pelagius had accompanied St. Agapetus I to Constantinople. Before that pope died there, he appointed Pelagius apocrisarius—papal ambassador to the imperial court. Pelagius remained there during the dramatic events surrounding the death of St. Silverius and the accession of Vigilius. In 543, having been instrumental in persuading Justinian (who held him in high regard) to condemn Origenism, Pelagius returned to Rome.

When Vigilius was compelled to leave for Constantinople, he left Pelagius as his representative in Rome. As the siege continued, Pelagius exhausted his private fortune relieving the starving of the city. At last, in 546, the Ostrogoths reentered the city; however, their king, Totila, had come to admire Pelagius so much for his bravery during the siege that he spared the lives of the Romans, and sent Pelagius to Constantinople to ask Justinian for peace. The emperor's reply was that Belisarius was in command in Italy and would make all decisions regarding peace or war.

Pelagius returned again to support Vigilius in his exile in 551. Empowered

by his subordinate, Vigilius continued to resist Justinian's demands. But after the Council of Constantinople was called, and Justinian ordered Pelagius and others supporters of the pope thrown into prison, Vigilius gave in. At first Pelagius, from his cell, wrote against both the Three Chapters' opponents and the pope's weakness, but, at last realizing that he did more harm than good in doing so, agreed to support Constantinople II. Following his release, he set off with Vigilius on the long voyage home.

As it happened, in the end he escorted the pope's body back to Rome. Pelagius returned to a country devastated by the Gothic War and rent by schism. Church organization had broken down, starvation was everywhere, and churches and houses alike were in poor repair. His own reputation was in tatters, partly for his acceptance of Constantinople II, and partly for the suspicion that he had had something to do with Vigilius's death. Although eventually elected pope by the Roman clergy, he had difficulty finding three bishops to consecrate him.

After Pelagius was enthroned, he went to St. Peter's, and before Narses (Belisarius's far more benevolent successor in Italy) he swore on the Gospels that he had done no ill to Vigilius. He then began to repair the material damage done by the Gothic War. Pelagius reorganized the Church's estates (from which came much of the Church's income), using his own money as well as that of the Church to relieve the poor, repair the damaged churches, and organize tribunals to deal with the clerical abuses that had grown over the years since Vigilius left—these comprised a good part of his work and paid off both in terms of the opinion of the people and in donations from overseas.

But just as difficult was the need to repair the damage done by the condemnation of the Three Chapters. The bishops of Northern Italy were vehemently apposed to Pelagius, try as he might to explain that there was no essential difference between the definitions of Chalcedon and those of Constantinople II, and that as the Three Chapters were implicitly heretical they might as well be explicitly condemned. Paulinus of Aquileia convened a synod that condemned the pope, separated itself from Rome, and excommunicated both Pelagius and Narses. Angered greatly by this, Pelagius urged Narses to march on Aquileia, but the canny general, aware of the political ramifications of such an act, refused.

In Gaul, however, the Frankish king Chilebert was convinced of Pelagius's orthodoxy by a profession of faith sent him, and he was pleased by the pope's handling of yet another fight over precedence in southern Gaul.

It was an exciting term, to be sure, and at the end he was hailed by the Romans as "Father of the poor and of his country." The day after his death, he was buried at St. Peter's.

## John III

### (July 17, 561–July 13, 574)

Born to the noble Roman family of the *Catelinii*, John had to wait a few months after his election to receive confirmation from Justinian, and upon receipt of which he was consecrated. Although his predecessor had done much to restore the ravaged peninsula, there was much yet to be done.

In the meantime, Narses, who administered Italy from Ravenna, had to be most concerned with the effectiveness of the imperial armies in Italy, since restless tribes—particularly the Lombards—were ranging north of the Alps, hoping for an entry into the sunny south.

John continued Pelagius's policy of quiet renovation, helping the poor and repairing the damaged fabric of Italy. But this quiet, if impoverished period, was soon to come to an end.

In 565 Emperor Justinian died, and his nephew, Justin II, assumed the throne. The new emperor soon received a deputation of nobles from Italy who condemned Narses for his taxes, saying that the Greeks were more oppressive than the Goths. Hoping to relieve his subjects, Justin II recalled Narses to Constantinople. Emboldened by departure, the Lombards streamed south.

Nominally Arian Christians, the Lombards were a savage lot. Under their king, Alboine, they had conquered their neighbors in Pannonia, the Gepidae, and brought them and various other conquered peoples with them into Italy. Some notion of Lombard manners and customs might be guessed from the fact that years later, in 574, Alboine's queen, the Gepid princess Rosamunde, stabbed Alboine to death in reprisal for her consort's forcing her to drink wine from the skull of her father, the conquered Gepid king.

These barbarians swept through the Adriatic plain. Although at first repulsed near Ravenna and Pavia, they soon took the latter city. Here Alboine set up his capital, which would be the dwelling place of all the Lombard kings so long as their realm lasted.

In a very short time, the Byzantines were confined to the south and the ports. The atrocities committed by the Lombards were legendary, and the disarmed Italian population—outside those areas protected by imperial troops—were at their mercy. As the blood of his flock ran, the pope could think of only one solution: Narses must return. John traveled to Constantinople and prevailed upon the old general to return and organize the defense, albeit on a private basis.

Unhappily, the imperial bureaucrats in Rome refused to deal with either John or Narses when they returned. The pope retreated to the catacombs in protest, performing all of his functions there and reemerging only a year later when Narses died. The general's body was sent back to Constantinople in a leaden casket, and John's hopes for a military victory against the Lombards went with him.

The three years remaining to the pope were saddened by the seemingly endless privations of his people. He stood beside them, however, helping where he could, without hope for human aid. He was buried in St. Peter's and given an epitaph that sums up his character: "In the midst of straits he knew how to be bountiful, and feared not to be crushed amidst a crumbling world."

## Benedict I

### (June 2, 575–July 30, 579)

The Lombards had succeeded in isolating Rome, and although the election of the new pope, a Roman by birth, occurred shortly after John III's death, eleven months would pass before confirmation of his accession was received from the emperor at Constantinople.

What the Lombards did for communications, they and the Gothic Wars had also done for agriculture—famine stalked the peninsula, even in places otherwise unaffected by combat. With the imperial garrisons restricted to the ports, and the interior being ravaged, hunger was an everyday reality for most Italians, regardless of rank. Apart from ordinations, the only existing record of Benedict's activities show him selling or reassigning Church properties in an attempt to bring some relief to the starving. He was buried in St. Peter's.

# Pelagius II

## (November 26, 579–February 7, 590)

Born at Rome of a Gothic father (Winigild), Pelagius faced the same problem as Benedict had in securing imperial confirmation. Four months passed after his election to the papacy; at last, the consecration was duly performed without the emperor's permission.

His first act was to convince—through words and money—the Lombards to cease for the moment their on again, off again siege of Rome. Immediately thereafter, he sent the deacon, Gregory, with an embassy to Constantinople to explain the events surrounding his consecration and to beg for military relief for the city. But the Empire was exhausted by Justinian's wars and the constant skirmishing with the Persians to the East. Justin II had died in 578, and was by no means a man of his uncle's ability (given his fits of madness)—still less so was his adopted son and successor, Tiberius II. In addition to the Eastern threat, the Avars, occupying modern Hungary and Romania, were a clear and present danger to Constantinople itself. There would be no help from the East, for the time being.

Pelagius therefore looked to the West, to the kingdom of the Franks in Gaul. A letter he wrote to the bishop of Auxerre, adviser to the Frankish kings, had the effect—along with a similar appeal by Tiberius II—of bringing the Franks into Italy in 581. At first, their success against the Lombards was tremendous and relieved pressure upon the still-Imperial coastal cities. But the Lombards had learned at least the art of bribery from their civilized prey and paid the Franks to go home. Conditions worsened further.

The next year Tiberius died and was succeeded by his son-in-law, the able general Maurice. Pelagius sent Gregory to Rome as apocrisarius, with a commission to "haunt the imperial palace" until he should get the needed aid. Making himself popular in various ways with the Easterners, Gregory at last prevailed upon Maurice in 584 to send a new sort of governor—an exarch—to Ravenna, armed with full military, judicial, and political power.

Alas, the exarch Decius arrived with few troops, more equipped to act as police in the areas still retained than as troops to defend them, let alone to defeat the Lombards. When the pope asked Decius for aid, he replied that he could not defend Ravenna against a determined assault, let alone Rome. Although further requests directly to Constantinople brought no help, the exarch finally managed to conclude a truce with the Lombards, who themselves were anxious at this point to rest and organize their plunder. For the moment, Italy was at peace.

The break in hostilities allowed the pontiff to turn his attention at last to the schism with Aquileia. He and his secretary—the returned Gregory—sent letter after letter to the schismatics, begging them to return to Catholic unity and ensuring them that condemnation of the Three Chapters was not a repudiation of Chalcedon. Persuasion did not work, whereupon Smaragdus—the new exarch—seized Severus of Grado—leader of the northern schism—and forced him to enter into communion with the Orthodox John, who was bishop of Ravenna. But as soon as Severus returned home, he repudiated his action. The schism continued.

At the same time, the patriarch of Constantinople assumed the title "Ecumenical Patriarch," which appeared to be a challenge to papal primacy. Pelagius unsuccessfully protested this. He had more luck with imposing celibacy on the subdeacons of Sicily and with redecorating and rebuilding various Roman churches, such as San Lorenzo.

If Famine had been somewhat allayed, and War quieted, the Third Horseman arrived—Plague. In 589, it swept Rome, carrying off—among many others—the pope himself. He was given a proper burial in St. Peter's.

## St. Gregory I (the Great)
### (September 3, 590–March 11, 604)

Gregory was born at Rome of the noble house of the *Anicii*, in 540. Gregory's father, Gordianus, was the son of St. Felix II and was married to Silvia, who would herself become a saint. Given his distinguished heritage, it was little surprise when in 571 Gregory was appointed Prefect of Rome.

Four years later, his father died. Gregory turned the mansion bequeathed him into the monastery of San Andrea al Celio; he erected no less than six abbeys on family estates in Sicily. Gregory took the habit and was soon appointed archdeacon of Rome. One day, in the slave market, he saw some Anglo-Saxon slaves from England. Impressed by their beauty, he asked what sort of men they were. Told they were Angles, he said, "not Angles, but Angels!" He bought and freed them, and they joined his monastery. One named Augustine would become famous in his own right.

In keeping with his reputation for holiness, Gregory kept open table for the poor. The stone table at which he hosted a beggar who turned out to be an angel in disguise is still preserved at his monastery (now San Gregorio al Celio).

In 579, Pelagius II sent him to Constantinople as apocrisarius and his piety and manner soon won him many friends. While there he composed the Liturgy of the Presanctified, a sort of prayer and communion service that is still used in the Byzantine Rite—both Catholic and Orthodox—during Lent. Although his mission was more or less unsuccessful, to this day he is considered a Church Father in the East.

In 585, Pelagius recalled Gregory to Rome to be his secretary, with special regard to ending the Aquileia schism; in this too, he did not succeed. But he was elected abbot of his monastery and began training his Anglo-Saxon brothers with the idea of accompanying them to England to begin the reconversion of that country.

The outbreak of the plague and the death of the pope, however, put all that into the background. Gregory was elected pope. He led a procession of the clergy, nobles, and people of Rome, asking God to forgive their sins and to end the plague. As the parade passed Hadrian's mausoleum, Gregory saw St. Michael the Archangel atop the building. To commemorate this occurrence, he ordered the golden statue of Michael placed where he had seen the spirit; ever since then, the building has been called "Castel Sant'Angelo."

Despite this success, however, Gregory feared the office of pope and fled in hopes of escaping it. He was found, brought back to the city, and consecrated on September 3. From then on, he began an incredible round of activity.

His interest in liturgical matters was enormous, as shown at Constantinople. He codified the Roman Canon of the Mass (called today, Eucharistic Prayer I) into its present form; hence the alternative name for it of "Gregorian Canon." The pope regulated the chants to be used in the liturgy, "Gregorian Chant." He also arranged the "Stations" of Rome found in the pre-1970 Roman Missal, the schedule of particular churches where individuals might hear Mass every day in succession.

Because a monk of his monastery appeared to Gregory after his death (as he related in his *Dialogues*, bk. 4), and asked for prayers, Gregory said thirty Masses for the monk in as many days, and was rewarded with a second apparition of the monk, who told him that the pope's Masses had released him from purgatory. The pope then ordered the practice of "Gregorian Masses," a cycle of thirty Masses to be said at a privileged altar for the express purpose of releasing an individual from purgatory.

His writings were voluminous—scripture commentaries, sermons, letters to various dignitaries and others throughout the world, and his famous *Dialogues* (for which the Easterners call him St. Gregory *Dialogos*) and *Pastoral Guide* for priests.

In addition to fighting Arianism, paganism, Simony, Manichaeanism, Donatism, and sundry other evils, Gregory promoted the growth of the Benedictine order and resisted the growing pretensions of the patriarch of Constantinople. To relieve peasants and the poor, he put the administration of Church properties, the "Patrimony of St. Peter," in order. He was even able to begin the conversion of the Lombards.

Though his work was great in Italy, his effect elsewhere was, if possible, even greater. He sent forty monks under Augustine to England, where they speedily converted much of the population; the now-Anglican cathedral of Rochester is called "St. Andrew" in memory of the Roman monastery where the forty-one had learned their Faith.

In Spain, the Visigothic king, Reccared, with most of his people, gave up Arianism in response to the work of Gregory and his friend St. Leander, bishop of Seville. The pontiff was just as successful in tightening ecclesiastical discipline and ending at last the Donatist heresy in North Africa.

When Gregory died, the Church was on a much more stable foundation than it had been at his accession. He was buried on March 12, which is his feast in both the Latin and Byzantine calendars (although those Orthodox who retain the Julian calendar transfer the observance to March 25). Still popular in the East, he was also especially revered in England before the Reformation.

## Sabinian
### (September 13, 604–February 22, 606)

Born at Bieda, near Viterbo, Sabinian was the son of Bonus. Sent to Constantinople as apocrisarius by St. Gregory I in 593, he was not very effective and was recalled in 597. Nevertheless, he was elected pope soon after Gregory's death, although he had to wait some time owing to the now-customary delay in imperial confirmation.

The Lombards seized St. Gregory's death as an excuse to go on the warpath again and although they subsided after a few months, their depredations were enough to cause famine once more. The pope, although opening the granaries and selling grain to the people cheaply, annoyed them by not giving it away. He replaced many of the monks St. Gregory had appointed with secular clerics.

## Boniface III
(February 19–November 12, 607)

Son of John Catadioce, Roman-born Boniface was elected nearly a year after his predecessor's death. He had been a deacon and served as apocrisarius under St. Gregory I, being sent to Constantinople in 603. Far more successful at the job than Sabinian had been, he won the friendship of the emperor Phocas, who at his urging ordered the patriarch of Constantinople to drop the title "Ecumenical," as belonging solely to the pope.

Boniface's major act as pope was to hold a synod, which excommunicated anyone who, during the lifetime of a pope or bishop, discussed or lobbied for his successor. The synod further forbade any election of a new candidate until the old one had been buried.

## St. Boniface IV
(September 15, 608–May 25, 615)

Born at Valeria in the province of Marsi, near Viterbo, Boniface was the son of a physician named John. He became a monk of San Sebastiano monastery and was ordained deacon by St. Gregory I, who appointed him administrator over the patrimony of St. Peter.

One of his first tasks was to appeal to Emperor Phocas for permission to turn the old pagan temple to Jupiter, Mars, and Venus—the Pantheon—into a church. Permission was duly granted, and the building was transformed on May 13, 609, into the church of Santa Maria ad Martyres. Twenty-eight cartloads of relics were brought up from the catacombs and placed beneath the new altar.

In Boniface's time, Mellitus, first bishop of London, arrived in Rome to consult with the pope on the affairs of the English Church and to take part in a synod. Boniface gave answers to various religious and administrative questions that Mellitus had, and the whole visit underscored the close relationship between England and Rome that would last until Henry VIII.

St. Columban, an Irish monk who had settled at Bobbio in Liguria (after

being driven out of Ireland, Scotland, and Gaul, where he had founded the great abbey of Luxeuil) wrote a letter to Boniface respectfully *and* insultingly demanding that the pope retract the condemnation of the Three Chapters and disavow Constantinople II. Boniface of course refused, but bore no ill will toward St. Columban for the outburst (something for which this author, whose familial patron St. Columban is, is truly grateful!).

If the Lombards were quiet, disease, famine, and flood were not. But truly horrifying news reached Rome from the East: in 614 the Persians swept over the frontier into Syria and Palestine and took Jerusalem. Not only were the holiest sites in Christendom now under heathen occupation, but also the Persians had taken the True Cross as a trophy of war back to their capital at Ctesiphon (in modern Iraq).

Heartbroken by this news, St. Boniface died the next year. His feast is June 1 on the Roman calendar, but May 25 at his hometown of Marsi.

## St. Deusdedit (Adeodatus) I

### (October 19, 615–November 8, 618)

Deusdedit was born a Roman, son of the subdeacon Stephen. He entered the priesthood and rose to be archpriest of the basilica of Sts. Giovanni e Paolo. His short pontificate was nevertheless extremely busy. This pope ordered that in churches too small to hold their congregations, Masses could be held twice on Sunday (a custom maintained to this day). During a plague year his attentions to his flock won him their devotion, and he was the first pope to affix leaden seals (*Bullae*) to his decrees—hence the common word for such a document, a "Bull." Although he died on November 8, his feast is kept at Rome on November 26 with Sts. Simplicius and Gelasius.

## Boniface V

### (December 23, 619–October 25, 625)

If events were not bad enough, the exarch Eleutherius of Ravenna, after the death of the pope, declared himself independent of the emperor and marched on Rome. Fortunately for the city, his own troops followed his example, mutinied, and slew him.

The next papal election was thus delayed by many months. When Boniface was elected, he immediately went to work dealing with administrative questions that the dramatic events of the previous few pontificates had led to being ignored. This pope established the right of sanctuary, whereby criminals could elude their pursuers for a period if they could reach a church; he further enacted that notaries—important officials under Roman-derived law (as in Louisiana today)—must follow the laws of the empire in their work. Moreover, he ruled that acolytes could not translate (move from one church to another) relics, nor take the place of deacons at baptism. Much loved by his clergy, he was buried on the day of his death.

## Honorius I

### (November 3, 625–October 12, 638)

It was well for the new pope, a native of Campania, that Italy had settled down for the moment. Modeling himself on Gregory I, Honorius was much concerned with English affairs and granted the pallium to the archbishops of Canterbury and York. Thus was established the duality between the two Sees that dominated English church history until the Reformation—men bearing those two titles remain the top Anglican churchmen today.

In Spain, Honorius oversaw the reorganization of the Church in that country after the Visigoths converted and made Catholicism the state church. In the year 630, he urged the southern Irish bishops to keep Easter on the same date as the rest of Christendom; in response they held a synod and adopted the Roman date, with much expression of love and fidelity to the pa-

pacy. He also reconciled many of the schismatics of northern Italy and restored a number of northern churches.

Events in the East shadowed his pontificate, however, and ultimately made him the first (and so far only) pope ever to be condemned as a heretic by an ecumenical council.

The fall of Jerusalem had led to the Persians conquering Egypt and Asia Minor, camping across the Bosphorus from Constantinople. The emperor Heraclius considered moving the capital of the empire to his hometown of Carthage in North Africa. But rallying both himself and his forces, he pulled off a series of stunning campaigns, driving the Persians out of the empire and regaining the True Cross, which he proudly reinstalled at the Church of the Holy Sepulchre.

The battles had underscored an important problem: the Monophysite subjects in Syria and Egypt were disaffected, and that disaffection had helped pave the way for the easy fall of those provinces to the Persians. Moreover, rumor had reached the court of a supposed prophet in the Arabian desert, whose followers felt obligated to subject the whole world to their idea of God, Allah. Clearly, some sort of compromise formula that both Catholics and Monophysites could accept was essential if the Byzantines were to retain the newly regained territories.

In 634, Patriarch Sergius of Constantinople wrote to Pope Honorius, explaining that while campaigning in Armenia back in 622, the emperor had refuted a Monophysite cleric he was debating by saying that although there were indeed two natures in Christ, there was one "operation" or will between them. This phrase, moreover, had been used by Vigilius in a letter to St. Mennas who was then patriarch of Constantinople (a letter, however, which later turned out to be a forgery). The problem with this was that in uniting the two Wills of Christ, He would cease to be perfect Man as well as perfect God—the utility of His Sacrifice for the salvation of humanity depending upon His Manhood. Thus the whole of the Divine economy of Salvation would be overthrown. Four years before Sergius wrote, he explained, Cyrus had become patriarch of Alexandria and had found Egypt almost entirely Monophysite. He found that using the emperor's formula allowed him to reconcile many Egyptian Monophysites to the Catholic faith. At this point a Palestinian monk named Sophronius objected, pointing out that the orthodox belief was that, having two perfect natures—Human and Divine—Christ must have two wills. Sergius was willing to instruct Cyrus to stop using "one operation" so long as Sophronius would not jeopardize such unity as had already been accomplished. The monk agreed, but Sergius wanted a definitive statement on the whole affair. Thus this letter to the pope.

Honorius's reply for the most part dodged the question—he neither defined nor condemned. He did say, however, that there was only one will in Christ. Now, unless he meant something else (and oceans of ink have been

poured to prove it so), then here is a plainly heretical statement on his part. But it is important to remember that in this letter he was neither speaking officially, nor attempting to bind the Church—hence the importance of the lack of condemnations and definitions. Nevertheless, this action led to his branding as a heretic by Constantinople III (680–681). (Having often been thrown up as proof of papal doctrinal malfeasance by various controversialists, this episode would be considered minutely by the Fathers of Vatican I in 1870, as they worked to define papal infallibility exactly.)

Meanwhile, the Muslim Arabs had lived up to Heraclius's worse fears—swarming out of the desert, they defeated the Byzantines at the battle of Yarmuk in 636, having taken Damascus the year before—in short order, Jerusalem and all of Syria and Palestine had fallen to them. Although they did not interfere with the local Christians initially, this would change.

Bear in mind that the regions of the empire which ultimately would fall to the Muslims—Syria, Palestine, Egypt, Lebanon, Libya, Tunisia, Algeria, Morocco, and Turkey—were, under Roman and Byzantine rule, flourishing and fertile places. Their rich Christian cultures were as advanced as contemporary Italy, Gaul, Spain, or Greece, and in many ways, more so. Over the centuries, however, Islamic rule stifled the Near East and North Africa. Most of the flourishing cities that had sent bishops to various councils and synods, and supported famed schools of learning, were eventually reduced to clumps of ruins, sometimes with tiny villages sheltering in the wreckage. Fertile fields and green forests became, thanks to poor land use and cistern maintenance, sheer desert. In remaining population centers, many a grand church or cathedral became a mosque. (Today the Umayyad Mosque at Damascus, once the grand cathedral of St. John the Baptist, still bears the inscription in Greek over its entrance, "Thy Kingdom, O Christ, is an Everlasting One.")

Small bands of native Christians remain in the Near East—Maronites, Melkites, Syriac Catholics, Armenian Catholics, Chaldean Catholics, and Coptic Catholics (in union with Rome) and Antiochian Orthodox, Coptic Orthodox, Syriac Orthodox, Assyrians, and Armenian Apostolics, out of it. Like the American Indians, these groups, dwindling in their native lands, nevertheless represent the original inhabitants of the Near East. Fortunately, many have come to Europe, North America, and Australasia; even those who are unable to travel to their countries of origin can, by knowing them, get to know something of the origins of Christianity firsthand. Nevertheless, it cannot be said that the Byzantine defeat at the hands of the Arabs was a good thing for the Near East.

In 638, Sergius issued an exposition of his teaching, the *Ecthesis*, which set forth this teaching, *Monothelitism*, as it is called. It is based upon Honorius's letter. Emperor Heraclius decreed that all residents of his empire must accept it. A copy was sent to Honorius for approval, but the pope died before its arrival. His successor would have to deal with the question.

## Severinus
### (May 28–August 2, 640)

Elected shortly after Honorius I's death, on August 18, Severinus sent legates to Constantinople for confirmation of his election. Upon their arrival, Heraclius demanded that Severinus approve the *Ecthesis.* Severinus refused to do so, and Heraclius withheld his confirmation.

To weaken Severinus's resolve, Isaac, the exarch of Ravenna, occupied the Lateran and seized the papal treasury. Still Severinus refused his assent. At last the legates at Constantinople prevailed upon Heraclius (whose attention was by this time firmly on the unraveling of the Eastern provinces), the confirmation was sent, and Severinus was duly consecrated almost two years after his election. This done, he declared once again that Christ had two wills and two natures. (Now, to moderns this seems so trivial, but it was tremendously important for the folk of that time as well as Christians today.) For if Christ had had only a Divine will, it meant that He was not "a man like us in all things save sin," and His sacrifice was thereby not perfect. For the Monothelites, however, their formula seemed to be the only method for reuniting the Copts and Syrians with Constantinople—an essential political measure in the face of the Muslim threat. To the emperors and officials who embraced this belief, the orthodox appeared to be stiff-necked fanatics who were willing to endanger the military security of the empire for the sake of mere words.

In any case, Severinus would enjoy the papacy in its fullness for only a little more than two months.

# John IV

## (December 24, 640–October 12, 642)

Born in Dalmatia, the son of a lawyer named Venantius, John was consecrated very shortly after his election (the job of granting imperial confirmation having been very sensibly deputized to the exarch at Ravenna). He was at the time of Severinus's death archdeacon of Rome.

His attention was soon taken up by the attacks of the Slavs and Avars on his native province (today the coast of Croatia). John sent a representative to Istria and Dalmatia with money to relieve the suffering there and to retrieve the relics of the great Dalmatian saints. These last had been enshrined in churches ruined by the barbarians; the pope erected an oratory to hold them that still stands. Before his elevation to the archidiaconate he had himself done missionary work among the Slavs, at the request of Emperor Heraclius. John also wrote to the northern Irish bishops, asking them to join their brethren in the southern part of the island in celebrating Easter on the Roman date, and warning them against Pelagianism.

John renewed his predecessor's condemnation of the *Ecthesis.* Heraclius, much more worried now about the impending Arab takeover of Egypt, disavowed it and blamed the patriarch Sergius for its composition. The emperor then died in February of 641. His was a most difficult reign, to be sure, but if the empire was gravely threatened at his death, it was not quite in imminent danger of dissolution as it was at his accession.

To the emperor's son and successor, Constans II, the pope wrote a *Defense of Pope Honorius,* in which he maintained that Heraclius, Sergius, and Honorius, although incorrect in their phraseology, had simply been trying to deny that Christ had had *contradictory* wills. Nevertheless, Pyrrus—Sergius's successor as patriarch of Constantinople—refused to withdraw the *Ecthesis,* was condemned by Rome, and so was deposed by Constans.

At his death John was buried in St. Peter's.

# The Heathen Peril

# Theodore I

## (November 24, 642–May 13, 649)

Born at Jerusalem of Greek descent, Theodore's father was a priest of the same name as himself. His election was speedily confirmed by the exarch at Ravenna.

The emperor replaced Pyrrus with a new candidate, Paul, and Pyrrus fled to Rome where he recanted. Theodore wrote to Constans that he could not recognize his deposition of Pyrrus because it was against the canons. Meanwhile, as was customary, Paul sent the pope a confession of faith, but since this did not mention that there were two wills in Christ, it was rejected by Theodore. In 649, encouraged by the support of the bishops of Palestine, Cyprus, and North Africa, Theodore excommunicated Paul and ordered him deposed.

The patriarch Paul was extremely angry. He had the apocrisarii (the papal envoys) at Constantinople mistreated and asked Constans to withdraw the *Ecthesis* once and for all. The emperor did so, but issued a new profession of his own: the *Type*. This document forbade speaking either of two wills or one, but maintained that no one who had used either phrase in the past was to be blamed. Bishops who disobeyed this order were to be deposed; all others would be exiled, excommunicated, or have their goods confiscated. This action was based upon a misinterpretation of John IV's *Defense*.

Theodore died before he could react to the emperor's order. Beloved as a benefactor of the poor and repairer of churches, he was buried in St. Peter's.

# St. Martin I
## (July 21, 649–September 16, 655)

Born at Todi in Tuscany, Martin had served as apocrisarius at Constantinople. As a result, he was very much aware of the Monothelite problem. The October following his consecration, Martin held a council at the Lateran, at which Cyrrus of Alexandria and Sergius, Pyrrus (who had relapsed), and Paul of Constantinople were all condemned as heretical—as were the *Ecthesis* and the *Type*.

Constans's response was predictable. He ordered the exarch Olympius to Rome, to arrest Martin. Once before the city, however, the exarch's nerve failed him, and he did not carry out his orders. His replacement, Theodore Calliopa, was made of sterner stuff, however, and seized the pope late on the night of June 17, 653. Martin was exiled to the Greek island of Naxos, in the Aegean, where he spent a year—ill and malnourished.

Finally Martin was taken to Constantinople to face trial. Despite his sickness, he faced his accusers bravely, was found guilty, and sentenced to be literally cut to pieces. But the dying patriarch Paul begged Constans to spare Martin's life. The emperor commuted his sentence to exile, and Martin was sent to Cherson in Crimea on March 26. Worn out with his sufferings, he soon died.

He was buried in the Blachernae church, near Cherson, but some of his relics were brought home to Rome. Initially buried in the cemetery of St. Priscilla, his relics were enshrined in the church of San Martino ai Monti by Sergius II. Like his predecessor in Crimean exile—St. Clement I—Martin is still revered by the Ukrainians. In the Roman Calendar, he is honored on November 12. The Greek Catholics and Orthodox and the Maronites keep his feast on April 13, and the Russian, Serbian, and Bulgarian Orthodox on April 14. The Greek Synaxarion says of him:

> St. Martin lived during the reign of emperor Constans, the grandson of Heraklios, in 644. Constans was killed in Syracuse of Sicily, specifically at Daphne's bath (as people call it) where he was wounded on the head with a bucket by Andrew Troilus. St. Martin, this excellent man of the orthodox faith, was forcefully brought from Rome to Constantinople together with other western bishops according to royal order.
>
> The blessed man suffered a lot of sorrows and hardships to-

gether with the rest of the bishops on their way to Constantinople. The emperor, who protected the impious heresy of the Monotheletes, sent men to bring the saint to Constantinople because St. Martin renounced and anathematized Sergius, Pyrrhos and Theodore the Monotheletes and he also issued a decree together with the Council which convened in Rome refuting the heresy of the Monotheletes. Thus, the emperor tied up St. Martin and the bishops who were with him as if they were criminals and thieves and he imprisoned them in the praetorium binding them with chains and bonds.

The blessed men remained locked up in prison for three years. Then, the emperor banished them to the city of Cherson which lies near Crimea. There St. Martin suffered a lot of hardships, he led a life of martyrdom and then he departed to the Lord. His holy relics were buried outside the city of Cherson in the church of most holy Theotokos.

## St. Eugene I

### (August 10, 654–June 1, 657)

Elected during the exile of St. Martin I, Eugene was forcibly consecrated by order of Emperor Constans II on September 8. If the emperor was taken in by Eugene's mild temperament, he was much mistaken. The pope reiterated the condemnations hurled by his predecessor. He sent apocrisarii to Constantinople where they were rejected by Pyrrus (once again on the patriarchal throne) and Constans. He was saved from sharing St. Martin I's fate by the Muslim seizure of Rhodes in 654 and their naval defeat of the Byzantines the next year. Caught between Arabs, Avars, and Slavs, Constans was too busy to annoy this pope further. St. Eugene I's feast is June 2.

## St. Vitalian

### (July 30, 657–January 27, 672)

Vitalian was born at Segni and his first interest was reunion with the emperor and patriarch of Constantinople. Not only did he notify Constans of his election on July 5, 663, he gave him a splendid reception at Rome. Despite the split between the two, he allowed the emperor to assist at Mass at St. Peter's on two successive Sundays—but to no avail.

The question was rendered moot in 668, when Emperor Constans II was murdered. His son and successor, Constantine IV Pognatus, had no appetite for further quarrels with the pope, having imperial survival uppermost in his mind.

On a happier note, in the same year Vitalian sent the Greek St. Theodore of Tarsus to England as archbishop of Canterbury, with a special mission of bringing the English churches in line with Rome in the celebration of Easter.

St. Vitalian's feast is January 27; it is marked in his home town of Segni with a fair.

## Adeodatus II

### (April 11, 672–June 26, 676)

A monk of the monastery of Sant'Elmo on the Celian Hill, Adeodatus defended orthodoxy against the Monothelites. He was an avid church restorer and took the monasteries of Sts. Peter and Paul (St. Augustine) in Canterbury, England, and that of St. Martin at Tours, France, under direct papal protection.

In his pontificate, Constantinople itself was under direct siege by the Arabs; for four long years the imperial city, under Constantine IV's command, held out. After the siege, they were forced to withdraw from Asia Minor (their first major defeat) and pay the emperor tribute for thirty years. At the same time, the citizens of Thessalonica broke the siege of the Slavs and Avars around their city. But in 674, the Bulgarians swept out of the Steppes, over the Danube, and into northern Thrace, where they set up a kingdom in the region that still bears their name.

## Donus
### (November 2, 676–April 11, 678)

Born in Rome to Mauricius, Donus paved the courtyard in front of St. Peter's and restored both Santa Eufemia on the Via Appia and St. Paul Outside the Walls. He had the joy of welcoming Reparatus, archbishop of Ravenna, back into union, ending the last of the schism of the Three Chapters. Donus also discovered a nest of Nestorian monks in the Monasterium Boetianum, a Syrian establishment in the city. He dispersed them and put Romans in their place.

## St. Agatho
### (June 27, 678–January 10, 681)

Born in Sicily, and originally a Basilian monk at a Greek-speaking monastery in Palermo, Agatho transferred to a house of his order in Rome. Constantine Pogonatus asked the pope to send legates to preside over an ecumenical council—Constantinople III—which opened on November 7, 680. There a letter from Agatho condemning the Monothelites was read and accepted; however, Macarius, Monothelite patriarch of Antioch, cited Pope Honorius I's writings in his own defense. As a result, that pope was posthumously condemned as a heretic by that council on March 28. The council documents were sent to Rome for approval, but by that time the pope was dead.

He also received St. Wilfrid, archbishop of York, and upheld him against St. Theodore, who was intent on bringing York more closely into line with Rome liturgically. Agatho restored his archdiocese to him and sent choristers to England to reintroduce Gregorian Chant. He performed many miracles. His feast day is January 10 in the Latin calendar, February 20 in the Byzantine, and February 14 at Palermo, where he is the major patron.

## St. Leo II

### (August 17, 682–June 28, 683)

Born at Aidone in Sicily, Leo had been elected in December of 681, but could be consecrated only after Constantine IV's confirmation. He received the findings of Constantinople III and duly ratified them. Of the condemnation of Honorius I, he wrote, "We anathematize . . . Honorius, who did not attempt to sanctify this Apostolic Church with the teaching of Apostolic tradition, but by profane treachery permitted its purity to be polluted."

Very friendly to the Easterners, he built the church of San Giorgio in Velabro for the Greeks in Rome. Moreover, he reconciled the last holdouts of the Northern schism. Leo also reformed Gregorian Chant, and, being a master of both Greek and Latin, composed several hymns that are still used in the Liturgy of the Hours. His feast is June 28, although it is observed at Aidone on July 3, that being the date of his burial in 684.

## St. Benedict II

### (June 26, 684–May 8, 685)

Benedict was born a Roman and had been a monk at Monte Cassino. Although elected just after the death of St. Leo II, he had to wait for his consecration until Constantine IV confirmed his accession. This experience led him to persuade the emperor to give up that privilege. He succeeded in impelling the Western Church to accept Constantinople III, which some local dioceses were reluctant to do because of its condemnation of Honorius I. Benedict also supported St. Wilfrid of York in his various tribulations. His feast is May 7.

## John V

### (July 23, 685–August 2, 686)

John was born in Syria, the son of Cyriacus. As a deacon, he had been part of the papal delegation at Constantinople III and returned with the documents of that council to Rome. While in the imperial city, he had so impressed Constantine IV that the emperor reduced the taxes on papal estates in Sicily and Calabria.

Because the emperor had renounced his right of confirmation, John was consecrated immediately after his election. The major issue of his pontificate concerned Sardinia. There, the archbishop of Cagliari had possessed a certain power over the other dioceses of the island; however, consecrating them was not one of his privileges. Thus, when Citonatus of Cagliari laid hands on the newly elected bishop of Turris, John took that diocese directly under his jurisdiction. He was best known among the Romans for his generosity to the poor, and after his death following a long illness he was buried in St. Peter's.

In 685, Constantine IV died and was succeeded by his sixteen-year-old son, Justinian II. Although an able soldier who inflicted great defeats on both the Arabs and the Bulgars, he had a savage disposition—something that did not bode well for his subjects.

## Conon

### (October 21, 686–September 21, 687)

The clergy of Rome and the imperial garrison were at odds after the death of John V; this endangered the tranquility of the election. Fortunately, a compromise candidate was found in the person of Conon. An elderly, venerated priest with a reputation for holiness, he was also the son of an officer in the Thracian Troop, one of the emperor's units at Rome. While the clergy of the city had no doubts regarding his independence, he pleased the soldiers by asking for confirmation of his election from the exarch, even though imperial approval was no longer required.

A group of Irish missionaries headed by St. Kilian arrived at Rome in Conon's time. The pope consecrated Kilian a bishop and dispatched him and his companions to Franconia in Bavaria. They preached the Faith there for a few years before being martyred. St. Kilian is the first bishop of Wurzburg.

Conon was adept at dealing with Justinian II, who not only accepted Constantinople III on his account, but gave to the Holy See certain taxes and dues owed by the imperial treasury. Conon died after a long illness and was buried in St. Peter's.

## St. Sergius I

### (December 15, 687–September 8, 701)

Born in 635, a Syrian educated at Palermo, Sergius was received into the Roman clergy by Pope Adeodatus and ordained a priest by St. Leo II in 683. His first years were rather quiet, but in 692, Justinian II's nature got the better of him. Justinian convened a group of Eastern prelates in Constantinople at what is called the Council *in Trullo* (after the hall in which it was held), which passed one hundred disciplinary canons, many expressly directed against Roman practices. The pope refused to accept them, except where they covered purely doctrinal and moral questions and were in accord with earlier canons and decrees.

Justinian was outraged. He sent agents to seize the pope, but the garrison at Ravenna mutinied. This led to uprisings against Justinian throughout his empire, and at last two soldiers took control of Constantinople, deposed him, cut off his nose, and sent him to the favored place of Byzantine exile—Cherson in the Crimea. But neither they nor the rest of the world had heard the last of the wily emperor.

Sergius was much concerned with internal Church affairs. He added the *Agnus Dei* to the Roman Mass and instituted processions on the feasts of the Nativity, Purification, Annunciation, and Assumption of the Virgin Mary. Moreover, Sergius sent St. Willibrord to be bishop of the Friesians (and so the apostle of the Netherlands and first bishop of Utrecht) and other missionaries to Germany. In 689, King Ceadwalla of the Saxons came to Rome to be baptized by Sergius, who also continued the tradition of backing up St. Wilfrid of York. St. Sergius's feast is September 9.

# John VI

## (October 30, 701–January 11, 705)

Despite being a Greek, the most dramatic episode in John's pontificate involved the new exarch Theophylactus. Upon the latter's arrival at Rome from Sicily, the local folks, sure that the exarch would be repeating some of his predecessors' treatment of prior popes, mobilized. These militias from the surrounding areas marched on Rome to defend John from any maltreatment. They camped around the city and showed their annoyance with the exarch. The pope sent priests to them, to ensure them that all was well; though this calmed the militiamen down, they demanded that all informers working for the exarch in the city be turned over to them.

Pleased at this falling out between the imperial representative and his people, Gisulf—king of the Lombards—marched on Rome. Knowing that the militias would be no match for the barbarians, John sent priests with money to bribe Gisulf to return to his own lands and to ransom captives. In both tasks they were successful.

St. Wilfrid had once again appealed to this pope. John confirmed the decrees of former popes in Wilfrid's favor. He was buried in St. Peter's.

# John VII

## (March 1, 705–October 18, 707)

Another Greek, John was the son of Blatta and Plato. His father Plato was a Byzantine official and restored the imperial palace on the Palatine Hill. Before his accession, John was manager of papal properties in the city and renovated the church of Santa Maria Antiqua, the oldest one dedicated to the Virgin in Rome. Once pope, John continued building.

Despite his connections to the empire, John was as surprised as anyone when Justin II managed to escape his place of exile, return to Constantinople, execute his two replacements, and resume power. He immediately began a reign of terror against his opponents. The emperor took up where he had left off with the Council *in*

*Trullo*, once again demanding papal approval of its decisions. When the decrees arrived John simply returned them, neither approving nor condemning.

The Lombards returned certain papal estates in Northern Italy that they had seized, and John managed to convince English priests in Rome to use clerical dress. He died in a palace he had built near the imperial one on the Palatine Hill and was buried in St. Peter's.

## Sisinnius
### (January 15–February 4, 708)

Syrian born, Sisinnius was so sick with gout that he was unable to feed himself. He was hardheaded, however, and made plans for strengthening the walls of Rome; he also managed before he died to consecrate a bishop for Corsica.

## Constantine
### (March 25, 708–April 9, 715)

Another Syrian, Constantine was renowned for his easygoing nature; he would need it. Shortly after his accession, famine broke out around Rome, which lasted for about three and a half years. Despite this, when kings Coenred of Mercia and Offa of Essex arrived in Rome from England, with St. Egwin, bishop of Worcester and abbot of Evesham, the duo were so impressed they entered monastic life.

It was also in this pope's reign that the Moors invaded Spain, defeating and killing the Visigothic king, Roderick, and seizing virtually the entire peninsula. Eight centuries of misery followed for the Spanish, during which (starting at the cave of Covadonga, last refuge of the Catholics under Don Pelayo), step by step the Muslims were pushed back. (To date, no apology has been forthcoming for the invasion and occupation of Spain from the Muslim side.)

Justin II, meanwhile, was keen in pursuing papal acceptance of his council, which, among other things, would have had the effect of making the patriarchate of Constantinople virtually independent from Rome. As noted previously, Constantine's predecessors managed, one way or another, to avoid doing so.

But the emperor could not be put off forever; he demanded that Constantine come to Constantinople, and in 709, the pope did so. By imperial command, at every port in which the papal party disembarked, they were received with great joy. On arrival at Constantinople, at the order of Justin himself, the pope was received with imperial honors. He then went across to Nicomedia (modern Izmit, Turkey), where Justin was living. There, oddly enough, the emperor fell at the pope's feet, weeping. At Mass, Constantine gave him Communion, and nothing more was heard about the pope accepting the spurious council of Justin II.

Shortly after Constantine returned to Rome in triumph, in 711, news arrived that Justin II had been overthrown and killed by Phillipicus. The new emperor resolved to revive Monothelitism and sent a letter to the pope outlining his beliefs. Constantine had the missive examined by a synod and burned. In short order, Phillipicus had the decrees of Constantinople III publicly ignited in similar fashion, the names of leading Monothelites added to the diptychs of the Liturgy, and removed the image of Constantinople III that hung in front of his palace.

In response, Constantine ordered pictures of all six councils erected in front of the portico of St. Peter's and refused to have Phillipicus's name mentioned in the Canon of the Mass or on charters; neither would he permit the emperor's statue in the chapel of St. Caesarius on the Palatine Hill (the imperial chapel in Rome), nor his face on the Roman coinage.

The emperor's reaction was swift. He sent a new duke to Rome, who certainly would have made the Romans' lives miserable. Fortunately, on Pentecost Eve, 713, Phillipicus was overthrown. The new emperor, Anastasius, dispatched a new exarch to Italy who delivered to the pope an imperial letter in which Anastasius affirmed his orthodoxy and denounced Monothelitism.

At the same time, John, patriarch of Constantinople, sent his own letter to the pope in which he declared that while cooperating with Phillipicus he had remained orthodox at heart. Moreover, John affirmed that the "apostolical pre-eminence of the pope is to the whole Church, what the head is to the body," and that "according to the canons he is the head of the Christian priesthood."

The other question solved in this pontificate was the Pavia question. The saintly Benedict, Archbishop of Milan, came to Rome with a problem. Until the 400s, the diocese of Pavia had depended on Milan. But since their See had become the Lombard capital, the Pavian bishops had been directly under Rome. Constantine showed Benedict the antiquity of this arrangement, which he accepted.

By the time of Constantine's death, the famine had ended and Rome was abundantly fed.

## St. Gregory II
### (May 19, 715–February 11, 731)

Born in Rome, Gregory had been archdeacon under St. Sergius I and had ably assisted Constantine on that pope's trip east. His experience with both internal administration and diplomacy would serve him well.

Despite being a secular cleric, he had a great love for the Benedictines; in 720, he restored Monte Cassino and attached monasteries to St. Paul's Outside the Walls and Santa Maria Maggiore. Moreover, Gregory was much interested in missionary work. He consecrated St. Boniface a bishop and sent him into Bavaria, corresponding with Theodo, duke of that country. He also communicated with the English, Scots, and Irish bishops about the Easter controversy.

Closer to home, however, he faced two problems: the Lombards and the Byzantines. The former group he was able to halt, much as they wished to annex Rome; the latter were a bit more difficult.

In 717, after Emperor Anastasius II was overthrown by a general who took the name Theodosius III, the usurper himself was deposed by another general, who called himself Leo III. Called "the Isaurian" from the remote district in Asia Minor where he was born, Leo had been a great soldier and proved to be an able administrator. He sent Gregory the customary confession of Orthodox faith and fended off another Arab assault on Constantinople. Leo brought Slavonic settlers to repopulate districts in Greece and Asia Minor that had been devastated by the Saracens. All in all, the first part of his reign was a success.

Not so the second. In 726, Leo—perhaps through contact with Islam—decided to violently oppose the use of images in the Church; this was the beginning of the iconoclastic heresy. He deposed the patriarch of Constantinople, who opposed him, and martyred a number of monks in the East for the same reason.

The pope's reaction was to call a synod, which condemned Leo's actions. In response, the emperor gave Illyricum to the patriarch of Constantinople (with whom it has remained ever since). He tried to do the same with Sicily

and southern Italy. Then Leo ordered his exarch at Ravenna to arrest the pope.

Instead, the exarch and his troops mutinied. The pope convinced them not to officially renounce imperial allegiance, but to be content with refusing an unjust order. While opposing the emperor's heresy, Gregory nevertheless insisted on the maintenance of his political rights—a policy that many popes from that time forward have followed. So matters stood when the pontiff died. St. Gregory II was buried in St. Peter's, and his feast is February 13. He is much revered in Fulda, St. Boniface's diocese.

## St. Gregory III

### (March 18, 731–December 10, 741)

A Syrian by birth, the new Gregory was renowned for his learning and his loyalty to the memory and policies of his predecessor. His was the last election for which confirmation was sought by the Byzantine emperor. Surprisingly, Leo III granted it, doubtless in hopes of winning the new pope for his heresy. In this, as in much else, the emperor was doomed to disappointment.

At a synod in 732, Gregory condemned Iconoclasm and excommunicated the emperor. Liutprand, king of the Lombards, saw this as a golden opportunity to seize the remaining parts of Italy, and he began to do so. Unable to appeal to the emperor for aid, the pope looked elsewhere.

The Franks were reunited under the effective control of Charles Martel (son of Pepin of Heristal), mayor of the palace to the figurehead Frankish king. Charles had just defeated the Muslims at the battle of Tours, thus saving the West from the fate of the Near East. Gregory appealed to him to cross the Alps and defend Rome against the Lombards. Charles refused.

Nevertheless, Gregory faced the invaders bravely, although the problem was unresolved when he died. He also appointed St. Boniface archbishop of Mainz, thus paving the way for the establishment of a German episcopate. St. Gregory III's feast is November 28.

# St. Zachary

## (December 10, 741–March 15, 752)

Of Greek descent, a native of Sanseverino in Calabria, Zachary was renowned for his learning, having translated St. Gregory I's dialogues into Greek. At home, his pontificate was primarily concerned with the Lombard problem. After his personal intervention prevailed upon the Lombards to desist, he signed a forty years' truce with them in 742, as part of which they restored some cities they had taken.

But Zachary did not forget the Byzantines. Leo had died in 740; his son, Constantine V (called *Copronymos*—"born of dung"—in tribute to the love his subjects bore him) was on campaign at the time. The new emperor's brother-in-law briefly seized control of the capital and voided Leo's iconoclastic legislation. But Constantine retook Constantinople and renewed his father's persecution, complete with Reformation-style image smashing and defiling. Zachary maintained St. Gregory III's policy of political loyalty and religious opposition, and four times wrote to convince the dung-born one of the error of his ways—but in vain. The rupture between Constantinople and imperial Italy led directly to the capture of Ravenna and its surrounding district—the Pentapolis—in 751.

With the Franks, however, Zachary had more success. St. Boniface was a great friend of Charles Martel's son and successor, Pepin the Short. With the help of the new mayor of the palace and papal approval, Boniface reorganized the Frankish Church, which had become virtually a department of state. Its independence renewed, new life and missionary fervor animated Frankish Catholicism.

In return, when Pepin decided that the time had come to end the reign of the Merovingian *rois faineants* ("do-nothing kings") Sts. Boniface and Zachary agreed to Pepin's being crowned king of the Franks. Thus would begin the line of the Carolingian kings.

Zachary solved two disputes that broke out between St. Boniface and the Irish Bishop of Salzburg, St. Virgilius (whose name in Gaelic is Farrell—all of that proud family claim him as their patron). The first regarded an invalid formula of baptism (in the name of Christ rather than the Trinity), which St. Boniface championed and St. Virgilius condemned. Zachary found for the Irishman. But later, it developed that in addition to believing that the world was round and had a continent on the other side (which Boniface did not condemn), he also claimed that the earth was hollow and had a sun and moon inside (which Boniface did attack). This time, the pope ruled in favor of the

Englishman. But both saints submitted to papal correction, even when their own opinions were condemned.

St. Zachary was buried in St. Peter's, and his feast is March 13.

## Stephen II
### (March 23–27, 752)

When Zachary died, the priest Stephen was unanimously elected pope. But a few days later, before he could be consecrated, he died of a stroke while dealing with Church affairs. Because of the brevity of his pontificate, Stephen has been a bit of a problem for accounting popes named Stephen; some lists do not include him.

## Stephen III (II)
### (April 3, 752–April 26, 757)

This Stephen, too, was unanimously elected. Immediately he had to deal with the Lombards, who, flush with their seizure of Ravenna, made ready to seize Rome despite the truce. Stephen appealed to Constantinople, without success; nor did his offer to bribe the Lombards impress their king Aistulf. At last, Stephen crossed the Alps himself to appeal in person to Pepin for aid.

Well received by the Frankish ruler, he crowned him king. In response, Pepin crossed into Italy with his army and defeated the Lombards, forcing Aistulf to surrender Ravenna and his other conquests. The Franks then returned home.

Constantine V then pressed for a return of his lost possessions. Because in this year of 754 he held a council condemning the use of images, and then suppressed all the monasteries he could (seizing their property and treasures, an eerie foreshadowing of Henry VIII's work), his appeals fell on deaf ears.

Aistulf, however, could not be trusted, and in 756 he besieged Rome. With Lombard armies besieging the Eternal City, Stephen again appealed to Pepin for aid. Once more the Franks returned to Italy and defeated the Lombards. Then Pepin bestowed not only Rome, Umbria, and the Marches

(as the Adriatic coastal region of the pope's domain was called) as papal property, he bestowed on the pope Romagna and Ravenna. From this time on, the popes would be temporal rulers as well as spiritual ones. The papal states henceforth would be sovereign, independent of any ruler other than the pope. But no sooner had Stephen taken possession of and organized the government for Ravenna, than his governor, Archbishop Sergius, rebelled. This was swiftly put down, however, and the archbishop of Ravenna was brought to Rome, to live there as long as Stephen did.

Meanwhile, King Aistulf of the Lombards died. His brother Ratchis, who had become a monk at Monte Cassino, emerged to claim the throne, as did Desiderius, the duke of Istria. The Lombard nation was deeply divided over the question and put it before the pope. He reminded Ratchis that his vows were for life, and so the prince returned to Monte Cassino. In the meantime, Desiderius promised to return a number of cities in Romagna, but he reneged and gave up only about half of them.

Stephen was loved by the Roman poor, for whom he built a number of hospitals around St. Peter's. They turned out in droves for his funeral and burial at St. Peter's.

## St. Paul I

### (May 29, 757–June 28, 767)

Paul was the brother of Stephen III and was educated with him for the priesthood at the Lateran school. Under his brother, he was appointed archpriest of San Crisogono. His work there led to a large party favoring him as Stephen's successor; however, others were partisans of Archdeacon Theophylact. At the election of 757, the former prevailed.

Paul continued his brother's policy of alliance with the Franks, so he enjoyed peace with the Lombards. He was a mild and peace-loving man, and forgave the injuries the Lombards had done to the Church. Paul was not in a position to do so with Constantine V, and he warmly welcomed the monks who fled to Rome to escape persecution for their love of images.

Paul transferred relics of St. Petronilla from the catacomb of St. Domatilla to St. Peter's. She became the special patroness of the Frankish kings.

So dedicated was Paul to his duties that he died of heatstroke while saying Mass at St. Paul's Outside the Walls. His feast is July 4.

## Stephen IV (III)

(August 7, 768–August 1, 772)

The death of St. Paul I was the signal for disorder in the Eternal City. A man named Toto of Nepi broke into Rome with a band of Tuscans. On June 30, 767, despite the opposition of Christopher, the *Primicerius* (head of the college of Notaries), they declared Toto's brother, a layman named Constantine, to be pope. The Lombards, in reply, declared a monk named Philip to be pope.

In the spring of 768, Christopher and his son Sergius escaped from Rome and convinced the Lombards to depose both their own candidate and Constantine. A Sicilian Benedictine—Stephen—was then properly elected and consecrated. But he was unable to restrain the Roman mob, who put both of his rivals to death despite his protests.

Born in 720, Stephen was ordained a priest by St. Zachary. In response to recent events, a council held at the Lateran in 769 ruled that henceforth only cardinals could be elected pope.

The remaining part of Stephen's brief pontificate paved the way for the papacy's future course, in that the new Frankish co-rulers, Carloman and Charles (known as Charles the Great, "Charlemagne") renewed their father's devotion to the Holy See and prevailed upon Desiderius to give up some of his purloined territories to the papacy. Desiderius in return convinced Carloman to marry his daughter and engineered the fall of Stephen's two ministers, Christopher and Sergius. Moreover, the wily Lombard allied himself with Paul Afiarta, the pope's chamberlain, who carried out tremendous cruelties while Stephen lay dying. But Desiderius was less successful in his attempts to foment a schism against the patriarch of Aquileia-Grado, who Stephen supported until his own death.

# Adrian I

## (February 1, 772–December 25, 795)

Adrian was born to a noble Roman family and had won great popularity among the Romans for his services to the last several popes. Despite the opposition of Paul Afiarta, he was unanimously elected by the people and clergy of Rome. This was rather a setback for Desiderius, though the Lombard king had yet to realize it.

Adrian's first act was to release from prison all of the captives placed there by Afiarta while Stephen was dying. On learning that the villainous chamberlain had arranged for the death of Sergius, son of Christopher, in prison, the pope ordered his arrest at Rimini. Afiarta had been on his way back from the court of his Lombard master, whom he had promised to deliver the pope to, "were it even in chains."

Annoyed by Adrian's move, Desiderius decided that the time had come to snuff out the last non-Lombard sections of Italy. His troops marched on Rome—secure in the knowledge that the Alpine passes were in Lombard hands should the Franks attempt once more to come to Rome's aid.

Moreover, Desiderius had an ace in the hole. At Carloman's sudden death from natural causes, his brother Charles seized his portion of the Frankish realm rather than allowing it to be divided up with heirs as had been the custom among the Merovingians (a custom that had led to that dynasty's continuing enfeeblement). Carloman's widow, Gerberga, returned with her two sons to her father's court at Pavia. Desiderius offered to leave Rome in peace if the pope would anoint the children as heirs to their father's throne. Thus the Holy See would be deprived of its major ally, and Desiderius could dream of perhaps even ruling Gaul one day.

But Adrian was not fooled. He refused, strengthened the Eternal City's defenses, and appealed to Charlemagne. The Frankish king was enjoying a truce with the Saxons—whose conquest had absorbed his attention until now—and crossed the Alps in 773. He rapidly seized Verona, where Carloman's widow and sons were holed up, and proceeded to besiege Pavia. The following Easter he celebrated with Adrian at Rome, and there he made the famous "Donation of Charlemagne," which confirmed all that his father had given, and added more territory besides. It is upon these two donations that the future Papal States were founded. Nominally, Adrian was master of two-thirds of the Peninsula.

Two months later Pavia fell, and Charlemagne became officially, "King of the Franks and Lombards." He was crowned in succession to Desiderius and

was now the official protector of Rome and the papacy. Charlemagne regarded Adrian as a father—a relationship that would determine the future course of the Church, Europe, and the world. Here was established the theoretical standing that, in the minds of European Christians for many years to come, was the ideal connection between pope and emperor.

If things were finally straightening out in the West, however, the East, too, gave Adrian cause for joy. In 775, the dung-born Constantine V died, leaving his son Leo IV on the throne. Leo's consort was one of the most truly remarkable women in history—the empress Irene. At heart an image venerator, when her consort died in 780, and she became Regent for her young son (Constantine VI), Irene resolved to end both Iconoclasm and the Byzantine empire's estrangement from Rome.

At her request, Adrian sent legates to preside at a new ecumenical council, Nicaea II, in 787. This council both restored communion between East and West and condemned Iconoclasm. Ever since, the First Sunday in Lent has been celebrated in the Byzantine Rite (both Catholic and Orthodox) as the Sunday of Orthodoxy. In addition to stirring prayers at both the Eucharistic Liturgy and that of the Hours, a list of anathematized heresies is read and their condemnation reaffirmed.

At Adrian's death the state of the Church was much happier than when he ascended the pontifical throne. The Lombard threat had ended and a powerful new protector was established, and unity with the Eastern Empire was restored. A sunny future appeared assured. Alas, as is so often the case in human history, new trials awaited. But the Sunday of Orthodoxy remains, even today, a powerful annual tribute to the unity of East and West.

# The Empire Returns

## St. Leo III
### (December 27, 795–June 12, 816)

A Benedictine, Leo was born at Rome, was the pastor of Santa Susanna (now the American church in Rome), and was appointed chief of the papal treasury by Adrian I.

His first few years were peaceful. In 798, he elevated Cologne and Salzburg to archdioceses, and the next year Leo condemned Felix—bishop of Urgel in Spain—for his preaching of Adoptianism, which held that Christ is only the "adopted" son of God.

Unfortunately, this period of peace rudely ended on April 25, 799. Certain devotees of the memory of Adrian I, who believed the new pope to be guilty of various crimes, attacked a procession he was leading and captured him. They plucked his eyes out (although the next day his sight was miraculously restored).

Leo fled Rome, first to Spoleto and then to Paderborn, Germany, where he was received by Charlemagne. Himself revering the memory of Adrian, Charlemagne nevertheless received the pope with full honors. Leo pled his case in front of the Frankish ruler, who believed him and returned him to Rome with an escort of Frankish nobles. Charlemagne promised that he himself would soon follow.

This he did, in late 800. Once in the Eternal City, the king held a conclave of Frankish, Roman, and Lombard clerics, nobles, and laymen. There, Leo swore on the Gospels that he was innocent of the charges imputed to him.

On Christmas Day, 800, while Charlemagne knelt at prayer in St. Peter's, the pope appeared with a golden crown, which he laid upon the king's head, saying, "All hail Charles Augustus, crowned of God, the great and life-giving Emperor of the Romans!" He then proceeded to anoint the new emperor and swore allegiance to him. This was allegiance, and not obedience, for the pope would remain sovereign in his own territories, albeit under imperial protection.

The Byzantines were resentful of what they considered to be a usurpation, although Empress Irene recognized the action; her son having rebelled against her, she had defeated him and had him blinded and deposed. At one point she considered marriage with Charlemagne, and at another (prior to this event) she negotiated a marriage between her son and Charlemagne's daughter.

Neither of these eventuated, and Irene herself would be overthrown in 802 and replaced by a noble named Nicephorus. Exiled to Lesbos, she died the following year, having supported herself by spinning cloth.

But the Romans and the West in general were ecstatic at having a new emperor. Since Leo III's break with Rome, imperial authority had been nonexistent; and yet it was considered as much a part of the order of things as the stars and planets—indeed, as the papacy itself.

Charlemagne, at this point, must be considered in and of himself. Every year on this day, in the German cities of Aachen (Aix-La-Chapelle—Charlemagne's old capital) and Frankfurt am Main, there is celebrated the feast of Blessed Charlemagne, the first Holy Roman Emperor. In 1998, the Mass in the emperor's old cathedral was offered by the archbishop of Rheims, the primate of France. Just as of old the emperors were crowned at Aachen, so too were the kings of France crowned at Rheims. Strange to say, this apparently most German of feasts is also the most French. Charlemagne, after all, is accounted as "Charles I" in the lists of both holy Roman emperors and French kings.

Many people are shocked to hear that Charlemagne is a "Blessed" of the Church. We are taught to think that kings are as a rule fairly despicable folk, and Charlemagne perhaps more than most. But in reality, as both Dom Gueranger in *The Liturgical Year* and Alban Butler in *The Lives of the Saints* are eloquent in pointing out, Charlemagne did indeed live a life of heroic virtue, performed miracles after his death, and in every way was worthy of being raised to the altars. Just as interesting, however, is the fact that later editions of both these works tend to leave him out. Above all, he was the progenitor of the Western expression of the imperial idea, which would affect the papacy, the Church, and the world mightily down to today—and may one day do so again.

The new emperor was regarded by both the pope and his subjects as the legitimate successor to Constantine and Justinian. However, the connection between Leo and Charlemagne was much greater than merely personal friendship, theoretical restoration, or the spur to education and liturgy (the Roman and Gaulish rites were fused) that resulted from Charlemagne's coronation. His exploits had united German and Latin, Frank and Bavarian, Saxon and Spaniard, Italian and Slav into one polity. A unified administration, civil order, and freedom of travel resulted in the establishment of a state that served as the foundation of modern Europe. But for its every activity, it was dependent on the closest possible cooperation between pope and emperor, Church and state. Christopher Dawson writes:

> The Carolingian Empire . . . was regarded by Charlemagne and his successors and their ecclesiastical advisors not merely as a Frankish imperial State, nor even as the revival of the Roman Empire in the

West, but as the political organ and counterpart of the Catholic Church. In the words of Charlemagne's letter to Leo III, the emperor is "the representative of God who has to protect and govern all the members of God," he is "Lord and Father, King and Priest, Leader and Guide of all Christians."

This unitary conception of Christian society naturally tended under a strong Emperor to result in a kind of Caesaropapism like that of the Byzantine Church. The emperor was regarded as the apex of the pyramid of Christian society, the culminating point at which the ecclesiastical and civil hierarchies converged. The Carolingian Empire, however, unlike the Christian Empire of the East, possessed no trained bureaucracy or class of lawyers and was consequently far more dependent on the assistance of ecclesiastics in the task of civil administration than was the Byzantine State. Alike in the Carolingian Empire and its Germanic successor the bishops were the mainstay of the government, and the ecclesiastics of the royal capella under the archchaplain formed the imperial chancery and the central organ of administration. Thus, on the one hand the emperor was continually interfering in purely ecclesiastical matters in virtue of his general prerogative as defender of the faith and overseer of ecclesiastical order, while, on the other hand, the clergy took a leading part in the secular administration of the Empire. Under such conditions the distinction between Church and State tended to become blurred and effaced. The Church was a State church and the State was a church State, membership of the latter involved membership of the former and the personnel of government was practically the same.

This state of affairs would have many repercussions—some positive, some negative—in the future. It did have one immediate religious result. Charlemagne urged Leo to add the word *Filioque*, "and the Son," to the words of the Nicene Creed describing the Procession of the Holy Spirit. This question had first arisen in sixth-century Spain, where it was pointed out that the Nature of the Trinity implied that the Holy Spirit would proceed from both the Father and the Son. But the Nicene Creed in its original form only specified procession from the Father. The custom of adding Filioque spread from Spain to Gaul. Though the pope accepted the teaching, he did not wish to add the word out of deference to the Greeks, who had not as yet considered the question. But this seemingly minor point would bear bitter fruit later.

Charlemagne died on January 28, 814, and was sincerely mourned by both the pope and the emperor's subjects; he was succeeded by his son, Louis the Pious. St. Leo III was canonized in 1673, although he had been venerated much earlier. His feast is June 12.

## Stephen V (IV)

### (June 22, 816–January 24, 817)

Born in Rome of a family that had given two popes to the Church, Stephen was the son of Martinus. He was patronized by both Adrian I and St. Leo III, the latter of whom made him a deacon. He was renowned for his generosity to the poor and was elected immediately upon St. Leo III's death. His first act was to administer to the Romans the oath of allegiance to the new emperor; next he sent Louis notice of his election. Finally, Stephen went to the Frankish realm and gave Louis his coronation. Louis in turn gave him many expensive gifts, and the two renewed the alliance between papacy and empire. While on his return trip, the pope stopped in Ravenna to expose the sandals of Christ for the people's veneration.

Dying soon after his return, Stephen was buried in St. Peter's.

## St. Paschal I

### (January 25, 817–February 11, 824)

Born in Rome, Paschal was educated at the Lateran school, became a Benedictine monk, and eventually was elected abbot of St. Stephen's near the Vatican, where he cared for pilgrims.

After his election, he immediately renewed his alliance with Emperor Louis. The latter, who did not have the governmental skills of his father, asked the pope to crown his son Lothair as co-emperor in order to secure his eventual succession to the imperial throne. Paschal did so in 823. But all was not rosy in Rome. Shortly after Lothair was crowned, two papal officials who were closely connected to the Franks were killed. Paschal took an oath before Louis's ambassador that he had had no part in the deed. What had made this necessary was that the pope had seen fit to exile certain nobles who, under the pretext of loyalty to the emperor, had attempted to take control of the city for themselves.

In more strictly religious matters, Paschal commissioned Ebbo, the archbishop of Rheims, to evangelize Denmark. In Constantinople, the new emperor, Leo V, reverted to Iconoclasm, renewed the persecutions, and thereby

set off a new wave of refugees to Rome, whom Paschal gladly received. Thanks, however, to Louis's protection, Leo's worst atrocities could not directly affect the Holy See.

Along with these activities, Paschal also brought a number of martyrs' relics from the catacombs to the churches of St. Peter's and Santa Prassedes. Moreover, he discovered the incorrupt body of St. Cecilia and had it transferred to the church that bears her name, which he had built over her former home. Unable to find her relics while searching the catacombs, Paschal had a dream in which the site was revealed to him. His feast day is May 14.

## Eugene II

### (June 6, 824–August 27, 827)

After St. Paschal I died, there was a hotly contested election: One party, more clerical in nature, supported a candidate who would continue his predecessor's policies. The other, made up of the customarily rambunctious Roman nobility, wanted a candidate who would favor them in their quest for control of Church and city. They made much of their loyalty to the emperor, in hopes that this would secure their goals.

Despite being barred by the council of 769 from any direct role in the election, they managed to bring about the election of their candidate, Eugene, the archpriest of Santa Sabina. But they had miscalculated in two important respects. One was the character of the new pope, who was as zealous for the rights of the Church as St. Paschal I had been.

The other misreading they made was the position of the emperor. Louis considered Eugene's election a victory and sent his son Lothair over the Alps to help consolidate it. Although many of the nobles whom St. Paschal I had exiled to the Frankish realm were allowed to return and their property restored, they soon learned that Lothair was not in the city for their benefit.

In 824, the pope and the emperor agreed on the *Constitution Romana*, under which the governance of Rome and the relationship between pope and emperor were codified. The following were its basic articles:

1. Those under Papal or Imperial protection were to be inviolable, and the pope and his officials were to be obeyed.
2. Church property was not to be plundered after the death of a pope.
3. Only those permitted to do so by the decree of Pope Stephen in 769 could participate in papal elections.

4. Two commissioners were to be appointed, one by the pope and the other by the emperor, who were to oversee justice in Rome.
5. Any failure in administration should be corrected by the pope, or failing him, by the emperor.

In all, the pontiff was to be obeyed. Eugene and Lothair further commanded that, with the exception of their duties to the pope, they were to swear allegiance to Louis and Lothair; they would ensure that papal elections follow the canons; and they would not allow the pope to be consecrated without the witness of imperial representatives.

At the same time, the Byzantine emperor Michael II attempted to get Emperor Louis to join his iconoclastic activities; this the Western emperor refused to do, while the pope assured St. Theodore the Studite, leader of the orthodox party at Constantinople, of his support. Upon Michael's accession, Theodore had written him in hopes of persuading him to cleave to orthodoxy. "Unite us," he begged, "[the Church of Constantinople] to the head of the Churches of God, that is, Rome, and through it with the Three Patriarchs (Antioch, Jerusalem, and Alexandria)." Ironically, Christians under Muslim domination were safe from iconoclastic persecution—a double irony considering Islam's view of images.

In 826, Eugene held a council at Rome, which among other things prescribed the deposition of ignorant or illiterate priests and bishops and the establishment of schools at cathedrals. He also sent St. Ansgar to Scandinavia, with the mission of converting the Vikings who by this time were ravaging northern Europe. At his death, he was buried at St. Peter's.

## Valentine
### (October 827)

Valentine was a Roman who entered the clergy while still quite young. His piety and morality brought him to the attention of St. Paschal I, who ordained him subdeacon and deacon, employed him at the Lateran, and at last made him archdeacon. Valentine retained this position under Eugene II, and at the latter's death he was unanimously elected pope by the nobles, people, and clergy of Rome. As a universally popular candidate, he was capable of reconciling all parties. The election took place while he was absent. He was at last found praying in Santa Maria Maggiore and within a few days the ceremonies were concluded. He died unexpectedly, however, forty days later. Valentine was buried in St. Peter's.

## Gregory IV
### (late December 827–January 25, 844)

Born in Rome, Gregory was ordained a priest by St. Paschal I, who was much impressed by his piety. Having been made archpriest of San Marco Basilica, Gregory decorated his church with beautiful mosaics and made a name for himself through his work for the poor.

Although he did not want to be elected pope, the Roman nobility insisted upon it. Because the imperial representatives in Rome would not permit him to be consecrated until the emperor confirmed his election, Gregory was not actually consecrated until March 28, 828.

Imperial concerns would dominate this pontificate. As previously mentioned, Louis the Pious (the First, both of the empire and France), lacked his father's sagacity. Upon his accession in 817, Louis had signed a deed, leaving his empire in common to his three sons—Lothair, Louis (called "the German"), and Pepin. But after their mother died, Louis married the ambitious Judith. By her he had a son, Charles (called "the Bald"), to whom he was completely devoted. He decided to amend the law to make Charles an equal co-heir with his three half brothers.

At that, in 830 the trio revolted. They quickly defeated their father's army and took him prisoner. Louis was compelled to restore the Constitution of 817; they further forced him to separate from their stepmother. But Lothair, Louis the German, and Pepin soon quarreled among themselves. The Frankish bishops and barons met at a diet in Nijmingen (now in the Netherlands) and forcibly returned Louis the Pious to power. In addition, by the pope's intervention, Louis's wife returned to him.

But the emperor could not be dissuaded from his goal of making young Charles the equal of his half brothers. They in turn went to war again, and Lothair, who had been ruling in Italy, persuaded the pope to cross the Alps with him. By appearing in the rebel camp, however, Gregory appeared to favor the sons over the father—an appearance that disenchanted both the emperor and the bishops loyal to him. While negotiations continued, Lothair bribed some of the emperor's guards to seize him. Once again Louis the Pious was deposed, and the pope returned to Rome. Once again, however, the three

quarrelsome princes lost control through their infighting. In 834, Louis was restored as emperor. But too kindhearted as he was, he allowed Lothair to retain control of Italy. As a result, Louis had to intervene repeatedly to protect the independence of the papacy. When on the road to fight another of his sons, Louis died in 840.

Lothair inherited the imperial title, but he wanted the power as well. He crossed the Alps with his army after having captured the papal emissary en route to his brothers to counsel peace. The forces of Lothair and his brothers met at Fontenoy in 841. In this frightful conflict, the flower of the Frankish nobility was decimated. Lothair was defeated and fled. In 843, the Oath of Strasbourg was taken, by which Charles the Bald, who received France Louis the German, who was given Germany, and Lothair, who was allowed to retain the Imperial title and Italy—as well as a strip of territory running north from the Alps to the North Sea—swore to uphold their territorial arrangements and keep the peace. This agreement is notable as including the earliest examples of French and German writing.

While the sons of Louis had been fighting, Viking raids increased. Moreover, the Muslims took Sicily from the Byzantines and began intervening in the affairs of southern Italy. By the end of Gregory's pontificate, the political situation was bleak. He did manage to fortify the ancient port of Ostia with a fortress named "Gregoriopolis" after himself. Moreover, he rebuilt and added churches and aqueducts in Latium, and he founded farm colonies in the Campagna.

The pope had not been idle, however, in the more purely religious sphere. His longest lasting achievement was to appoint November 1 as the Feast of All Saints, celebrated from that time to this, on which day all in heaven would be honored. Gregory approved the work of St. Ansgar in converting the Danes and Swedes, and he appointed Ansgar archbishop of Hamburg and papal legate to the North.

Gregory gave the Pallium to the archbishops of Canterbury, Salzburg, and Grado, and he supported the bishop of Le Mans who was persecuted for his support of Louis the Pious. Moreover, when that emperor sent clerics to Rome to be trained in Gregorian Chant, Gregory happily complied. From there these priests and bishops returned to their own homes to spread Gregorian Chant throughout what had been Charlemagne's empire. Not all of that monarch's efforts would be snuffed out.

## Sergius II

### (January 844–January 27, 847)

Sergius was born into a noble Roman family that had given two popes to the Church. Graduating from the Choir School, he was made cardinal priest of the church of Sts. Martino e Silvestro by St. Paschal I, and he served as archpriest under Gregory IV. At the election following Gregory's death, Sergius won a majority; however, the Roman mob attempted to enthrone a deacon named John. Nevertheless, order prevailed: John was sent to a monastery and Sergius was enthroned.

Sergius had a taste for fine foods, but, alas—as was so often the case in those days—such tastes brought gout. So in pain was the new pope much of the time that his brother, Benedict, took over some of the administrative tasks of the Church (also making a profit by them).

Sergius had bigger problems, however. Because his election had not been confirmed by the emperor (which he saw as a violation of the agreement of 824), Lothair sent his son, Louis II, with an army into Italy to sort out the matter. Upon his arrival at the Eternal City, Sergius refused to give an oath of loyalty, but he did crown Louis as king of Italy, under his father. In 844, Sergius made Louis's adviser, Drogo of Metz, his legate to France and Germany.

Busy with their internal strife, the sons of Charlemagne had ruined the Frankish military—this would have terrible results. In 846, the Muslims landed near Rome and came very close to seizing the city. Despite the resistance of the Romans and resident foreigners, the Muslims did manage to sack St. Peter's and St. Paul Outside the Walls. (Although they were at last driven off, no Muslim authority has to date offered to apologize for this act, any more than for the conquest of Spain.)

Troubling as all these events were, however, Sergius did manage, before he died, to carry out improvements on various churches, aqueducts, and the Lateran Basilica.

# St. Leo IV

## (April 10, 847–July 17, 855)

Born in Rome, a Benedictine of San Martino in the Eternal City, Leo was cardinal of the church of Quattro Coronati (held at the present time by Roger Cardinal Mahony, archbishop of Los Angeles). His immediate task after his election was to strengthen the defenses of Rome against any possible return engagements by the Muslims. He embellished the city's walls and towers and enclosed the new quarter that had grown up around St. Peter's with new walls.

In 849, troops from Naples (still nominally under the Byzantine empire) sought his blessing before trouncing the Muslims outside of Ostia, and Leo then built new fortifications near the port of what is now Civitavecchia. He further made a new treaty with Lothair and Louis II (the latter of whom he crowned co-emperor in 950): While respecting imperial rights in the city, he nevertheless prevailed upon the father and son to respect the canons covering papal elections. He also opposed Hincmar of Rheims' attempt to set up a quasi-national church in France. Leo also crowned the visiting Saxon prince Ethelwulf as king, thus tying the English monarchy even closer to Rome at its inception.

Leo was a great builder. He repaired and beautified St. Peter's, and he renovated San Martino, Quattro Coronati, San Clemente, and Santa Maria Nova. This pope also convoked four synods in Rome. Among other miracles, Leo extinguished a fire that threatened St. Peter's by blessing it with the sign of the cross. As soon as he died, the cardinals gathered around his deathbed and elected Benedict, priest of San Callisto, as pope. Today St. Leo IV's relics are in the chapel of Our Lady of the Pillar in St. Peter's, and his feast is July 17.

## "*Pope Joan*"

Several chroniclers claimed between the thirteenth and sixteenth century, on the death of St. Leo IV, a monk named John who was noted for his piety was elected pope. Some time later, during a procession, the new pope was taken ill—but rather than stomach cramps, it was discovered that John was actually giving birth, being, in fact, "Joanna." Although thoroughly discredited (as noted, Benedict III was actually elected the day St. Leo IV died, in sight of his predecessor's corpse), the tale was believed by some and used immediately after the Reformation by some Protestants to try to point up the supposed corruption of Rome. Oddly enough, some very fervent Calvinists were later instrumental in proving the story untrue. Nevertheless, Pope Joan is used as a rallying point by some contemporary feminists. In one of G. K. Chesterton's Father Brown stories, the priest detective finds a secret passage in a library by reading the titles of three supposed books: *The Religion of Frederick the Great*, *The Snakes of Iceland*, and *A True History of Pope Joan*. All three being mythical, they obviously covered the lever for the passage's door.

It is today a peculiarly Catholic insult to claim that one or another cardinal whom the speaker dislikes has said that if elected pope, he will take the name "Joan II."

## Benedict III
### (July 17, 855–April 17, 858)

As previously noted, Benedict was elected immediately after St. Leo IV's death. Envoys were sent to Lothair and Louis II to seek confirmation of the election; however, these emissaries were bribed by allies of the ambitious Cardinal Anastasius—the representatives in turn corrupted the two imperial commissioners at Rome. They imprisoned and insulted Benedict. But most of the people and clergy of the city remained loyal to Benedict and forced his release and consecration. Although a synod condemned Anastasius, the new pope allowed him communion as a layman.

The Church in Frankish lands suffered as much as the state in the interminable squabbles between the Carolingians. But because of the intertwined nature of things referred to earlier, many of the bishops were too cowardly to speak out against evils of various kinds. Benedict strongly condemned their silence.

In the rest of the Catholic world, Benedict's stock was very high. He was asked to mediate a dispute between St. Ignatius, patriarch of Constantinople, and Gregory, bishop of Syracuse, which he did to the satisfaction of both parties. Ethelwulf returned to Rome on a visit with his young son Alfred. This Alfred, later known as "Alfred the Great," would one day be the Charlemagne of England and a loyal son of the Holy See. Upon his death, Benedict was buried near the main entrance to St. Peter's.

## St. Nicholas I (the Great)
### (April 24, 858–November 13, 867)

The abuses that Benedict III faced could only grow ever stronger unless checked. Both secular rulers and archbishops of the Church throughout the West seemed hell-bent on running ecclesiastical affairs as their own private concerns; so too did the emperor at Constantinople. Facing these difficulties, the Romans elected the Roman noble, Nicholas, as their pope. The son of the defensor Theodore, Nicholas had received an excellent theological training. He had entered the service of the Church at an early age; made subdeacon by Sergius II, he was ordained deacon by Leo IV.

After Benedict III's death, Emperor Louis II, who was near Rome at the time, came into the city to influence the election. Despite this pressure, Nicholas was elected pope, and on the same day he was consecrated and enthroned in St. Peter's in the presence of the emperor. Three days later, the new pontiff gave a farewell banquet to Louis, and afterward, with the Roman nobility, visited him in his camp outside the city. To symbolize his submission to the papacy, the emperor came to meet the pope and led his horse for some distance.

Influential under his predecessor, Nicholas had been known for his fearlessness as well as his piety. These were traits he would need during his pontificate. In 861, Archbishop John of Ravenna began oppressing the clergy and people of his See; shortly thereafter, Hincmar, archbishop of Rheims, claimed the right to intervene in the affairs of the diocese of Soissons. In both cases, Nicholas came to the aid of the oppressed.

He faced very difficult resistance among the secular rulers as well. King Lothair of Lorraine had flouted the Church's marriage laws. The pope excommunicated him, and for two days Louis II, the brother of Lothair, besieged Nicholas in St. Peter's, forbidding him food. Nicholas did not waver in

his determination, and the emperor, after being reconciled with the pope, withdrew from Rome. Though Nicholas never ceased his efforts to bring about a reconciliation between Lothair and his lawful wife, he was unsuccessful.

Events in the East were even more stressful. Moreover, they are worth following in some detail, because the Orthodox date the schism between East and West from this pontificate.

As mentioned previously, under Benedict III, St. Ignatius was the patriarch of Constantinople at the time of Nicholas's accession, and a most remarkable man. He was born in 799, the youngest son of Byzantine emperor Michael I. After his father was deposed by Leo the Armenian in 813, Ignatius was confined to the monastery of Satyrus. So well, however, did he take to monastic life, that he was elected abbot of the place, and he eventually became patriarch of Constantinople in 846.

Ignatius's sanctity was recognized universally after his death; he is considered a saint not only in the Catholic and Orthodox Churches, but in the Coptic as well. The following is from the official biography of him in the Russian Orthodox *Synaxarion* for October 23:

> Saint Ignatius, Patriarch of Constantinople (847–857; 867–877), in the world Nikita, was of imperial lineage. When his father, the emperor Michael I (811–813), was deposed from the imperial throne by Leo the Armenian (813–820), the 15 year old youth Ignatios was imprisoned in a monastery. Life in the monastery strengthened Saint Ignatios in faith and in piety. Soon he was made hegumen of the monastery, and later on he was chosen Patriarch of Constantinople.
>
> The emperor Michael III (855–867) was still a minor in age, and the country was actually governed by his uncle, Bardas—a man impious and unchaste. The holy patriarch urged Bardas to forsake his sinful life, and he boldly denounced him in his iniquity. When Bardas attempted to force Saint Ignatios to impose monastic tonsure upon the holy Empress Theodora—mother of the emperor, so as to remove her from governance of the realm, holy Patriarch Ignatios did not only not consent to this, but also publicly excommunicated Bardas from Communion. They tortured the holy patriarch for fifteen days to force him to resign, and then they sent him off into exile. When the new emperor came to power, Saint Ignatios was recalled from prison, and was Patriarch for another 10 years. He died in the year 877 in a monastery.

After his deposition in 858, Ignatius wrote to Nicholas, appealing to him as head of the Church, citing Christ's

> saying to Peter, the greatest of the Apostles: "Thou art Peter and upon this rock I will build My Church, and the gates of hell shall not prevail against it." And again "I will give thee the keys of the kingdom of heaven, and whatsoever thou shalt loose on earth shall be bound in heaven." For such blessed words He did not circumscribe and define to the Prince of the Apostles alone by a kind of chance, but through him he transmitted them to all who, after him as his successors, were to be made chief pastors, and divine and sacred pontiffs of elder Rome. (Mansi XVI, 47)

At Bardas's urging, Emperor Michael III installed a learned layman named Photius as patriarch of Constantinople. Photius was quite a different creature from Bardas; today he is also revered as a saint by the Orthodox churches, despite their similarly reverencing Ignatius. But he had long disliked the patriarch and was happy to take his place.

Nicholas pondered the problem for some time. At length, on May 8, 862, he wrote to the patriarchs of Antioch, Alexandria, and Jerusalem, instructing them to withdraw recognition from Photius and restore it to Ignatius. The pope then convened a synod at Rome, which in April of 863 excommunicated Photius.

Additionally in 862, Michael III ("the Drunkard") sent Constantine (later Cyril, died 869) and his brother Methodius (died 885) to Moravia to teach Christianity to the Slavs there. They translated the Bible and other religious writings into Old Church Slavonic and they invented a Slavic alphabet to record these books in (called "Cyrillic," still in use today by the Slavic nations). These "Apostles to the Slavs" would later have the support of popes Adrian II and John VIII and be made co-patrons of Europe by John Paul II. In the immediate, however, their mission was the cause of great controversy, because Moravia lay squarely in the West.

In response to the apparent aggression of the two brothers' work in Moravia, Nicholas stepped up Latin missionary work in Bulgaria. That country had been converted by Greek missionaries, but its ruler, Prince Boris, in August 863 sent an embassy to the pope with 106 questions on the teaching and discipline of the Church. Nicholas answered these inquiries exhaustively in the *Responsa Nicolai ad consulta Bulgarorum.*

Enraged, in 867 Photius convened a council ( the "Conciliabulum") that claimed to depose Nicholas and further attacked papal primacy and many Western practices—especially including the Filioque in the Nicene Creed. The Orthodox churches now date the East–West split from this event (the Photian Schism).

In addition, Nicholas encouraged the missionary activity of the Church. He sanctioned the union of the Sees of Bremen and Hamburg, and he confirmed to St. Ansgar (archbishop of Bremen) and his successors the office of

papal legate to the Danes, Swedes, and Slavs. At Rome, Nicholas rebuilt and endowed several churches and constantly sought to encourage religious life. His feast is November 13.

## Adrian II

### (December 14, 867–December 1, 872)

Cardinal Adrian, born in 792 and now an old man, was elected unanimously by the Roman people and clergy. Although he came of a family that had produced popes Stephen III and Sergius II, he had already refused the papacy twice. The same themes that had dominated St. Nicholas I's pontificate—dealing with emperors East and West, the Photian schism, and the missionary apostolate—were to dominate his. In response, he followed his predecessor's policies as closely as he could.

He was partially successful in dealing with the descendants of Charlemagne. On the one hand, at Monte Cassino, he received back into communion the repentant Lothair, who agreed to give up his mistress and return to his lawful wife. On the way home to Lorraine, however, Lothair died, and his kingdom was partitioned between his two uncles—Louis the German and Charles the Bald. The latter was particularly unhelpful toward Adrian in the pope's struggle against Hincmar of Rheims, who continued to claim that no bishop of Gaul could appeal beyond himself to the pope. Louis II, busy besieging the Saracen-held city of Bari in southern Italy, could not maintain the independence of his brother's realm.

However, Louis was helpful in ending another problem. In 866, Basil the Macedonian, a mercenary who had won the favor (and some say, the bed) of Emperor Michael III, assassinated—with his imperial friend's consent—Bardas. Within a year, Basil murdered Michael and was now emperor of Byzantium. Despite his rather unsavory rise, Basil surprised everyone by the way he began restoring Byzantine administration, law, finances, and the military. Important to his program was reestablishing good relations with the West. To that end, in 869, he concluded a treaty of alliance with Louis II, by which the two emperors agreed to jointly expel the Muslims from Bari. After a two-year-long siege, this goal was accomplished in 871.

To receive papal favor, Basil deposed Photius and restored Ignatius. He then requested Adrian to convene a council at Constantinople. Considered the Eighth Ecumenical Council by the Catholics, Constantinople IV opened

in 869, under the presidency of Adrian (represented by legates) and Basil. Numbering 102 bishops, 3 papal legates, and 4 patriarchs, the council fathers ordered burned the acts of the conciliabulum. They condemned Photius and likewise approved all the Latin practices that Photius had condemned.

Peace was restored, but Adrian's efforts to attach Bulgaria to the West failed. Nevertheless, by his timely support of Sts. Cyril and Methodius, Adrian ensured that some of the Slavic peoples would remain part of the patriarchate of the West. And so it is that although the Bulgarians, Serbs, Macedonians, Ukrainians, Belarusians, and Russians are Byzantine Rite (whether Catholic or Orthodox), the Czechs, Slovaks, Croats, Slovenes, and Poles are Latins.

Although Emperor Basil's reign was fairly tranquil at this point, his Western colleague's life was rather difficult. Having withdrawn in August of 871 to Benevento, in preparation for further campaigning, Louis was treacherously taken captive by the Lombard duke of Benevento, the emperor's supposed vassal. The arrival of Muslim invaders a month later compelled the traitorous duke to release his prisoner, but only after having had Louis swear that he would take no revenge, or ever again enter Benevento with an army. The liberated emperor proceeded to trounce the invaders yet again. In celebration, he returned to Rome, where he was crowned a second time by Adrian on May 18, 872.

This was a prelude to yet another victory for Louis; he shortly afterward departed the Eternal City in a successful effort to dislodge a band of Saracens who had taken Capua. But it was the aged pope's last major public action; after such an adventurous reign, the old man surely found death a release.

## John VIII
### (December 14, 872–December 16, 882)

As Adrian II aged, governance of the Church in Rome fell increasingly into the hands of a clique of unscrupulous clerics; some of these enjoyed the friendship of Louis II, others of Formosus, the bishop of Porto. Although these two last worthies were not, all in all, a bad sort, some of their cronies most definitely were—a problem not unknown in either Church or state, before or since. Indeed, it is a universal phenomenon.

Of this group, perhaps the most notorious were Gregory, primicerius of

the Roman Church; his brother Stephen (both of whom were great for selling Church offices); and his son-in-law, George of the Aventine, who had a flair for both murder and adultery.

Anyone who ascended the papal throne would have to contend with this set of black sheep, who enjoyed the emperor's favor. Moreover, there remained the problem of Bulgaria and the East in general, as well as of the successors of Charlemagne and the more or less constant Saracen raiding.

By election of the Roman clergy and people, dealing with all of this fell to John, the archdeacon. The new pope's election was stoutly opposed by Formosus, who would remain an enemy as long as John lived (although he would later have great problems of his own).

John was in a ticklish position: he could not clean house so long as Louis II, from whom essential military protection came, lived. At the same time, should Louis die, none of his likely successors had the same military ability; the Muslims would be virtually unopposed. It was a classical papal dilemma. While the emperor lived, an uneasy truce prevailed within Rome.

But other problems occupied John's time elsewhere. In Moravia, after his brother St. Cyril's death in 869, St. Methodius labored on among the Slavs, using the Slavonic Liturgy approved by Adrian II. This bothered the German princes and bishops tremendously—the prospect of a fully independent Slavic state outside of German political control and dependent religiously on Rome directly was not pleasing to them. They had Methodius seized on trumped-up charges and imprisoned.

It took two years for the captive saint to get word of this to the pope. On receiving this knowledge, John (to please the Germans) forbade the use of Slavonic in the Liturgy, but ordered Methodius restored as ruling bishop. This done, he ordered Methodius to Rome to answer fresh accusations. Once before the pontiff, Methodius not only cleared himself completely, but also had his liturgical privileges restored. Thus the Slavonic ritual was confirmed in the approval it has enjoyed from that day to this, and Methodius returned to Moravia, working until his death in 885.

John would have less success with Bulgaria, which he too attempted to woo for Rome. He wrote to Prince Boris of the Bulgarians that, though the faith of Constantinople and of Rome were the same, the former diocese's continual habit of falling into heresy or schism would affect Bulgaria one day. The prince was sympathetic, but felt he could not leave the oversight of so holy a man as St. Ignatius.

Meanwhile, in 875, Louis II died near Brescia, but not before nominating his cousin Carloman of Bavaria (son of Louis the German, who renounced his own rights in his son's favor) as his successor. The emperor was entombed at the cathedral of San Ambrogio in Milan. Carloman prepared an army to cross the Alps, while his uncle Charles the Bald asserted his claim to the imperial

title as the last remaining eligible son of Louis the Pious. The Muslims, needless to say, were elated and stepped up their raids.

What John feared most had come to pass, but the pope was not one to let fear of approaching ruin paralyze him. Deriving what benefit he could from Louis's death, he immediately moved to clean up the Roman administration. Deprived of their imperial protector, the Gregory-Stephen-George clique were charged with their crimes. They managed to evade justice for a while and even plotted to deliver Rome to the Muslims; however, found at last, they fled Rome for France with the papal treasury. With them fled Formosus. While he had not joined his friends in their crimes, his open opposition to the pope and his relationship with the exiles led him to fear papal justice.

Although Louis's death had beneficial effects in Rome, its impact on the larger stage was catastrophic. Charles the Bald was able at length to convince his nephew of the justice of his claims to the imperial throne; on Christmas Day, 875, John duly crowned Charles emperor at Rome. Carloman, in turn, was consoled for his loss by at last inheriting Bavaria on his father's death in 876. The same year, Charles showed his gratitude by giving up to John "many of the rights and customs of the empire."

In 877, however, Carloman crossed the Alps and had himself crowned king of the Lombards at Pavia. He asked John to accept him as emperor, which the pope, having crowned Charles, refused to do. By this time, Carloman had become ill and he placed the administration of his Italian kingdom into John's hands, withdrawing to Bavaria. Carloman died at last in 880, leaving behind an illegitimate son, Arnulf.

Things did not fare much better with Charles the Bald. Although he led an expedition into Italy to fight the Muslims, his efforts had poor results. While on a trip to see the emperor, John encountered Formosus in France, whom he compelled to make an oath never to return to Rome. Without practical imperial aid, John was forced to become a general, fortifying St. John Outside the Walls, and an admiral, forming a fleet and defeating the Muslims in a naval battle in 876. Well aware that direct military command did not well befit his office, he tried with limited success to rally the southern Italian princes against the invaders.

Charles the Bald attempted to mount another attack, but before he could do so, he died on October 6, 877. There were several claimants to the vacant throne, whose filling the Muslim raids and general disorder made essential. The only one who John thought was capable was Boso, the heir to Provence. Being uninterested in the role, Boso stepped down. Carloman's brother, Charles the Fat, *was* interested, however. In time Charles would inherit both his two brothers' lands in Germany. He was helping his nephews dispute the throne of France when the call came from the pope to take up the imperial crown. Leaving his nephews, Charles headed for Rome.

John crowned him Charles III in February 881. By the time the pope died, Charles was, on paper, ruler of most of the empire of Charlemagne. But because Charles was not the man his father was, neither were his realms in that empire.

John's relations with the Eastern empire were somewhat less problematic, but only just. Given Prince Boris's refusal to leave St. Ignatius' of Constantinople's leadership, John wrote to Ignatius asking him to give up Bulgaria. For all that the patriarch felt subject to Rome in matters spiritual, he felt he could not in justice surrender the territories he had inherited. Thus John did one of the very few deeply unjust things of his pontificate. He signed the excommunication of St. Ignatius of Constantinople when Ignatius died.

On Ignatius's death, Photius was restored as patriarch. The legates of Pope John VIII accepted him on the condition that Bulgaria be returned to the Latin church; however, the theological issues remained unresolved and have plagued the Church ever since. Moreover, the large and pious party led by St. Ignatius—many of whose relatives had been executed for their adherence to him, were, to put it mildly, scandalized.

Despite this continuing dissonance, Photius's Greek version of the letter of Pope John VIII to the emperor was read into the acts of the local council of 879–880. The pope's words were recorded with no objection, which acceptance must be considered Photius's opinion at that time:

> One can ask from what master you have learned to act in that way. First of all, certainly from the coryphaeus of the Apostles, Peter, whom the Lord had constituted head of all churches when he said [to him]: "Feed my sheep." (John 21:17). Not only [from Him] but also from the holy synods and constitutions. And also from the holy and orthodox decrees and constitutions of the fathers, as it is testified by your divine and pious letters.

Since, however, Photius did not give up Bulgaria, in 881 he was once again excommunicated. It is a bad spot on an otherwise inspiring papal career, although it must be admitted that the situation with the East was confusing.

In contrast, there were brighter accomplishments. In Spain, the Christians of the north were already slowly reconquering Spain from the Muslims. Things had gone so well thus far that John made Oviedo, their capital, an archdiocese. English refugees from the Danes came to Rome: Burhred, king of Mercia, and Edred, archbishop of Canterbury. This last confided to the pontiff his fears for young Alfred, whose seat on the Saxon throne was as unsteady as his way of life appeared. John had already written the young king a letter full of good advice, which that monarch treasured ever after.

At John's death, some problems had been solved, but more had taken

their place. Except for the Eastern schism, it is hard to see what else John VIII could do. Reportedly, he was murdered, but the facts are unclear as to how, or even whether, he was killed. These rumors unleashed gang warfare in the streets of Rome.

## Marinus I

### (December 16, 882–May 15, 884)

The son of the priest Palumbo, Marinus joined the clergy at twelve. Ordained a subdeacon by Leo IV, he was sent, after being made a deacon, on three important missions to Constantinople. The second time he arrived there, in 869, he presided, in the name of Adrian II, over Constantinople IV. John VIII consecrated him bishop of Cervetri, treasurer of the Roman Church, and archdeacon, then sent him on mission to Constantinople where he was imprisoned for his firmness.

Although a bishop, Marinus was elected pope the very day John VIII died. He was consecrated without waiting for permission from Charles III. He immediately set about trying to end the factionalism in the city, and to that end, Marinus pardoned Formosus and allowed him to return.

However much he might depart from his predecessor's internal policy, Marinus maintained his Eastern one. He repeated the excommunication of Photius. Hoping for imperial assistance against the Muslims, he met Charles III in 883—but that meeting produced little result. The emperor had not earned his nickname "the Fat" out of industriousness.

Marinus sent the pallium to Fulk, the new archbishop of Rheims—a welcome relief from the annoying Hincmar. King Alfred applied for and received an exemption of taxes on the English School at Rome. So things stood when Marinus died and was laid to rest in the portico of St. Peter's.

## St. Adrian III

### (May 17, 884–September 17, 885)

Born at Teano, Adrian was faced with a number of problems. He reiterated the censures against Photius and dealt heroically with a famine that had struck Rome. During Adrian's short pontificate, violent feuds based upon the alleged assassination of John VIII continued. George of the Aventine, a priest whom John had exiled and whom Marinus I had allowed to return to Rome, was blinded, possibly by order of the new pope. In the summer of 885, Charles III convoked the Diet of Worms to ensure the succession of his illegitimate son, Bernard. Realizing the danger that newly increased Muslim raids posed to the city, he resolved to travel to the diet, to plead with the magnates of the empire for help. Adrian died en route at Spilambergo in the diocese of Modena (where a church bears his name). His feast is July 8.

## Stephen VI (V)

### (May 17, 885–September 14, 891)

Born to a Roman noble named Hadrian, Stephen's early education was given over to his cousin Bishop Zachary, librarian of the Holy See. In time he became renowned for his learning and piety and was appointed cardinal of Sts. Quatro Coronati by Pope Marinus I. Unanimously elected pope, he would not wait for imperial confirmation, but Charles III acquiesced when he learned the circumstances of Stephen's election.

Stephen's first great challenge came with a plague of locusts, who ate the crops and reduced the city to starvation. Because the papal treasury was empty, he resorted to his father's fortune, using it to buy food, to free prisoners, and to repair churches.

Moreover, there were many issues to resolve in the Church at large. Aurelian, the archbishop of Lyons, refused to consecrate Teutbold, who had been canonically elected bishop of Langres. Stephen solved the matter by consecrating the prelate himself. Similarly, when the archbishops of Bordeaux and Ravenna broke canon law, their subjects appealed to Stephen, who set matters

straight. But imperial affairs—both Eastern and Western—would take up most of Stephen's time.

Shortly after his decision with regard to the papal election, Charles III's incompetence as emperor was becoming ever more manifest. At a diet held at Frankfurt in November of 887, he was deposed, only to die a few months later. Arnulf, the illegitimate son of Carloman, succeeded him as king of Germany. But the new king, hard put to keep peace in Germany, and at war with the Moravians, could not spare the time to claim the imperial throne.

This put Stephen in an awkward position because the Saracens were once again raiding to their hearts' content. At last, he turned to the most powerful south Italian noble, Guido III, duke of Spoleto. In 891, he both crowned the Duke emperor and adopted him as his son, despite his preference for Arnulf.

In 886, Basil I died and was replaced on the Byzantine throne by his son, Leo VI. Immediately, Stephen appealed to the new emperor to depose Photius and end the schism. Leo did, packing Photius off to a remote monastery where he died in 891. Thus the Eastern Schism was healed once again. Stephen then asked for a fleet and military support to drive off the Muslims, but the hard-pressed Leo refused, because of his own strategic needs.

At Stephen's death, the situation seemed bleak, but not hopeless. He was laid to rest near the portico of St. Peter's.

# The Pornocracy

# Formosus

## (October 6, 891–April 4, 896)

As previously seen, Formosus had led an adventurous life. Prior to his troubles with John VIII, he had been sent upon various sensitive missions by several popes, and he had fulfilled them well. He was both learned and ascetical and had fallen afoul of Pope John more for his poor choice in friends and his indecision than for any truly personal flaws.

He had in due course been rehabilitated and restored to his diocese of Porto. There matters stood when Stephen VI died. Formosus, whose standing among the Romans was very great by this time, was elected unanimously. Like his predecessor, he had to deal with Emperor Guido, but unlike him, Formosus had some hope that Arnulf would come to Rome to claim his rights.

Nevertheless, in 892, Guido arrived at the Eternal City with his son Lambert in tow, to demand another imperial co-coronation. Formosus duly crowned the Spoletan pair, but he prayed for Arnulf to arrive.

Meanwhile, the declining fortunes of the Carolingians in France claimed Formosus's attention. One of the last failures of Charles III in that country had been his inability to relieve the city of Paris, which had been besieged by the Vikings. The defense of the city was carried on by Eudes, count of Paris (a Carolingian on his mother's side). After Charles III was deposed at Frankfurt, the French decided to have a king of their own. The nearest Carolingian was Charles of Lorraine, called "the Simple." But Eudes, too, because of his prowess in defending the people—as well as his maternal descent—had a large following. Formosus was ever reverent of the descendants of Charlemagne and came out for Charles, appealing to Arnulf to support his cousin. Although Eudes would indeed mount the throne, he was overthrown in favor of Charles a few years later.

In Constantinople, the bishops who had recognized Photius appealed to the pope (now that Basil I's son Stephen was patriarch) to confirm them in their places. In 892, Formosus replied that this would be the case for laymen who had served Photius; however, he ordered all clerics anointed by Photius to resign.

In addition, Formosus intervened in the affairs of Germany, where the dio-

ceses of Hamburg and Bremen were locked in combat over which would be metropolitan over the other. Formosus found in favor of Hamburg.

But events in Italy were not so easily resolved. It soon became apparent that Guido desired the same control over the Church the Lombards had. Moreover, he had established a party favoring himself among the Roman nobles, thus putting papal independence at serious risk.

Formosus secretly corresponded with Arnulf, urging him to come to Italy to claim the imperial throne. At last, in 894, the German king crossed the Alps. Soon, all Italy north of the Po was in his hands. At this juncture, Guido died, leaving his son and co-emperor Lambert in charge, together with the Empress-Mother, Agiltrude. By February of 896, Arnulf had arrived at Rome, but Agiltrude had locked herself up in the city. Arnulf nevertheless was able to enter; Agiltrude and Lambert fled to their stronghold of Spoleto. Formosus at last had his pleasure of crowning Arnulf as emperor.

Safely crowned, Arnulf set off to Spoleto. But he was stricken with paralysis on the route and was unable to continue the campaign. Formosus died a few days later.

## Boniface VI

(April 4–19, 896)

The death of Formosus left, to put it mildly, a power vacuum in the city. The Roman mob proposed and elected Boniface, a cleric who had twice been deprived of holy orders. He reigned 15 days; according to some he died of gout, while others maintain he was deposed by his successor.

## Stephen VII (VI)
### (May 1, 896–August 897)

The Spoletans quickly reassumed control of Rome. Lambert and Agiltrude's supporters elected Stephen, bishop of Anagni, the son of John, a Roman priest. Consecrated bishop by Formosus, he would preside over one of the most colorful, albeit disgusting, episodes in the history of the papacy. Agiltrude demanded that Formosus be tried for alleged crimes.

The pope's corpse was disinterred, and a synod convened at the Lateran to judge him. The rotting cadaver was set up in full pontifical robes, with a deacon to answer the charges made, and Stephen sitting as judge. The verdict was that Formosus could not have been a valid pope, as he had been bishop of another See at the time of his election; Stephen further ruled that all of Formosus's clerical appointments were also invalid (this served Stephen well because it meant that his own appointment to Anagni was annulled, thus allowing him, by his own rights, to be pope). Further, Stephen declared Formosus's sacramental ministrations as pope to have been invalid, especially ordinations of priests and consecrations of bishops—all of those who the late pope had anointed were to be considered laymen (this last judgment, incidentally, was itself heretical, since Catholic dogma holds that the sacraments work of themselves [*ex opere operato*], regardless of the legal standing of the cleric administering them.

The papal vestments were stripped from Formosus's body; his hairshirt, however, had merged with his flesh and could not be extracted. The three fingers of his right hand, used to bless when he was alive, were cut off, and his corpse flung into the Tiber after being dragged through the streets. Later, a monk would rescue it.

Despite this exciting interlude, Stephen himself was destined for a bad end. A few months later, an insurrection against Guido took over Rome. The pope was stripped of his pontifical robes and insignia, then strangled.

## Romanus
### (August 897)

Born at Gallese, near Civita Castellana, Romanus was the son of a man named Constantine. As cardinal of S. Pietro ad Vincula, he won a reputation for virtue. He was elected after calm came to Rome in the wake of Stephen's death, but lived a mere four months afterward. In that time, he gave the pallium to the patriarch of Grado, confirmed the election of two Spanish bishops, and nullified Stephen's acts. Formosus's body was reburied. Romanus was deposed by Stephen's adherents. His coins bear his own title and that of the emperor Lambert.

## Theodore II
### (December 897)

Formosus's adherents were able to elect Theodore, son of Photius, as pope; but he lived only twenty days. In that time he had Formosus's funeral conducted with full pontifical honors. He reinstated all the clerics deposed by Stephen and declared Formosus's sacramental acts valid. His reign, though short, was remembered by the Roman people fondly, not least because of Theodore's numerous acts of charity.

## John IX
### (January 898–January 900)

Born in Tivoli, John had been a Benedictine monk and was ordained priest by Formosus. At his election, the proponents of Stephen's party attempted to place one of their own, Sergius, on the papal throne. But enjoying the favor of Lambert, John was able to secure his position; Sergius was driven from the city and excommunicated.

The new pope's first interest was to eliminate the anarchy that had overwhelmed Rome and Italy because of factionalism and the breakdown of the empire. In the course of several synods held in Rome in 898, John restored the clerics degraded by Stephen, ordered an end to the plunder of the papal and Episcopal palaces upon their tenants' decease (a custom that, in view of the raging disorder, had become usual), required that popes-elect could not be consecrated without the presence of imperial envoys (to reduce the attendant disorders), and declared for Lambert against Berenger, a warlord who wished to be emperor. John also had the synod declare that Boniface VI had not been the legitimate pope, a decision subsequently rescinded.

John signed an accord of union with the patriarch of Constantinople, Anthony II Cauleas. For the moment, affairs in the East were satisfactory.

Despite the wishes of the German bishops, John erected an independent hierarchy for Moravia and consecrated a metropolitan and three bishops for that country, thus underlying papal support for nascent nationalities. At his death he was buried near St. Peter's.

## Benedict IV
### (February 900–July 903)

The new pope was a Roman, son of Mammalus, and had been ordained by Formosus. His generosity and learning were bywords, and it was fervently hoped that he could restore the Church's tranquility. Certainly, the difficulties in the papacy led to all sorts of disorder. Baldwin, count of Flanders, assassinated Fulk, archbishop of Rheims; Benedict excommunicated the murderous noble on June 17,

900. When the bishop of Amasia in Asia Minor sought refuge in Rome (his diocese having been overrun by the Muslims), Benedict hosted him royally. He also confirmed the great abbey of Fulda in its privileges.

But imperial affairs would keep Benedict busy. The paralyzed Arnulf died in early 900. After this, Louis, called "the blind," the maternal grandson of Emperor Louis II, came to Pavia where he was elected king of Italy. He then came to Rome, where in February 901, Benedict crowned him Emperor Louis III. But Berengar of Friuli, Lambert's rival, was able to drive him out again, forcing him to swear never to return. So affairs stood when Benedict died, being buried by St. Peter's near the gate of Guido.

## Leo V
### (August 903)

Born in Priapi, a village of Ardea, Leo was a gentle man who was renowned for his holiness. Not being a cardinal, but attached to a church outside of the city, he was elected by the Romans in hopes that an outsider would be above the bitter factionalism that was destroying the Church. This he was; but his neutrality did not help him. After about a month on the pontifical throne, Leo was seized and imprisoned by Christopher, cardinal-priest of St. Damasus. Although Christopher declared himself pope, he himself was soon overthrown.

## Sergius III
### (January 29, 904–April 14, 911)

A Roman noble, Sergius was the son of Benedict. Consecrated as bishop of Caere by Formosus, he joined the party of Formosus's enemies and ceased to act as a bishop at that pope's death. The Roman mob, disgusted by Cardinal Christopher's abuse of Leo V, overthrew him and elected Sergius in his place. One of the new pope's first acts was to order both Leo and Christopher executed. Thus there was no question as to who the real pope was.

As a partisan of Stephen VII, Sergius officially rehabilitated the grisly posthumous trial of Formosus, declaring its findings valid. This meant that once again Formosus's appointments were annulled, and his ordinations and consecrations held to be invalid. Given that the bishops consecrated by Formosus had in the meantime consecrated or ordained a number of clerics themselves, this added sacramental confusion to political anarchy.

That Sergius's grasp on propriety was weak is borne out further by his dealings with Emperor Leo VI. He had taken his mistress, Zoe, to wife after his third empress died. Not only had their affair been scandalous; Byzantine canon law forbade fourth marriages. But Leo had had a son by the union, and was desperate for an heir. The patriarch, Nicholas I Mysticus, baptized the boy on the proviso that Leo and Zoe would separate afterward. Not only did Leo renege on his promise, but he crowned Zoe as empress. Both sides appealed to Rome.

Sergius examined the case. He declared that while the Byzantine canons did indeed forbid the union (although those of Rome did not ban fourth marriages), the good of the empire demanded its recognition. He sided with the emperor against the patriarch, losing the respect of many of the Byzantines. Given his own relations with the Roman noblewoman, Marozia, which produced in turn a son (himself one day to be pope as John XI), Sergius's acceptance of moral diversity can be understood. His unorthodox lifestyle paved the way for the dominance of the papacy by the family of Theophylactus, Marozia's understanding father. This was the infamous "pornocracy," to date probably the darkest hour in the annals of the popes. Sergius did, however, restore the Lateran basilica and was buried at St. Peter's.

## Anastasius III
### (September 911–November 913)

A Roman born, the son of Lucian, Anastasius was a marked contrast to his predecessor. He was known as a man of moderation, and the most exciting event of his quiet reign was the determination of certain diocesan boundaries in Germany. His pontificate would be happily remembered, given the events that followed. This was ironic, as the Theophylacts consolidated their power, allowing Anastasius very little control over Roman affairs.

## Lando
### (July 913–February 914)

Born in the district of Sabina, Lando was much like Anastasius III—a quiet man, disinclined to challenge the growing power of the Theophylacts. He did, however, grant a privilege to a church in his native town.

## John X
### (914–928)

John was a deacon of Bologna and became archbishop of Ravenna in 905. As a cousin (and some say lover) of Theodora—mother to Marozia and wife of Theophylact—he had, however, an entrée into Roman politics. At Lando's death, Theodora was able to secure John's election to the papacy.

But unlike his predecessors, John was no wallflower; moreover, given Theodora's age at the time, it may well be that their relationship was platonic. Whatever the case, John's energy was soon employed in fighting the Muslims, who had ensconced themselves in a set of forts on the Garigliano River. The pope organized an alliance of Italian princes, headed by the redoubtable Berengar of Friuli, who had been such a trial to the emperors Lambert and Arnulf. At last, Berengar came to Rome in 915 and was crowned emperor himself by John. The next year, the pontiff attacked and destroyed the Saracen forts, ending that particular threat.

John's activities with the Western Church in general were mixed. On the one hand, he gave initial approval to the charter of Cluny, an ascetical Benedictine abbey that excelled in liturgical life. The pope entered into direct and friendly relations with Conrad, the king of Germany. But when Count Heribert of Aquitaine took the king of France prisoner, John allowed him to make his five-year-old son, Hugh of Vermandois, archbishop of Rheims in return for the king's release.

Eastern affairs were even more muddled. On the one hand, John was partly successful in binding the Church in Dalmatia more closely to Rome.

But for all his efforts in Bulgaria, that perennial object of papal ambition remained out of his grasp, due in no small part to the efforts of the emperor and patriarch at Constantinople.

But another opportunity to more completely perfect the union with Constantinople was lost by him. Although Leo VI had deposed Patriarch Nicholas I for his opposition to the fourth marriage, before his death Leo had relented and allowed Nicholas to return to his post. The new emperor, Alexander, likewise supported Nicholas. But a large number of bishops in the East would not accept him. The patriarch appealed to John to compel their obedience; this he refused to do, reasserting Sergius III's decision regarding the marriage.

More problems awaited in Italy. In 924, Emperor Berengar was murdered. John supported as a successor Hugh of Burgundy. When the latter ruler landed in Pisa, the pope sent a legate to welcome him and invite the Burgundian to Rome to be crowned emperor. In the meantime, Marozia, whose first husband Alberic had died, went on to marry Guido, Margrave of Tuscany, whom she wished to see as emperor.

Fearing the confluence of John with Hugh, she resolved to remove the pope. Marozia and her husband had Petrus, John's brother and prefect of Rome, murdered in June of 928. Shortly afterward, they had the pope himself seized and imprisoned in the Castel Sant'Angelo. Apparently, he was smothered there with a pillow.

## Leo VI

### (June 928–February 929)

Leo was the son of Christopher, primicerius to John VIII. He was cardinal-priest of Santa Susanna at his election. Allowed by the Theophylacts only to attend to purely spiritual duties, he spent his pontificate organizing the Church in Dalmatia. Leo was buried at St. Peter's.

## Stephen VIII (VII)
### (February 929–March 931)

A Roman, the son of Teudemund, Stephen was, when elected, cardinal-priest of Santa Anastasia (which in 1953 would become the title of James Francis Cardinal McIntyre, archbishop of Los Angeles). Confined as per usual to spiritual duties by the Theophylacts, Stephen confirmed the privileges of a number of French and Italian monasteries, and was duly buried in St. Peter's.

## John XI
### (931–December 935)

Not content with the popes being essentially merely their chaplains, the Theophylacts decided at last to place one of their own on the Chair of Peter. John was the son of Marozia, legally by Alberic, but probably by Sergius III, and was made to succeed his father as pope. Guido of Tuscany having died, Hugh of Provence, who had become king of Italy, was a threat to Rome. But Marozia enticed and married him, bringing him to rule in the Eternal City. John was completely under their control.

But their rule was extremely oppressive; the pope's brother, Alberic II, led the Romans in revolt. Marozia was thrown into prison, but Hugh escaped Rome. John was now ruled by Alberic, who even made ecclesiastical decisions. When the Byzantine emperor Romanus asked that his sixteen-year-old son Theophylactus be made patriarch of Constantinople, Alberic duly had John send him the pallium. But of his own accord, the pope did give Cluny many privileges. Nevertheless this pontificate was truly one of the most depressing in papal history.

# Leo VII

### (January 3, 936–July 13, 939)

Born in Rome, Leo had been a Benedictine monk, and was at last made priest of San Sisto. Alberic II put him on the throne, but Leo soon proved to have a mind of his own. The city was besieged by Alberic's stepfather, King Hugh; the pope sent word to Odo, abbot of Cluny, to come to Rome. This holy prelate managed to pass through the siege lines. Using Odo's influence with Alberic and Hugh, Leo was able to bring them together for peace. Alberic married Hugh's daughter Alda, and for the moment tranquility returned to the Eternal City.

Leo granted privileges to many monasteries, especially Cluny, and appointed Frederick, archbishop of Mainz, as his vicar for Germany. This gave the prelate the authority to work with the king of Germany, Henry the Fowler, and his son Otto, for the reform of conditions in both Church and state north of the Alps. Leo forbade the forcible conversion of Jews.

# Stephen IX (X)

### (July 14, 939–October 31, 942)

A Roman, when Stephen was elected at Alberic II's insistence, he was the cardinal-priest of SS. Silvestro e Martino. Although acting pretty much as Alberic's chaplain, he was loyal to the memory of Charlemagne; for that reason, he compelled (via threat of excommunication) the French nobles to remain loyal to their king, the Carolingian Louis IV.

## Marinus II
### (942–April 946)

Yet another of Alberic's chaplains, Marinus was born in Rome, and at the time of his election was cardinal-priest of San Ciriaco. He did work for reform at home and abroad, in the former case using his legates and in the latter his own example. He looked after both the poor and the repair of churches. As was common with the popes of his stamp, he encouraged the Cluniac reform in particular.

## Agapetus II
### (May 10, 946–August 955)

A man of virtuous life, Agapetus, although lacking any temporal power under Alberic's rule as "Senator and Prince of Rome," nevertheless managed to accomplish a great deal in the spiritual realm. Beloved by the Romans, he worked on the repair of churches and relief of the poor. He particularly encouraged King Otto I in Germany to continue his work of reform in that realm. Agapetus also settled a succession dispute in the archdiocese of Rheims and encouraged the growth of Catholicism among the Danes.

Unfortunately, he was forced, with the clergy and nobles of the city, to consent to an act that would pave the way for one of the worst Pontificates. On Alberic's deathbed, he had compelled Agapetus and the notables to swear to make his son, Octavian, pope in due course. Aware of Octavian's vicious and immoral life—exacerbated by his temporal rule in succession to his father—Agapetus and various leading Italian magnates appealed to Otto to come to Rome and set things to rights. Agapetus died before this could happen, however.

## John XII
### (December 16, 955–May 14, 964)

As noticed, John XII's election had been arranged in advance. Complying with this illegal compact, Octavian became John XII. In what had been a dismal age for the papacy, the new pontiff was surely one of its lowest points. The Lateran Palace was called a brothel in his day, thanks to his diverse taste in lovers—both in terms of gender and number.

Yet, despite himself, he paved the way for reform in the Church. On the one hand, he confirmed the charter of Cluny, from whence many active reformers would emerge. On the other, by repeating Agapetus II's call to King Otto I of Germany to come down to northern Italy to save papal possessions there (and giving Otto the Imperial Crown in return), John unwittingly set in motion the cleansing of Rome by the Imperial army.

### Charter of the Monastery of Cluny

**Signed by Duke William of Aquitaine**
**On September 11, 910**

To those who consider things sanely it is evident that Divine Providence counsels the rich to use well those goods that they possess in transitory fashion, if they wish for eternal recompense. . . . Wherefore I, William, by the grace of God count and duke, having pondered these things and wishing while there is yet time to make provision for my salvation, have found it right, yea necessary, to dispose for the good of my soul of some of the temporal possessions which have been bestowed upon me. . . . That this benefaction may endure not only for a time, but may last for ever, I will provide at my expense for men living together under monastic vows, with this faith and hope that if I cannot myself despise all the things of this world, at least by sustaining those who despise the world, those whom I believe to be righteous in the eyes of God, I may myself receive the reward of the righteous.

To all those who live in the unity of faith . . . I make known that for the love of God and of our Saviour Christ Jesus I give and deliver to the Apostles Peter and Paul the village of Cluny, with its estate and its manor, and with the chapel that is dedicated in honour of St. Mary Mother of God and of St. Peter, Prince of the Apostles, with all the property that depends thereon, cottages, chapels, serfs both men and women, vines, fields, meadows, forests, water and watercourses, mills, crops, and revenues, land tilled and untilled, with no reservations. . . . I, William, with my wife Ingelberge, give these things to the aforesaid Apostles, first for the love of God, then for the soul of my Lord the King, for the souls of my father and mother, for me and my wife, that is for the salvation of our souls and bodies, for the soul of Ava my sister who left me these properties by will, for the souls of our brothers and sisters, our nephews and for all our kindred, men and women, for our faithful servants, and for the maintenance and integrity of the Catholic faith. Finally, since as Christians we are all bound together by the bonds of our faith and charity, may this gift be made also for the faithful of times past, present, and to come.

I give on condition that a Regular Monastery be established at Cluny . . . that monks shall form a congregation there living under the rule of St. Benedict; that they shall for ever possess, hold and order the property given in such wise that this honourable house shall be unceasingly full of vows and prayers, that men shall seek there with a lively desire and an inner fervour the sweetness of converse with Heaven, and that prayers and supplications shall be addressed thence without ceasing to God, both for me and for those persons commemorated above.

. . . May the monks and all the aforesaid possessions be under the power and the dominion of Abbot Berno, who shall rule according to his knowledge and power so long as he shall live. After his death may the monks have the power and liberty to elect as abbot and ruler the monk of their order whom they shall prefer, according to the good pleasure of God and the rule laid down by St. Benedict, with no contradiction or impediment of this election by our power or that of any man. . . . May they have as protectors the Apostles themselves, and for defender the Pontiff of Rome. . . .

It has pleased us to set forth in this testament that from this day forward the monks united in congregation at Cluny shall be wholly freed from our power, from that of our kindred, and

from the jurisdiction of royal greatness, and shall never submit to the yoke of any earthly power. I beg and pray that no secular Prince, no Count, no Bishop, no Pontiff of the Roman Church, by God and through God and all his saints, under threat of the awful day of Judgment, may ever invade the possessions of these servants of God. Let him not sell, nor diminish, nor exchange, nor take any thing which is theirs; let him set up no ruler over them against their will. That this prohibition may bind the bold and evil with straiter bonds, once again I say it, and add: I conjure you, ye Holy Apostles and glorious Princes of the Earth, Peter and Paul; and thou, Pontiff of Pontiffs of the Apostolic See, do ye cut off from the communion of the Holy Catholic Church and from life eternal, by the canonical and apostolic authority received from God, those who steal, invade, or sell these things which I give to you with eager wish and a joyful heart. Be ye the guardians and defenders of Cluny and of the servants of God who shall dwell there, and of their goods that are destined for the giving of alms, for the imitation of lovingkindness and mercy of our most Holy Redeemer.

From "Charter of Abbey of Cluny," in E. F. Henderson, ed., *Select Historical Documents of the Middle Ages* (London: George Bell, 1892), pp. 329–332. Reprinted in Brian Tierney, ed., *The Middle Ages, Vol. I: Sources of Medieval History*, 4th ed. (New York: Alfred A. Knopf, 1983), pp. 137–139.

On January 31, 962, Otto entered Rome at the head of his troops, having rescued the endangered papal territories in the north. Otto and his consort, Adelaide, were solemnly crowned in St. Peter's the following February 2 by John. A synod met in the emperor's presence, which among other things demanded that John reform his life. By the "Ottonian Privilege," the emperor expanded the papal states, undertook to defend the Holy See, and codified the rules for papal elections, which would require imperial approval. From this time forward, the popes were to swear allegiance to the emperors.

As soon as Otto had left with his troops for Germany, John began plotting with the emperor's Italian enemies. In advance of Otto's return in November of 963, John fled with the papal treasury to Tivoli. The emperor convened another synod, which demanded that John return to Rome and face charges of various kinds. John refused and threatened to excommunicate all the participants. In return, the synod declared John deposed on December 4. A well-known and able curia official was elected pope as Leo VIII in John's place. Since he was a layman, all of the required sacramental offices had to be administered to him before he could ascend the throne.

From his refuge in Tivoli, John continued to agitate against Leo and encouraged the Roman mob against him. When the emperor and his army

departed yet again in mid-January, riots broke out and Leo was forced to flee the city. Another synod was held, and on February 26, 964, Leo was declared deposed, and John was reinstated. Otto returned once more, John fled yet again, and in May, died in the arms of his married mistress, at the hands of her husband.

## Leo VIII

### (December 4, 963–March 965)

Leo was a Roman noble, and worked as a protonotary in the papal administration. When Otto I deposed John XII, he had Leo, a layman, elected to his place. All of the holy orders, from lector through bishop, were hurriedly bestowed upon him by Sico, bishop of Ostia, on December 6.

A few weeks later, the Romans rose against Otto; they were swiftly defeated and severely punished, hostages were taken for their good behavior—if the Romans would revolt again, the hostages would be killed. But the new pope convinced the emperor to release the captives. In return, as soon as Otto left Rome, in February of 964, the Romans rebelled again and expelled Leo from the city. John XII returned, took over the reigns of the papacy, and degraded all the clerics ordained or appointed by Leo. But news of Otto's imminent return sent John fleeing Rome, only to die in the unfortunate manner referred to earlier.

In response, the clergy and people of the city elected as pope the cardinal-deacon Benedict. But Otto arrived, retook the city, and returned Leo to his position in July. Leo in turn publicly took the pallium from Benedict and returned him to the deaconate—apparently with Benedict's consent. Leo was then able to enjoy the few months of life remaining to him in peace.

## Benedict V
(May–July 964)

Having just read of his short pontificate, it is worth noting that as cardinal-deacon, Benedict had had a great reputation for learning. After returning to the diaconate, Benedict was taken by Otto I back to Germany. There he was given to the care of Adaldag, archbishop of Hamburg-Bremen. He was treated with honor (and acknowledged by some of the German clergy as pope) until his death on July 4, 965.

## John XIII
(October 1, 965–September 6, 972)

Marozia, dominatrix of the papacy, had had a younger sister named Theodora, after their mother. The younger Theodora married John, who after his wife died became a priest. This couple produced two daughters and three sons, one of whom was also named John. He followed his father into the priesthood. Despite his family background, young John soon distinguished himself for both piety and learning; the result was his election to the diocese of Narni.

The death of Leo VIII led the Romans to petition Otto I to return Benedict V to them as pope. But the exasperated emperor was in no mood to give his ever-rebellious subjects their wish. Instead, he proposed the bishop of Narni; in the presence of the imperial envoys John was duly elected and consecrated pope.

Some of the Roman nobility resented the new pontiff and plotted against him. In December 965, they took him captive and imprisoned him—first in the Castel Sant' Angelo, and then in the Campagna. But John managed to escape, and sought refuge in Capua with the duke of that city.

Meanwhile, the plotters had managed to annoy the Romans by their misrule, and a great desire grew among the populace to bring the pope back. At the same time, Otto I, infuriated at having once again to set Italy to rights, mounted another expedition to Rome. Fearful of the emperor's probable ac-

tivities upon his arrival, the Romans asked John to return, which he did on November 14. In December, Otto arrived at the city gates, to be greeted by the pope and his people. The emperor dispensed justice very quickly, executing some of the conspirators, banishing others.

On January 11, 966, John convened a synod in the emperor's presence at St. Peter's. Pope and emperor cooperated in a manner worthy of St. Leo III and Charlemagne from then on. Together, in April of 967, they traveled to Ravenna, where another synod was held, resulting in Magdeburg, Germany, becoming an archdiocese, the settlement of various ecclesiastical disputes, bestowal of privileges on various monasteries, and Ravenna itself becoming a papal state.

The papal-imperial alliance was sealed on Christmas Day, 967, when the emperor's thirteen-year-old son, Otto II, was crowned co-emperor with his father. Where Otto I was in many ways a rough Germanic chieftain, the second Otto was well schooled—not just in letters, but in the theory of the empire.

Shortly after the coronation, John raised the monastery of Meissen, founded in Saxony by Otto I, to a diocese of its own. In 968, St. Adalbert was made archbishop of Magdeburg and extended his missionary work throughout what are now central Germany and the Czech Republic. John also made Benevento and Capua (the latter as a reward for providing him refuge) archdioceses.

But the greatest triumph for both pope and emperor was that of uniting the two imperial traditions by securing a marriage for Otto II with a Byzantine princess. As it was, the younger Otto had a remarkable mother, Empress St. Adelaide. Born to Rudolf II of Burgundy in 931, she had married Otto I when she was twenty, and served as regent for Otto II after his father's death.

Just as impressive on her own was Princess Theophano (956–991), daughter of Emperor Romanus II. Learned and pious, she had also been witness to the intrigues of the Byzantine court and had there gained political acumen, which would be an asset to her future husband. Her charm endeared her to all parties concerned—John, the two Ottos, and St. Adelaide. The marriage of Otto II and Theophano was performed by John himself at Rome on April 14, 972. It was the crowning achievement of his pontificate, and one that would bear much good fruit in the future.

## Benedict VI
### (September 972–August 974)

Cardinal-deacon of San Teodoro, Benedict was a Roman, the son of Hildebrand. Although he was elected shortly after John XIII, Benedict had to wait until January 19, 973, to be consecrated, because Sicco, the imperial envoy whom the law now required present as witness, was unable to arrive until then.

Most of his pontificate was uneventful, concerned as it was with granting various privileges to different churches and monasteries throughout the Catholic world. But its end was as dramatic as any event in papal history. Crescentius, son of Theodora and brother to John XIII, and his partner, the deacon Boniface, were keen on taking control of the city for themselves. The death of Otto I gave them, they thought, their opportunity. As a first step to destroying imperial rule in the city, the pair seized Benedict and flung him into Castel Sant' Angelo in June of 974. As the imperial envoy, Sicco, upon hearing the news began advancing toward Rome with troops to free the pope, Crescentius and Boniface had Benedict either strangled or starved to death.

## *Boniface VII*
### *Anti-Pope (August 974–July 985)*

Born Boniface Franco, he was a native of Rome and son of Ferrucius. A friend and collaborator of Crescentius (particularly in his dealings with Benedict VI), when that pope was killed in prison, Boniface was elevated to the papal throne by his ally. But the approach of the imperial forces, led by Count Sicco, ended for the moment the pair's dreams of power. Boniface fled the city and headed to Constantinople with the papal treasury.

After nine years in exile, news of the death of Otto II emboldened the antipope to return to the Eternal City. There he overthrew Pope John XIV and threw him into Castel Sant' Angelo, where the rightful pope soon followed Benedict VI to the grave. Boniface lorded it over Rome, happy to be back in charge. Although he considered himself to have always been the pope, his subjects did not share his views. At last, anxious to avenge the usurper's two victims, the people rose up, killed him, stripped his corpse, and dragged it

through the streets. Then, they threw Boniface's cadaver beneath a statue in the Lateran, from whence, on the following day, some compassionate priests gave it a Christian burial.

## Benedict VII
### (October 974–October 983)

The army of Otto II, led by Count Sicco, entered the city. The anti-pope Boniface VII fled, and Otto's representative immediately began to repair the damage done by Crescentius and his friend. Benedict, bishop of Sutri, was elected pope; but as soon as the imperial forces withdrew, Crescentius's party began once again to menace the new pontiff. The people once again appealed to the emperor, and yet another army entered Rome.

The rest of Benedict's time was peaceful, allowing him to promote the growth of the monasteries and to give aid to the persecuted Christians of North Africa, who were slowly being strangled out of existence by the Muslims.

## John XIV
### (November 983–August 20, 984)

After the death of Benedict VII, Peter Campanora of Pavia, imperial chancellor for Italy, was elected pope. Because he did not wish to be "Peter II," he took the name John. Unfortunately, Emperor Otto II, who was then at Rome, took fatally ill shortly after John's accession. The pope himself prepared the emperor for death, hearing last confession, giving him the viaticum, and administering the Last Rites. Theophano, away in Germany, became regent for the young Otto III.

Great as this tragedy was, worse would soon follow. The anti-pope, Boniface VII, drawn to Rome by the news, arrived in the Eternal City in April of 984. With the help of the followers of Crescentius, he overthrew the pope and deposited him in Castel Sant' Angelo. There John was murdered at Boniface's order four months later.

# John XV

## (August 6, 985–April 996)

After Boniface VII met his dramatic and well-deserved end, the Romans elected John, son of Leo, as pope. Although the usurper was gone, the city was under the control of John Crescentius, son to Boniface's friend. At first, John Crescentius's control was so complete that none could see the pope without bribing the nobleman first. Unable to deal with this any longer, the pontiff fled to Tuscany, wherein he launched an appeal to Empress Theophano. Fearful of yet another imperial invasion, Crescentius promised free access to his person if the pope would return. Mollified, the pope returned to his city.

This was a very good development, indeed, because all sorts of international affairs soon demanded John's attention; fortunately, for the rest of his pontificate his now-good relationship with Crescentius, as well as his friendliness with empresses St. Adelaide and Theophano, guaranteed quiet at home. One of John's greatest accomplishments was the first canonization by a pope—that of St. Ulrich, bishop of Augsburg, on January 31, 993. Prior to this time, saints were canonized by the acclamation of the faithful following either their martyrdom, or miracles at their tombs or with their relics. Henceforth, it would become a far more careful procedure.

Ethelred the Unready, king of England, and Duke Richard of Normandy were locked in a dispute that foreshadowed the Norman invasion of England in 1066. Rather than come to blows, however, they asked the pope to mediate. He did, in the person of his legate, Leo of Travi, who concluded between the two the Peace of Rouen on March 1, 991.

More complex was the succession struggle in the archdiocese of Rheims. The death of Louis IV, the last French Carolingian, provoked a dynastic struggle. On the one hand, Charles, Duke of Lorraine, was, by right of male succession (the "Salic Law") the closest heir to the dead king. But he was a foreigner in the eyes of the French. Hugh Capet, descendant of the doughty Eudes, count of Paris, was only a Carolingian in the female line. But he was a Frenchman. The French clergy and nobility chose him as king; all succeeding sovereigns of that country—Capet, Valois, and Bourbon—descend from him and the title "Count of Paris" is borne today by one of the three claimants to the French throne, his descendants.

The duke of Lorraine was not pleased by this turn of events and went to war to gain the crown. Now, in 989, Hugh made Charles's nephew Arnulf the archbishop of Rheims. When the Lorrainer captured Rheims, he took his nephew prisoner. But Hugh considered the Archbishop a traitor; after he captured the pair at Rheims, he held a synod at that city, which deposed Arnulf. The king then appointed the learned Gerbert, abbot of Aurillac, as archbishop. But the pope repudiated these proceedings and ordered the French bishops to hold an independent synod at Aix-la-Chapelle to consider the matter further and decide to whom the archdiocese belonged. They refused to do so, and in response, John ordered them to Rome to hold their synod there. This too they would not do, claiming that the situation in both France and Italy was too unsettled for them to travel.

The extremely annoyed John sent his legate Leo, abbot of Santa Bonifacio, to France to convene a synod of the French and German bishops at Mousson. Hugh refused to allow the French to attend, but Gerbert went anyway, in order to plead his case before the legate. Nevertheless, the German bishops condemned him on June 2, 995, and he was declared deposed. When Hugh died on October 23, 996, Arnulf was restored to his See.

Emperor Otto III was a most remarkable character. Well educated and trained in both the Western and Byzantine imperial traditions, he saw himself as the successor of Constantine, Theodosius I, Justinian, and Charlemagne. Nothing less than the complete and entire regeneration of the empire in both East and West was to be his mission.

In keeping with this vision, Otto descended into Italy in 996, to receive the imperial coronation at the hands of the pope. But he delayed his arrival at Rome in order to celebrate Easter at his capital of Pavia, on April 12. By that time, the pope had died.

# False Dawn

# Gregory V
## (May 3, 996–February 4, 999)

When John XV died, the Romans sent a message to Otto III, asking him to name the next pope. The emperor sent his chaplain and cousin, Bruno, who took the name "Gregory." On May 21, his first major act was to crown Otto as emperor. A few days later the two held a synod, at which the condemnation of Gerbert was repeated, for all that he had been Otto's tutor. But Gregory made a mistake when he prevailed upon the emperor to allow Crescentius to remain in the city.

No sooner had Otto left, then Crescentius rebelled; Gregory fled Rome, and the impudent noble appointed a new anti-pope, the Italo-Greek John Philagathus, who took the name John XVI in 997.

Gregory had made his way to Pavia, however, where he held a synod, excommunicating Crescentius and John, and threatening to do so with King Robert III of France if he did not put away Bertha, his God-daughter and cousin, whom he had illegally married. Robert, called "the Pious" did so, and found a more suitable mate. Gerbert, whose condemnation had again been repeated, announced his submission and was given the archdiocese of Ravenna. The Roman rebels proved to be a harder nut to crack, however.

At last Otto marched upon Rome. The anti-pope fled the city—while Crescentius shut himself up in the Castel Sant'Angelo. The imperial troops apprehended John in 998, and they cut off his nose, ears, and tongue, and put out his eyes. The troops brought John back to Rome and before Otto and the pope he was publicly deprived of his assumed office. John was then packed off to the German Abbey of Fulda, where he lived until 1013. The same year the imperial troops besieged and took the Castel Sant'Angelo, whereupon Crescentius was hanged on its walls.

Now that Rome was secure, the normal run of papal and imperial administration could take place. Among other activities, Aelfric, archbishop of Canterbury, came to Rome to secure both pallium and permission to replace the secular canons of his cathedral with Benedictines. Both were given. At Otto's request, Gregory granted numerous privileges to various imperial abbeys in

Germany, and he held a number of synods in the emperor's presence for the regulation of Church affairs.

At his death, Gregory was buried in St. Peter's near the sacristy. Otto was on tour in southern Italy, accepting the homage of the princes there, but he hurried back to Rome on reception of the news, to suppress any possible disorders there.

## Sylvester II
### (April 9, 999–May 12, 1003)

Born around 945 near Aurillac in Auvergne, France, Gerbert came of humble stock, and he was the first Frenchman to sit on the throne of St. Peter. His life and work are known today because of the 220 letters that he wrote before his pontificate, the bulls he promulgated in Rome, and his philosophical and scientific treatises. In addition, he appears in some pages of the *History of France,* written before 998 by his disciple Richer, a monk of S.-Remi of Rheims. Called in his own day "the Wonder of the World," he is surely one of the most remarkable of the popes.

When quite young, Gerbert was sent by his parents to the great abbey of St. Géraud d'Aurillac. He spent his childhood there, until Borrell, count of Barcelona, took him along to Catalonia and entrusted him to the schoolmaster of Vich. This school, like that of Ripoll, was famous for its teaching of the *quadrivium*—arithmetic, geometry, music, and astronomy. There, in contact with Arab science, Gerbert was so well educated that he became one of the greatest scientists of Christendom. He was particularly impressed by the decimal notation and simplified numerals that the Arabs had borrowed from the Indians, possibly by the intermediary of the mathematician Al-Biruni who had lived several years in India, and whose work was a synthesis of Greek and Indian sciences. Gerbert strongly contributed to the adoption of the decimal system in Europe, as well as inventing the pendulum clock. After three years of studies, he accompanied Borrell to Rome in 970, astonishing John XIII and Otto I by his science. To perfect his knowledge in logic, he decided to go to Rheims two years later. Archbishop Adalbero then entrusted the direction of the cathedral school to him.

Thanks to his knowledge and his innovative teaching methods, Gerbert was a great success as an instructor, and students multiplied. He explained the classic authors of antiquity to them, initiated them into rhetoric and logic,

and placed at their disposal an abacus for arithmetic, spheres for astronomy, and a monocorde for the music. The scholar of Magdeburg, Otric, defied him in philosophy; Gerbert answered him triumphantly at Ravenna in front of Otto II during January of 981.

To reward him, the emperor entrusted to him the abbey of Bobbio, in northern Italy, founded by the Irishman, St. Columban. There Gerbert found the richest library in the West and was very happy, as his first letters testify in 983. But later letters reveal his difficulties in dealing with neighboring lay aristocrats. Not being able to fight against them, Gerbert was able after Otto II's death in December 983 to leave the abbey and to go back to Rheims. He retained the title of abbot and his relationship with the monks.

In Rheims, Gerbert not only resumed his teaching, but he also dealt with policy. Adalbero supported Hugh Capet against the Carolingian Lothair. He also supported the three-year-old king, Otto III, who was threatened by his cousin the duke of Bavaria. The correspondence of Gerbert enables us to follow this policy and the maneuvering of the archbishop. After the death of Lothair in 986, then of his son Louis V the following year, Adalbero and Gerbert worked to withdraw the candidacy for the throne of Charles of Lorraine and to have Hugh Capet elected as king of France (June 987).

While remaining with Adalbero, Gerbert wrote some letters in the name of the new king. Because Adalbero had died in January 989, Gerbert hoped to receive from Hugh the archdiocese of Rheims. But the king, engaged in a war against Charles, tried to disarm his adversaries by naming Arnoul, a nephew of his adversary, as archbishop. Arnoul's uncle soon took control of the city.

Gerbert, after some hesitation, joined Hugh and became once more the secretary of the king. The king having triumphed at last over Charles, then decided to try the archbishop for treason. Hugh notified the pope, who made no reply, and then convened a national council at the abbey of St. Basil of Verzy, close to Rheims. Gerbert played a great role in the preparation of this council while providing the thirteen bishops who represented the four ecclesiastical provinces of the country with the documents necessary for the indictment. He also inspired the speech of his friend, another Arnoul, the bishop of Orleans, which not only accused Arnoul of treason, but cited the appeal to the papacy that had not been answered.

When Abbo, abbot of Fleury-en-Loire, defended the archbishop and declared that to judge an archbishop it was necessary to call on the pope, the bishop of Orleans and Gerbert held that the pope was inefficient and that the case was an interior question for the Church of France alone to decide. After the judgment of Arnoul of Rheims, the king decided to replace him with Gerbert. The newly elected prelate then had to make a profession of faith; some, apparently, were wary of the new archbishop's orthodoxy.

Gerbert was an active archbishop, as his preserved letters testify. The letters deal with the conflicts between clergy and laity, consultations of a canonical

nature, and recalling to the order the disobedient suffrage bishops. But most of Gerbert's activity was absorbed in his conflict with the papacy. Indeed, John XV regarded him as an "intruder," and sent his legate to inquire into the question. King Hugh and his son Robert supported Gerbert at the synod of Chelles. The archbishop denounced himself at the synods of Mouzon (June 995) and Rheims (July 995), but he then published the acts of the council of St. Basil and defended his theses in a letter sent to Wilderod, bishop of Strasbourg.

The argument of Gerbert rested on that of Hincmar, his ninth-century predecessor as archbishop of Rheims. While recognizing the primacy of the pope, Gerbert maintained at this stage of his career that the pontiff need not intervene directly in the business of the province of Rheims, because the African councils and the council of Nicaea had already defined the role of provincial councils. The pope, Gerbert wrote, could not go against what he claimed was tradition: "The bishops of Gaul," he wrote to Wilderod, "have the right to follow the Gospel, the apostles, the prophets, the approved councils, the decrees which are not in disagreement with the four councils, which were always received and will be it always."

Gerbert appealed once more to Rome, but the new pope, Gregory V, maintained the positions of his predecessor. Moreover, Hugh Capet died in October 996; his successor, King Robert the Pious, withdrew his support of Gerbert to try to obtain the recognition by Rome of his marriage with his cousin.

The bishops, who had participated in the council of St. Basil, were being threatened with excommunication; Gerbert, not wanting a schism in the Church, preferred to leave Rheims and joined the young emperor Otto III, with whom he had become acquainted in Rome. The monarch asked Gerbert to become his tutor in autumn 997. Since the former archbishop, Arnoul, had been restored to Rheims by King Robert, Otto III decided to give Gerbert the archdiocese of Ravenna in April 998. Gerbert then convened a local synod, which condemned simony and attended to priestly recruitment. On July 2, 998, Gerbert attended a synod in Pavia chaired by Otto III. Its principal goal was to restore goods taken from the churches.

In March 999, after the death of Gregory V, Gerbert was invited by the emperor to accept the tiara. He gave up Ravenna and Bobbio and was crowned under the name Sylvester II.

Gerbert took the name "Sylvester" in tribute to the pope who baptized the first Christian emperor. He planned to play a similar role with Otto, who saw himself as a "new Constantine" and who wanted to "renovate" the empire, directing Christendom from Rome. The emperor did not intend to give up his power to his old tutor, however. In a famous decree, he denounced the "distorted donation of Constantine" and recalled that he was the one who had authority in Italy and the West.

Otto settled in Rome and built a palace for himself on the Aventine Hill. There he surrounded himself with the splendor of an imperial court befitting his mother's home in Constantinople. Not only did he reproduce a number of the titles and positions of the Byzantine court at his own, he revived the Roman patriciate and planned as well to restore the senate and consulate of the city. But Otto, in addition, spent a fortnight praying in the Grotto of San Clemente and did penance in a number of Italian monasteries.

The new pope settled a number of questions. He forgave Arnoul of Rheims and restored him officially to his archdiocese. Thanks to forty extant bulls, we see that Pope Sylvester intervened everywhere in the West, here delivering decrees of exemption to abbeys, there defending bishops against lay lords, elsewhere arbitrating conflicts between monks and secular clergy.

In collaboration with the emperor, Sylvester created two new national churches: those of Poland and Hungary. In the year 1000, at the time of a pilgrimage to Gniezno's tomb of St. Adalbert, Otto III decided to establish a Polish Church. Gniezno was to be the metropolis with three suffragan dioceses (Cracow, Wroclaw, and Kolobrzeg). Boleslaw "the Brave" Chrobry, would be the first king of Poland to receive a Christian coronation. The crown itself, a gift of Pope Sylvester II, has long since disappeared. Several years later, amid political turmoil, Polish regalia were taken by Queen Rycheza, the consort of Boleslaus the Brave's successor, King Mieszko II, to Germany and handed over to the Emperor.

In 1001, Prince Stephen of Hungary received the royal crown sent by the pope; to this day, the Holy Crown of St. Stephen remains the most sacred symbol of Hungarian nationhood, and is kept as such in the Parliament building in Budapest. Two archdioceses were created (Esztergom and Kaloca), and several dioceses. Hartvik, the biographer of St. Stephen, tells us that the pope hailed the new king as a veritable "Apostle" of Christ, referring to his labors in spreading the Catholic Faith throughout Hungary. The bull of Sylvester II, dated March 27, 1000, granted St. Stephen the crown and title of king, returned to him the kingdom he had offered to the Holy See, conferred on him the right to have the cross carried before him, and gave him administrative authority over dioceses and churches. From that time until the death of Karol IV (Karl I of Austria) in 1922, the kings of Hungary were addressed as "Apostolic Majesty."

Following his trip to Poland, Otto went on to Aix-la-Chapelle, where he had the tomb of Charlemagne opened. Therein the great emperor was, so it is written, incorrupt and seated on his throne. Otto bestowed many gifts upon Charlemagne's church, a number of which are still treasured there today.

On his return to Italy, the emperor soon found trouble brewing. The Romans rebelled against their "Saxon" ruler, and Sylvester and Otto fled to Ravenna where they planned to reconquer Rome. But Otto III died at Paterno, near Viterbo, on January 22, 1002, at a mere twenty-two years of age,

leaving the throne to his cousin, St. Henry II. Heartbroken, Sylvester returned then to Rome and continuous work, as the bulls left in the papal archives prove. Worn out, he died at fifty-eight (then considered a tremendous age) and was buried in St. John Lateran. Pope Sergius IV erected an epitaph at Worms, which can still be read; it is engraved against a pillar of the basilica, recalling the brilliant career of Sylvester II.

Sylvester was a scientist who, although not of aristocratic birth, was held by his contemporaries to have acquired his nobility by his intelligence, his knowledge, and his talents. Like Boethius (the late Roman statesman and author of *The Consolation of Philosophy*), whom he admired, Sylvester wanted to apply philosophy to the policy. He wrote a treatise for his student Otto "On the reasonable individual and the use of reason." He made a gift of his large library to Otto III; part of this was transported by Emperor Henry II to Bamberg where it remains to this day.

Because of his extraordinary scientific knowledge, Sylvester came to be regarded by the less educated as a magician. Some maintained that he had evoked a demon who gave him the papacy and who promised that he would die only in Jerusalem. The story went further that he was taken by his last illness in a church in Rome, which he remembered too late was Santa Croce in Gerusalemme. Even those who rejected such tales, such as William of Malmsbury, the famed medieval chronicler, recounted with relish that Sylvester had invented a bronze head that could speak. His magical powers, it was maintained, allowed him to find buried treasure and to visit an underground palace, whose splendor vanished at his touch. Moreover, such folk claimed that Sylvester's tomb in the Lateran retained some of his power, and would weep when any of his successors was to die. This legendary aspect of Sylvester's life has been used by such writers as James Blish in *Black Easter* and Judith Tarr in *Ars Magica*.

Interesting as these legends are, however, it is as a reconciler and unifier, a bridge builder between the Eastern Empire and the Western, between the Italian provinces, between France and Germany, and between the core of Christendom and its then-frontiers, that Sylvester stands out. This role, taken together with his philosophical, educational, and scientific achievements, forms a contribution to western civilization on the part of a single individual perhaps unequaled before or since.

## John XVII
### (June 13–November 6, 1003)

The death of Sylvester II left a power vacuum in Rome that was quickly filled by a noble faction led by John Crescentius, whose father Otto III had defeated and executed. He arranged for Sicco to be elected, who took the name John. The new pope had been a layman; his three sons all entered the priesthood. But he died a few months after his election.

## John XVIII
### (December 25, 1003–June 1009)

Born Phasianus to a Roman priest named Leo, John also owed his position to John Crescentius. His attention was taken up entirely with administrative details, confirming or extending privileges to churches and abbeys, conferring the pallium on the archbishops of Trier and Canterbury, and confirming the establishment of the dioceses of Merseburg and Bamberg in Germany by St. Henry II. When the archbishop of Sens and the bishop of Orleans attempted to force the abbot of Fleury to give up the privileges bestowed upon his monastery by previous popes, John came to the abbot's aid and summoned both prelates to Rome under pain of interdict for France. His relationship with Constantinople was extremely cordial, and he became a monk of St. Paul Outside the Walls before he died.

## Sergius IV
### (July 31, 1009–May 12, 1012)

Born Peter Bucca Porci ("Pig's Snout") son of Peter the Shoemaker, Sergius had been bishop of Albano before his election. The new pope was able to restrict the power of Crescentius to a degree, and he conferred exemption from Episcopal jurisdiction upon a number of monasteries. A number of nobles placed their lands under Sergius's protection, and he greatly relieved the sufferings of the poor during a famine. He was buried in the Lateran.

## Benedict VIII
### (May 18, 1012–April 9, 1024)

Born the son of Gregory, count of Tusculum, Benedict was elected to the papacy by force, his family having defeated Crescentius in a struggle for control of the city. Despite his unusual means of accession, the new pontiff soon turned out to be a man of piety as well as strength.

On February 14, 1014, Benedict crowned St. Henry II as emperor, after the latter's arrival in Rome subsequent to defeating a rebellion in northern Italy. Thus began another of those happy but few real partnerships between emperors and popes, in which both sides did their part wholeheartedly. Henry, for his part, had always shown himself a true friend of the Church; this would only accelerate after his coronation, at which time he confirmed papal rule over Ravenna.

With the emperor's aid, Benedict defeated the Crescentii and yet another Muslim assault. The pope also befriended the Normans, who at this time were beginning to take over southern Italy. Benedict then visited Germany, consecrating the cathedral of Bamberg and visiting Fulda. He gave more privileges to Cluny, which the emperor had further honored by giving the abbey the golden orb bestowed upon him at his coronation. Together with Henry, Pope Benedict held a synod at Pavia, which condemned simony and clerical marriage. His papacy was crowned by the reconciliation of Henry and King Robert the Pious of France, an alliance that was underlined by the great af-

fection all three parties came to have for one another—an affection that made factual the theoretical alliance between the head of the Church and the two successors of Charlemagne.

## John XIX
### (April 12, 1024–November 6, 1032)

During his pontificate, Benedict VIII's brother, Romanus, had exercised temporal power in Rome as consul and senator. At his brother's death, though a layman, Romanus was elected pope. He then received all the holy orders in rapid succession, took the name of John, and did his best to win the affection of the Romans—no small order.

Shortly afterward, Basil II, the Byzantine emperor (whose largely successful program for restoring the Eastern Empire included a complete reconciliation with the papacy) sent envoys to Rome, requesting official recognition of the patriarchate of Constantinople's assumption of the title "Ecumenical." Although this title, implying worldwide jurisdiction, might be seen as an attempt to usurp papal prerogatives, this attempt was not unwelcome to John, partly because he wanted to remain on good terms with the now-resurgent Byzantines in southern Italy, and partly due to his desire to be on the best of terms with both the Eastern and Western emperors. Unfortunately, the many reformers in Italy and France, not content with the good work they had done in their own countries, regarded the Eastern Church as hopelessly corrupt. Word leaked out of the impending recognition, and the reformers compelled the pope to abandon the idea. The current patriarch ordered the pope's name removed from the diptychs (prayers at Mass, the removal of which signified excommunication), much to his emperor's annoyance.

John invited the musician and originator of *solfeggio* (*do-re-mi*), Guido of Arezzo, to Rome, to explain his invention to him. John did much to popularize this new development in the West.

Upon St. Henry II's death, Conrad the Salian was elected king of Germany. The pope and the archbishop of Milan invited Conrad to Italy, where in 1026 he received the Iron Crown of Lombardy. On March 26, 1027, Conrad was crowned emperor at Rome by John; assisting the emperor were the kings of Burgundy and Denmark, the latter of whom received various privileges for the Church in his country.

John intervened in a large number of jurisdictional differences between bishops in Italy and France. Moreover, in 1030, he confirmed and extended the *Pax Dei*, a custom which had begun in France as a result of the continuous petty warfare that the gradual breakup of Charlemagne's empire had begun. The *Pax Dei* stated that, clerics, religious, and noncombatants would be exempt from warfare, churches and monasteries would be inviolate, and Sundays would be a day of truce. Failure to observe this rule would result in excommunication. Despite the failure of John's Eastern policy, his death found the papacy and the Church in high repute and relative peace. This pleasant situation, alas, would not endure long.

## Benedict IX
### (October 1032–1045)

Though the two Tusculan brothers had been very good popes and men; indeed, their brother Alberic was not. Sadder yet, he had raised his son, Benedict, not only to be exceedingly immoral, but also to regard the papacy as a family heirloom, which should pass to him when both his uncles were dead.

Sure enough, upon John XIX's demise, Alberic placed his son, then about twenty, on the papal throne. Unfortunately, his morals were also as bad as expected. Benedict did, in fact, perform some of the routine tasks of his office, confirming or conferring various privileges to different churches and monasteries, and ordering Bretislav, duke of Bohemia, to found a monastery in reparation for carrying off the body of St. Adalbert. The pope also went north in 1037 to meet Emperor Conrad and he held a synod to excommunicate Archbishop Heribert of Milan, with whom he was having a dispute.

His personal life was so disgusting (filled as it was with mistresses and rumors of incest and sodomy) that one of the city's factions was able to rally support against him and drove Benedict out of Rome. In his place the people put John, the bishop of Santa Sabina.

## Sylvester III
(January–April 1045)

As just stated, Sylvester had been bishop of Santa Sabina and was elected after Benedict IX was driven out of the city. Benedict returned, however, and expelled Sylvester and his friends. After Benedict sold the papacy to John Graziane, Sylvester resigned his claim to the post, in favor of Gregory VI (Graziane) and returned to his old diocese. Sylvester reasserted his claim after Benedict's return, however, and was deposed along with Benedict and Gregory at the Synod of Sutri by Emperor Conrad's successor, Henry III; the new German king then packed him off to a monastery. Sylvester III is sometimes called an anti-pope, but historians may be forgiven for confusion on this point, given the circumstances.

## Benedict IX
(April–May 1045)

After successfully regaining his position from Sylvester, Benedict came back to power. But he had unfortunately learned nothing in his exile. Anticipating many future priests, Benedict decided he wanted to marry, and he sold the papacy to John Gratian, archpriest of Rome. Later he repented of his bargain and decided to retake the papal throne.

# Gregory VI
## (May 1, 1045–December 20, 1046)

John Gratian was archpriest of Rome and had been godfather to Benedict. A holy and sincere man, John had looked with horror on his godson's deeds and manner of life. When Benedict approached John with the idea of stepping down from the papacy in return for money so that he could marry, John was only too happy to oblige him, convinced that any price was worth having Benedict out of the picture.

The Romans thought so, too, and Gregory VI, as John was now known, was hailed joyfully. Despite the way Gregory had received the papacy, a great man named St. Peter Damian, a Camoldolese monk renowned for struggles against clerical immorality and simony, welcomed him to the throne. But the new pope faced an empty treasury and a ton of problems. Sylvester and Benedict were soon plotting their respective returns, and the Roman clergy under Benedict's rule had become extremely immoral. Nevertheless, with the help of his chaplain, the able Hildebrand, Gregory set to work. He tried to end the religious disorders by letters and synods—the civil problems through force of arms. But the opposing factions of his two predecessors were powerful, and the city of the popes became a battleground, like present-day Belfast or south-central Los Angeles. Each of three papal claimants occupied a major basilica.

At last, despairing of order ever being restored, a large number of the clergy in the city renounced allegiance to Gregory, Benedict, or Sylvester, and appealed to the king of Germany to sort the situation out. The energetic monarch proceeded to do so. In the autumn of 1046, Henry arrived at Sutri, by now the traditional meeting place for popes and emperors when the latter came to be crowned. Convinced of his own innocence, and anxious to end the disorders in the city, Gregory went to see Henry and was received by him with all pontifical honors. Next, the Pope summoned a synod with the king, which opened on December 20.

Sylvester showed up, but Benedict did not. Both were deposed. Convinced that he had committed simony by paying Benedict to leave, Gregory voluntarily abdicated. Suidger, the bishop of Bamberg, Germany, was then selected, taking the name of Clement II. Gregory and Hildebrand (who insisted on accompanying him) then left for Germany with the emperor. The former pope died at Cologne in early 1048.

## Clement II
### (December 25, 1046–October 9, 1047)

With Gregory VI's abdication, Henry III needed to choose a new pope, as much to crown him emperor as to rule the church. The king's first choice was Adalbert, archbishop of Bremen, who refused, but suggested his friend Suidger, bishop of Bamberg.

A nobleman from Saxony, Suidger had first been a canon in Halberstadt, and then chaplain to Henry III. When Eberhard, the first Bishop of Bamberg (appointed by St. Henry II) died, the king put Suidger in his place. There the new prelate built up a reputation for holiness. Though he had accompanied the king to the Synod of Sutri, Suidger was very anxious to return to his diocese. Henry insisted on his elevation, however, and led him by the hand to the acclaiming clergy. Nevertheless, the new pope refused to give up Bamberg.

Shortly after his consecration, the pope and the emperor arrived at Rome, where Clement crowned Henry and his empress. He then held a synod in January, at which simony was severely condemned. Next, Clement solved one of the innumerable precedence disputes between Milan, Aquileia, and Ravenna, ruling that, in the emperor's absence, the archbishop of the latter city would stand at the pope's right hand.

Clement then accompanied the emperor on a triumphant tour of Italy, and thence to Germany. He died at Pesaro and his body is entombed at his cathedral of Bamberg.

## Benedict IX
### (November 1047–July 1048)

Benedict had been unable to win his intended's affections. Taking advantage of Clement's death, he returned to Rome, reigning in his usual style for a year. But the new emperor, Henry III (to say nothing of the Roman people), exasperated with his high jinks, drove Benedict once again from the city. This time, worn out with his lifestyle and adventures, the feckless pontiff sought refuge at the Byzantine rite abbey of Grottaferrata, becoming a disciple of its saintly abbot, Bartholomew. Under his new confessor's influence, Benedict abdicated definitively, gave up his sinful ways, and died a penitent death.

## Damasus II

### (July 17–August 8, 1048)

Many would have liked to have seen Gregory VI restored; however, his death precluded that possibility and Henry III appointed Poppo, bishop of Brixen, to be pope in January of 1048. He took the name Damasus II and was conducted by Boniface, Margrave of Tyrol, to Rome. Benedict was driven out and Damasus was enthroned. Shortly thereafter, Damasus left Rome for the resort of Palestrina to escape the summer heat. The pope caught malaria soon after his arrival and died.

## St. Leo IX

### (February 12, 1049–April 19, 1054)

Born Bruno of Dagsburg on June 21, 1002, in Egisheim, Alsace, to a noble family (cousins of the Salians, who would soon be Holy Roman Emperors), this pontiff was introduced early to both politics and piety. Bruno was educated by Bishop Bertold and consecrated Bishop of Toul (now in France, then in Germany) on September 9, 1027. A zealous prelate, he introduced the Cluniac reform into the monasteries of his diocese. Bruno naturally supported his cousins Conrad and Henry as kings of Germany (and so, Holy Roman Emperors) against the House of Burgundy. As a result, in December of 1048, Henry III designated Bruno over Bruno's friend Halinard, Archbishop of Lyons, as pope at the Diet of Worms, after the death of Damasus II. Bruno, however, refused to accept the papacy unless properly elected by the cardinals at Rome.

This accomplished, he began very quickly to reorganize the extremely muddled affairs of the Roman Church. He was assisted by Hildebrand, who had returned to Rome with him. Anxious to add new (and honest) blood to the College of Cardinals, he appointed Hildebrand and Humbert, another energetic reformer, to that body. Leo swiftly tightened the administration at Rome and held synods at the Lateran, Pavia, Rheims, and Mainz to attack

simony, lay investiture, clerical immorality, and various other abuses that had become rampant during the reigns of Benedict IX and his rivals. Leo visited Henry III in Germany, and at Vercelli he held a synod that condemned Berengar, a heretic who denied the Real Presence of Christ in the Eucharist. Pope Leo's work constantly demonstrated the holiness that would lead to his canonization.

Though successful in all of these matters, Leo faced two challenges: one brought him down, the other would have unpleasant consequences down to present day.

The first involved affairs in the south of Italy where the Normans had, minor principality by minor principality, been eating up the country. Both the remaining independent south Italian princes and the Byzantines were anxious that the new power be stopped. Both prevailed upon Leo to go to war against the Normans. The Pontiff at last agreed, accompanying the Byzantine army that met the Norman army in battle at Civitella on June 18, 1053. The imperial army was defeated and the pontiff was captured by the Normans, who imprisoned him at Benevento. Leo became sick in prison and was at last released on March 12, 1054, when his captors realized that he was dying. After resting for twelve days at Capua, Leo finally arrived at Rome, but he died shortly thereafter.

It was only after he died that his legate, Cardinal Humbert, returned from Constantinople with even more disastrous news. The patriarch of Constantinople, Michael Cerularius, had been excommunicated in Leo's name by a zealous cardinal, and Michael had in turn excommunicated Leo.

The events leading up to this affair were typical of the nasty nature of ecclesiastical politics. In 1054, Leo, the Byzantine archbishop of Bulgaria, sent a message to the pope declaring that only Constantinople had the true Faith and the real sacrifice of the altar, because the West used unleavened bread. This latter was considered by the Easterners to be a suspect custom because of its resemblance to Jewish practice. Pope Leo wrote a letter to the patriarch of Constantinople, asking for an explanation. In response, Michael repeated all the former charges made by past patriarchs against Rome, closed all the Latin churches in Constantinople, and desecrated the hosts in their tabernacles, to show that they were invalid. Angered by this sacrilege, Leo sent Cardinal Humbert to Constantinople to negotiate; Michael refused him, so the cardinal laid a bull of excommunication upon the altar of Hagia Sophia. In response, Michael returned the favor. This was the final stroke of the "Great Schism" between East and West, which has lasted—with a few happy intervals—until the present day. Of course, trouble had been brewing since before the Photian schism in the ninth century.

In and of itself, this action meant little. As the great nineteenth-century Russian philosopher Vladimir Soloviev observed, "The final rupture . . . [Of]

1054, was nothing, in fact, but a mere event without any kind of legal or binding sanction. The anathema of the legates of Pope Leo IX was not aimed against the Eastern Church, but solely against the person of the patriarch Michael Cerularius and against 'the partners of his folly' (folly obvious enough, to be sure); and on the other hand, the Eastern Church has never been able to assemble an oecumenical council, which, even according to our own theologians, is the only tribunal competent to pass judgment on our differences with the Papacy" (*Russia and the Universal Church*, Centenary Press, 1948, p. 48, n. 1). Moreover, it took some time for the other four eastern patriarchates to pass into schism with Rome. Further complicating the matter from a legal viewpoint was the joint lifting of the excommunications by Pope Paul VI and Patriarch Athenagoras II on the Mount of Olives in 1964.

Nevertheless, the rupture was quite effective. But what really was the cause? In part, the rashness of an angry Cardinal Humbert was perhaps partially to blame. But, perhaps Soloviev has put his finger on the nature of the problem:

> This was no matter of a dispute in theology or of a rivalry between prelates. It was simply the refusal of the old Empire of Constantine to give place to the new Western power born of the close alliance of the Papacy with the Frankish kingdom; everything else was secondary or by way of excuse. This view of the matter is confirmed by the fact that after Photius' death the schism took no effect for a century and a half—exactly the period when Western Christendom, newly organised, seemed on the verge of collapse, when the Papacy was subservient to a degenerate oligarchy and had lost its moral and religious prestige, and when the Carolingian dynasty was consumed with internal strife. But no sooner was the imperial power restored under the energetic government of the German kings, no sooner was the see of St. Peter again occupied by men of apostolic character, than the anti-Catholic movement at Constantinople broke forth with violence and the schism was consummated. (Soloviev, p. 28)

In many ways, a certain unity remained: apart from the obvious joint enemy in the Muslims, the Apostolic succession, a commonality of doctrine on most points, and above all, the consciousness on the part of many that the schism was simply *wrong*, remained. Soloviev spoke for many, before, during, and after his own time, when he wrote the following:

> This difficulty [what "Orthodoxy" really is] does not exist for those folk who are really orthodox in all good conscience and in the sim-

> plicity of their heart. When questioned intelligently about their religion, they will tell you that to be Orthodox is to be baptised a Christian, to wear a cross or some holy image on your breast, to worship Christ, to pray to the Blessed Virgin most immaculate and to all the saints represented by images and relics, to rest from work on all festivals and to fast in accordance with traditional custom, to venerate the sacred office of bishops and priests, and to participate in the holy sacraments and divine worship. That is the true Orthodoxy of the Russian people, and it is ours also. But it is not that of our militant patriots. It is obvious that true Orthodoxy contains nothing particularist and can in no way form a national or local attribute separating us in any sense from the Western peoples; for the greater part of these peoples, the Catholic part, has precisely the same religious basis that we have. Whatever is holy and sacred for us is also holy and sacred for them. To indicate only one essential point: not only is devotion to the Blessed Virgin one of the characteristic features of Catholicism—generally practiced by Russian Orthodoxy, but there are even special miraculous images venerated in common by Roman Catholics and Russian Orthodox (for example, the holy Virgin of Czestochowa in Poland). If "piety" is indeed the distinctive characteristic of our national genius, the fact that the chief emblems of that piety are common to us and the Westerns compels us to recognise our oneness with them in what we regard as the most essential thing of all. As regards the profound contrast between the contemplative piety of the East and the active religion of the Westerns, this contrast being purely human and subjective has nothing to do with the divine objects of our faith and worship; so far from being a good reason for schism it should rather bring the two great parts of the Christian world into a closer and mutually complementary union. (Soloviev, p. 47)

This is of course echoed in Pope John Paul II's declaration in recent years that the East and West are "the two lungs" of the Church. Despite the many wrongs committed on each by members of the two communions after 1054, something of this phantom unity has remained and has affected the history of both down to present day.

It may be that the split was inevitable; unfortunately for his memory, it occurred during St. Leo IX's papacy.

# Victor II

## (April 13, 1055–July 28, 1057)

Born Gebhard, Count von Calw, Tollenstein, und Hirschberg in 1018, this pope was also a cousin of Henry III. His uncle, who was the Bishop of Regensburg, presented him to the emperor on Christmas Day, 1042, as a candidate for the diocese of Eichstatt. Henry was at first displeased by this idea, given Gebhard's age (twenty-four), but he was persuaded to oblige by the saintly archbishop of Mainz. It proved to be an excellent choice, because Gebhard was able to both please his subjects and administer the diocese well. He accompanied Henry III to his coronation in Rome in 1046 and to consultations with St. Leo IX in 1049 and 1052. The next year, however, Gebhard convinced Henry not to send the German army to join St. Leo IX and the Byzantines in their war against the Normans. Gebhard bitterly regretted this when he received news of the defeat and the pope's imprisonment.

In the same year, Henry deposed Duke Conrad of Bavaria and gave the Duchy to his son, also Henry (later to become king-emperor as Henry IV). Because the prince was only three at the time, the emperor made Gebhard his regent in Bavaria, a position which led him into conflict with, among others, his uncle.

When St. Leo IX died Cardinal Hildebrand asked King Henry to name Gebhard as pope. Henry did so at the Diet of Mainz in September 1054; but Gebhard refused the honor. At the Diet of Regensburg (March 1055), Gebhard finally gave in, but only on the condition that Henry restore to the Holy See certain territories he and his predecessors had usurped. The emperor agreed, and in company with Hildebrand, Gebhard traveled to Rome (retaining his own diocese, however) and was duly crowned Victor II.

As had St. Leo IX, the new pope fought simony, priestly fornication, and other misdeeds. On June 4, 1055 (Pentecost Sunday), Victor held a synod in the presence of the emperor and 120 bishops, confirming previous disciplinary decrees and deposing a number of immoral prelates. With Henry's power behind him, Victor was able to suppress a large number of abuses. In return, he assisted the emperor in his program of imperial reform. When King Ferdinand of Castile refused to acknowledge Henry as emperor, Victor threatened that monarch with excommunication, a threat which worked.

In 1056, Victor sent Hildebrand to northern France to work against clerical immorality there, and he named two southern French bishops as his legates to perform the same work there. In the summer of that year, Victor hurried to Germany to be by Henry's side, who felt his end approaching. The

pope assisted the emperor on his deathbed, which ended on October 5. In accordance with the late ruler's will, Victor served as regent for the six-year-old Henry IV as king of Germany. To solidify his young charge's position, after burying the father in the cathedral at Speyer on October 28, he crowned the lad king of Germany and the Romans at Aachen. Then Victor presided over imperial diets at Cologne and Regensburg in December. At those gatherings he swore the great men of the empire to the allegiance of the new king.

Leaving Henry IV's mother, Agnes, in charge, Victor returned to Rome in February of 1057. On April 18 he presided over a council at the Lateran and on June 14 he made Frederick, brother of Duke Godfrey of Lorraine and abbot of Monte Cassino, a cardinal. This cemented his alliance with that major province of Germany. Victor then went to Tuscany, where on July 28 he arbitrated a jurisdictional dispute between the bishops of Siena and Arrezzo. He died there five days later. Although his will specified his body was to be returned to Eichstatt, he was so beloved that the people of Ravenna attacked the cortege and forcibly buried him at the great church of Santa Maria Rotonda in their city.

## Stephen X (IX)
### (August 3, 1057–March 29, 1058)

Son of Gozelon and brother of Godfrey, both in their turns dukes of Lorraine, Frederick (as he was born) first saw the light near the beginning of the eleventh century and was eventually made a canon of Liege cathedral. In this post, he met his cousin, St. Leo IX, who in 1051 made him chancellor and librarian of the Roman Church. Frederick traveled with St. Leo on his various jaunts and assisted Cardinal Humbert on the ill-fated embassy of 1054 to Constantinople. The next year he became a monk at Monte Cassino, and two years after, Frederick was elected abbot there. Victor II made him a cardinal, and on that pope's death, Frederick was elected, taking the name of Stephen.

His commitment to reform was shown early, as he made St. Peter Damian a cardinal and worked closely with Cardinals Humbert and Hildebrand. Stephen dispatched the latter to Milan to enforce reform of clerical morality there. After that, Hildebrand was to go on to Germany to get Empress Agnes to accept Stephen's election to the papacy, though she had not been consulted. After this he was to return to France to continue his work there.

Stephen, in the meantime, planned to reopen negotiations with Constantinople and to work against the growing Norman power. Unfortunately, he died prematurely; as he lay on his deathbed, he asked the cardinals to wait until Hildebrand's return before selecting a new pontiff. Stephen X was buried in the church of Santa Reparata.

## *Benedict X*

*Anti-Pope (April 1058–January 1059)*

Unfortunately, the imperially powered reform popes had been unable to root out the Tusculan party, despite the departure and repentance of their poster boy, Benedict IX. This became immediately apparent on the death of Stephen X. Ignoring the deathbed plea of the dying pontiff that they wait for the return of Cardinal Hildebrand, the Cardinals, forced by the Tusculani to do so through corruption and threats, elected John Mincius, the bishop of Velletri, as pope. A few of the cardinals protested, but they were forced to flee the city in terror of their lives. The new anti-pope took the name of Benedict after the worst of the Tusculan popes. Luckily, his hold on the city was to prove short-lived, although he would continue to get into mischief, as we shall see. He eventually died under house arrest at the abbey of Sant' Agnese in 1080. Despite being an anti-pope, he is nevertheless lodged in papal accounting, so that, for instance, the Pope Benedict who reigned from 1914 to 1922 is called "XV," when in truth he should be "XIV." But such are the vagaries of papal history.

## Nicholas II

**(December 1058–July 19, 1061)**

Born Gerhard of Burgundy in Savoy, he had been a canon at Liege and in 1046 became archbishop of Florence. Gerhard hosted several of the exiles driven from Rome by the intrusion of Benedict X onto the throne of St. Peter.

Cardinal Hildebrand, returning to Italy upon hearing news of the death of Stephen X and subsequent events, rushed to Florence to take stock of the situation. There he consulted with Duke Godfrey (who had been given Tuscany in addition to Lorraine) and agreed that Gerhard would be the best candidate for pope. Hildebrand invited the cardi-

nals to Siena; making their escape from the Tusculani, the prelates gathered in that city and elected Gerhard—he nevertheless retained Florence. The imperial confirmation was sent from the empress Agnes. After taking the name Nicholas, the new pontiff next proceeded to Sutri. There, in the presence of Godfrey and Guibert of Parma, the imperial chancellor for Italy, he pronounced the deposition of Benedict X. In January of 1059, Nicholas reentered Rome and was crowned on the twenty-fourth.

The new pope set about repairing the damage inflicted on the city by the Tusculani. Unfortunately, Benedict and his supporters were still armed and carrying on guerrilla warfare in the papal states. To fight them, Nicholas sent Hildebrand to make an alliance with the Normans, who had at last removed the last traces of Byzantine rule from Italy. The cardinal was successful; in return for recognizing Count Richard of Aversa as prince of Capua, Norman troops were sent to root out the Tusculani from the Campania. Although not entirely successful, their actions restored peace to the degree that Nicholas was able to carry out episcopal visitations—journeying around his diocese, correcting abuses and confirming children.

Meanwhile, events at Milan were demanding papal attention. The clergy there were sunk deep in simony and vice; the ordinary people were disgusted with them. In response, a reform party, the *Patarini*, emerged. These folk were led by the skilled soldier Count Herlemwald. His skills were needed, because Archbishop Guido of Milan and his cohorts were worthy colleagues of the Tusculani. Nevertheless, with Patarine help, St. Peter Damian and Anselm of Lucca were able to hold a synod in which Guido and his cronies were forced to swear to uphold Church discipline. The Patarines were no more reluctant to fight than to pray.

Emboldened by his success at Milan, Nicholas decided to do more of the same at Rome itself. Specifically, papal elections had to be more clearly spelled out and regulated. At a synod held at the Lateran on Easter, 1059, in the company of 113 bishops, regulations for the elections were promulgated. Henceforth, the cardinals alone were to vote for the pope, although the clergy and people of Rome retained the right of "acclaiming" the elect—that is, ratifying his election by cheering him. Similarly, a personal right of confirmation was to be given each succeeding emperor.

In the summer of 1059, Nicholas went to Melfi, capital of Norman Apulia, to hold a synod and negotiate with their duke, Robert Guiscard. This worthy duke was invested with the rule of Calabria, Apulia, and Sicily, if he could reconquer them from the Muslims. In return, he would pay tribute to the Holy See, hold the aforementioned lands as a papal vassal, and undertake to protect the Papal States and the integrity of papal elections. A similar alliance was struck with the Norman prince of Capua. The Normans then pursued Benedict and his allies, forcing them to surrender in the autumn of 1059.

Following this victory Nicholas made Hildebrand archdeacon. It was well

known at the papal court that the decrees of the synod regarding the election, removing as they did all lay influence, would encounter opposition. Cardinal Stephen was sent to France to hold local councils of the French bishops to induce those prelates to accept the new rules. These were held in January and February of 1060.

In Germany, however, there was much more opposition. Secure in his alliance with the Normans, however, Nicholas was able to disregard imperial opposition, and renewed the election rules at the Lateran Synod of 1060. He then sent Cardinal Stephen as his legate to Germany to work the same magic he had in France. In response, a council of German bishops was held the same year, which declared the new rules annulled. Nicholas nevertheless renewed the election rules at another synod in 1061, shortly before his death. He was buried at Santa Reparata in Florence.

## Alexander II

### (September 30, 1061–April 21, 1073)

As might be expected, the troubles of the last pontificate continued into the next. Anselm of Lucca was born in Baggio, near Milan, and was a monk at Cluny with Hildebrand. Born to an illustrious family, when he returned to Milan his co-founding of the Pataria gave that body much influence. Despite many threats, he and his colleagues steadily battled the immoral party of Archbishop Guido. Given the popular following Anselm soon assembled, Guido and his friends conceived of the idea of sending him to the court of Henry III—where he would remove the fiery preacher from the neighborhood.

Instead, it only increased his influence; Henry was so taken by his life and speech that the emperor appointed Anselm bishop of Lucca in 1057. Twice Stephen X and Nicholas II sent Anselm to Milan as a legate to repress abuses—the first time with Hildebrand, the second with St. Peter Damian. Although the latter mission compelled Guido to swear renunciation of his evil ways, the crafty archbishop was of course lying.

The death of Nicholas II opened the gate to conflict. On the one side were most of the cardinals with Hildebrand and St. Peter Damian. Zealous for reform, they decided that Anselm would be the best choice for pope. The other side, made up of immoral clerics, Roman nobles annoyed at losing their hold over the papacy, and pro-imperialists who believed that the office should simply be in the emperor's gift, settled on the notably immoral Bishop Cadalus of Parma as their candidate.

Aware that war was brewing, the cardinals elected Anselm, who took the name Alexander II. Hoping to forestall conflict, the cardinals sent notification of Alexander's election to the imperial court. But when the empress-regent and her advisers dismissed the cardinals' envoy without seeing him, they were considered to have forfeited their rights.

Meanwhile, the Roman nobility, together with the fun-loving clergy of Lombardy, sent a representative to Agnes asking for royal approval of a new papal election. She granted this and convened a council at Basle; although there were no cardinals present, Cadalus of Parma was declared pope, taking the name Honorius II on October 28.

Despite this, Alexander had a number of advantages; not least of these were the Norman alliance and the friendship of Countess Matilda of Tuscany, one of the most remarkable women of that or any other time. Thanks to these two powers, Rome stayed safely in papal hands.

At last, in October of 1062, Archbishop Hanno of Cologne overthrew Agnes and became regent for Henry IV; the vanquished empress entered a convent. The new Regent convened a Diet at Augsburg in October 1062, which in turn sent an emissary to Rome to look into the whole affair. He found in Alexander's favor, and at a council held at Mantua on Pentecost, 1064, Alexander was recognized indisputably as pope.

The remainder of his pontificate was spent, with the help of Hildebrand, in putting down simony and vice, as well as deposing prelates throughout Christendom who favored these activities. In 1069, the now-of-age Henry IV decided to divorce his wife, Bertha of Turin. He was deterred from this unsavory project by Alexander's threat of excommunication. Similar warnings led Henry to desist from intruding one of his clients into the archdiocese of Milan, which had suffered enough from simony.

Alexander blessed the banners of Roger Guiscard and William the Conqueror, as they respectively conquered Sicily and England. Because of its importance to the modern world (and what the episode says about the Middle Ages) we should look at this last episode a little more closely.

Normandy was at this time a typical French feudal state, with little to distinguish it from its neighbors save the odd names of some of its nobles. Its administration was not particularly well organized, and when Duke Robert I of Normandy died in 1035, he was succeeded by his illegitimate seven-year-old son, William. It was not an auspicious occasion, given that the Duchy's borders were unsettled, to have a minor on the Ducal throne. But William showed his mettle, taking direct control of affairs when he was fourteen. Among many other fateful developments of his early reign, taking in the fugitive Prince Edward from England was perhaps the most decisive. The

two became friends, and Edward would eventually promise his throne to William.

Edward's brother-in-law, Harold, was a great magnate and heir to Earl Godwine. Godwine had been in and out of exile as of power, but by the time of his death he had become an important force in the realm—an importance that descended to Earl Harold. Harold was shipwrecked on the coast of Normandy in 1064. Arrested by one of William's vassals, Harold accompanied William on a military campaign against the duke of Brittany. At that time, Harold swore allegiance to the Norman and promised to help him gain the English throne after Edward's death.

Upon his return to England, however, Harold forgot about his pledge and returned to his role as most powerful noble. Although he had no drop of royal blood himself, both his power and his relationship with Edward's late queen made him a favored candidate for the crown—a candidacy he gladly accepted. On Edward's death, the king's council confirmed Harold as king. Fearing William's claim to the throne, Harold had himself crowned in Westminster Abbey on January 6, 1066, the day after Edward's death.

In September, Harald Hardrada of Norway invaded England and was defeated by Harold at the Battle of Stamford Bridge near York. Hardrada's army had invaded using more than 300 ships; so many were killed that only 25 ships were needed to transport the survivors home. Harold had proved himself to be a formidable commander.

William too, however, had shown military prowess. When he decided to invade England, knights rallied to him from all over France. But in those days, such a venture required some sort of legality. Here William invoked Harold's perjured oath and appealed to the two supreme authorities in the West—the emperor and the pope.

The emperor was Henry IV. William, like Harold—like all Europeans of the time—considered the Holy Roman Emperor to be supreme in matters temporal and the successor of both Constantine and Charlemagne. (Although today this supremacy would be considered merely symbolic, like the headship of the queen over the Commonwealth, at that time mere lack of power did not mean a lack of authority.) Later English kings quite readily acknowledged the superiority of the emperor. In 1024, Canute had done this at the coronation of Conrad II. So too would Richard the Lion-Hearted, who "by the advice of his mother Eleanor stripped himself of the Kingdom of England and delivered it over to the emperor as Lord of the World"; the emperor, in true feudal fashion, as quickly returned it while retaining suzerainty. Various later English kings would deny this supremacy, but Henry VIII tacitly acknowledged it—first by competing for the post in the election against Charles I of Spain (who won the imperial title under the name of Charles V) and Francis I of France, and later feeling the need to officially declare independence of the empire at the time he declared himself head of the Church of

England. (A lingering memory of the imperial-english relationship turned up in 1806, when England refused to recognize the dissolution of the empire.) In any case, William was successful in his requests, and Emperor Henry IV authorized the duke to take England and offered material assistance, if necessary.

The pope, too, needed to be convinced, as the spiritual head of Christendom. There was a formal hearing at Rome, with William as plaintiff against Harold's perjury. Hildebrand argued William's case, and the pope ruled in favor of the duke. Alexander II then sent a banner to the duke to symbolize the pontifical judgment.

A reinforced William landed in Sussex. Harold rushed south and, on October 14, 1066, his army of seven thousand was defeated on the field of Senlac near Hastings. Harold was hit in the eye by an arrow and cut down by Norman swords. Although the new regime would face some determined resistance, Anglo-Saxon England was over; Norman—and so modern—England was begun.

Another event occurred during Alexander's pontificate, which, although he had nothing to do with it, would affect many of his successors. Since the fall of Syria in the 640s, the Byzantines had kept the Muslims out of Asia Minor; under Basil II, in the late tenth century, they had even reconquered Antioch. But this triumph was short-lived. The now-decadent Arab caliphs were subsumed by a power out of the East—"the recently converted to Islam" Seljuk Turks. They fell upon the Byzantine frontier with a fury unseen in centuries. While emperors replaced each other at Constantinople through bloody coups, the new adversary gathered strength.

The latest emperor, Romanus Diogenes, was, unlike his immediate predecessors, an able soldier. Aware of the threat, he began to raise a new army. But time was too short, and he and his army were cut to pieces by the Turks at the battle of Manzikert in May of 1071. The conquerors rolled over Asia Minor, burning, raping, and pillaging. Ancient centers of Christianity, such as Tarsus, Iconium, and Caesarea, fell to them and have remained Muslim ever since; the Christians of Cappadocia withdrew into their famous caves. But like Syria, Palestine, Egypt, and North Africa before them, lands once as Christian as Italy or Ireland were engulfed by the crescent. Although parts of eastern Asia Minor would be regained for a time later, never would the land of St. John and St. Paul, St. Polycarp and St. Basil, be secure again.

Alexander II also instituted the feast of the Holy Trinity on the Sunday following Pentecost, which feast is still with us today; it is also observed by the Anglicans and Lutherans, few of whom, perhaps, realize its origins.

Despite the power that Alexander wielded, it was already obvious from his high-handed manner that young Henry was going to be a problem. Alexander's death meant that his successor would have to deal with it.

## *Honorius II*

*Anti-Pope (October 28, 1061–1072)*

Born at Parma of noble heritage, Cadalus was appointed bishop of his native place (it was more than suspected that money had changed hands). Both a nobleman and a simoniac cleric, he was very popular with both groups, who proposed that he should become successor to Nicholas II. As noted earlier, he was "elected" pope by the Council of Basle, and took the name Honorius. In the spring of 1062 he marched on Rome; Benda, bishop of Alba and imperial agent, had gone before to prepare the city to receive the latest anti-pope. On April 14, the forces loyal to Alexander II were defeated, and Honorius took possession of St. Peter's. But in May, Godfrey of Tuscany took the city, forcing Honorius to flee to Parma. Meanwhile, Alexander withdrew to Lucca, where he awaited events.

After the empress Agnes's deposition by Archbishop Hanno, and the subsequent finding for Alexander by the imperial envoy charged with investigating the election, Honorius counterattacked. In 1063, he actually assaulted, took, and held for a short time the Castel Sant' Angelo, before fleeing back to Parma. He was deposed and excommunicated formally by the council of Mantua on Pentecost 1064, but until his death he retained possession of his diocese. Honorius claimed the papacy all that time and made Parma a refuge for the discontented anti-reform folk.

## St. Gregory VII

(April 22, 1073–May 25, 1085)

Hildebrand was born in Sovana, Tuscany, to low-class parents. He received his education at the abbey of Santa Maria in Aventino where his uncle was abbot and was there professed a monk. In 1047, Gregory VI named him his chaplain; however, Hildebrand sought spiritual perfection above advancement and withdrew to the abbey of Cluny. When St. Leo IX became pope, he found a master after his own heart, and he reentered the pontifical service in 1049. Leo appointed him administrator of the patrimony of St. Peter. Continuing his monastic residence in 1050 Hildebrand was made prior of St. Paul Outside the Walls. Five years later, he was appointed legate to

France to combat the heresy of Berengar of Tours, who denied the Real Presence of Jesus in the Eucharist. In 1057 he became legate to Germany, and in 1059 archdeacon. During five event-filled pontificates he was the heart (and sometimes the head) of the reform party. As right arm of these popes, he learned more than most about the papacy—a knowledge that would serve him well.

As the obvious successor to Alexander II, his election was a foregone conclusion to all but him. Once in the chair of St. Peter, he took the name of Gregory and immediately began promulgating reform edicts—1074 and 1075 saw a flurry of decrees against simony, clerical immorality, and lay investiture.

The result was a revolt by guilty clerics under Cencius at Christmas of 1075; although they imprisoned Gregory overnight, he was released by the angry populace the next day. Because of Gregory's refusal to accept the emperor's appointment and investiture of bishops with their clerical insignia, Henry IV refused obedience and declared Gregory "deposed" at the Diet of Worms on January 24, 1076. In response, Gregory excommunicated Henry, who was in turn deposed by the German nobles at Tribur in October. Gregory, who had sought refuge with Countess Matilda at her castle of Canossa, allied with the nobles who were in the process of replacing Henry as king with one of their own.

Realizing that the alliance of pope and princes would doom him, Henry went to Canossa and did penance in the snow in January of 1077. His object, of course, was simply to divide the pope—who he knew wanted peace more than Henry's deposition—from Henry's outraged subjects. The ruse worked. Accepting Henry's penance, the pope called on the German princes to support him as their rightful ruler.

Henry soon returned to his old tricks, however, and so Gregory deposed him and bestowed the imperial crown upon Rudolf of Swabia.

In return, Henry set up as anti-pope the excommunicated simoniac archbishop of Ravenna, Guibert (who called himself Clement III), besieging Gregory in the process. Robert Guiscard rescued him, however, and Gregory accompanied his liberator to Salerno, where Gregory died. Among his last words were, "I have loved truth and hated iniquity, and therefore I die in exile." St. Gregory VII was buried in Salerno Cathedral, and his feast is May 25. His sanctity was confirmed by many remarkable miracles, some of which occurred during his lifetime.

# *Clement III*

*Anti-Pope (June 1080–September 8, 1100)*

Guibert was born at Parma in 1025. He became a cleric, and the empress Agnes appointed him chancellor of Italy in 1057, a post he held until 1063. (In those days, chancellors, the chief legal officer of a realm, were almost always priests—St. Thomas More was the first lay lord chancellor in England.) As noted previously, Guibert was present at the synod held by Nicholas II in 1059, but at the latter's death he was instrumental in having Honorius II elevated to the anti-papacy. As a leader in opposition to Alexander II, Guibert shared in his party's ruin, losing the chancellorship at the empress Agnes's defeat.

When, however, in 1072 the archdiocese of Ravenna became vacant, Henry IV appointed him to the post. Alexander II was reluctant to confirm Guibert, given his record. But Cardinal Hildebrand pointed out the reconciliatory value of such an act. Often accused throughout his career of ambition and malice, Hildebrand in reality practiced forgiveness and patience almost to a fault. In 1073, Guibert was duly consecrated.

After Hildebrand became Gregory VII, Guibert at first cooperated with the new pontiff, attending the synod of 1074, which condemned yet again simony and clerical vice. But he soon quarreled with Gregory and joined his opposition. After the abortive Christmas coup, Guibert was accused of having sided with Cencius. In response, he refused to attend the synod of 1075, despite his obligation by oath to do so. Gregory subsequently suspended him.

Fortunately for Guibert, Henry IV began open conflict with the pope at this time. At the council of German bishops called by Henry at Worms in January of 1076 to depose Gregory, Guibert joined with his brother bishops of northern Italy in voting for the deposition. Gregory promulgated an excommunication and interdict against the lot in his own synod of 1076. In April of that year, Guibert presided over a meeting of bishops at Pavia, which answered Gregory's excommunication with one of their own against him. So, in the Roman synod of 1078, Gregory excommunicated Guibert by name.

In March 1080, Gregory renewed his anathema against Henry IV, who in return convened a gathering of bishops at Brixen, declaring Gregory deposed and electing Guibert as "pope." He in turn took the name Clement III. Henry swore that he would bring him to Rome and receive the imperial coronation from him. With much pomp, Guibert returned to Ravenna in pontifical regalia.

It was one thing to make bold declarations, another to execute them. At the synod of 1081, Gregory excommunicated Henry and all his followers;

Clement's pontificate extended no farther than the lands controlled by Henry at any one time. At last, on March 21, 1084, Henry managed to seize Rome, leaving Gregory besieged in the Castel Sant'Angelo. Three days later, Clement was solemnly enthroned at St. John Lateran and on March 31, Clement did indeed give Henry the imperial diadem at St. Peter's.

But the triumph was short-lived. News came that Robert Guiscard was en route to rescue Gregory. Henry and Clement decamped to Tuscany to fight the forces of the countess Matilda. The Normans escorted Gregory to the safety of Salerno, where he renewed all the relevant excommunications.

In Germany the bishops were divided; those loyal to Gregory held a council at Quedlinburg in which they confirmed all the censures against Clement and Henry. But the emperor gathered his own followers at Mainz to second his measures. The conflict continued after the death of St. Gregory VII on May 25, 1085. Clement continued to act as anti-pope through the next three pontificates.

As we will see, Blessed Victor III, whose election to the papacy had to be postponed for many months owing to the conditions at Rome, was at last finally inaugurated on May 3, 1087. But he had to flee the city eight days later as Clement's supporters seized control. The countess Matilda in turn retook Rome, besieging Clement's allies in the Pantheon.

The next pope, Bl. Urban II, had control of much of Rome during the first part of his pontificate, but he was driven off again by Clement's folk and had to seek refuge in southern Italy and France, where he preached the First Crusade in 1097. Emboldened by the zeal Urban's words had roused in them, a party of Crusaders under Hugh of Vermandois, brother of the king of France, retook Rome. Only the Castel Sant'Angelo remained under Clement, and that too fell in 1098. After Henry IV left Italy, Clement's control was restricted to Ravenna and a few other northern Italian spots.

After Urban's death and the accession of Paschal II, Clement rushed to Albano, hoping to regain control of Rome; when he failed, he and his followers withdrew to Civita Castellana, where Clement died. His adherents elected Bishop Theodorus of Santa Rufina to succeed him, but that effort went nowhere.

# Bl. Victor III

## (May 24, 1086–September 16, 1087)

Born Desiderius Defaurie at Benevento, he took the Benedictine habit, and was elected abbot of Monte Cassino in 1057. Defaurie was a great statesman, negotiating the alliance between St. Gregory VII and Robert Guiscard. When the former died, he was the obvious choice for successor. Given both the state of Rome and his own reluctance, however, a year passed before Victor's election. Even then, he refused the tiara, consenting finally to be crowned only on May 9, 1087. He reconfirmed all of Gregory's condemnations and policies. As we have seen, he had to flee Rome a few days later.

Back at Monte Cassino, he remained until his death a few months later. His status as a Blessed (next-to-last stage on the road to canonization) was confirmed for the Benedictines and Benevento in 1727, and his feast is October 16.

# CRUSADES AND CORRUPTION

# Bl. Urban II

### (March 12, 1088–July 29, 1099)

Born at Chatillon-sur-Marne in 1042, he was originally named Odon de Lagery. Named canon and then archdeacon of Rheims, his clerical career seemed secure. But he tossed it all over to become a monk at Cluny in 1070. His qualities were so apparent to his brothers that he was soon elected prior. His former fellow at Cluny, St. Gregory VII, however, had need of his abilities; he was summoned to Rome and made cardinal-bishop of Ostia in 1078. In 1084, he was given the thankless task of legate to Germany.

Elected in succession to Bl. Victor III, he was crowned at Terracina and took the name Urban. Although he was at first in control of Rome, taking possession in 1088, Henry and Clement's followers managed to oust him. Urban did hold the city for a short time in 1094, where he sat on the papal throne for the first time since his election. He was soon put out again, and Clement III's followers went back to business as usual.

In November 1095 Urban traveled to Clermont, France, where he added to the prohibition of lay investiture a stricture against bishops and abbots doing homage to lay magnates. He further excommunicated Phillip I, King of France, for adultery in his own country.

Far more notable, however, he preached the First Crusade at the synod. After the Great Schism, papal interest in Eastern affairs did not wane. But the difficulties facing the papacy meant that there was little that could be done, even after the terrible defeat of Manzikert. With Byzantine power in Asia Minor restricted to a few fortresses on the Aegean coast, and the West distracted by the conflict between Henry and the papacy, the Seljuks had a free hand to deal with the Christians in their power—natives and pilgrims—as they pleased. At first content after the initial atrocities with extorting money from them, the Seljuks went on to the odd wholesale pogrom and torture of individuals. Then, at last, they began destroying the Holy Places in Palestine, even including the Holy Sepulchre itself. Added to this sacrilege was the fact that the Seljuks planned, if they could, to invade the West.

To Urban, this seemed a far greater problem than that posed by Henry IV and Clement III. Unlike these opponents, Urban's holiness had become a by-

word; his word meant much. His plan was simple: persuade the fractious Western kings and nobles to drop their petty differences and unite under the Cross to free the Holy Places, secure the Byzantine Empire, and drive the Muslims back from where they had come. Starting at Clermont in 1095, he preached a great Crusade that would accomplish these goals. So inspiring were his words that many of his hearers, with the words "God wills it!" on their lips, immediately began their plans to set off to the Holy Land and do battle with "the Infidel." A simple cleric, Peter the Hermit, who had been tortured while on pilgrimage, immediately took up the pope's challenge. Joining him was a financially ruined knight, Sir Walter the Penniless. They gathered a huge mob of peasants, who set off for Palestine via Constantinople. The ill-planned expedition came to grief in Asia Minor. A detachment led by Godefroi of Bouillon, his brother Baldwin, and a number of other nobles was better planned.

## Urban II's Speech at Clermont

Most beloved brethren: Urged by necessity, I, Urban, by the permission of God chief bishop and prelate over the whole world, have come into these parts as an ambassador with a divine admonition to you, the servants of God. I hoped to find you as faithful and as zealous in the service of God as I had supposed you to be. But if there is in you any deformity or crookedness contrary to God's law, with divine help I will do my best to remove it. For God has put you as stewards over his family to minister to it. Happy indeed will you be if he finds you faithful in your stewardship. You are called shepherds; see that you do not act as hirelings. But be true shepherds, with your crooks always in your hands. Do not go to sleep, but guard on all sides the flock committed to you. For if through your carelessness or negligence a wolf carries away one of your sheep, you will surely lose the reward laid up for you with God. And after you have been bitterly scourged with remorse for your faults, you will be fiercely overwhelmed in hell, the abode of death. For according to the gospel you are the salt of the earth [Matt. 5:13]. But if you fall short in your duty, how, it may be asked, can it be salted? O how great the need of salting! It is indeed necessary for you to correct with the salt of wisdom this foolish people which is so devoted to the pleasures of this world, lest the Lord, when He may wish to speak to them, find them putrefied by their sins unsalted and

stinking. For if He shall find worms, that is, sins, in them, because you have been negligent in your duty, He will command them as worthless to be thrown into the abyss of unclean things. And because you cannot restore to Him His great loss, He will surely condemn you and drive you from His loving presence. But the man who applies this salt should be prudent, provident, modest, learned, peaceable, watchful, pious, just, equitable, and pure. For how can the ignorant teach others? How can the licentious make others modest? And how can the impure make others pure? If anyone hates peace, how can he make others peaceable? Or if anyone has soiled his hands with baseness, how can he cleanse the impurities of another? We read also that if the blind lead the blind, both will fall into the ditch [Matt. 15:14]. But first correct yourselves, in order that, free from blame, you may be able to correct those who are subject to you. If you wish to be the friends of God, gladly do the things which you know will please Him. You must especially let all matters that pertain to the church be controlled by the law of the church. And be careful that simony does not take root among you, lest both those who buy and those who sell [church offices] be beaten with the scourges of the Lord through narrow streets and driven into the place of destruction and confusion. Keep the church and the clergy in all its grades entirely free from the secular power. See that the tithes that belong to God are faithfully paid from all the produce of the land; let them not be sold or withheld. If anyone seizes a bishop let him be treated as an outlaw. If anyone seizes or robs monks, or clergymen, or nuns, or their servants, or pilgrims, or merchants, let him be anathema [that is, cursed]. Let robbers and incendiaries and all their accomplices be expelled from the church and anthematized. If a man who does not give a part of his goods as alms is punished with the damnation of hell, how should he be punished who robs another of his goods? For thus it happened to the rich man in the gospel [Luke 16:19]; he was not punished because he had stolen the goods of another, but because he had not used well the things which were his.

You have seen for a long time the great disorder in the world caused by these crimes. It is so bad in some of your provinces, I am told, and you are so weak in the administration of justice, that one can hardly go along the road by day or night without being attacked by robbers; and whether at home or abroad one is in danger of being despoiled either by force or fraud. Therefore it is necessary to reenact the truce, as it is commonly called,

which was proclaimed a long time ago by our holy fathers. I exhort and demand that you, each, try hard to have the truce kept in your diocese. And if anyone shall be led by his cupidity or arrogance to break this truce, by the authority of God and with the sanction of this council he shall be anathematized.

. . . Although, O sons of God, you have promised more firmly than ever to keep the peace among yourselves and to preserve the rights of the church, there remains still an important work for you to do. Freshly quickened by the divine correction, you must apply the strength of your righteousness to another matter which concerns you as well as God. For your brethren who live in the east are in urgent need of your help, and you must hasten to give them the aid which has often been promised them. For, as the most of you have heard, the Turks and Arabs have attacked them and have conquered the territory of Romania [the Greek empire] as far west as the shore of the Mediterranean and the Hellespont, which is called the Arm of St. George. They have occupied more and more of the lands of those Christians, and have overcome them in seven battles. They have killed and captured many, and have destroyed the churches and devastated the empire. If you permit them to continue thus for awhile with impurity, the faithful of God will be much more widely attacked by them. On this account I, or rather the Lord, beseech you as Christ's heralds to publish this everywhere and to persuade all people of whatever rank, foot-soldiers and knights, poor and rich, to carry aid promptly to those Christians and to destroy that vile race from the lands of our friends. I say this to those who are present, it [being] meant also for those who are absent. Moreover, Christ commands it.

All who die by the way, whether by land or by sea, or in battle against the pagans, shall have immediate remission of sins. This I grant them through the power of God with which I am invested. O what a disgrace if such a despised and base race, which worships demons, should conquer a people which has the faith of omnipotent God and is made glorious with the name of Christ! With what reproaches will the Lord overwhelm us if you do not aid those who, with us, profess the Christian religion! Let those who have been accustomed unjustly to wage private warfare against the faithful now go against the infidels and end with victory this war which should have been begun long ago. Let those who for a long time, have been robbers, now become knights. Let those who have been fighting against their brothers and rel-

> atives now fight in a proper way against the barbarians. Let those who have been serving as mercenaries for small pay now obtain the eternal reward. Let those who have been wearing themselves out in both body and soul now work for a double honor. Behold! on this side will be the sorrowful and poor, on that, the rich; on this side, the enemies of the Lord, on that, his friends. Let those who go not put off the journey, but rent their lands and collect money for their expenses; and as soon as winter is over and spring comes, let them eagerly set out on the way with God as their guide.
>
> From Bongars, Gesta Dei per Francos, 1, pp. 382 f., trans in Oliver J. Thatcher, and Edgar Holmes McNeal, eds., A Source Book for Medieval History (New York: Scribners, 1905), 513–17.

(Today most people deplore the Crusades for the many excesses that occurred during their execution—Pope John Paul II has apologized to the Muslims for them. Remember, however, they were in actuality defensive, and they were launched for justifiable reasons. In recent times, most Americans consider that the bombings of Dresden and Hamburg, Nagasaki and Hiroshima (to mention a few) were justified in eradicating evil. Although many more were killed than those who died in the Crusades, it is highly unlikely that America, or her allies, will ever apologize for those bombings to the Germans, and Japanese. Moreover, since victory required handing over eastern Europe to Stalin at Yalta, it is even less likely that an apology is forthcoming to the Poles, Czechs, and the rest for what they endured from 1945 until 1991. Interestingly, World War II was itself often called a crusade; General Eisenhower named his book of memoirs of the period, Crusade in Europe. The fact that after President Bush's initial misstep, the early twenty-first century American leadership studiously avoids calling the war on terror a "crusade" (Secretary of State Colin Powell even apologized for using the term in an "unguarded moment") reflects current feelings that will best be evaluated by future historians.

Initially, the first Crusade was quite successful. The eastern third of Asia Minor was recovered for the Byzantines; Antioch and Edessa were also liberated. At last Jerusalem itself was delivered. (If their successes were not lasting, surely those who have lived through the atomic fears of the Cold War, and rejoiced to see the fall of the Soviet Union, only to see hopes for lasting peace dashed on September 11, 2001, will understand how fleeting victory and peace alike can be.)

1095–1096 The Peasants' Crusade
1096–1099 The First Crusade

| | |
|---|---|
| 1147–1149 | The Second Crusade |
| 1189–1192 | The Third Crusade |
| 1202–1204 | The Fourth Crusade |
| 1202–1202 | The Children's Crusade |
| 1218–1221 | The Fifth Crusade |
| 1228–1229 | The Sixth Crusade |
| 1248–1254 | The Seventh Crusade |

But later defeat could not be foretold when the Crusaders took Jerusalem. Godefroi of Bouillon refused to be named king when the city fell. "I will not wear a crown of gold where Our Saviour wore a crown of thorns," was his reply to the invitation by the other Crusade leaders. He died soon after, and his brother Baldwin consented to be crowned king of Jerusalem at the Church of the Nativity in Bethlehem.

In any case, an unexpected byproduct of the Crusade was that some of its leaders would see the recovery of Rome as a more immediate goal. So it was, as noted earlier, that Urban II returned at last to his city. He died shortly thereafter, and was beatified on July 14, 1881, by Leo XIII. His feast is July 30, and is observed at Rome, at the monastery of Cava, and in certain French dioceses.

## Paschal II

### (August 13, 1099–January 21, 1118)

Born Rainerius in central Italy, he became a monk at Cluny when quite young. At only twenty he was sent to Rome on the abbey's business, but was drafted by St. Gregory VII and made cardinal of San Clemente. After the death of Urban II, the Cardinals met at his church and unanimously elected him. Despite his protests (for he claimed that his monastic education unsuited him for the office) Paschal was consecrated at St. Peter's the next day.

Following the lead of St. Gregory VII and Bl. Urban II was his constant goal; as a result, through many gatherings in Italy and France he labored to continue the flow of Crusaders to the East to help maintain and consolidate the conquests there.

The conflict with Henry IV ate up much of his energy, as it had his predecessors. Anti-Pope Clement III, as we have noticed, died a few months after Paschal's election; although the imperialist party put in a successor, Theodorus, he was exiled by Paschal to a monastery in 1102. His successor, Aleric,

who was treated the same way in 1105, left little mark. But Maginulf, the third in this line, who took the name Sylvester IV, made much more of an impact, even if he had few followers. As for Henry IV, he remained unrepentant, although he did not return to the offensive. He died, insisting on his right of investiture, at Liege on August 7, 1106.

The new German king, Henry V, while prince, had seemed favorable to the papacy; once in his father's palace, however, he continued to give out dioceses to friends. This annoyed the pope, who at several councils denounced lay investiture again. Because Henry would not stop the practice, Paschal changed his planned visit to Germany into a journey to France, where the king (having done penance and been restored to the Church) welcomed the pontiff happily. Although the lay investiture question was a universal problem, Henry affected to be upset at discussion of a German institution on foreign soil, and he readied an army to compel imperial coronation at Rome from Paschal.

In August 1110, the German king crossed the Alps with an army of troops and lawyers. The two worked out an accord at Sutri, whereby Henry would renounce investitures while the pope ordered all bishops and abbots of the empire to restore their properties to imperial jurisdiction. This last could not please those German and Italian higher clerics who were thus reduced from princes to paupers. Their anger was further increased by the fact that the Roman diocese was expressly exempted from this confiscation.

These prelates were behind the uprising that broke out at Rome on February 12, 1111, the date chosen for the imperial coronation. In response, Henry left the city after three days of rioting, taking the pope and his cardinals as prisoners with him. After two months in captivity, Paschal gave the king the right to invest prelates, leading all Europe to condemn Henry. The recalcitrant Henry finally released Paschal, after extracting from the pope a promise not to seek revenge—a promise Paschal steadfastly kept after his return to Rome.

The remainder of the pontificate was more or less peaceful, with the pope among other things helping St. Anselm of Canterbury and approving the new orders of the Cistercians and of Fontrevault (which order held a unique arrangement featuring both nuns and monks under one abbess). In 1117, Henry came to Rome to demand his terms and Paschal fled to Benevento. The pope sent Maurice Bourdin as his personal emissary; so impressed with Henry was the envoy that he defected to his side—a defection that would have unpleasant results later. Paschal's traveling endeared him to the Catholic people (in a way similar to that of John Paul II in present day).

## *Sylvester IV*

*Anti-Pope (November 18, 1105–January 1111)*

Born Maginulfo at Rome, Sylvester IV had been elected as successor to the incarcerated anti-pope Alberic. Although his supporters, led by Werner, Marquis of Ancona, had managed to regain control of Rome, the day after his election, Sylvester and his allies were expelled from Rome. Although Henry V gave him some support, the agreement between the German king and Paschal at Sutri ended that. Bereft of this aid, Sylvester died later in 1111.

## Gelasius II

(1118–1119)

Born John, at Gaeta, as a member of the noble family of the Gaetani (lords of the town), this pope early in his life became a monk at Monte Cassino, where his proficiency in Latin brought him first to the attention of the Papal Court, and then to the office of Chancellor of the Papacy.

When Paschal II died, the cardinals, knowing that Henry would attempt, with the help of his faction in Rome, to put one of his own followers on the papal throne, met secretly at the Benedictine monastery on the Palatine Hill. They sent a messenger summoning John from Monte Cassino; on his arrival, despite his protests, they unanimously elected him pope.

Cencius Frangipani, leader of the imperialists in the city, soon learned what had taken place. Breaking down the door of the abbey in the company of his men, he grabbed the new pontiff by the throat. Throwing him down on the ground, he stamped on him with his spurred and booted feet, dragged him by the hair to his tower, loaded him with chains, and flung him into the family dungeon. The following day the Romans found out and besieged Frangipani; the hunter was now hunted himself. He released the pope and threw himself at his feet, begging forgiveness. Gelasius, as he wished to be called, freely agreed. A joyous procession brought the new pontiff to the Lateran where he was enthroned.

Frangipani's master was not idle, however; Henry V hurried down to Rome from Lombardy, and by March 2 had occupied St. Peter's. Gelasius and his officials fled in two boats down the Tiber, their passing marked both a raging storm and the stones and arrows of Henry's troops. At last, they arrived at Gaeta, where the Normans welcomed them. At this time Gelasius was only a deacon, but he was there made priest and bishop.

Henry was also busy. He elevated Maurice Bourdin to anti-pope, as Gregory VIII (rather an ironic name, all things considered). The new would-be pontiff crowned his master as emperor. This accomplished, Henry and Gregory left the Eternal City.

Gelasius returned secretly and, realizing that he could not hold Rome against the king, fled to France via Pisa (where he consecrated the cathedral) and Genoa. There King Louis VI and his chief adviser, Suger (abbot of St. Denis, and builder of its glorious church, the burial ground of the French monarchs), received him. Suger himself guided the pope to Cluny, where he set plans for a general council to be held at Rheims. Unfortunately, Gelasius died before he could set this meeting in motion.

## *Gregory VIII*

*Anti-Pope (March 8, 1118–1137)*

Born Maurice Bourdin at Limoges, and educated and professed a Benedictine at Cluny, he traveled over the Pyrenees with his fellow Cluniac Bernard, who had been made archbishop of Toledo and primate of Spain. Owing to his background and friendship with Bernard, Bourdin was made bishop of Coimbra in 1098 and archbishop of Braga in 1111. But he quarreled with Bernard in 1114 and was suspended by Paschal II. Going to Rome, however, Maurice so impressed the pope that he soon became a powerful adviser to him. In this position, Paschal entrusted him to negotiate with Henry V; however, as we have seen, the wily archbishop went over to the king and was made anti-pope by him.

But Gregory's anti-pontificate was ill-starred. Repeatedly excommunicated, he fell into the hands of Callixtus II in 1121, who confined him to the fortress of Fumo until his death.

# Callixtus (Callistus) II
## (February 1, 1119–December 13, 1124)

Guido, son of Count William of Burgundy, was related to most of the royal houses of Europe. After his brother Hugh was appointed archbishop of Besançon, Guido was given the archdiocese of Vienne in 1088. Afterward, Paschal II made him legate to France. In this office Guido stirred up opposition to Henry V—suppressing lay investiture became a key issue of Guido's career, both before and after his elevation to the papacy.

In 1112 Guido attended the Lateran synod, then held a regional council at Vienne, in which lay investiture was declared heretical and Henry V excommunicated because of the concessions he had extorted from Paschal II at Sutri. The pope confirmed these actions and made Guido a cardinal.

Four days after Gelasius II died at Cluny, the cardinals elected Guido pope; he took the name Callixtus II. Because of his familial connection with the kings of Germany, France, England, and Denmark, it was considered that he would be able to deal with Henry on equal terms. The German king met Callistus's emissaries at Strasbourg and agreed to meet the pontiff himself at Mousson.

Meanwhile, in October of 1119, the pope held a council at Rheims where four hundred bishops and abbots, most of the French nobles, and King Louis VI attended. While the conference deliberated, Callistus departed for Mousson. Fortunately, he discovered before he got there that Henry had arrived with an army of thirty-thousand men; with these he hoped to repeat his performance with Paschal II at Sutri. But Callistus hurried back to Rheims and the security provided by Louis VI. There, after publishing decrees against lay investiture, simony, and clerical vice, the German king and his anti-pope were again excommunicated, on October 30, 1119.

At the same time, Callistus attempted to mediate unsuccessfully the conflict between King Henry I of England and his brother Duke Robert of Normandy. Both sons of William the Conqueror, war had broken out between Henry and their now-deceased older brother, William II, on the one hand, and Robert on the other. At the battle of Tinchebray in 1106, Henry had defeated Robert and seized his Duchy. For the remaining twenty-eight years of his life, the Duke would be his brother's prisoner—a situation that Callistus, cousin to them both, had hoped to rectify.

Henry I had another importance to the pope however, because his daughter, Mathilda, was wife to Henry V. A tempestuous creature, after her imperial

husband's demise, she would return to England to claim her father's throne amid an extraordinarily bloody civil war. In the meantime, however, it was hoped that she might convince her consort to see reason in the matter of the lay investitures.

The fact that Henry I had made a useful compromise with St. Anselm in England increased this hope. King William II had fought with the saintly archbishop over royal investitures of bishops. This question, which plagued popes in regard to emperors, arose because most bishops in Medieval Europe were also feudal lords. In spiritual matters, the pope was of course the bishops' lawful superior. But as lords, these prelates owed their lands and fealty to the emperor or one of the various kings. This led to the lay investiture dispute, as temporal authorities sought control over the spiritual side of the bishops' office as well. It was a tricky problem, and so it proved in England. Asking Anselm to return from Rome, where he had sought refuge with Paschal II, Henry I came to an agreement with Anselm on the Feast of the Assumption, 1106. The king would invest the bishops, as their feudal overlord, with their temporalities—the lands of the diocese. But the ring and mitre, symbols of the bishop's spiritual authority, would be given to the consecrand by the proper Church official. Thus the dual nature of the Church's hierarchs was admitted by Church and state alike. Callixtus saw this as a useful model for peace with the German king.

The pope decided next to take possession of Rome, at the moment in the hands of Gregory VIII. Callixtus's arrival in Italy sparked jubilation among the people, and the anti-pope's support melted away; he fled to the fortress of Sutri. The pope, meanwhile, entered Rome, and after his gala enthronement, he passed over to Salerno to renew the alliance with the Normans. The Normans in turn made war upon Henry and Gregory. Capturing the latter, they turned him over to Callixtus. Norman troops also smashed the forces of Cenzio Frangipani.

Following the securing of Italy, Callixtus was now ready to deal with Henry. The would-be emperor was having trouble in Germany, where many of the princes and people were displeased with the way he had dealt with successive popes. He agreed at last to meet with papal representatives at the Diet of Worms, in September of 1122. On the twenty-third, the Concordat of Worms was signed, which ended the investiture controversy on more or less the English model.

The long struggle was over, and the papacy had, in some ways, clearly emerged the victor. But the tremendous weakening of the stature of the imperial office by Henry IV and V did not really benefit the Church and certainly contributed to instability in Germany and Italy.

Callistus convened the Ecumenical Council of Lateran I on March 18, 1123. Three hundred bishops and twice that many abbots attended from

every part of Europe. The council Fathers approved the Worms treaty, condemned existing abuses, and further attacked violators of the Truce of God. They also renewed the indulgences given Crusaders, among other things.

The security given by Callixtus's measures to his pontificate allowed him to spend his remaining days dealing with a dizzying number of ecclesiastical problems in Italy, France, England, and Spain, which were brought about by the paralysis of the last few pontificates. But when he breathed his last, Callixtus had done for the Church what Charlemagne, Otto I, and Henry III had done for the empire.

## Honorius II

### (December 15, 1124–February 14, 1130)

Lamberto Scannabecchi was born to poor parents at Fagnano near Imola. Entering the clergy, he became archdeacon of Bologna and acquired a great reputation for learning. As a result of this, Paschal II brought him to Rome and made him a canon of the Lateran. In 1117 he became cardinal bishop of Ostia and Velletri, and then followed Gelasius II into exile. Callixtus II used Lamberto as legate to Henry V in all of his negotiations, and it was Cardinal Lamberto who concluded the Concordat of Worms and reconciled Henry V to the Church.

While Callixtus had suppressed the power of the Frangipani and the other noble families in Rome, his death was the signal for them to reemerge. Two days following Callixtus's death, the cardinals elected Teodoro Cardinal Boccadipecora, who took the name Celestine II. He was dressed in the papal robes, and the choir was singing the Te Deum, when Roberto Frangipani burst into the hall, declared that he had no use for Teodoro, and that Lamberto was to be pope. The frightened cardinals agreed, and to prevent a schism, Teodoro abdicated. But after five days, Lamberto declared that he doubted his own legitimacy. He could not be persuaded to retain the tiara until all the cardinals, including Teodoro, assured him that they wanted him. He took the name Honorius.

Shortly after this tumultuous accession, Emperor Henry V died childless. Immediately, the pope sent two legates to Rome, who, with Adalbert, the archbishop of Prague, attempted to secure the election of an Emperor who would not attack the Church's rights. Lothair, count of Supplinburg was in

due course elected. The new German king not only accepted the pope's spiritual supremacy, but also his temporal overlordship. He gave over even more rights to the Church than required by the Concordat of Worms.

In return, when Conrad von Hohenstaufen rose in revolt against the new king, and had himself crowned king of Italy at Monza, Honorius excommunicated both the usurper and the prelate who crowned him. As a result, the revolt was speedily put down.

Troubles arose again in England, however, where Henry I was nibbling away at the Church's rights. In an attempt to prevent the pope from stopping him, he refused any papal legates to England, saying the archbishop of Canterbury, who bore as part of his office the title of Legatus Natus (an honorary title without jurisdiction) was the only legitimate papal legate in the realm. As part of this policy, when Honorius sent Cardinal John of Crema as his legate to England, the king had him detained in Normandy for quite some time. Eventually he was permitted to go to England. He passed through to Scotland, where he held a synod of the local bishops to look into their conflict with the archdiocese of York, who had jurisdiction over them. Crema then convened the English bishops at Westminster, where at last discipline was enforced upon the English Church.

Honorius also, after some conflict that included a short war, regulated further the Holy See's relationship with the Normans in southern Italy. When the abbots of Cluny and Monte Cassino tyrannized their subjects, he deposed and excommunicated them. But the most lasting accomplishment of his pontificate was his confirmation of the charter of the Norbertines on February 26, 1123.

## The Norbertines

This order of men would perform many great services for the Church down through history; even today, a number of its houses are still renowned for orthodoxy and piety. Founded by St. Norbert, this order, whose official name is the Canons Regular of Premontre, follows the rule of St. Augustine, who lived in community with the higher clergy of his diocese of Hippo. As a youth, St. Norbert had led a wild life; in reparation, his followers today are active in education of the young and scholarship. They wear white cassocks. In several European countries, membership in the order is considered tantamount to noble status.

# Innocent II

## (February 14, 1130–September 24, 1143)

Born Gregorio Papareschi, this pope was a member of the noble Roman clan of the Guidoni. Made a cardinal by Paschal II, he went into exile with Gelasius II and accompanied Cardinal Lamberto on his German trips. The morning after the death of Honorius II, he was elected by the cardinal-bishops, taking the name of Innocent.

Alas, his archrival in the College of Cardinals, Pietro Pierleone, was elected by the other cardinals, taking the name of Anacletus II. On February 23, Innocent was consecrated at Santa Maria Nuova, and Anacletus at St. Peter's. The Frangipani declared for Anacletus, so Innocent withdrew to his family's stronghold of Trastevere, thereafter to Pisa, Genoa, and France. In France, Louis VI rallied to him, and an assembly of bishops led by Abbot Suger at Etampes swore allegiance to him. The bishops of southern France did the same at Puy-en-Velay under the presidency of St. Hugh of Grenoble. France's allegiance to Innocent was cemented by another such gathering at Clermont in November 1130.

The German bishops did the same at a synod held at Wurzburg by request of King Lothair. The pope and the king met together at Liege on March 22, 1131; a week later, Lothair and his queen were crowned by Innocent. At Easter, 1131, Innocent traveled to Paris, and he crowned Louis VII as king of France at Rheims on October 18. He also held a synod there at that time, attended by clerics from France, Spain, and England. Innocent then reentered Italy, keeping Pentecost of 1132 at Piacenza.

In 1133, Innocent and Lothair reentered Rome, and on June 4 the pope performed the imperial coronation. As long as Lothair stayed in the nominal capital of his empire with his army, Innocent was safe there. But when emperor and troops withdrew in 1134 to return to Germany, Innocent accompanied them as far as Pisa, leaving Rome in the hands of Anacletus. At that city, Innocent held another synod for the bishops of France, Germany, Spain, England, Hungary, and elsewhere.

The pope was not content to linger in exile forever. He continually begged the emperor to liberate Rome. Finally, in 1137, Lothair responded. On May 30 Innocent and Lothair met with their troops and soon had control of Rome. Anacletus maintained control of a part of the city; after his death on January 25, 1138, his followers elected a successor, who called himself Victor IV. He, however, was induced by St. Bernard of Clairvaux to surrender to Innocent. At last the pope was master in Rome as well as the world.

The schism had had any number of bad effects. To end these, Innocent convened Lateran II on April 4, 1139. One thousand prelates attended: they annulled all the acts of Anacletus II and deposed most of his clergy; they condemned various heresies and abuses; and they excommunicated King Robert of Sicily, who had invaded the Papal States after Lothair's return to Germany. In that same year St. Malachy, archbishop of Armagh, arrived on pilgrimage. He supposedly left a set of prophecies regarding the future popes.

In the East, the Latin patriarchs of Jerusalem and Antioch had begun claiming equality with Rome; they were soon set straight. So too was Louis VII of France, who attempted to interfere with the election of a bishop in France. Innocent placed the country under interdict.

At this time Portugal was asserting its independence from Castile. As its new king had placed Portugal under the papacy as a fief, the pope intervened and secured Portuguese freedom.

Saints Norbert, Hugh of Grenoble, and Bernard of Clairvaux were the great upholders of Innocent's authority in all his conflicts. It speaks well of this pope that he could command such loyalty from such men. His policy may be summed up in his own words (quoted from Henry Denzinger's Enchiridion Symbolorum): "If the sacred authority of the popes and the imperial power are imbued with mutual love, we must thank God in all humility, since then only can peace and harmony exist among Christian peoples. For there is nothing so sublime as the papacy nor so exalted as the Imperial throne."

## *Anacletus II*

*Anti-Pope (February 14, 1130–January 25, 1138)*

Pietro Pierleone was born to a powerful Roman noble family, who had consistently supported the popes against the Frangipani. Educated at Paris and joining Benedictines at Cluny, Pietro was called to Rome by Paschal II, who made him cardinal-deacon of SS. Cosma e Damiano. He fled with Gelasius II and was used extensively as an envoy by him and succeeding popes.

Having already secured the votes of thirty of the cardinals before Honorius died, Pietro was confident of the outcome of the election. But the cardinal-bishops took the dying pope to a place near the Frangipani tower; the day after he died, as previously mentioned, they elected Innocent II. Next followed the twin consecrations, and the unexpected defection of the Frangipani, which prompted Innocent's flight.

Anacletus was left in control of Rome, but Innocent, with the aid of his

three saintly supporters, conquered the Catholic world. The new anti-pope plundered the churches and emptied his family's coffers to treat the Romans to food and entertainment; his letters to Lothair went unanswered.

Looking for a new ally he turned to the Norman duke, Roger of Apulia. On Christmas Day, 1130, Anacletus crowned Roger as king of the Two Sicilies, thus creating a major Italian power that would survive—under various families—until 1860, and which even yet boasts supporters in the Italian south.

In the Spring of 1133, Lothair and Innocent entered Rome for the imperial coronation, but Anacletus held on to the Castel Sant'Angelo, blocking the road to St. Peter's. The ceremony was therefore held in St. John Lateran—after a short period, pope and emperor left. In 1137, Lothair returned to Italy to fight King Roger, while St. Bernard went to Rome to preach obedience to Innocent II. Anacletus died soon after, and the people of Rome, as well as his "successor," Victor IV, swore allegiance to the pope at last.

## *Victor IV*

### *Anti-Pope (March 15-May 29,1138)*

Gregory Cardinal Conti was elected by the Pierleoni family's partisans as successor to Anacletus II. But after two months he submitted to Innocent II.

## Celestine II

### (September 25, 1143–March 8, 1144)

Guido del Castello was born in Roman Tuscany (Tuscia) and was educated at Paris. There he imbibed a great love of France and became a disciple of Abelard, Heloise's beau and a noted philosopher of the day. Unlike his master, however, Guido earned a reputation for holiness, and was made a cardinal in 1128. In 1140 he became papal legate to France.

## Abelard

Born at Le Pallet, near Nantes, in 1079, Abelard went (c. 1100) to Paris to study under William of Champeaux at the school of Notre Dame. He soon attacked the ultrarealist position of his master with such success that William was forced to modify his teaching. Abelard's ideas were called "conceptualism." Abelard became master at Notre Dame, but, when deprived of his place, set himself up (1112) at a school on Mont-Ste-Geneviève, just outside the city walls. Abelard's fame as a dialectician attracted great numbers of students to Paris. This part of his career was cut short by his romance with Heloise (d. c.1164), the learned niece of Fulbert, canon of Notre Dame, who had hired Abelard as her tutor.

After Heloise bore a son, they secretly married to appease her uncle. Fulbert's ill treatment of Heloise led Abelard to remove her secretly to the convent at Argenteuil. Fulbert, who thought that Abelard planned to abandon her, had ruffians attack and castrate him. Abelard sought refuge at Saint-Denis where he became a monk. In 1120 he left Saint-Denis to teach. At the instigation of his rivals, the Council of Soissons had his first theological work burned as heretical (1121). After a short imprisonment, he returned to Saint-Denis but fell out with the monks and built a hermitage near Troyes. To house the students who sought him out, he established a monastery, the Paraclete. When Abelard became abbot at Saint-Gildas-en-Rhuys, Brittany, he gave the Paraclete to Heloise, who became an abbess of a convent there.

St. Bernard of Clairvaux thought Abelard's influence was dangerous and secured his condemnation by the Council of Sens (1140). Abelard appealed to the pope, who upheld the council. Abelard submitted and retired to Cluny. He was buried at the Paraclete, as was Heloise; their bodies were later moved to Père-Lachaise in Paris by the French Revolutionaries.

Guido was elected pope and took the name of Celestine. Among his very first acts was lifting the interdict against France. At his death, a few months later, a conflict was brewing with King Roger of the Two Sicilies.

## Lucius II

### (March 12, 1144–February 15, 1145)

Named Gherardo Caccianemici, at the time of his election he was cardinal-priest of Santa Croce in Gerusalemme and chancellor and librarian of the Roman Church. Although short, his pontificate was extremely dramatic. He intervened in a number of foreign questions, making giving the archdiocese of Tours Primatial See of Brittany, giving the same status over the Iberian peninsula to Toledo, and accepting feudal lordship over Portugal for the Holy See.

But events at home were even more exciting. Rome had at this time an independent Senate, whose membership was demanding that the clergy cease to occupy any political role. Failing to interest either the Holy Roman Emperor or the king of the Two Sicilies in suppressing the incipient revolution, Lucius decided to lead his own army against the Senate. While leading his troops on an assault of the Capitol, where the Senate was dug in, he was struck by a heavy stone. He died of his injuries.

## Bl. Eugene III

### (February 15, 1145–July 8, 1153)

Bernardo Pignatelli was born at Montemagno, near Pisa. Entering the Cistercian order, he became a disciple of St. Bernard of Clairvaux, and, in time, abbot of Santa Anastasia in Rome. St. Bernard wrote his famous tract, De Consideratione, for his instruction.

## St. Bernard Of Clairvaux

Bernard, a Burgundian nobleman, was born in 1090. Although his three brothers were trained as soldiers, Bernard was trained as a scholar. One Christmas Eve as a child he had a dream about the infant Christ in the manger; the memory of it, and consequent devotion to the mystery of the Word made flesh, remained with him throughout his life.

He decided at age twenty-two to enter the monastery of Citeaux, an offshoot of the Benedictines with a much stricter rule than theirs, and became the founding house of the Cistercian order. He persuaded four of his brothers, one uncle, and twenty-six other men to join him. They were the first novices that Citeaux had had for several years. After three years, the abbot ordered Bernard to take twelve monks and found a new house at La Ferte. The first year was one of great hardship. They had no stores and lived chiefly on roots and barley bread. Bernard imposed such severe discipline that his monks became discouraged. He realized his error, however, and became more lenient. The reputation of the monastery, known as Clairvaux, spread across Europe. By the time of his death, sixty new monasteries of the Cistercian order were established under his direction.

For four years after 1130 Bernard was deeply involved with a disputed papal election, championing the claims of Innocent II against his rival Anacletus II. He traveled throughout France, Germany, and Italy mustering support for his candidate and returned from one of these journeys with Peter Bernard of Paganelli as a postulant for the monastery.

The papal election was not the only dispute in which Bernard became involved. As reported previously he was highly critical of Peter Abelard, one of the most brilliant theologians of the day (see April 21). Bernard believed that Abelard was too rationalistic in his approach and failed to allow sufficiently for the element of mystery in the faith. Peter the Venerable, the abbot of Cluny, was a friend of both Abelard and Bernard, and managed to reconcile them before they died.

One of Bernard's most influential acts was his preaching of the Second Crusade. When Muslim forces captured Edessa in 1144, King Louis VII of France was eager to launch a crusade to

retake Edessa and prevent a Muslim recapture of Jerusalem. He asked Bernard for help, and Bernard refused. He then asked the pope to order Bernard to preach a Crusade. The pope gave the order, and Bernard preached, with spectacular results. But things went wrong from the start. The various rulers leading the movement were distrustful of one another and not disposed to work together. Of the soldiers who set out (contemporary estimates vary from 100,000 to 1,500,000), most died of disease and starvation before reaching their goal, and most of the remainder were killed or captured soon after their arrival. The impact on Bernard was devastating, and so was the impact on Europe. In the meantime, however, Bernard had also launched the new military order of the Knights Templars.

In 1153, Bernard journeyed to reconcile the warring provinces Metz and Lorraine. He persuaded them to peace and to an agreement drawn up under his mediation, and then, in failing health, returned home to die.

In his book On Consideration (De Consideratione), dedicated to his disciple, Eugene III, the first Cistercian Pope, Bernard wrote of the need for spiritual authorities to balance prayer with action, and of the various temptations they would face.

Elected pope in the wake of Lucius II's dramatic death, Eugene immediately fled Rome for the imperial abbey of Farfa. While there, he learned that Edessa and various other Crusader strongholds had fallen to the Muslims. Eugene called for the Second Crusade, which St. Bernard preached all over Europe. At the same time, Arnold of Brescia took over leadership of the Roman Senate's revolution and proclaimed the city's Second Republic. Arnold, a monk who had studied under Abelard in Paris, had refused to recant when his master did and had been in fact sent to Rome as a penance by Eugene. But once there he rapidly assumed the headship of the revolutionaries.

From Farfa, Eugene went to France for a warm reception by Louis VII. Germany was his next call, where Emperor Conrad von Hohenstaufen (at last upon the imperial throne) was also happy to see him. The pope convened synods at Paris in 1146, and Trier, Rheims, and Cremona in 1147, to combat clerical corruption. Making an alliance with King Roger of Sicily, he briefly retook Rome in 1149; he would return for good in 1152.

The last major act of his life was to sign a treaty on January 23, 1153 with Frederick I, Conrad's son, binding the empire to protect the papacy. Dying at Tivoli on July 8 of that year, he was beatified on September 28, 1872. His feast is July 8 at Arezzo, July 21 at Rome.

## Anastasius IV
### (July 12, 1153–December 3, 1154)

During his pontificate the Pantheon was restored. Anastasius also gave special privileges to the Knights Hospitallers (now the Knights of Malta). He was much concerned with German affairs, particularly the activities of Frederick I (Barbarossa). Among other things, he wrote a treatise on the Trinity.

## Adrian IV
### (1154–1159)

Nicholas Breakspear was born at Abbot's Langley, near St. Albans, in 1100. Of a humble family, he had held various jobs (including shepherd) in his youth. But he had a taste for learning, and so he became a traveling scholar, a not uncommon occupation in the learning-loving Middle Ages. Nicholas's studies took him to Arles in southern France, then a center for learning. While on vacation, he visited the Augustinian monastery of St. Rufus, near Avignon. Feeling called, he enrolled as a canon. His qualities of learning led to his eventual election as abbot.

Visiting Rome on his monastery's business, he met Bl. Eugenius III, who was as impressed with him as his brother had been. Eugenius commanded Adrian to stay in the Eternal City as part of the papal court and in 1146 made him cardinal-bishop of Albano. In 1152, Eugenius sent him to Scandinavia as papal legate, to reform and reorganize the Church in that area, which up until now had been under the archdiocese of Hamburg. Apart from ending various abuses and quarrels in Norway and Sweden, he made Trondheim, whose cathedral held the relics of St. Olaf (converter of the nation), the primatial See of that country.

Returning to Rome, he was called "the Apostle of the North." When Anastasius IV died soon after, Nicholas was unanimously elected pope and took the name Adrian. His problems were manifold. King Frederick of Germany, while professing love of the papacy, apparently was somewhat inspired by the memory of the emperors Henry IV and Henry V. William of Sicily was in

open enmity and keen on seizing more land. The Roman republicans under Arnold of Brescia were in control of Rome, and the robber barons of the Campagna were plundering where they could. Matters came to a head when Cardinal Gerardus was murdered while walking down the street one day.

Adrian put the city under interdict and moved to Viterbo. He forbade any liturgical services to be held in Rome until the following Wednesday of Holy Week. At that time, the Senators, clergy, and people of Rome made submission and welcomed Adrian back. Arnold fled to some of the barons of the Campagna and stayed with them until they betrayed him and turned him over to the pope. Adrian was at last in full charge of the Eternal City.

At this juncture, Frederick came down to Italy for his coronations as king of Italy and as emperor. Reception of the Iron Crown at Pavia went without incident, despite the building opposition to him on the part of the northern Italian cities (who formed the Lombard League to limit the king's power). The next traditional event in the royal tour was the customary meeting with the pope at Sutri. This occurred on June 9, 1155.

The prescribed ritual required that the emperor-elect should step forward and hold the Pontiff's stirrup. After the pope dismounted, the monarch would guide him to a silver chair, then prostrate himself and kiss the pope's slipper. Once that was accomplished, the pontiff would bestow on the sovereign the kiss of peace on the cheek. (In an age when symbolism was essential to hierarchical relationships, every slight move on such occasions was fraught with meaning.)

Thus, when Frederick refused to hold Adrian's stirrup, it was held to be both a personal insult and an affront to the papal office. The pope proceeded to the chair and allowed Frederick to kiss his foot, but he refused to grant the kiss of peace in reprisal. The implied threat was that imperial coronation would also be withheld if Frederick did not comply with the traditional rites of homage. The king relented and met the pope again at Nepi two days later. There he complied with established form, and so was duly crowned at St. Peter's taking the usual oaths to defend the pope.

While these festivities were occurring, however, the republicans, who had control of the old city within the walls, seized the bridge to the Leonine city from its guard of imperial troops. The two sides fought late into the night, and while Frederick's troops regained the bridge, the city proper was shut tight against them. Bereft of provisions from that quarter, and the crown settled firmly on his head, Frederick made ready to leave for points north. Parting from the pope at Tivoli, the emperor left Adrian to deal with the Normans on his own.

Though the Western emperor had deserted the pope, the Eastern one came to his aid. Manuel I Comnenus was, like Basil II and Justinian I, consumed with the idea of restoring the Eastern empire to its lost greatness. To that end, he at times collaborated and at times fought with the Latin Cru-

saders in Syria; he drove the pirates from the Aegean; he reestablished a toehold in southern Italy; and above all, he allied with the papacy. Although this alliance did not bring about the reunion that both the pope and the emperor craved (the Byzantine populace was too angry about the intrusion of Latin patriarchs at Antioch and Jerusalem for that), it did provide a counterbalance to the Norman William of Sicily, who saw in Frederick's departure an opportunity for conquest.

In February 1154, William I had followed his father on the throne of the Two Sicilies. When Adrian refused to recognize him as king, this rather annoyed William, who besieged Benevento, a papal fief in the south. Neither this action nor their ravaging of the southern Campagna led to any real result, and, after Frederick left, Adrian gathered his vassals and soldiers to go on the warpath. They arrived at Benevento, where Adrian would stay until June of 1156.

It was while encamped here that Adrian performed the most influential act of his career—at least the one with the longest lasting effect. Ireland was at this time considered to be both an imperial and a papal fief. Although there was a high king at Tara, his actual control was restricted to Meath. The four provinces each had their own kings—Leinster of the MacMurrogh-Kavanaghs; Ulster of the O'Neills; Munster of the O'Briens; and Connaught of the O'Conors. Each of these was in turn divided into ever smaller kingdoms and subkingdoms.

Although this system had worked well for centuries, by the twelfth century it had broken down into endemic warfare. The usual evils for the Church in such periods had arisen, and Adrian sought some method of imposing order in this mess. Making King Henry II of England "lord" of Ireland seemed like a good way to bring peace to the turbulent Irish. So Adrian donated Ireland to Henry. It resulted in an invasion of Ireland by the Anglo-Normans and the beginning of the troubles that continue to this day. (The Orangemen may take comfort from the fact that however anti-papal they may be, they owe their position to a pope—something their Catholic opponents might reflect upon as well.)

However exciting the Donation of Adrian might have been later and elsewhere, it did not affect the situation with the Normans one bit. What did was William's capture of Brindisi from the Byzantines. There he garnered weaponry, gold intended for the pope, and many Greek captives—a few of whom he ransomed, but most of whom he sold as slaves to the Muslims. The pope immediately made terms, granting William the title of king, as well as the lands he already held, including the Mark of Ancona, and certain other northern places. In return, William swore to be the pope's liege man, to pay him an annual tribute, and to defend him. Adrian then repaired to Viterbo, where he cut a deal with the Romans and returned to the city early in 1157.

This turn of events deeply displeased Frederick, however, as some of the

lands William occupied were imperial fiefs. Other annoyances included Frederick's wish to regain the right of lay investiture. Conflict broke out between the pope and the emperor, with the Lombard League, anxious to rule themselves, allied with Adrian. The pope proceeded to Anagni to direct operations, but death claimed him before hostilities could break out.

## Alexander III

### (September 7, 1159–August 3, 1181)

Orlando Bandinelli was born to a noble family in Siena. After his ordination he became a canon lawyer at Bologna, which was in the process of developing into the first great European university. His abilities in this field attracted the attention of Eugene III, who summoned him to Rome in 1150. The pope soon appointed him cardinal, then chancellor of the Roman Church.

Orlando was Adrian IV's most trusted adviser, and the leader of the "independence" party among the cardinals, who wanted to free the papacy from imperial influence through the Norman alliance. At the Diet of Besançon in 1157, Cardinal Orlando told Frederick that the imperial crown was a mere privilege granted by the pope. Otto von Wittelsbach, a nobleman who became Orlando's lifelong foe, would have split him with a battle-axe on the spot had the emperor not prevented it.

Wanting a friendly pope the next time the position should open up, Frederick sent Otto and archbishop-elect of Cologne Rainald von Dassel (whose election Adrian IV would not confirm) to secure as many votes among the cardinals as possible. In the event, nineteen cardinals voted for Orlando, who took the name Alexander, and only three for Cardinal Octavian, the imperial candidate. Nevertheless, those three cardinals declared that Octavian had won, and he duly took the name Victor IV. A mob hired by Otto then chased Alexander and his friends out of the city.

They retreated toward the Norman south, and the ceremony of consecration was performed at Nympha, a little Volscian town, on September 20. Rome was no more secure for Victor either, and so he was consecrated at the imperial abbey of Farfa on October 4.

Frederick had a bit of a problem, because it was his representatives who had engineered the difficulty. He summoned both Alexander and Victor to a Diet at Pavia, where he would supposedly render impartial judgment. But as the emperor from the beginning addressed Victor as pope and Alexander as

Cardinal Orlando, it was obvious what Frederick's conclusion would be. On February 11, 1160, he duly found for Victor. In response, Alexander excommunicated him and released his subjects from their obedience.

Within two years, Alexander was forced to find refuge in France, where he would stay until 1165. While there he dealt with the murder of St. Thomas à Becket at the request of King Henry II. Frederick, in the meantime, in addition to papal forces and the Normans, also had to deal with rebellious German nobles and the Lombard League. The schism wound on, until Frederick was defeated and captured by the Lombard League at Legnano in 1176. Peace was concluded at last between pope and emperor at Venice the following year.

Alexander convened the Council of Lateran III in 1179. Among its many decrees was one limiting the vote for pope to two-thirds or more of the College of Cardinals. Alexander also encouraged the growth of the new university movement, whereby scholars would concentrate with teachers in a given town, rather than wandering about as formerly. This too would have a great effect in later years. Additionally in 1179, he approved the foundation of Westminster School, which remains a leading secondary school in England.

Worn out by his years and work, Alexander died at Civita Castellana.

## *Victor IV*

*Anti-Pope (September 7, 1159–April 24, 1164)*

Octavian was born in Rome to the family of the Counts of Tusculum and was appointed cardinal of Sant Cecilia in 1138. He was very popular for his free and easy manner and generosity, and in addition was a great friend to the emperor. As noted previously, he came to take the name Victor IV, as anti-pope.

Despite Imperial patronage, Victor was never recognized by all the Germans, and France, England, Spain, Hungary, Norway, and Ireland all came out for Alexander. Victor died at Lucca on April 2, 1164.

## *Paschal III*

*Anti-Pope (April 22, 1164–September 20, 1168)*

Guido of Crema was elected to succeed Victor IV as Frederick's pet pope. Rainald von Dassel, imperial vicar in Italy, secured Paschal's election. His only major action was to canonize Charlemagne in 1165. (Though this action was never ratified by an authentic pope, later pontiffs have treated the great emperor as a Blessed.) Paschal was enthroned in Rome when the city fell to Frederick, and he crowned his master emperor a second time in August of 1167. Paschal fled with Frederick from Rome the next year when the plague decimated the imperial army.

## Lucius III

(September 1, 1181–November 25, 1185)

Ubaldo Allucungoli was born in Lucca. Innocent II made him a cardinal and sent him as legate to France. Eugene III sent him as legate to Sicily, and Ubaldo negotiated the 1177 treaty at Venice between Emperor Frederick and Alexander III.

Ubaldo was elected pope at Velletri and consecrated on September 6, taking the name Lucius. The new pope went to Rome in November, but the republicans there made life so unpleasant that he returned to Velletri in March 1182. After reconciling the king of Scotland and touring his domains, he tried again to return to Rome, but conditions there had not improved and Lucius left again in late 1183.

Spending a short time in southern Italy and at Bologna, he arrived at Verona in July of 1184. There, with Emperor Frederick (with whom he had a strained but formal relationship) he convened a synod in October and November, condemning the resurgent Manichaean heresy, which, under the mane of Catharism, had begun to spread among the common folk while their clerical and noble betters squabbled. The emperor pledged to leave on Crusade, but the pope never left Verona. Moreover, he would not crown Henry, Frederick's son, as king to secure his succession.

Relations between pope and emperor became strained when Constance, heiress to the Norman kingdom of the Two Sicilies, arrived in August of 1185, becoming betrothed to Henry. The independence of the papacy had

been maintained by playing the Normans against the emperors; this betrothal threatened to ruin this policy completely. Lucius could not be expected to be pleased at the forthcoming nuptials.

## Urban III
### (November 25, 1185–October 19, 1187)

Uberto Crivelli, a nobleman of Milan, became cardinal under Lucius III in 1182, and archbishop of Milan three years later. The Crivellis had suffered horribly at Frederick's hands when the emperor took Milan in 1162; a number of Uberto's relations were tortured and mutilated by imperial troops.

When Lucius died, Uberto was elected the same day and crowned on December 1, taking the name Urban. The speed with which the cardinals acted was intended to prevent any attempt by the emperor to interfere with the proceedings. Given both his prior history with Frederick and the impending union between the Hohenstaufens and the Normans of Sicily, Urban inherited and amplified the papal side of the feud with the empire.

On January 4, 1186, Constance and Henry were married. Thus ended the papal strategy that had been followed since St. Gregory VII's time; what would replace it remained to be seen. Moreover, the estates of the countess Matilda, which had been left to the papacy, were also claimed by the emperor. Because control of these estates meant control of much of Tuscany and the Po Valley, it was a fertile ground for conflict.

Open struggle commenced when, in response to Urban's continuing refusal to crown Henry as king of Italy, Frederick persuaded the patriarch of Aquileia to do so. The coronation belonged by right to the archbishop of Milan to perform, and, since Urban had held on to his archdiocese after his election, Urban declared the patriarch's action an attack on his own prerogatives. The pope's next move was to excommunicate the patriarch and all the clergy who had assisted at the coronation.

Urban then went on the offensive. When the archdiocese of Trier became vacant, Folmar won the majority of votes of the canons, but the emperor favored Rudolf, who had won the minority. Frederick invested him with the temporalities of the archdiocese and secured the promise of Urban to confirm him as archbishop. In reprisal for the coronation, however, Urban broke his promise, and on May 31, 1187, made Folmar a cardinal. The next day, he

confirmed him as archbishop. In reprisal, Frederick closed the Alpine passes to papal messengers and sent Henry to attack Italy.

At this point, the German bishops were meeting at the Diet of Gelnhausen. Urban hoped that they would endorse his action; instead, they refused to hear the papal legate and voted in favor of the emperor, calling on the pope to "do justice to him." In response, Urban summoned Frederick to appear before him at Verona. To prevent the pope from excommunicating their sovereign, the Veronese rose up against him—Urban fled the city. Realizing that he would be safe there, Urban set out for Venice, where he would be able to excommunicate Frederick in peace. He died on the way, at Ferrara, after receiving news of the defeat of the Crusaders at Hattin.

Urban's short pontificate was far from completely unsuccessful, however. To support the war against the Muslims, he strove to maintain peace between the kings of Europe; his effort was partly rewarded on June 23, 1187. At Chateauroux on that date, the armies of the French and English kings were drawn up and ready for what promised to be a bloody battle. At Urban's instructions, the papal legates confronted the two rulers and declared that they both would be excommunicated. The kings desisted, and agreed to a two-year truce.

## Gregory VIII

### (October 21–December 17, 1187)

While Urban III and Frederick I were quarreling, events had been unfolding in the Holy Land. On July 4, 1187, Saladin, leader of the Muslims, had decimated the Crusaders at Hattin. By October 3, he had retaken Jerusalem for Islam. All the petty squabbles of Christendom, for the moment, receded into the background as Christendom became aware of the great setback it had sustained. (It was a moment not unlike, for the people of that time, Pearl Harbor or September 11, 2001.)

At Ferrara on the day after Urban's death, the cardinals elected Cardinal Alberto, who took the name of Gregory. A native of Benevento, the new pope had been a monk and was made a cardinal in 1155 by Adrian IV. Alexander III made him chancellor in 1172. That pope had sent him to England to investigate the murder of St. Thomas à Becket and to Portugal to crown, on his behalf, King Affonso II.

No sooner was he in office than Gregory sent a letter to Frederick to heal

the quarrel between papacy and empire, in the light of the common menace. He sent letters to all the kings, princes, and city-states of Christendom to make peace between themselves to prepare for a Third Crusade. Because the conflict between Pisa and Genoa was particularly fierce, he personally made his way to the former city to impose a settlement. He died, however, and was buried with full honors in the cathedral of Pisa.

## Clement III
### (December 19, 1187–March 27, 1191)

Paolo Scolari was born in Rome, and was cardinal-bishop of Palestrina at Gregory VII's death. As the first Roman elected since Arnold of Brescia's time, his accession was greeted with joy by his fellow citizens. In February 1188, after a treaty was signed between them, he reentered the Eternal City and was solemnly enthroned at the Lateran.

His most immediate interest was the organizing of the Third Crusade. Emperor Frederick, Philip Augustus of France, and Richard the Lion-Hearted of England all set off for Palestine, the first by land via Turkey, the last two by sea to Acre. In their wake, thousands of Europeans of every degree followed.

In more strictly ecclesiastical questions, Gregory ended the Trier dispute amicably and separated the Church in Scotland from the archdiocese of York, placing Scotland directly under the Holy See.

New troubles now arose. William II of the Two Sicilies died, leaving his daughter Constance as his only heir. Henry VI, left in charge while his father went off on Crusade, claimed the throne. But the idea of having the Hohenstaufens both on the imperial and the Sicilian thrones was too much for both the pope and Henry's putative suspects. An illegitimate member of the house of Guiscard, Tancredo of Lace, was elevated to the kingship by popular acclaim. Gregory duly crowned him. Yet, at the same time, news came of Frederick's drowning on the way to Palestine. Henry VI was now king instead of regent and marched into Italy to claim both kingships. But Gregory died before having to deal with the problem, while prospects for success on the Crusade were still bright.

# Celestine III
## (March 30, 1191–January 8, 1198)

Giacinto Bobone was Roman, and a member of the noble family of the Orsini. Elected at age eighty-five, he had been a cardinal for forty-seven years. As a deacon, he was ordained to the priesthood on Holy Saturday, April 13, and consecrated the next day. On Easter Monday he anointed Henry VI (who had arrived in Rome) as emperor, and Constance as empress. This was permitted by the Roman populace, however, only on Henry's agreeing to destroy the nearby town of Tusculum for them, which he did. Celestine professed himself neutral in the struggle between Henry and Tancred, and the emperor set off to claim his wife's kingdom. Tancred, however, defeated Henry and drove him out of the south, taking his cousin the empress prisoner. He later released her on Celestine's request.

Back in Germany, Henry proved himself a cruel ruler and abusive to the churches. Celestine tolerated this; moreover, when, in 1192 Henry had Archduke Leopold von Babenberg of Austria take Richard the Lion-Hearted prisoner and hold him for ransom, the pope again did nothing. This was a particularly egregious act, because returning Crusaders were protected from molestation under pain of excommunication. This imprisonment led Richard's favorite minstrel, Blondel, to look for him (as immortalized in Gore Vidal's book, A Search for the King). Finally, Richard was released after the archduke was paid a large ransom. In 1193, Celestine was able to secure the return of the money, after which he excommunicated Leopold.

Meanwhile, the pope did show more energy in defending the marriage bond: He persuaded Alfonso IX of Leon to abandon his plan to marry his niece, a Portuguese princess, and he refused to grant a divorce to Philip Augustus, quashing the one granted by the French bishops. Celestine granted many privileges to the Templars and the Hospitallers, while granting a charter to the new Teutonic Knights, all in hopes of stimulating a new Crusade.

It was that very end that led him to treat Henry with kid gloves, because the Holy Roman Emperor was by right the proper leader for such a Crusade. In the face of many promises for such action from Henry, he tolerated his return to Italy to claim the crown after Tancred died in 1194. For that reason also, Celestine recognized Henry's infant son, Frederick, as his heir to both the empire and the Sicilies. The emperor was more concerned, however, with practicing atrocities on Christian lands than on Muslim. Where his temperament would have taken him in his relationship with the papacy is anyone's guess, but Henry died on September 28, 1197, at age thirty-six. The much older Celestine departed a few months later, having urged the cardinals to elect Giovanni di Colonna as his successor.

# HEIGHTS AND DEPTHS

## Innocent III

### (January 8, 1198–June 16, 1216)

Lotario de Conti was born at Anagni in 1160, the son of Count Trasimund of Segni and nephew of Clement III. Studying at Rome, Bologna, and Paris, he soon acquired a reputation as one of the greatest jurists and scholars of his day. He returned to Rome in 1180 and held a number of offices under the pontiffs following Alexander III, eventually being made cardinal. Because Celestine III's family was opposed to Lotario's, he spent the years under Celestine in retirement at Anagni in study and meditation.

Lotario was elected pope the very day of Celestine's death, and he took the name of Innocent. At the time, no successor to the imperial throne had been chosen. Innocent used the interregnum to secure the Papal States and to reassert his suzerainty over Tuscany and elsewhere. Queen Constance of Sicily died shortly after Innocent became Pope, but she had chosen him guardian for young Frederick II. Innocent defended the young king and maintained his rule over the Two Sicilies. To safeguard the young ruler further, he arranged his marriage to the daughter of the king of Hungary.

Meanwhile, in Germany, two parties had emerged, each of whom held their own Imperial election. The Ghibellines declared Philip of Swabia the new emperor, while the Guelphs declared the winner to be Otto IV, of the House of Brunswick. Civil war would be the inevitable result. Innocent III bent all his efforts to prevent this, but with little success. He attempted to be an "honest broker" between the two sides, but this turned out to be impossible. Philip's adherents accused him of favoring Otto IV, which became a self-fulfilling prophecy, and the pope declared for Otto in 1201. In May of the next year, Innocent issued a decree whereby he declared that the imperial coronation by the pope gave the pontiff the right to rule upon the suitability of the candidate, because he obviously could not crown a heretic or reprobate in good conscience. In the case of disputed or double elections, like the one currently tearing the empire apart, it was up to the pope to decide the proper candidate—basing his judgment on the qualities of the candidates, not the legality of the election.

Initially, most of the German princes sided with Otto, and so accepted Innocent's decree. But the irritable Otto had a great talent for annoying people, and managed, by 1203, to alienate most of his supporters and drive them into Philip's camp. The pope himself reversed sides and declared for Philip in 1207. Unfortunately for Innocent, however, his new imperial ally was murdered the following year, and the situation in Germany changed completely.

On November 11, all the German princes acknowledged Otto as the rightful king of Germany and the Romans. Innocent agreed to give him the imperial coronation, and did so at Rome on October 4, 1209. Otto promised to guarantee the possession of the Marches and Umbria to the Papal States, as well as to safeguard papal suzerainty over Sicily, uphold the spiritual and temporal privileges of the clergy, and help stamp out heresy. But no sooner was he crowned and anointed, than he set about breaking these promises.

After taking Umbria and the Marches, and giving them to friends, he set out to conquer Sicily from young Frederick. In response, Innocent excommunicated Otto on March 31, 1211, and began negotiating with Philip Augustus of France and the German princes for his deposition. In September of 1211, the princes gathered at the Diet of Nurnberg, renounced Otto, and elected Frederick II in his place. They repeated this action on December 2, 1212, at the Diet of Frankfort in front of a papal legate and Philip Augustus of France. What makes the French king's participation in this process so important is that he appears, as the "other successor of Charlemagne," in some sense a guardian of the imperial office. Two years later, when Otto IV invaded France, Philippe defeated him at Bouvines, a battle that is often seen as a definitive separation of France from the empire. But was it seen as such at the time? Did Philip see his victory as one for French independence, or for imperial legitimacy, of which, as foremost king of Europe, and successor of Charlemagne, he was a protector? Despite frequent assertions of complete French independence from the Holy Empire, in 1515 Francis I ran for the imperial leadership against Charles V and Henry VIII. An interesting set of circumstances, in the light of later history. In any case, Frederick II was crowned king at Aachen in 1215; three years later, Otto IV, who had lost all following outside his own estates, died, leaving Innocent's young protégé unchallenged. In return for his coronation, Frederick both renewed all of Otto's promises to Innocent and added one that he would never unite the imperial and Sicilian thrones.

Innocent acted in the affairs of many nations: in France, he compelled Philip Augustus to return to his wife; in England, he forced King John to give up the money and privileges he had taken from the Church, and to give England over and receive it back as a papal fief. The pope intervened in various disputes in Hungary, Leon, Portugal, and Aragon (whose king he crowned at Rome), Norway, Sweden, and Poland. Moreover, he preached a Crusade against the Spanish Muslims, which in 1212 broke their power at the battle of

Navas de Tolosa. In a nutshell, Innocent functioned as if he were as much an emperor as a pope.

But his greatest interest was the healing of the Eastern schism and the recovery of the Holy Land. To that end, a fourth Crusade was gathered in 1203 and launched against the East. It was financed by the Venetians, who ordered the Crusaders to attack Constantinople. The politics surrounding the three imperial claimants there were truly Byzantine. The final result was the sacking of the imperial city by the Crusaders on April 12, 1204. This was, to be sure, a horrible sacrilege, and one that the Greeks have never forgiven (though they do tend to forget such things on their own part vis-à-vis the Latins). What is also forgotten is that Innocent excommunicated the leaders of the Crusade when he received the news.

Baldwin of Flanders was made Latin emperor of Constantinople, and a Latin patriarch appointed. In the end, Innocent decided to make the best of a bad job and to recognize the new order in the East. Meanwhile, Byzantine princes fled to Nicaea, Trebizond, and Epirus, setting up successor states that nursed bitter hatred toward the Latins. One unexpected benefit was that, since the new regime at Constantinople was perpetually in need of funds, they often paid back loans with relics from the imperial chapel. Thus, such irreplaceable things as the Crown of Thorns found their way to such collections as the Hofburg in Vienna, the treasury of St. Mark's at Venice, the Welf treasury at Brunswick, and the Sainte-Chapelle in Paris. (Much as Christians should decry the method in which this transportation occurred, they should be grateful these relics were not present when Constantinople fell to the Turks.)

In any case, there was call for Crusades closer to home than Spain or Palestine. In the south of France, the Albigenses, the local manifestation of the Cathari, had become ensconced. There is a present-day tendency to romanticize these folk, to see them as stern old Protestant fathers, bravely defending themselves and their loved ones against the evil Catholics. Others see them as martyrs to free thought, or New Age–style love-folk. In point of fact, they were rather different from either of these. Being dualists, they held that matter was irredeemably evil, created by an evil god—the Church that worshiped this creator, and purported to bestow His grace via the Sacraments through the same matter that imprisons the spirit, was as evil as her lord. So too were the governments and lordships that claimed legitimacy from her.

By contrast, the good god, who had created spirit, was the object of the Albigense worship. The ideal Albigense was a vegetarian, did not drink wine, was celibate, and avoided wealth; those who followed this regimen were called the "Perfect." As might be guessed from all the political history reported to this point, many of the Catholic clergy at this time were far from edifying. The contrast between their lives and those of the Perfect was striking, to say the least.

The majority of Albigenses, however, could not be and were not expected to live up to the lifestyle of the Perfect. These "Believers" were considered imprisoned by their flesh and doomed to a life of excess, which was not really their fault. The one thing that was considered sinful for them was procreation, so homosexuality and infanticide were extremely common among them. It was held that only those who were among the perfect could be saved, so often a dying believer was initiated into their ranks. If he recovered, he very often committed suicide—a practice that was encouraged among the Perfecti as well, as the ultimate insult to the evil creator.

As might be expected, these traits endeared the Albigense to neither Church nor state; indeed, they were seen as clear and present dangers to both. In the first year of his pontificate, Innocent sent missionaries and papal legates to try to convert the Albigenses peacefully, to little effect. In 1208, the missionaries were abused by their hearers, and the legate, Peter of Castenau, was murdered. The pope resolved to rely on the secular arm. He excommunicated Count Raymond of Toulouse, whom he suspected of instigating Castelnau's death, and called the Knights of Europe to Crusade against the Albigenses. Led by Simon de Montfort, the knights conducted a bloody, but at the last, victorious, struggle against them. (Today, in books and movies, the Albigenses are often portrayed as heroes, possibly because their values are not uncommon in current society. But few folk whose values contradict their society's completely are allowed to live in peace in any age—even our own, as the Branch Davidians might tell us if they could.)

On November 15, 1215, Innocent opened the Council of Lateran IV. Apart from a number of sorely needed disciplinary decrees and a call for a new Crusade, the Council Fathers issued a new creed, in the face of the challenges posed by the Albigenses and others. Among other articles of Faith promulgated by the Council, there was one that has caused much controversy since the nineteenth century—"There is but one universal Church of the faithful, outside of which no one at all can be saved." Another section of the Creed described the process at Mass that changes the bread and wine to the Body and Blood of Jesus as "Transubstantiation." This word was coined by the Neo-Platonist philosopher, Hildebert of Lavardin, and was considered to best explain what the Church had always taught on the subject. The word's definition is simply that the actual substance of the thing changes, while the outward appearance remains the same. The canonization of this term is perhaps the greatest remaining legacy of Innocent's pontificate.

But there are others. Innocent was all too aware of the decline in the quality and apostolic character of the clergy of his time. On several nights, he dreamed of a bearded man in a brown robe who was holding up the tottering structure of St. John Lateran (then the symbol of the Church as St. Peter's is today). The pope later recognized the man in his dream as a supplicant who wanted him to approve his idea for a new and different kind of order. The

man was St. Francis, and the order, of course, the Franciscans. Innocent approved both, as he did St. Dominic and his Dominicans. These mendicant friars, as they were called, would combine living off the free offerings of the faithful with a total devotion to evangelization—the Franciscans maintaining a special devotion to poverty, and the Dominicans to skilled preaching. Together, they would do far more to return the people of southern France and elsewhere to the Faith than could de Montfort and his armies. The contributions of both orders to the Church in later years—both in safeguarding orthodoxy and in spreading the Faith in non-Catholic lands—is incalculable. Innocent gave his approval to another still-existing order as well—the Trinitarians. Originally, they raised money to pay ransoms for Christians kidnaped by the Muslims and sold into slavery; the Trinitarians also substituted themselves for those so captured.

In 1209, Innocent authorized the sending of missionaries to still-pagan Prussia (in time this would lead to the Christianization of Lithuania, Latvia, and Estonia as well).

But perhaps the greatest gift he left the world in general is the institution of the modern hospital, of which he founded the first, Santo Spirito, in Rome. The notion of putting a number of doctors under one roof, with the poor paying little or nothing for their services, was quite revolutionary at the time.

Innocent practiced what he preached. After Lateran IV, he traveled about preaching the Crusade the Council had ordered. It was on one such trip in Perugia that the pope fell ill and died. He was buried in the cathedral there, until Leo XIII, who admired him a great deal, brought him to St. Peter's in 1891.

## Honorius III
### (July 18, 1216–March 18, 1227)

Cencio Savelli was born in Rome to a noble family. Celestine III made him a cardinal-deacon in 1193, and Innocent III made him both a cardinal-priest and tutor to Frederick II. His election was unusual in that, owing to the highly divided status of the College of Cardinals at that point, the method of compromise was used—two members were elected by the others with the authority to select a pope. The pair's choice fell on Cencio, who took the name Honorius. The Romans were very pleased that one of their own had again been elected. Honorius was consecrated at Perugia on July 24, crowned at

St. Peter's on August 31, and took possession of the Lateran on September 3.

Honorius's two great goals were the moral reformation of the Church and the prosecution of a Crusade. Unlike Innocent, who thundered and commanded, Honorius hoped to bring these ends about through kindness and gentleness. His initial call for a Crusade was well heeded—a fortune in money was gathered, and thousands signed up. But the fortune was not large enough, and many of the volunteers simply would not make good soldiers—something often not realized until they arrived in foreign ports. Nothing would do except that Frederick II, as Holy Roman Emperor, should himself lead the faithful into combat against the Muslims.

While Otto IV was still lurking about, Honorius did not expect Frederick to go on Crusade, but after his foe died, the pressure began to mount. In the meantime, the ever-fickle Romans rebelled against the rule of Honorius (although he was one of their own), and he was forced to flee in June of 1219. Fortunately for the pontiff, Frederick came down in 1220 to receive the imperial coronation on November 22. Their mood having changed, the Romans welcomed Honorius back in time to perform the ceremony.

But Frederick kept getting extensions on his oath to go on Crusade. In an effort to bring him around, Honorius approved the election of Frederick's son Henry as king of the Romans—this practically institutionalized the union between the empire and the Two Sicilies, which pontiff after pontiff had tried to prevent. But all to no avail. Frederick further interfered with Episcopal appointments in Apulia and trespassed on papal prerogatives here and there. Honorius went to his grave without an open break with the emperor, though one seemed to be forthcoming.

Another part of Honorius's program for the Crusade was establishing peace between all the European powers. He mediated between Pisa and Genoa, Milan and Cremona, and Bologna and Pistoia. In England he safeguarded the rights of the minor Henry III against the nobles who wanted to control the young prince. And he intervened in the interests of justice and public order in virtually every country in western Christendom. In addition, he encouraged the evangelization of Prussia. Honorius granted privileges to the universities of Paris and Bologna, canonized a number of saints, and wrote a great deal. If he did not accomplish the second of his two goals, he went very far toward the first.

# Gregory IX

## (March 19, 1227–August 22, 1241)

Ugolino, count of Segni, was born at Anagni in 1145. A nephew of Innocent III, he held several offices and was at last made a cardinal in 1198. In May 1206, he was made cardinal-bishop of Ostia and Velletri. As papal legate to Germany, Ugolino managed to construct several truces between battling imperial candidates. In January 1217, Honorius III made him legate for Tuscany, in which capacity he made peace between Genoa and Pisa. Frederick II received the Cross (in token of his promise to go on Crusade) from Ugolino at his coronation in Rome, and the next year Honorius commissioned Ugolino to travel through Italy preaching the Crusade—which, alas, did not occur.

At Honorius's death, it was at first decided that three cardinals should choose the next pontiff, under the mode of "compromise." Ugolino and Conrad of Urach were among the three selected to decide, but because Ugolino and the other cardinal chose Conrad, he refused the honor, fearing it would be thought that he had voted for himself. A standard conclave was then held, and Ugolino was elected: he took the name Gregory.

As an experienced diplomat, Gregory did not trust the wily Frederick II to fulfill his promise to lead the Crusade. Three days after his election, the pope demanded that the emperor keep his promise that was delayed so long. Frederick set sail on September 8, 1227, but returned three days later, pleading illness. On September 29, Gregory excommunicated him.

Both emperor and pope sought to justify their actions to the princes of Europe, but a Roman mob, led by the Frangipani, drove the pope from the city. Gregory fled, first to Viterbo and then to Perugia. Moreover, most of the German princes and bishops refused to recognize the excommunication of Frederick. To solidify his position, the emperor at long last departed on the Crusade in June of 1228. Once there, he acknowledged the justice of the pope's excommunication. After regaining Jerusalem for the Christians, he reembarked and arrived in Italy in June of 1229.

Frederick defeated the papal troops who were attempting to seize Sicily; after this victory, however, pope and emperor spent the summer of 1230 reconciling. Their visions of church and empire were, in the final analysis, irreconcilable. For Frederick, the empire's control over Germany and Italy was to be complete and absolute—to this end, he began suppressing the local liberties of the Italian cities he controlled. For Gregory, however, the empire was simply one of the powers among which the Church must work—and none of

whom must be allowed to be supreme in Italy, lest the independence of the Church suffer. So the pope supported the cities of Lombardy, Tuscany, and Umbria in their efforts to league against Frederick and secure their own independence. One immediate by-product of the reconciliation, however, had been Gregory's return to Rome in February of 1230.

Tensions in the peninsula between the Italian cities and the emperor rose. At first Frederick would submit disputes between the two parties to the pope for mediation, then his resentment of the pope's partiality toward the Italian cities led the emperor to stop doing so. In the end, open war broke out between Frederick and the cities, and he trounced the army of the Lombard League on November 27, 1237, at Cortenuova. As Gregory tried to reorganize the resistance more or less openly, Frederick announced his intention of uniting all of Italy—including the Papal States—to the empire. In response, on March 20, 1239, Gregory excommunicated the emperor and ordered a Crusade preached against Frederick. Again, most of the Germans ignored this measure, and the Crusade never materialized.

Frederick then declared his intention of seizing the Papal States, and accordingly marched with his army. In response, Gregory called a General Council at Rome, which was to open on Easter Sunday, 1241. Frederick prevented the bishops' attendance. He then marched on Rome, but before his arrival the old pope died.

Gregory IX was a remarkable man. A close friend of SS. Francis and Dominic, he patronized their orders and canonized both of them as well as St. Anthony of Padua (and Lisbon). Among other orders, he approved the Mercedarians, who, like the Trinitarians, were given up to trading themselves for Muslim prisoners. Gregory gave privileges to the universities of Toulouse and Paris in 1231 (thus endorsing Philip Augustus's formal foundation of the latter in 1200) and enacted a curriculum for parish schools—the world's first for primary education.

On a harsher front, in 1231, due to the growth of Manichaeanism in Italy and elsewhere, Gregory decreed that heretics might, if unrepentant, be handed over to the secular authorities for punishment. Heresy, it must be understood, was considered as treason to the state. It is interesting that Frederick, who has been most popular among modern historians for his problems with the papacy and his alleged tolerance, was one of the most zealous persecutors of heresy.

Gregory is looked upon as the originator of the Inquisition—or at least of the Roman one (we will look at the Spanish example later). (To understand the medieval horror of heresy, it would be well to remember that our ancestors looked at heretics as we look at Nazis. Even as we spare no expense to root them out, no matter how aged, because we see them as a threat, so it was with heresy, five and more centuries ago.)

In time, the Inquisition would be staffed with Dominicans and Franciscans; its scope included both transgressions against Faith and against morals—indeed, more were turned over to be executed for bestiality than for heresy. Because its procedures were so standardized, with many protections for the accused, people would strive to be tried in these courts, rather than state institutions. (These are all things to keep in mind, when contemplating apologies.)

## Celestine IV
### (October 25–November 10, 1241)

Gofredo Castiglioni, another nephew of Innocent III, was a native of Milan and a Cistercian, before being given the Red Hat by Gregory IX in 1239. He was elected (in the first recognizable modern conclave, organized by the Senator Matteo Orsini) and died two weeks later, while Frederick II was planning to seize Rome.

## Innocent IV
### (June 25, 1243–December 7, 1254)

The death of Celestine IV found the situation unchanged—Rome was virtually under siege and Frederick applied all the pressure he could to bring about an outcome he could favor. But the cardinals slipped out of the Eternal City, found refuge in Anagni, and elected Sinibaldo Cardinal di Fieschi, the Count of Lavagna, native of Genoa. Innocent (the name he had taken) had been a cardinal since 1227, and bishop of Albenga since 1245. Formerly a close friend of Frederick, he knew the emperor better than most. As a result, he did not trust him.

Immediately after Innocent's election, Frederick sent messages of peace and greeting and a personal envoy to negotiate a peace. But since the envoy was as excommunicate as his master, the pope would not receive him. Finally, on March 31, 1244, Frederick signed a treaty with Innocent. Among other things, he promised that he would release all the prelates he had captured en

route to Pope Gregory's council, restore the Papal States, and give amnesty to all the pope's allies.

Once again, Frederick reneged on his promises. Through third parties, he began to raise riots among the factions in Rome and refused to release his captive bishops. Fearing for his own safety in the city, and worried about Frederick's military, Innocent quietly slipped out of Italy and sought refuge in France with King St. Louis IX. In December 1244, he arrived at Lyons, and on January 3 opened up an Ecumenical Council there. The first order of business was of course the condemnation of the emperor. On July 17, Frederick was solemnly deposed by the Council, and the pope called for a new election, to be held the next year.

Another order of business for the Council concerned a possible reunion with the East; although the Latins retained their hold on Constantinople, the Byzantines at Nicaea were gradually retaking their territory. In 1244, Patriarch Manuel II suggested a compromise on the "filioque" question. His new formula was that "the Holy Ghost proceeds from the Father 'through' the Son," rather than "and." He won his co-religionists, including Emperor John III Vatatzes, to the plan. At the Council of Lyons, emperor and patriarch proposed that "If the Pope yielded the throne of Constantinople to the Greek Emperor, and its See to the Greek Patriarch, the Greek Church would acknowledge the primacy by restoring [Innocent's] name to the diptychs and would take the oath of canonical obedience." The pope accepted the terms and declared that a council would be held on Greek territory to ratify all the agreements. Unfortunately, the pope, the patriarch, and the emperor all died within a short time, and none of their successors were interested in pursuing the matter.

On May 22, 1246, an imperial election was held, at which Henry Raspe, Landgrave of Thuringia, was elected. But most of the German princes refused to recognize the legality of the election. Raspe died soon after, and on February 12, 1247, William of Holland was elected by the handful of papal loyalists in Germany. But William's problem was the same as Raspe's. Frederick was unquestionably accepted by most of Germany. St. Louis's attempts to mediate between the two implacable enemies failed, and in 1249, Gregory preached a Crusade against Frederick and declared that no Hohenstaufen would ever again be emperor.

On December 12, 1250, Frederick II died, but Innocent continued the struggle against his sons, Conrad IV and Manfred. On April 19, 1251, the pope returned to Italy and took possession of Rome in October of 1253. Since the crown of Sicily had returned, legally, to the Holy See on the death of Frederick, Innocent was keen on bestowing it on some foreign prince who would then drive Conrad and Manfred out. There were no takers. Finally, on May 20, 1254, after Conrad's death, Innocent recognized his two-year-old son, Conradin, as king of Sicily. Manfred surrendered and Innocent entered Naples in triumph on October 27, 1254. The wily Hohenstaufen, however, revolted again and defeated the papal troops at Foggia two months later.

While imperial questions took up much of his time, Innocent intervened elsewhere—safeguarding Henry III's throne in England and ending disputes in Hungary, Austria, and Portugal. He confirmed the rules of the Silvestrines and the Poor Clares and canonized, among others, St. Peter of Verona, the martyred patron of the Inquisition; and St. Stanislaus, archbishop of Cracow and one of the patrons of Poland.

Innocent died before he could know the outcome of Manfred's revolt.

## Alexander IV
### (December 7, 1254–May 25, 1261)

Born Rinaldo Conti, and related to Innocent III and Gregory IX (who had made him a cardinal in 1227), the new pope took the name Alexander after his unanimous election. At once he had to consider what he would do about the descendants of Frederick II—son Manfred on the warpath in Apulia, and grandson Conradin in Sicily. Given the Hohenstaufen family's history, many churchmen thought they were simply bad seeds—bad from birth. Whether or not that was true, Alexander would not compromise with them.

On March 25, 1255, the pope declared the kingdom of the Two Sicilies to Edmund of Lancaster, second son of England's Henry III. The next year, when William of Holland died, Alexander supported Henry's brother, Richard of Cornwall, over Alfonso of Castile. Though these measures brought money from Henry, they also brought the hatred of the English for the methods in which the money was extracted from them.

Meanwhile, Manfred went from strength to strength. It was rumored that Conradin had died in Germany—Manfred was accordingly crowned King in Palermo in 1258. Two years later, at the battle of Montaperti, Manfred became master of southern Italy. Rome came under the domination of factions allied with him, and despite the defeat of the tyrant Ezzolino at the hands of papally inspired northern Italian Crusaders, in political matters the papacy did poorly under Alexander.

Purely spiritual matters were different, however. Alexander was a great friend and defender of the orders of friars against their critics. He canonized

St. Clair of Assisi, having seen her stigmata himself. In 1255, he confirmed the charter of the University of Salamanca—some consolation in a pontificate, which, by the time of Alexander's death, had lost control of Italy.

## Urban IV
### (August 29, 1261–October 2, 1264)

Jacques Pantaleon was born at Troyes, the son of a cobbler, some time in the 1190s. After joining the priesthood, he became a canon of Laon, then archdeacon of Liege. In this latter post Jacques was the confessor of Bl. Julianna de Cornillon, who communicated her vision and revelation regarding the necessity of a feast day in honor of the Blessed Sacrament to him.

Winning the attention of Innocent IV at the Council of Lyons in 1245, two years later he was sent as legate to Germany. He was made bishop of Verdun in 1253 and Latin patriarch of Jerusalem two years later. When Alexander IV died, he returned to the West and met his seven fellow cardinals at Viterbo. Intensely jealous of each other, the college took three months before they elected Jacques, who took the name Urban.

Two weeks after the election, Constantinople fell to the Greeks, and the Latin empire there ended. Manfred remained a problem, not just in Sicily and Naples but throughout the peninsula, because of his headship of the Ghibelline or imperial party. He was keen, however, to come to an understanding with the Holy See. This keenness would do him little good, however, because Urban was determined that the house of Hohenstaufen should be utterly destroyed. The new pope opened up negotiations with St. Louis IX of France, in hopes of bringing that king's brother, Charles of Anjou, with a French army to conquer the two Sicilies.

Urban swiftly began the creation of new cardinals—six were related to or allied with the current seven, but an additional seven were Frenchmen and these started a "French party" in the college. As regarded parties also, to counter the Ghibellines, Urban created a Guelph or Papal party, which stood for the independence of Italy from the Germans. These two groupings could be found throughout north and central Italy and after a while brought the joys of civil war to most of them.

On a more religious plain, Urban approved the feast of Corpus Christi, in keeping with the message of Bl. Julianna di Cornillon.

But this was a shining light of faith in a dark realm of politics. The two par-

ties contested much of Italy, and St. Louis seemed reluctant to let his brother go. At last, he agreed in May of 1264. The position of the papacy was eroding; Urban had never entered Rome, and his position at Orvieto, where he was staying, was becoming precarious. He removed to Perugia, where he later died.

## Clement IV

### (February 5, 1265–November 29, 1268)

Guido Le Gros was born at St. Gilles. Son of a knight who had become a Carthusian when his wife died, Guido became a renowned lawyer and a good friend of St. Louis IX. When his wife died, he followed his father's example and entered holy orders. His advancement in the Church was rapid: In 1261, he was the first cardinal created by Urban IV. In 1264, Urban sent him as legate to England.

The death of that pontiff led to a long conclave, as those members of the college who were assembled at Perugia debated whether Charles's conquest of Sicily should be abetted, or they should attempt to work out a compromise with Manfred. At last, they sent word that Cardinal Le Gros should join them. When he arrived, he was informed that he was their unanimous choice for pope. He took the name Clement.

Moving to Viterbo, he was crowned there on February 22. The new pope would not set foot in Rome during his brief pontificate. His time was primarily taken up with the Neapolitan problem. In France, Clement called for a Crusade against Manfred. Although many found it difficult to understand how the war against Manfred could be called "holy," it was pointed out that the largest part of Manfred's army was made up of Muslims whom his father had settled in southern Italy.

Charles of Anjou came to Rome, and after he signed a treaty that guaranteed the Church's liberties and her overlordship of Sicily, he was crowned king of that country by a bishop acting in the pope's stead on January 6, 1266, in St. Peter's. On February 22, Charles fought the battle of Benevento with Manfred. The latter's forces were completely defeated and Manfred himself killed. Charles entered Naples and the Angevin dynasty was established.

The new king was as unlike his saintly brother as might be imagined, and Clement constantly reproved him. In 1268, Conradin (who was indeed alive) reentered Italy. Greeted everywhere with joy by the Ghibellines (including at Rome), Conradin and his army entered his kingdom, only to be defeated by

Charles's army at Tagliacozzo on August 23. Despite Clement's begging, Charles ordered Conradin beheaded at the marketplace in Naples on October 29. This marked the passing of the house of Hohenstaufen, but the manner of its passing haunted Clement for the month he had remaining. His letters condemning Charles's deed were about his last.

## Bl. Gregory X

### (September 1, 1271–January 10, 1276)

Born Theobald Visconti at Piacenza in 1210, he was archdeacon of Liege and made preacher of the last Crusade. At the time of his election, he was with Prince Edward in the Holy Land.

The cardinals had dallied at Viterbo for three years and had failed to elect a pope—partly out of division, partly because they enjoyed the accommodations. At length, the Viterbans took the roof off the Papal Palace at Viterbo, forcing the cardinals to choose between a new pope and death from exposure. They took the first course, appointing a commission to choose a compromise candidate. They found this in Visconti, who was not a bishop or a priest when he was elected.

On March 27, 1272, he was crowned at Rome and went about pursuing his goals: reforming the life of the Church, securing papal control in the Papal States, restoring order in Germany, reuniting with the Greeks, and launching another Crusade. In the first two, he was partially successful. By approving the election of Rudolf von Habsburg, the pope went far toward ending the anarchy that had prevailed in Germany since the death of Frederick II.

Seeing the last goal as dependent upon the second, Gregory rejoiced when he received news that Patriarch John XI Beccus had accepted the Filioque and that Emperor Michael VIII was supportive of the reunion. Gregory convoked Lyons II, and on July 6 1274, the union was officially declared. Various other important measures were passed. But on his way home from the Council, Gregory X died at Arezzo. His cultus was approved by Benedict XIV. His feast is observed at Lyons on January 28, at Arezzo on January 19, and at Rome on February 4.

## Bl. Innocent V

### (January 12–June 22, 1276)

Born Peter of Tarentaise, he joined the Dominican order and studied at Paris. Peter was master of theology there in 1259, provincial for France in 1267, bishop of Lyons in 1272, and cardinal bishop of Ostia the following year. Once elected pope, he tried, during his short reign, to reconcile Guelphs and Ghibellines, to reconcile Charles of Anjou with Rudolf von Habsburg, and to maintain the union with Constantinople. After his death at Rome, he was venerated by the people, but his beatus status was not approved by the Church until 1898. His feast is June 22.

## Adrian V

### (July 12–August 18, 1276)

Ottobuono Fieschi, a native of Genoa, was elected pope at Viterbo. A nephew of Innocent IV, he took the name Adrian. He annulled Bl. Gregory X's rigid rules on conclaves, but he died before issuing any substitutes.

## John XXI

### (September 13, 1276–May 20, 1277)

Petrus Juliani was born between 1210 and 1220 at Lisbon. Completing his studies at the Cathedral school in his native city, he moved on to the University of Paris, where he studied theology, medicine, and natural philosophy under Albertus Magnus. In an age when magic and alchemy were to some degree included under the last heading, Petrus acquired a reputation as a magician. Certainly, he was much attracted to the philosophy of Aristotle. In

1247, he accepted the post of Professor of Medicine at the University of Siena. Petrus became a friend of Teobaldo Cardinal Visconti, the future Gregory X. Under Bl. Gregory, Petrus acquired several honors, being made archbishop of Braga in early 1273 and cardinal-bishop of Tusculum later that year.

Adrian V's death at Viterbo led to riots in the city. As a result, the cardinals fairly hurriedly (for them) elected Petrus as pope. He took the name John at his coronation on September 20. Very quickly, John issued new rules for the conclave and ordered punishment for those who had rioted.

The new pope was now ready to face the outside world. Charles of Anjou came to Viterbo shortly after the coronation to convince John to allow him to fulfill his plans for control of all Italy. On October 7, Charles took the oath of fealty for Sicily, which declared that the Two Sicilies would never be united with Lombardy, Tuscany, or the empire. Moreover, John refused to renew Charles's status as senator of Rome and vicar for Tuscany and Lombardy, as he had been earlier.

The pope also sent an envoy to Rudolf von Habsburg, asking him to send an ambassador to Rome to meet with Charles of Anjou's representative. This would allow an Italian settlement and therefore pave the way for Rudolf's imperial coronation. John also mediated between the kings of France and Castile, who twice almost came to blows over Navarre, but who both had promised to go on Crusade. The pope intervened in affairs in Portugal and England, as well. A great encouragement to John came from Constantinople, from which was received news declaring the Orthodox hierarchy's acceptance of Lyons.

In between affairs of state, John conducted experiments in a special apartment he had added on to the palace at Viterbo. On May 14, while he worked alone in this laboratory, the building collapsed. John died a few days later from his injuries. To many this seemed to prove that his experiments were magical in nature.

# Nicholas III

(November 25, 1277–August 22, 1280)

Born at Rome in 1216, Giovanni Gaetani Orsini was the descendant of two of the noblest families in Rome. His father, Matteo Rosso Orsini, had been senator and led the defense of Rome against Frederick II. He was also a great friend of St. Francis and his order, which affection was retained throughout his life.

With such a background, it was inevitable that Giovanni should advance when he decided to become a priest. Innocent IV made him a cardinal in 1244, and Giovanni was one of the five such prelates who accompanied that pope on his flight to France. In 1252 and 1258 he was sent on diplomatic missions to Italy and France and became renowned for his honesty. Instrumental in the election of Urban IV, Giovanni was named inquisitor general in 1262 and protector of the Franciscans the following year. Under Clement IV he was one of the cardinals involved in the coronation of Charles of Anjou, and he occupied important positions under Bl. Gregory X and John XXI.

Taking the name of Nicholas, it was his policy to keep the papacy independent of both Charles of Anjou and Rudolf of Habsburg. He convinced the latter ruler to surrender Romagna in 1278, and on July 18 of that year Nicholas promulgated a decree forbidding imperial or royal intervention in the selection of Roman senators and magistrates. In this way he hoped to safeguard papal elections from secular influence.

In 1280, Nicholas brought about an agreement whereby Rudolf bestowed Provence upon Charles of Anjou as a fief; further, Rudolf's daughter Clementia was betrothed to Charles's grandson, Charles Martel of Anjou. This was in keeping with the general papal policy of reconciliation with a view to launching another Crusade. Nicholas attempted, fruitlessly, to reconcile the kings of Castile and France, for the same reason. Similarly, the pope intervened in Hungarian affairs, where the Kumans, an Asiatic tribe, were disrupting the state. He at last prevailed upon King Ladislaus to defeat them.

Regarding Constantinople, Nicholas sent envoys to the East to further confirm the Union of Lyons, and he also supported the Eastern emperor against Charles of Anjou's efforts to expand into the Ionian Islands and restore the Latin empire at Constantinople. Nicholas sent five Franciscans to China at the request of the Great Khan, and he expanded and beautified the Vatican Palace. He also delegated to the archbishop of Canterbury the right

to authorize notaries in England (the Anglican dignitary bearing that title does so today). He was buried in the chapel of St. Nicholas, built by him at St. Peter's.

## Martin IV
### (February 22, 1281–March 28, 1285)

Born at the castle of Montpensier in Touraine, Simon de Brie was a priest at Rouen before being appointed canon and treasurer of the church of St. Martin at Tours, of which the king of France was canonically the superior. St. Louis IX appointed him chancellor of France in 1260, and Urban IV made him a cardinal two years later. Simon was legate in France under Urban, Clement IV, and Bl. Gregory X. After the death of Nicholas III, Charles of Anjou entered Viterbo and had the two most influential cardinals of the Italian faction thrown into prison. The remainder of the cardinals elected Simon unanimously, and he took the name of Martin.

Not wanting to stay in Viterbo—having placed the city under interdict because of the arrest of the two cardinals—and unable to enter Rome because of his nationality, Martin went to Orvieto to be crowned on March 23. Dependent on Charles, he made him senator of Rome.

Eastern affairs took up a good deal of Martin's attention. Charles of Anjou was as anxious as ever to rebuild the Latin empire of Constantinople, with himself as emperor. But since the Council of Lyons, the popes had been pledged to alliance with the Byzantines; nevertheless, Charles prevailed upon Martin to excommunicate Emperor Michael VIII Palaeologus, ostensibly for his blinding and deposing John IV Lascaris back in 1264—an act for which Patriarch John's predecessor, Arsenius Autorianus, had in fact excommunicated Michael at the time. Thus ended the Union of Lyons.

Michael was to have his revenge, however, in the Sicilian Vespers, a cruel massacre of the French in Palermo by the locals on March 31, 1282. (It must be admitted that the nasty behavior of Charles's troops did give some reason for the Sicilians' cruelty). They then elected Peter III of Aragon as king. Martin excommunicated him and preached a Crusade against the Sicilians, with little effect. The pope gave Aragon to Charles of Valois, the son of Philip III of France. When Venice refused to provide a fleet for Charles of Anjou, Martin placed the Adriatic city under interdict. Charles of Anjou sent an army at last to Sicily, led by his son, Charles of Salerno. But the army was defeated

and the prince captured. Thus matters stood when Charles of Anjou died on January 6, 1285, leaving his prisoner-son as his heir.

Martin named seven as cardinals—one of these, Benedetto Gaetano, would become one of the more famous of the popes. Martin himself died at Perugia.

## Honorius IV
### (April 2, 1285-April 3, 1287)

Giacomo Savelli was born at Rome, the great-nephew of Honorius III, around 1210. Having studied at the University of Paris, he was made a cardinal by Alexander IV in 1261, who made him captain of the papal army. Clement IV sent him with three other cardinals to invest Charles of Anjou as king of the Two Sicilies in 1265. In July of 1276 he was sent to negotiate with Rudolf von Habsburg about the latter's imperial coronation.

Four days after the death of Martin IV, the cardinals elected Giacomo as pope—he took the name Honorius. The Romans were overjoyed at his election, and, unlike his predecessor, he was crowned at St. Peter's on May 20. He was so old that he had to sit at Mass and have his hands lifted at the elevation by a machine.

Nevertheless, difficult matters awaited the new pope, and decrepitude would not stop him. Under him, the entirety of the Papal States were returned to pontifical control, and internal order restored there, such as had not been seen in many a long year.

The Sicilians thought that as a fellow Italian the pope would see things their way. They were wrong, because the kingship of Sicily, being in the papal gift, would be a sore point with whoever was pope. Though he did not lift Martin IV's strictures on Sicily and Aragon, however, on September 17, 1285, he did pass a new constitution for the kingdom, which was designed to make the people safe against their king and his officers. If these should violate the law, the Sicilians were entitled to direct appeal to the pope. But Honorius would not lift the interdict against Sicily and Aragon, nor the excommunication against Peter III.

Peter's death on November 11, 1285, at first made little difference in the situation. His older son, Alfonso, succeeded him as king of Aragon, his younger son, James, as king of Sicily. On February 2, 1286, James was crowned and anointed by the Sicilian bishops in Palermo. On the following April 11, these prelates were excommunicated by Honorius. Meanwhile, on February 27, 1287,

the long-imprisoned Charles of Salerno renounced his rights to Sicily in return for his freedom. Honorius refused to accept.

With James's brother Alfonso, however, Honorius was less severe, and he opened negotiations toward resolving the conflict there. Moreover, on March 16, 1286, he lifted the interdict on Venice.

Honorius enjoyed a good relationship with Rudolf von Habsburg, and he agreed to crown Rudolf emperor at Rome on February 2, Candlemas, 1287. War broke out in Germany, however, keeping Rudolf from visiting Italy.

The Dominicans and Franciscans found a great friend in Honorius, as did the Carmelites and Augustinians, whose charters he approved. He also advocated the study of Oriental languages at Paris, both to work for reunion with the East, and to convert Muslims. On March 11, 1286, he condemned the Apostolici, a sect founded at Parma by Gerard Segarelli in 1260. These claimed to live the life of the original Apostles—they were to live in absolute poverty and hold all things in common, including—according to some—their wives. They created quite a stir, which lasted about fifty years altogether. (The Apostolici would inspire later imitators, including the nineteenth-century Oneida movement, known today primarily for its manufacture of silverware.)

## Nicholas IV

### (February 15, 1288–April 4, 1292)

Girolamo Masci was born at Ascoli to humble parents and early on became a Franciscan. In 1272 he was sent to Constantinople to ask the Greeks to participate in Lyons II. In 1274, he succeeded St. Bonaventure as general of the Franciscans. Four years later he was made cardinal. After the death of Honorius IV, the conclave was divided, but then fever struck and all the cardinals fled Rome except Girolamo. They reconvened several months later and unanimously elected him pope. He refused to accept their decision, so they proceeded to reelect him a week later. He took the name Nicholas in honor of Nicholas III.

Rome was dominated during his pontificate by the Colonna family, and his overseas policy was unsuccessful. Nicholas would not accept James of Aragon as king of Sicily, and he crowned Charles of Salerno as Charles II of the Two Sicilies at Rieti on May 29, 1289, in return for Charles's recognition of Papal Suzerainty over the island. In 1291, Alfonso III of Aragon died, leaving his realm to his brother. Anxious to end the quarrel with the pope and shed his

troublesome island kingdom, James II agreed to give Sicily back to Charles II in return for his daughter Blanche's hand in marriage and a large dowry.

This did not endear Nicholas to Rudolf of Habsburg, who was anxious for a solution to the ongoing problem. Furthermore, when Ladislaus IV of Hungary died on August 31, 1290, and Rudolf appointed his son Albert to the Apostolic Throne, Nicholas claimed it also as a fief and bestowed Hungary upon Charles II's son, Charles Martel.

Rudolf died in 1291. As prearranged, his son Albert, archduke of Austria, declared himself king of Germany. The next year, however, the electors put Adolf von Nassau on the German throne. Albert submitted, but awaited an opportunity to seize the throne.

Even more dispiriting was the fall of the last Crusader strongholds on the Palestinian coast in 1291. Nicholas immediately launched a call for another Crusade and urged the merger of the two great military orders, the Templars and the Hospitallers (whose divisions and quarrels had helped sap the strength of the Crusaders). Nothing came of this effort, although the pope did outfit twenty ships of war against the Muslims. But now all the fratricidal wars that had racked Christendom bore their bitter fruit. While some popes did their best to reconcile the squabbling princes, others joined in the quarreling.

In 1289, Nicholas approved the foundation of the University of Montpellier, the greatest medical college of its time (except perhaps Salerno). The next year he did the same for Coimbra's University. Apart from renewing the condemnation of the Apostolici, Nicholas beautified Santa Maria Maggiore. This is where he was buried.

## St. Celestine V

### (July 5–December 13, 1294)

Born in 1215 at Isernia in Molise, Peter del Murrone became a Benedictine at age seventeen. His love of solitude took him to the wilderness of Monte Morrone, then to Monte Majella. Disciples gathered around him and in 1254, these grew into the Celestine order of Benedictine hermits.

Charles II of Naples influenced the cardinals to elect Peter pope, much against his will. He took the name Celestine. At that time, it was thought that a holy man was needed to set the affairs of the Church in order. Living first at Aquila and then at Naples, Celestine was completely unable to govern the

Church and resigned. (It is for this act that Dante put him in hell.) His successor, Boniface VIII, fearful that use might be made of him as an anti-pope, decided to keep him in honorable confinement. Hungry for his old hermitage, he fled to the Abruzzi. He was caught near Monte Gargano and kept prisoner at Fumone Castle near Anagni. There he died on May 19, 1296, at ninety-one years of age.

Canonized in 1313, St. Celestine V's relics are at Santa Maria del Colle, in Aquila. His feast day is May 19. Among the Celestines, who lasted until the French Revolution, he had the additional feasts of his Consecration and Coronation as Pope, August 30; Renunciation of the Papacy, February 13; Translation of his relics, February 15; and his Apparition (during a war at Aquila), June 11.

## Boniface VIII
### (December 24, 1294–October 11, 1303)

Benedetto Gaetani was born at Anagni in 1235 to a family of Spanish origin who eventually became lords of Gaeta and Anagni. His mother's family were the Counts of Segni, who had given Innocent III, Gregory IX, and Alexander IV to the papacy. Coming from such a tradition, and having studied canon law at Todi, Spoleto, and Paris, Benedetto was zealous for the rights of the Church from an early age. In 1275 he was appointed to his first curia position, and in 1281 he became cardinal-deacon by Martin IV, followed by cardinal-priest in 1291. Having acted as legate in France and Sicily, St. Celestine V relied upon him to a degree, but Benedetto was unable to prevent the simple old hermit from granting all sorts of privileges to all who met him. When Celestine decided to resign, at first Benedetto pleaded with him not to. When it became apparent that he would do so anyway, Benedetto then asked him to first issue a constitution making it legal for popes to resign.

Ten days following Celestine's resignation, the cardinals went into conclave at the Castel Nuovo in Naples. Benedetto was elected by a majority and took the name Boniface. To show his independence of the House of Anjou, Boniface set out for Rome in early January and was crowned at St. John Lateran on January 23. King Charles II of Naples (as we must call him) and his son, Charles Martel, led the pontiff's horse at the coronation and waited on him at the banquet thereafter—in sign of submission.

As previously noted, fearful of the use that might be made of Celestine if

he fell into the wrong hands, Boniface felt compelled to first hold his predecessor under house arrest, and then, (after Celestine's flight and recapture) keep him in a castle. Though the political motives behind this act were understandable, the act itself did not make an extremely good impression.

Nevertheless, with his wide learning, his political experience and acumen, and his winning personality, it seemed at first that Boniface's pontificate would be a happy one. Moreover, his program of universal peace among Christians and his new Crusade against the Turks were popular, and no European prince could disagree with him openly. But dark events waited.

At first, light appeared at the end of the Sicilian tunnel. Boniface happily approved the agreement between James II and Charles II, and, as compensation for James's loss of Sicily, Boniface bestowed the papal fiefs of Corsica and Sardinia upon him. The Sicilians were not pleased with the idea of a French return to the island and asked Frederick, James's younger brother, to be their king. Despite Boniface's appeal, Frederick agreed. The papal legate was expelled, and Frederick was crowned king at Palermo on March 25, 1296. In response, the pope excommunicated Frederick and placed the island under interdict. Since the Sicilians ignored these censures, James II, as captain general of the Church, was ordered to make war upon his brother. The conflict ended at last in 1302 with a compromise. Frederick was to remain king of Sicily and recognized vassal of the Holy See for his lifetime, after which the island would revert to the king of Naples. Moreover, Frederick would marry Charles II's daughter, Blanche.

Realizing that a Crusade was impossible unless the squabbling cities of Genoa and Venice were reconciled, the pope ordered a truce in 1296. Both parties ignored him and continued fighting until 1299, stopping out of exhaustion. Even then, however, they refused his offer of mediation.

At this time, Florence and Tuscany were in civil war between the Guephs and Ghibellines—in this local case, the former representing the old nobility, and the latter the newer rising intellectuals (including Dante Alighieri). Boniface, hoping to establish peace close to home, sent a legate, whom both parties ignored. The legate returned home, leaving Florence under an interdict. In 1300, Boniface asked Charles of Valois, brother of the King of France, Philip IV, called "the Fair," to intervene as governor of Tuscany (the pope had the power to appoint this office while the empire was vacant). Instead of acting as honest broker, after taking over on November 1, 1301, Charles exiled the leading Ghibellines and ran a five-month-long reign of terror. The result was to embitter many of the most able Florentines against the pope.

In 1297, a portion of the Colonna family led a revolt in Rome, claiming that Boniface had been illegally elected because Celestine V had still been alive. The fact that the two cardinals in the family had voted for him, as well as that the pope had refused to allow their robbery of another branch of their family, was conveniently forgotten. At first they triumphed and Boniface fled

to Orvieto, but by the end of the year he had retaken the Eternal City and expelled the offending Colonnas.

Denmark, Hungary, Bohemia, and Poland all had internal political disputes in which Boniface attempted to intervene. The Danish case involved an archbishop flung into jail by the country's king, forcing the pope to put the country under interdict. In response, the king who had imprisoned the archbishop relented, but Boniface transferred the cleric out of the country and harm's way. The Polish, Bohemian, and Hungarian cases, involving succession disputes, were solved completely without reference to papal rights in both countries—Boniface's legates were simply ignored.

In Germany, meanwhile, things were not going well. Adolf von Nassau's governance was not very able, so on June 28, 1298, three electors gathered in Mainz and declared him deposed, making Albert von Habsburg king in his place. War was the certain outcome. At the battle of Goellheim, on July 2, Adolf was defeated and killed. The Diet of Frankfurt reelected Albert, and on August 24 he was crowned king at Aachen. The electors asked Boniface for approval of Albert's elevation as well as agreement to perform the imperial coronation at Rome. The Pope refused, charging Albert with taking up arms against his liege lord and murdering him. The three archbishop-electors (who had crowned him at Aachen) of Cologne, Mainz, and Trier were soon at war with Albert, and in 1301, Boniface ordered him to Rome to defend himself against various charges. Following his defeat of the trio of prelates, the next year Albert sent agents to Rome bearing letters in which he said he was innocent of Adolf's blood, and that the war had been forced upon him, and so on. The pope accepted this defense, and on April 30, 1303, accorded Albert the recognition he had wished. Albert replied with an oath to defend the papacy (especially its rights in Germany) and not to appoint vicars in Tuscany or Lombardy for five years.

Much less success accompanied Boniface's attempts to safeguard the independence of Scotland. (As viewers of the film Braveheart will remember, Edward I of England used a dynastic problem in Scotland to conquer his northern neighbor—the result was an initially unsuccessful resistance led by Sir William Wallace, which eventually triumphed under King Robert the Bruce.) Not so well known is that Boniface used every means at his disposal to force Edward to leave Scotland's independence intact. Boniface was unsuccessful in this attempt. Moreover, Edward, in order to finance his wars against the Scots and the French (in Gascony), began confiscating from the clergy, abbeys, and other religious institutions, depending on the year, a tenth, a third, or a half of their incomes. Although there was no justification for these moves in law or custom, Edward acted in total defiance of both his archbishops and the pope himself. This did not bode well for peace between France and England.

This last cause was particularly dear to Boniface, for without it there could be no Crusade. Annoying as Edward was, Philip was no better; indeed, it was he who started the war by illegally seizing Gascony, an English fief held by the French Crown and all that remained of Henry II's continental inheritance after King John lost Normandy, Brittany, and other provinces. Like Edward, Philip had been fleecing the clergy to prosecute the war. Annoyed with both of them, in 1296 Boniface issued the bull Clericis laicos, which renewed former prohibitions against lay authorities taxing the clergy. Edward ignored the document, but Philip immediately responded by cutting off all money to Rome—whether for the use of the papacy, the missions, or the projected Crusade. The next year, Boniface was able to ease Philip's anger by explaining that he did not mean that there could be no voluntary contributions by the clergy to the Crown. He also canonized St. Louis IX, Philip's much worthier grandfather. Tensions relaxed to the point that in 1298, the pope was able to arrange a two-years' truce between France and England.

Boniface declared 1300 the first Great Jubilee Year. In addition, he decreed a Plenary Indulgence to all pilgrims who would visit Rome and the tombs of the Apostles there. He launched it on June 29, the feast of SS. Peter and Paul. (In subsequent years, this has become a regular feature of Catholic life, being fixed at twenty-five-year intervals in 1475. Those who were in Rome for the Great Jubilee of 2000 shall never forget it; they would do well to remember that we owe it to Boniface.) Twenty thousand pilgrims descended on Rome at that first one, and new gates had to be opened in the walls to accommodate them. Although it was a great success spiritually, it did not escape anyone's notice that the only monarch who attended was the king of Naples.

Meanwhile, problems with Philip continued, for he did not cease to plunder the French Church. Moreover, he dreamed of annexing the Holy Roman and Byzantine empires and turning the pope into a sort of personal chaplain. Even worse, the papal legate to France was thrown into prison. The pope demanded his envoy's immediate release, and on December 5, 1301, issued a bull, Ausculta fili, in which he reminded the king of the previous teaching regarding the pope's position as head of the Church, and as judge of the morality of Royal acts. When presented officially with a copy of this bull, not only did Philip order it thrown into the fire and all copies in France suppressed, but also he and a henchman forged a counterfeit bull that alleged that Boniface claimed all temporal power over monarchs.

In response, Boniface issued a call for a general council, to open on November 4, 1302. Philip called a national synod at Notre Dame de Paris of all the French bishops, who issued an appeal to Boniface to withdraw the call for the Council, because all the French nobility swore to back the king in his defiance of Rome. Boniface's reply was an attack on the bishops for their cow-

ardice, coupled with an appeal to the duke of Brittany or Burgundy to moderate. The Council met in October, with a number of French prelates whose properties were immediately seized by Philip. In November, Boniface issued the famous bull, Unam sanctam. The source of much controversy from that day forward, the bull simply encapsulated Church teaching up to that time, in a clear manner. Interestingly, the last line of the bull (from Henry Denzinger's Enchiridion Symbolorum), "Furthermore, we declare, we proclaim, we define that it is absolutely necessary for salvation that every human creature be subject to the Roman Pontiff" (while very controversial in modern times) was not at issue when written. The rest of the bull, while declaring that the secular power existed solely for the benefit of the Church, did not, according to some, invoke infallibility the way the last line did. And, of course, Philip would not argue with the essential need for submission to the pope to be saved; however, he would argue as to what the submission consisted of.

Philip had a refutation prepared that attacked the bull not for its doctrinal conclusion, but for its comments on Church-state relations. In it, he claimed that it was not the papacy against which he fought, but Boniface personally. This distinction between office and person was an important one to the medieval mind and was already enshrined in secular theory by the notion of "the King's Two Bodies," that is, the Body political, which embodied the nation and the law, and never died, and the Body Natural, which did die and might act against the interests of the Body Political—in which case it needed correction, sometimes violently. And so did Philip reason with regard to the pope—he rejected him as arbitrator with England and Flanders.

After Philip refused to give any definite replies to the new legate in France, Boniface sent his representative two letters on April 13, 1303. The first declared Philip excommunicated, the other ordered all the French bishops to come to Rome.

At this point, Boniface was politically isolated. Only the kings of Sicily and Germany were entirely on his side, and they were busy with problems of their own. At the same time, the Colonnas had fled to France and were working with Philip. In April, Nogaret, one of Philip's chief henchmen, and Sciarra di Colonna went to Tuscany and raised a force of two thousand mercenaries. The papal messenger carrying the two aforementioned letters was captured, and the legate fled. On June 13, an assembly of the nobles and prelates of France was called at the Louvre in the presence of the king. This body accused Boniface of infidelity, immorality, simony, heresy, the death of Celestine V, the loss of the Holy Land, and seemingly anything else that could be thought of. The document carrying these charges was forcibly signed by abbots, canons, nobles, mayors, and others throughout France. Jean de Pontoise, abbot of Citeaux, refused and was arrested.

In August 1303, Boniface convened a consistory of the cardinals. There he

swore his innocence of the crimes charged against him and went on to suspend the first bishop who signed the document and to temporarily end the University of Paris's granting of degrees. A number of other ecclesiastical censures were imposed as well. On September 8, a bull solemnly excommunicating Philip was prepared. But the day before, Nogaret and Colonna appeared with their mercenaries at Anagni. Allowed into the town by some confederates, they immediately besieged the papal palace, managing to enter it at nightfall through the cathedral. Four of the cardinals with Boniface fled, and only a single Spanish cardinal remained by his side. The pope declared, "Since I am betrayed like the Savior, and my end is nigh, I will die like a Pope"; he sat on his throne in full pontificalia when Colonna appeared, sword in hand, with Nogaret by his side. The latter prevented his friend from killing the pope on the spot. But Boniface said to them, "Here is my head, here is my neck; I will patiently bear that I, a Catholic and lawful pontiff and vicar of Christ, be condemned and deposed by the Paterini [a heretical sect to which Nogaret's parents belonged]; I desire to die for Christ's faith and His Church."

Boniface was taken prisoner and held for three days without food or water. His captors plundered the palace and destroyed the archives therein. Finally, the townspeople, who at first had fraternized with the troops, rose and threw them out of town. Four hundred horsemen of the Orsinis, blood enemies of the Colonnas, arrived and brought the pope back to Rome on September 13. Before leaving, he absolved all his attackers except those who had plundered Church property (and them too, if they returned their booty). But his mistreatment had shattered his health, and he died of a fever on October 11. To the end, however, he retained his sanity, and, in the presence of eight cardinals and the members of his household, he received the Last Rites and made his profession of Faith before dying.

Dante, who to be sure was no ally of Boniface's, nevertheless commemorated this occurrence in the Purgatorio: "I see the Fleur-de-lys Anagni enter, and Christ in his own Vicar captive made; I see him yet another time derided; I see renewed the vinegar and gall, and between living thieves I see him slain." (Canto XX, 86) Boniface was buried in St. Peter's (when his grave was opened in 1605, he was found to be perfectly incorrupt).

Boniface VIII was a great friend to learning and the arts—he founded the University of Rome in 1303 and that of Fermo the next year. He also refounded the Vatican Library, which had been burned by the Frangipani in 1227. All over the Papal States he added art to churches new and old, and he erected many public works. He was one of the most remarkable men ever to sit in the Chair of St. Peter, though his end was one of the most unfortunate.

# Bl. Benedict XI

## (October 22, 1303–July 7, 1304)

Niccolo Boccasini was born at Treviso in 1240. He became a Dominican and was elected master general of that order in 1296. Two years later, Boniface VIII named him cardinal-bishop of Ostia and sent him as nuncio to England, France, Denmark, Hungary, Poland, Austria, Serbia, and elsewhere. Although his missions were rarely successful, his holiness and learning won Niccolo the respect of all those leaders he met—if not their acquiescence.

His major goal upon his election to the papacy (whereupon he took the name Benedict) was to calm the troubles that ended his predecessor's pontificate so tragically. To that end, he ended the banishment of the Colonnas, absolved Philip IV's excommunication, and ended the penalties imposed upon France. His other major accomplishment was to accept in 1304 the profession of faith of the Nestorian Catholicos, Jahballaha III. He died at Perugia, and his feast is July 7.

# CAPTIVITY AND SCHISM

# Clement V

## (June 5, 1305–April 20, 1314)

Born Bertrand de Got at Villandraut, Gascony, in 1264, he came from a noble family. Bertrand's older brother had been archbishop of Lyons and cardinal-bishop of Albano (dying in 1297). Bertrand himself studied at the universities of Toulouse, Orleans, and Bologna, eventually becoming archbishop of Bordeaux. Although in that capacity actually a subject of the king of England, he was a boyhood friend of Philip IV. Even so, he had remained faithful to Boniface VIII. As such, he appeared to the cardinals assembled at Perugia the perfect compromise candidate. After five months of bickering and thinking, ten of the fifteen cardinals (most of whom were Italians) voted for him. They invited Bertrand to Rome for the coronation; instead, he summoned them to Lyons for the rite.

Crowned on November 14, 1305, in the presence of the cardinals and Philip, the new pope, who took the name Clement, was faced with all sorts of ill omens. As he returned in procession, a wall fell, causing his horse to throw him and killing one of his brothers and the ancient Matteo, Cardinal Orsini, who had seen twelve conclaves and thirteen popes. The most precious jewel in the papal tiara was lost that day, as well. From then until 1309, fearful of the disorders in Rome, Clement moved around France. At last he settled in Avignon, on territory surrounded by a papal fief (the Venaissin), but itself subject to the kingdom of Naples. This began what was called the "Babylonian captivity" of the papacy. About the only unalloyed good that emerged of this period was that eventually, long after the popes returned to Rome, vineyards which they had owned would produce Chateauneuf du Pape. (Because this is one of the author's favorite wines, he can say only that God brings good out of evil.)

Clement's fears of living in Rome were not unfounded, however. Not only were the Colonnas and Orsinis at each others' throats, there was conflict between the aristocracy as a whole and the people. Worse still, this sort of drama was repeated throughout the Papal States. The Venetians thought that they might take the opportunity presented by this disorder to snatch the duchy of Ferrara, and did so. But they miscalculated Clement V. He preached a Cru-

sade against them, placed Venice under interdict, and sent his legate, Cardinal Pelagrue, with an army to handily defeat them.

However, Clement could not be as upfront in dealing with Philip. Above all, Philip wanted a condemnation of Boniface VIII in the style of Formosus. On the one hand, Clement was no Stephen VII—he was no Boniface VIII either. After absolving Philip of all responsibility in the dispute, he deftly delayed any decision on the matter, finally declaring that any such action must be taken by the Ecumenical Council, which he intended to call at Vienne in 1311.

Philip's interest in having Boniface condemned was thrown a bit off course by another interest he had—seizing the money of the Knights Templar. This chapter in church history is shrouded in mystery. After the fall of the Holy Land in 1291, the Templars and the Hospitallers withdrew to Cyprus. The latter order soon established itself in Rhodes, from which stronghold its members continued to fight, harassing Muslim shipping. The wide network of commanderies across Europe continued to assist this effort financially. Because the Hospitallers, or (as we must call them now) the Knights of Rhodes, were actively engaged in the work for which they were founded, there was little resentment toward them.

But the Poor Knights of the Temple were a different story. Though they too had maintained their profitable network of properties, they were not actively fighting the Muslims. Indeed, they had gone into banking in a big way and had become far wealthier than ever—without, however, doing anything with this wealth.

Philip, ever on the lookout for cash, gazed greedy eyes on their possessions. Having cured himself of any fear of the sacred by his dealing with Boniface VIII, he was not worried by their religious status. There had long been rumors about the Templars—that in the Holy Land they had allied with the feared Old Man of the Mountain, whose hashish-crazed followers murdered whomever they were told, and who followed a secret religion (supposedly the forerunner of today's Druze). Reportedly the Templars worshiped Satan as an idol under the name Baphomet, practiced sodomy, and required kissing one's superior on the buttocks to gain initiation into the order.

In the first year of Clement's pontificate, Philip began demanding their suppression. In 1307, Clement tried unsuccessfully to unite the two knightly orders, wisely supposing that uniting the assets of the one to the activity of the other would benefit both. When that effort failed, Clement agreed to an investigation of the charges which Philip brought against the Templars. Philip would not wait, however, and had all the members of the order in France thrown into prison, including the grand master, Jacques de Molay.

The drama of the next five years included confessions made under torture in France, recantations, and so on. In the end, without passing judgment on the veracity of the claims against them, Clement ordered the Templars dis-

solved at the Council of Vienne in 1312. Outside of France, few knights confessed to much wrongdoing. The provinces of Portugal and Aragon were considered so free of abuse that the kings of those countries constituted them as separate orders—Christ and Montesa, respectively (which survive, in much altered form, today). Most of the Templar properties and personnel outside of France were transferred to the Knights Hospitallers of Rhodes to support their work. The temple in London, the English headquarters, was rented out by the Hospitallers to the lawyers in that city. These in turn bought it outright from the Crown after Henry VIII seized ownership at the Reformation. (It remains the foremost center of the British legal profession today. The round Temple Church in the center of the complex is typical of the order's churches around Europe which yet exist. And, in rural Normandy, the small village of Sainte Colombe-la-Commanderie not only retains its memory as a former Templar commandery, it gave this author's family its name!)

Were the Templars guilty or not? Much ink has been spilled both ways. Some were doubtless guilty of something, but how much and what probably cannot be answered this side of the grave. Some have said that Clement, after his initial refusal to allow them to be tortured, gave way because of admissions to him on the part of de Molay and his assistants. Others claim that Philip threatened Clement with Boniface VIII's fate. Whatever the case, Philip happily gobbled up their property and money. (Rumors of their treasures and secrets have lasted till present day, fueling speculation and fiction alike and inspiring a whole mythology tapped into by the Freemasons and others—which is why the young Masons in the United States are called "Demolay.")

De Molay and his assistant, when faced with life imprisonment, recanted their former confessions and were burned at the stake. De Molay is said to have cursed pope and king alike, saying that they would both die within a year of his death, March 18, 1314. So they did.

The Council of Vienne, 1311–1312, accomplished more than the dissolution of the Templars, however. Clement was skillfully able to avoid any consideration of Boniface VIII's guilt. As a result, that particular question died. A number of disciplinary regulations, especially concerning the Benedictines, were passed, as were some dogmatic definitions. Most specific, in the light of the Church's interaction with other religions and various heresies, was the Council's decree on Baptism: "All the faithful must confess only one Baptism, which regenerates in Christ all the baptized, just as there is one God and one faith. We believe that this Sacrament, celebrated in water and in the name of the Father, Son, and Holy Ghost, is necessary for children and grown-up people alike for salvation." (Henry Denzinger, Enchiridion Symbolorum, p.482)

Clement and the council were less successful in dealing with affairs of the Franciscans. A faction of that order, the so-called Spirituals, called for a radical observance of St. Francis's rule, particularly with regard to the lack of any property. Some of these were orthodox, but others drifted into the notion

that property of any kind was an evil for all, and especially for Churchmen. A few of these went further, declaring that the pope and curia were agents of Satan because of their wealth. At last, a still smaller set proclaimed that this corruption betokened either the end of the world, or the end of this age of the world. For this latter subgrouping, a whole set of prophecies, surrounding one or another charismatic leader, grew up. Some of these prophets called for withdrawal from the world to await its end, others called on their followers to help start it.

Clement had other interests at stake besides dealing with Philip. Above all, he needed an independent temporal power to safeguard the papacy from Philip's control. The empire was still vacant, and, acknowledging France's tenuous theoretical relationship with that title, Philip began lobbying to have his brother, Charles of Valois, succeed Albert von Habsburg. But while giving lip service to this candidacy, Clement threw all his weight behind Henry of Luxembourg. With the three archbishops in his corner, and the temporal electors not keen to give the empire up to France, the Luxembourg prince was elected Henry VII on January 6, 1309. Three years later, he came to Rome and was crowned emperor at St. John Lateran by cardinals specially delegated by Clement for that purpose. Although he was hailed as a savior by Dante and the rest of the Ghibelline party in Italy, the Guelphs (who controlled most of Rome) rallied against him by orders of King Robert of Naples. The emperor was forced to withdraw, but he returned with greater force to defeat the king, who nevertheless had invoked his status as a papal vassal. Before anything further could transpire, Henry died suddenly near Siena on August 24, 1313. Dante had written his De Monarchia in support of the emperor—for it was in reconstitution of the empire and its reconciliation with the papacy that Dante saw the only hope for Italy, Christendom, and renewal of the Crusade.

Clement's other major antagonist was Edward I of England, who had kept up his ways during all the drama on the continent. The archbishop of Canterbury, Robert of Winchelsea, had been fiercely persecuted by Edward and took flight to Bordeaux. He was only able to return after Edward II came to the throne in 1307.

Clement's other great accomplishment was the final codification of canon law. In addition, he granted a charter to the University of Perugia. Apart from the Templar question, Clement's pontificate must be considered a qualified success. If he gave Philip too much, it was not nearly all that grasping king wanted—under such circumstances, holding anything back was a triumph.

# John XXII
## (August 7, 1316–December 4, 1334)

Jacques d'Euse was born at Cahors in 1249. He was taught by the Dominicans, pursuing his studies in theology and law at the universities of Montpellier and Paris. After teaching civil and canon law at Toulouse and Cahors, he became a friend of Charles II of Naples, who recommended him to the diocese of Frejus in Provence in 1300. The Neapolitan king made him chancellor in 1309, and the following year Jacques transferred to the diocese of Avignon. He defended both the suppression of the Templars and Unam Sanctam (the bull of Boniface VIII defining the necessity of submission to the pope for salvation), and so was made cardinal-bishop of Porto by Clement V in 1312.

The death of Clement plunged the church into disorder. Assembling at Carpentras, the cardinals (eight Italian, ten Gascon, three Provençal, and three from other French provinces) could not agree where to have the conclave and dispersed without any decision. For more than two years this situation continued, despite the pleas of all Christendom. At last, after his coronation, Philip V of France managed to persuade twenty-three cardinals to assemble at the Dominican monastery in Lyons on June 26, 1316. Eventually, they elected Jacques, who took the name John. Crowned at Lyons on September 5, the new pope went to Avignon, where he set up his seat.

The state of affairs that faced John was incredibly complex. Foremost among them was the disorder in the Franciscan houses. The general of the order died about the same time as Clement V, and the split between the Conventuals (as the conservative Franciscans were called) and the Spirituals became public. Many of the latter violently drove the former from their houses. Almost to the end of his pontificate, John was forced to issue decrees against them. Some allied with such opponents of the Holy See as philosopher William of Occam and imperial claimant Louis of Bavaria.

During the vacancy after Clement V's death, another, greater, dispute had arisen. The imperial electors had split—one faction favoring Louis of Bavaria, the other Frederick of Austria. On November 25, 1314, Louis was crowned king of Germany at Aachen, and Frederick at Bonn. Once John was elected pope, both would-be emperors wrote to him for confirmation of their kingship and a date for imperial coronation. The pontiff answered to both that they must come to some sort of arrangement. Until then, John declared, the imperial throne would remain vacant. Even so, Louis in 1315 appointed an imperial vicar for Italy and supported the visconti in Milan, who at that point were in conflict with John and had been excommunicated. On March 13,

1317, John repeated former papal declarations that during such vacancies all imperial appointments rested with the pope, and so appointed King Robert of Sicily as imperial vicar for Italy. By 1322, Louis informed John that Frederick was defeated, and the pope replied, offering to recognize him as king and emperor-elect.

But Louis spurned the offer and appointed a new vicar for Italy. From here, the conflict between the two became almost comic in its intensity—Louis insisting on his complete rights over the Empire, John denying them. The Bavarian accused John of heresy, and the Spirituals seconded. John responded with various penalties and threats of excommunication. More oceans of ink were spilled by controversialists on either side: The pope's partisans reiterated the dependency of the imperial upon the papal power; Louis's friends, such as William of Occam, Marsilius of Padua, and the Spirituals, argued that the ecclesiastical power must be entirely dependent upon the state. The arguments of the latter group, although not entirely successful at the time, would be used again at the Reformation. (Since then they have actually formed the dominant theory for virtually all the governments under which the Church functions today, even though the empire for which they were formed is gone.) For pope and emperor alike, and the kings of Europe who watched the drama unfold, all victories were in the end pyrrhic.

But the outcome was not so obvious then. By 1327, Germany had been subjected to Louis's rule; he and an army marched into Italy. Welcomed by the Visconti at Milan and the Ghibellines generally, he was invested with the Iron Crown of Lombardy at that city by two excommunicated bishops. Louis then marched on to Rome, where the Colonnas opened the gates to him. On January 17, 1328, Sciarra Cardinal Colonna bestowed the imperial crown on Louis and in April declared John deposed. The pope was burned in effigy, and Louis proclaimed a Spiritual, Pietro Rainalducci, as anti-pope, under the title of Nicholas V. John of course had excommunicated the Bavarian.

In Italy, however, Louis was his own worst enemy. His administrators and local rulers grabbed what cash they could. Even the Ghibellines began to rally to John, and city after city declared for him. Finally, in 1330, Louis returned to Germany, and Nicholas V went to Avignon to seek the pope's forgiveness, which he granted. In May of that year, Louis opened negotiations with John, who insisted on his abdication. By 1333, Louis was willing to consider it—there matters lay at John's death.

All of this excitement was confined to mostly Germany and Italy. Safe under French protection, John serenely reconstructed the financial affairs of the Church. He managed to find ways to charge for an enormous number of appointments to positions throughout the Catholic world and regulated the money sent to the papal court, both for its own expenses and the wars in Italy. These exactions would breed resentment in various places and would bear bitter fruit. At one point, John also supported another attempt of the French

king to be elected to the imperial throne. Though this move once again underscored the connection between the two Carolingian thrones, it also fed into the belief that the papacy was becoming an entirely French enterprise.

John was a pontiff who taught erroneous opinions privately. It had been the common belief of Catholics (and Orthodox) that the just see God immediately after their death—this beatific vision is the essence of heaven, its other joys being secondary. But before he became pope, John had advanced the opinion that in fact, the saints themselves will not see God until after the Final Judgment, when the graves offer up their dead, and all reunite with their bodies for final disposition. This aroused some comment at the time, and after his ascension to the papacy what had been the view of a theologian became the papal view. He gave sermons on the topic and imprisoned a Dominican who disagreed with him. When the same notion was advanced at the University of Paris by some professors, however, the academic authorities there rejected it, affirming the traditional teaching and pointing out that John's opinion was only that, and not the decision of the papacy as such. In November of 1333, John wrote to King Philip VI agreeing that there had been no such decision, and that, as a result, theologians were free to hold whichever view they wished to (he sprang the Dominican from prison at this time). The next month, the university officially petitioned him to make such a decision. He duly appointed a commission of theologians at Avignon to consult the works of the Church Fathers, past popes and councils, and the Scriptures. On January 3, 1334, he declared in a consistory that he had never wished to teach anything contrary to Scripture, nor to make a binding decision on the issue. On his deathbed, he renounced his own teaching and subscribed to the traditional view of the matter. This was one of the incidents most carefully reviewed at Vatican I in 1870, when the Fathers there defined Infallibility.

Perhaps the most enduring event of his papacy occurred in compensation to the faithful for the way John had misled them on the Beatific Vision issue. The brown scapular is a piece of cloth worn by the faithful, to which they are entitled after enrollment into the Confraternity of Our Lady of Mt. Carmel. On July 16, 1251, Our Lady appeared to St. Simon Stock, head of the Carmelites, and promised that those who affiliated with the Carmelites by wearing the scapular (adopted from the order's habit), and who said certain prayers and lived chaste lives, would not, if dying in the scapular, go to hell. In 1322, the Virgin appeared to John and assured him that those who died in this manner, having fulfilled the other requirements, would be conducted out of purgatory to heaven by Mary herself the Saturday following their deaths. This is the famous "Sabbatine Privilege," and it has been a tremendous comfort to uncounted numbers of Catholics from that day onward. The issues and problems of John's reign have been more or less resolved, for better or worse; but the Privilege remains.

## *Nicholas V*

*Anti-Pope (May 22, 1328–August 25, 1330)*

Pietro Rainalducci was born at Corbario and entered the Franciscans, becoming part of the "Spiritual" faction. Proclaimed pope by Louis the German after the latter's attempted imperial coronation at Rome, he took the name Nicholas. Following his disillusionment with the whole scheme, he wrote to John and asked for forgiveness. Nicholas then went to Avignon and presented himself to the pope, who gave him absolution and the kiss of peace. Nicholas remained at Avignon for the remaining three years of his life, devoted to prayer and study.

## Benedict XII

**(December 20, 1334–April 24, 1342)**

Born Jacques Fournier at Saverdun near Toulouse to peasant parents, he became a Cistercian monk, studied theology at Paris, and was elected abbot of his monastery of Fontfroide. In December 1317, he became bishop of Pamiers, from where he was translated to the Diocese of Mirepoix and in 1327 made cardinal by John XXII.

At the conclave that met at Avignon after John's death, the favorite was Cardinal de Comminges, a prelate known for piety and political acumen. He was also known for his desire to return the papacy to Rome, which did not please the majority of cardinals—not merely because they were French, but because life at Avignon was sweet and undemanding (as well as profitable to many). This promise de Comminges refused to make, so there was a furious search for an alternative. Many of the cardinals voted for Fournier as the least likely candidate, in an attempt to find a real alternative. Lacking social position, wealth, or a following, Cardinal Fournier seemed an impossible choice, and thus a suitable stopgap. Two-thirds of the cardinals pursued this strategy, and he was elected to everyone's surprise (not least his own) on the first ballot.

Crowned as Benedict XII on January 8, 1335, his first concern was to go back to Rome. The new pope immediately funded the restoration of St. Peter's and St. John Lateran in preparation for his expected return, and the cardinals immediately began to squawk, pointing out (rightly, alas) the dangerous state

of Rome and the peninsula. Seeing their resistance, he proposed Bologna as a compromise. They refused. Finally reconciled to the inevitable, Benedict began the construction in 1339 of the enormous Palais du Pape, which is still Avignon's greatest architectural pride. His conscience continued to prick him, however, and he sent large amounts of money to Italy on a regular basis to aid the suffering there.

Even at Avignon he found ways to vent his zeal for reform. Immediately after he was elected, he sent back to their benefices all clerics not required at the papal court. He put an end to many of the financial abuses that had grown, whereby various church bureaucrats had found ways of extracting money, both at Avignon and around Europe. Additionally, Benedict resolutely fought nepotism, first for his own family, and then for others—going as far as to insist that his only niece find a husband of their own class, rather than one of the numerous nobles attracted by the prospect of becoming the pope's son-in-law.

Theology was his first interest, and he soon finished the problem started by John XXII. He examined the work of the commission his predecessor had appointed and defined the traditional teaching on the Beatific Vision. Under John, three streams of heresy had cropped up in many districts of Christendom: the Manicheans, the radical Spirituals, and the anti-papal theorists endorsed by Louis the German. In combating these he used the stick of the Inquisition, and the carrot of gentle persuasion and debate, of which he himself was a master. The pope further aided the Armenians, hard-pressed by Muslim aggression, with money and prayer.

But effective as he was in spiritual terms, he was a political novice, frequently outsmarted by Philip VI. Anxious to end the rift with Louis the German, in July of 1335 Benedict sent generous peace terms. But Philip (wanting to prevent any reconciliation between pope and empire) and the cardinals insisted that to do so would be to encourage heresy and schism. Despite overtures from Louis, in 1337 Benedict declared that it would be impossible to absolve the Bavarian. Philip had had his way, but as Benedict feared, it led to Louis allying with Edward III of England against France. War broke out between the two sides, despite the pope's efforts to avert it. Later, Philip completed his humiliation by allying with Louis, despite the Bavarian's claims to be able to annul marriages. Worse, Philip sabotaged Benedict's efforts to call a Crusade to free Palestine. The pontiff was successful when a fresh wave of Muslims came into Spain from North Africa—calling a Crusade there in 1339. It succeeded in blunting their attack, and it endeared Benedict to the Iberians. Petrarch made much fun of him, primarily because he did not return to Rome.

# Clement VI

## (May 7, 1342–December 6, 1352)

Born Pierre Roger in 1291 at the castle of Maumont, located in present-day Department of Correze, at age ten he entered the Benedictine monastery of Chaise-Dieu. Studying theology at Paris, he became a professor of the university. Pierre had been introduced to John XXII and rapidly rose through various offices, becoming bishop of Arras and chancellor of France in 1328, archbishop of Sens the following year, and archbishop of Rouen in 1330. Benedict XII named him cardinal eight years later. As a great prelate and officer of state at the French court, Pierre became a patron of arts and letters, a bon viveur, and a thrower of sumptuous entertainments. As well, he was completely devoted to the interests of France. These traits would remain with him for the rest of his life, even following his election to the throne of St. Peter, when he took the name of Clement in honor of the pontiff who had removed the papacy to France.

As a result, he was unable to mediate effectively between the French and English who were still at war (although he did manage a brief truce in 1343). Of the twenty-five cardinals he created, most were French, and in 1344 he conceded to the king of France the privileges of receiving from the chalice at communion, like a priest, and of touching the chalice as well (a reminder of how sacred these things really are—in a period like modern day, anyone may do so). Clement purchased the lordship of Avignon from Joanna of Naples in 1348, thus assuring the apparent permanence of papal residence there. Nevertheless, he did not forget Rome entirely. In 1347, he recognized the assumption of power there by the demagogue Cola di Rienzi. But his condemnation of Rienzi brought about the latter's downfall.

Still, hanging fire was the problem with Louis the Bavarian, whose misrule in Germany was threatening to repeat his sad fate in Italy. Perhaps the final straw was his annulment of a princess's marriage so that she might marry his son. To save his position, Louis wrote to Clement in September of 1343, declaring the invalidity of all his imperial acts, asking for absolution, but also requesting to be recognized as king of the Romans (that is, of Germany). In response, Clement required in addition that no imperial law should thenceforth be enacted without papal sanction; that all Royal laws emplaced by Louis should be suspended, pending Clement's review; that Louis should depose all the bishops and abbots he had put in place; and that further, he renounce all claim to the Papal States, Sicily, Sardinia, and Corsica. Louis submitted these demands to a gathering of the German princes. These wor-

thies, annoyed at Clement's separating the archdiocese of Prague from that of Magdeburg (a measure that delighted the Czechs) rejected the pope's requirements. In addition, they declared that they wanted a new king. On April 13, 1346, Clement issued a bull to these princes, calling upon them to elect a new king.

In response, on July 11, 1346, John of Bohemia, Rudolf of Saxony, and the three archbishop-electors made John's son, Charles of Luxembourg, king of Germany. Although the new king, Charles IV, accepted most of the papal demands, Louis still claimed the throne. The country was about to fall into civil war, when the Bavarian was killed on a boar hunt, on October 11, 1347. Without Louis to protect them, William of Occam and the Spirituals quickly made their submission.

As a foretaste of future events, the Canary Islands and their mysterious people, the Guanches, had recently been discovered. In 1344, Clement bestowed the sovereignty of the islands to a Castilian prince, and in 1351 appointed a bishop for them. The Spaniard was unable to pursue the venture, however, and the Canaries, Europe's first colonial effort, remained outside for the moment.

Clement's Eastern policy was not very successful either. Efforts at reunion with the Greeks and Armenians failed. He was successful in launching a Crusade, spearheaded by the Knights of Rhodes. The Crusaders succeeded in taking Smyrna from the Turks, thus relieving the pressure on Constantinople, but the effort bogged down in a truce.

To finance both his efforts for the Church and the glittering court he maintained at Avignon, Clement abolished not only Benedict XII's economies but also most of his monetary reforms, once again charging for presentation to various Church positions overseas. So onerous did these charges become that Edward III of England passed a bill requiring royal approval of all such transactions. These exactions bred much resentment, as did the pope's obvious French partisanship. Clement's grave failings must be contrasted with his genuine work for the poor and his personal bravery during the Black Plague when it hit Avignon in 1348–1349. The fun-loving pontiff was transformed into a fearless visitor of the highly contagious sick, and he spent much of the papal treasury on relieving plague sufferers throughout Europe. At the same time, when many of the superstitious in various places accused the Jews of being plague carriers and persecuted them accordingly, Clement passed several bulls in their favor and established Avignon as a refuge for them. In 1343, he approved the charter of the University of Pisa, and three years later, that of Valladolid.

Clement's final illness was brief, and at his request his body was interred at his abbey of Chaise-Dieu. In 1562, when the Huguenots took the Abbey during the Wars of Religion, they desecrated his grave and burned his body, scattering its ashes.

# Innocent VI

## (December 18, 1352–September 18, 1362)

Etienne Aubert was born at Mont, in the Diocese of Limoges. He studied civil law at the University of Toulouse, where he became a professor and eventually chief judge of that city's court. After he felt a call to religious life, Etienne joined the priesthood. Owing to his administrative abilities, in 1338 he became bishop of Noyons. Two years later he was translated to Clermont and in 1342 he became a cardinal. In 1352, Etienne was made cardinal-bishop of Ostia and Grand Penitentiary. So venal had the Papal Court become in Clement VI's day, that at the conclave after his death, each of the cardinals was made to sign an agreement saying that they would share half the revenues of the Holy See with the College, if elected. Etienne signed, but added the rider, "insofar as it is not contrary to Church law." Upon his election, he declared this act void, because it limited papal power conferred by God alone.

Immediately after he was crowned Innocent VI, the new pope ordered all nonresident clerics back to their own dioceses, abbeys, or parishes. He ended all luxury at the Papal Court and gave salaries to the auditors of the Rota, whose unpaid status had led them to eke out their incomes with bribes.

Innocent then turned his attention to Italy, where the peninsula's minor princes had taken over most of the Papal States. The pope sent the able cardinal Gil d'Albornoz as his legate to regain these territories. Able at war and diplomacy, that redoubtable prelate soon had things in hand.

Charles IV was on very good terms with Innocent, the first emperor in some time who could make such a claim. In 1354, he successfully asked Innocent to institute the Feast of the Holy Lance and Nails for Germany and Bohemia. Charles had been crowned at Aachen and was ready for his imperial anointing. Innocent happily agreed—on the proviso, however, that he remain in Rome no longer than one day. Charles, more concerned with his Bohemian Kingdom than with Italy (modern Prague owes many of its prettiest structures to him) readily consented. Traveling to Italy in 1355, he received first the Iron Crown of Lombardy at Milan, then the Imperial Crown at Rome on Easter Sunday, at the hands of the cardinal-bishop of Ostia. He then withdrew to Prague. The next year he issued the "Golden Bull," a constitution that at once regulated and confirmed the near anarchic state the empire had fallen into, and which would last more or less until 1806. No mention was made in this document of papal privileges as regarded the imperial office, so Innocent protested, as he did in 1359, when Charles floated a plan to independently reform the German clergy. But all such quarrels ended quickly as a result of the great affection between the two.

Innocent's more balanced relationship with the French resulted in his successful attempt to mediate between France and England, resulting in the treaty of Bretigny in 1360. But he suffered some setbacks as well; his attempts at fomenting a new Crusade failed, as did his mediation between Castile and Aragon—the former's king, Peter I ("Pedro the Cruel") ignored all penalties Innocent imposed on him for murdering his wife and sundry others.

Clearly, he restored a great deal of papal prestige.

## Bl. Urban V

### (October 28, 1362–December 19, 1370)

Born Guillaume de Grimoard at Grisac, Languedoc, in 1310, he was professed a Benedictine at the abbey of Chiriac. He studied canon law and became a professor of the subject at Montpellier, Toulouse, Paris, and Avignon, and then a monk at Cluny. In 1362, Clement VI appointed him abbot of St. Germain d'Auxerre. Clement also employed him as legate to Milan; as Innocent VI sent him to Naples in the same capacity. He was crowned Urban at Avignon on November 6, 1362.

From the beginning of his pontificate, various important folk urged him, known as he was for his holiness and dedication, to return to Rome. St. Bridget of Sweden, the holy widow whose order Urban approved, received revelations from Jesus calling on Urban to return to the Eternal City. Petrarch the poet, on behalf of his fellow citizens there, added his voice to hers, and so too did Emperor Charles IV. Of course, the French court showed little enthusiasm for the idea.

At last, Urban resolved to make the plunge. To assist him and provide security, Charles IV volunteered to accompany him. In 1365, the emperor arrived at Avignon, and together the two heads of Christendom made ready to enter what was, in theory, their common capital. Proceeding south to Arles, Charles was crowned king of Burgundy at that city's church of St. Trophime, the traditional location of the ceremony. He was the last emperor to claim all four coronations.

Urban's return to Rome was precarious—he too found himself spending time at safer retreats like Viterbo. In 1368, Charles IV met him there before going to his own palace at Siena. In 1369 an attack there convinced the em-

peror that Prague was a better location. He decamped accordingly. But the other emperor, John V Palaeologus, came to Rome to be reconciled with the papacy. Zealous both for reunion and the Crusade, Urban happily received and reconciled him. The refusal of the Western princes to rally to the aid of the Eastern Christians doomed this attempt, however, and the Turks were now loose in Bulgaria and Thrace, and they had Constantinople under virtual siege.

At last, in September 1370, opposition from the Visconti and others drove Urban back to Avignon. He died very shortly following his return, in accord with a prediction by St. Bridget. He was beatified in 1870, and his feast is December 19. In 1364, he confirmed the creation of the Jagiellonian University at Cracow.

## Gregory XI
### (December 30, 1370–March 27, 1378)

Pierre Roger de Beaufort was born in 1331 at his family's castle of Maumont. He was the nephew of Clement VI and received many honors and offices from his uncle. This nepotism could not cover up Pierre's own very real abilities. Although made a cardinal as a teenager in 1348, he went to the University of Perugia while wearing the Red Hat. He gained fame not only for his learning in theology and canon law, but also in piety. After his election, he chose the name Gregory, had himself ordained on January 4, 1371, at Avignon, and crowned the following day.

His first act was an unsuccessful attempt to bring about peace between England and France. He enjoyed greater success with Castile, Aragon, Navarre, Naples, and Sicily, all of whom had been at one another's throats. In addition, Gregory was concerned with the reunion with the Greeks, the Crusade, and clergy reform, each seemingly impossible at the time. Of the latter situation, St. Catherine of Siena, the new pope's confidante, declared, "They have condensed all the Ten Commandments to one: bring hither the money." In 1374, Gregory approved the Hieronymites, a new Spanish order whose best-known monastery, El Escorial, is still considered a great attraction.

But it was Italy that soon claimed his attention. Duke Bernabo Visconti of Milan had driven Urban V from Italy and was busy usurping pieces of the Papal States. All other efforts had failed, so Gregory excommunicated him. Visconti's response was to force-feed the parchment upon which the anathema

was written to the legate who delivered it. In response, Gregory declared war in 1372. At first Visconti was victorious, but the king of Hungary and the queen of Naples joined the fray on the pope's side. The latter hired the English mercenary, Sir John Hawkwood (about whom Sir Arthur Conan Doyle wrote The White Company). Visconti asked for and received a truce in 1374.

Gregory at this point played into the hands of Visconti by appointing French legates to govern his Italian possessions. The Italians had no more use for them than they had had for Louis the Bavarian's Germans—the result was the same. Moreover, Florence feared papal power as well, and that city allied with Visconti, reopening the war. In response, Gregory put Florence under interdict, excommunicated the city's leaders, and offered the city and its goods to whomever could or would conquer it. The frightened Florentines sent St. Catherine of Siena to consult with Gregory and she soon became his most trusted adviser. Unfortunately, her efforts were undercut by her countrymen's continued fighting against the papal forces. Moreover, Rome itself had joined the Florentines and Milanese.

St. Catherine called on Gregory to return to Rome; this alone, she foresaw, would bring peace. Despite the French king and the cardinals' pleas, Gregory left Avignon on September 13, 1376, took ship at Marseilles on October 2, and via Genoa arrived at Corneto on December 6. He waited there for arrangements to proceed to Rome. On January 13, 1377, he sailed from Corneto to Ostia, traveled up the Tiber, and arrived at the monastery of St. Paul Outside the Walls. On January 17 he made his official entrance into the Eternal City.

Peace, however, did not arrive with him. War raged elsewhere, and shortly after Gregory's return, Cardinal Robert of Geneva presided over the massacre of Cesena. This in turn sparked riots that led the pope to withdraw to Anagni in May. While there he issued condemnations of the teaching of the heretical English priest, John Wycliff. These errors included denial of Transubstantiation, the primacy of preaching over the Sacraments, the complete sufficiency of Scripture for doctrine (to that end he offered a somewhat doctored version of the Bible in English), and a denial of papal primacy.

Eventually, the Romans simmered down, and Gregory returned. But he was very disgusted with affairs there, and in all likelihood would have returned to Avignon had not death come to him first.

# Urban VI

## (April 8, 1378–October 15, 1389)

Bartolomeo Prignano was born at Naples in 1318 and early on went to Avignon, where he became a favorite at the papal court. In 1364, he was made bishop of Acerenza in his native land, and in 1377, Gregory XI translated him to the archdiocese of Bari. Since the papal chancellor remained at Avignon, Bartolomeo became treasurer at Rome. He was known for his business acumen, integrity, and ability.

The conclave that met on April 7, after Gregory XI's death, was highly divided. The French cardinals of course wanted another Frenchman, and a return to Avignon. Their Italian counterparts wanted one of their own, and the Roman mob seconded that opinion, making it clear that if the cardinals did elect a Frenchman, they were highly unlikely to leave alive. Bartolomeo seemed the obvious choice. He was Italian, but not Roman; a subject of the Queen of Naples; and yet friendly to Avignon. Despite not being a cardinal, he was elected, and a messenger was sent to bring him to Rome. The mob was appeased, and Bartolomeo took the name Urban at his coronation.

The honeymoon was short-lived. Urban was anxious to reform the Church immediately and he began with the cardinals—something many of them, particularly the French, resented. Urban's high-handed method of dealing with people soon annoyed the Romans as well and alienated Queen Joanna. Many cardinals left Rome for Anagni, ostensibly to escape the heat. But on August 2, the malcontents, including cardinals Robert of Geneva and the fiery Spaniard Pedro de Luna, declared that the election of Urban had been invalid because of the pressure exerted by the Roman mob and other irregularities. On August 27, they moved on to Fondi, where the king of France encouraged them to elect another Pope. On September 20, they chose Robert of Geneva, who took the name Clement VII, in honor of the pope who had moved the papacy to France. He and his cardinals then returned to Avignon and set up shop.

Thus began the Great Western Schism (1378–1417). In this civil war, the lines were drawn along political boundaries: France, Spain, Portugal, Scotland, Denmark, Norway, and Naples recognized Clement; most of Germany and northern Italy, England and Ireland, and Poland and Hungary remained loyal to Urban. The remainder of Urban's career consisted of various exploits involving the changing factions in Italy, which he managed to annoy one after another. Before his death, he did proclaim a Jubilee Year for 1390. Urban left a lasting legacy in the University of Heidelberg, whose founding he approved in 1385.

## *Clement VII*

*Anti-Pope (September 20, 1378–September 16, 1394)*

Born Robert of Savoy, at Geneva in 1342, he was the son of Count Amadeus III. In 1359 he became a protonotary apostolic (a monsignor today); he was bishop of Therouanne three years later, archbishop of Cambrai in 1368, and at last, a cardinal in 1371. In 1376, Gregory XI appointed him legate for northern Italy, where he authorized the execution of four thousand people at Cesena in order to suppress a rebellion.

The dissident cardinals at Fondi elected him pope and he returned to Avignon, where he depended completely on the French king. Though he did appoint worthy cardinals, he donated most of the Papal States to Louis II of Anjou, the king of Naples. Cruel and grasping, he was not a shining example. At his death, the Schism raged unabated.

## Boniface IX

(November 2, 1389–October 1, 1404)

Piero Tomacelli came of a poor but noble Neapolitan family. At the time of his election, he had a number of difficulties to deal with, thanks to the impetuosity of Urban VI. Clement VII (with whom Boniface exchanged mutual excommunications) had just crowned Louis II of Anjou as king of Naples. In return, Boniface championed the cause of Ladislaus, son of Charles III, the former king there. Because of Boniface's support, more than a decade of warfare finally placed Ladislaus on the throne. In that same period, the pope ended Rome's virtual independence and secured control over most of the Papal States. Moreover, in those areas of Europe loyal to him, he quickly restored confidence in the papacy.

He presided over two Holy Years: 1390, proclaimed by Urban VI; and 1400, one of his own. Boniface granted charters to the universities of Ferrara, Pavia, and Fermo and confirmed that of Erfurt. Owing to the great lack of money in the papal coffers, the pope issued a new tax on all that part of Christendom loyal to him—that of the Annates, or "First Fruits." Though his need for cash (given the difficulties he encountered in fund-raising) is understandable, it helped pave the way for the problems of the next century. In

England he struggled with the king over the question of appointments, but in the end had to accept royal veto over any he made there.

Imperial affairs occupied the pontiff's time as well. Charles IV's brave son Sigismund, king of Hungary, led a Crusade preached by Boniface against the Turks who were threatening to cross the Danube. It was a great success. In 1398 and 1399, the pope appealed for a new Crusade to assist the hard-pressed Eastern emperor Emmanuel. This received little response, but a Mongol attack gave the Turks other worries, and the pressure on Constantinople was relieved. The next year, however, the Western Empire became problematic. Wenceslas, the ne'er-do-well son of Charles IV, had become so obnoxious to the German princes that in 1400 they deposed him and replaced him with Rupert, duke of Bavaria. For two years Boniface maintained neutrality, but in 1403 he recognized the deposition. (The year before, he had approved the foundation of the University of Wurzburg.)

Although anxious to end the Schism, Boniface made little headway with Clement. When the Frenchman died in 1394, the Avignon cardinals elected Pedro de Luna, who took the name Benedict XIII in his place. Although they exchanged envoys from time to time, little was accomplished. Boniface's last interview with them was so distressful, he took to his bed and died two days later.

## *Benedict XIII*

*Anti-Pope (September 28, 1394–May 23, 1423)*

Pedro de Luna was born at Illueca, Aragon, in 1328. He studied canon law at Montpellier and became a professor at that university before Gregory XI, in 1375, made him a cardinal. Pedro was both learned and austere, values that Gregory prized. He accompanied the pope back to Rome and showed great courage during the conclave following his patron's death. He voted for Urban VI and was at first a great partisan of his. He went to Anagni with the other cardinals, however, and was convinced of the invalidity of Urban's election.

From that point on, he was by far the most able of Clement VII's cardinals, and in consequence was used by him as legate to practically every country that recognized him. But Pedro was interested in reunion, particularly after Urban's death. A rift grew between him and Clement. When Clement died, his cardinals elected Pedro because he promised to search for reunion—even if it meant resigning the papacy.

By this time, all of Europe—even France—was clamoring against the dis-

union. Within a year of becoming Benedict XIII, the new would-be pope received an embassy from the king and the University of Paris, asking for his signature on a document that declared that the best path to reunion was for both popes to resign. Benedict refused, saying that negotiations between the pontiffs were the best route. He dispatched and received envoys from Boniface, with whom, for a time, he was actually on good terms. But both men were convinced that they were in fact the rightful pope, and neither would resign.

Through 1397 and 1398, various European kings, including those of France and Germany, insisted that both pontiffs should abdicate. Neither budged. Then, the king of France withdrew obedience from Benedict, and all but five of his cardinals left Avignon. In 1399, French troops took Avignon, and Benedict was made to swear that he would resign if the Roman pope would also do so. But a few days later he swore before a notary that this oath had been made under duress, and so was not binding. He remained a prisoner in his palace. The French could not convince any other country in Benedict's obedience to back up their action, and in 1403 he escaped to Provence, under Louis of Anjou. Once safely ensconced there, Avignon and his cardinals again declared for him, and France accepted him once more.

He then reopened negotiations with Boniface, suggesting that both popes should meet with both sets of cardinals in one place to end the Schism. Boniface refused, then died. None of his successors would negotiate with Benedict, and in 1408, Charles V of France declared his country neutral toward both popes and called for their resignation. A number of cardinals of both obediences met at the Council of Pisa and declared both popes deposed. Benedict refused to recognize their action and fled to Perpignan in Rousillon. The Pisans selected their own Pope (now there were three!), and Avignon was seized for Alexander V, their creation in 1411. Benedict retained his hold on Scotland, however, issuing a bull approving the University of St. Andrews.

In September of 1415, Emperor Sigismund, fresh from the Council of Constance, visited Benedict at Perpignan and begged him to resign. The stubborn Spaniard refused, and two months later the few countries still loyal to him renounced their obedience. Next, he left for a remote castle owned by his family, Pensicola, on the Aragon coast. Likening his stronghold to the ark, and surrounded by five cardinals, he stayed there until his death. At that point, his five went over to Pope Martin V. At his death, Benedict's few remaining disciples rallied to a cleric named Munoz, who took the name Clement VIII. But he too soon submitted to Martin V.

# Innocent VII

## (October 17, 1404–November 6, 1406)

Cosimo di Migliorati was born in 1336 at Sulmona in the Abruzzi to parents who were poor. He studied law at Perugia, Padua, and Bologna. After teaching for some time, he went to Rome and was brought into the curia by Urban VI. After ten years in England as papal collector, he was made bishop of Bologna in 1386, and archbishop of Ravenna the following year. Boniface IX created him a cardinal in 1389. When elected to replace Boniface, he took the name Innocent.

Although, like the other cardinals, he had taken an oath to end the Schism in any way possible—even vowing to resign, if that were necessary—after his accession his problems with King Ladislaus of Naples forced his attention entirely into that area. The revolutionaries among the Romans rose up, and Innocent called on Ladislaus to suppress them. The King did, but on the promise that Innocent would run any possible solution to the Schism past him first and insist on his rights over Naples. But this was merely a prelude, since Ladislaus actually wanted to annex the Papal States.

To this end, in 1405 Ladislaus fomented another revolution with the help of the Colonnas. This was assisted by a crime committed in the pope's name (kidnaping with intent to kill a number of prominent citizens) by his nephew. Innocent fled to Viterbo, and Ladislaus occupied the Castel Sant'Angelo. After a year, the Romans invited the pope back, but Innocent was forced to excommunicate Ladislaus in order to make him withdraw his troops. This was the pontiff's last success before his death.

## Gregory XII
### (November 30, 1406–July 4, 1415)

Born Angelo Corrario to a noble Venetian family in 1327, he was made bishop of Castello in 1380 and titular patriarch of Constantinople a decade later. At Innocent VII's death, the Roman cardinals took an oath that, if elected, they would resign the Tiara to bring reunion with Avignon—if Benedict XIII would do the same. Cardinal Corrario, renowned for his dedication to the cause of union, was unanimously elected, taking the name Gregory.

On December 12, 1406, Gregory notified Benedict of his election and informed him that he was willing to abdicate if the Avignon pope would do likewise. Benedict agreed in principle and suggested a meeting. The two popes agreed to a rendezvous at Savona, but it never occurred—partly because Benedict soon indicated that he was not really willing to abdicate, and because both Gregory's family and King Ladislaus of Naples were reluctant for Gregory to, playing upon his fears of Benedict's real intentions.

Gregory's cardinals began to mistrust his sincerity in ending the Schism. On May 4, 1408, Gregory convened them at Lucca and ordered them to remain in the city. Seven did and contacted a number of Benedict's cardinals. These together agreed to hold a Council at Pisa for the purpose of reuniting the Church. There the cardinals summoned both popes. Neither showed, and on June 5, 1409, were both declared deposed. On June 26 in their place, the Pisan cardinals elected Alexander V.

Gregory sought refuge with his friend Charles Malatesta, the prince of Rimini, who attempted to mediate uselessly between Pisa and Gregory. On June 6, 1409, the pope held a synod of his own near Aquileia, where he condemned both Benedict and Alexander. Most Catholic bishops were backing one or the other of his rivals, but Gregory remained the actual pope (recognized by the kings of Germany and Naples and a few other rulers), although he eventually became convinced of the necessity of his own resignation. When Louis II of Anjou began his war against Ladislaus for the throne of Naples, he took several papal towns and in 1410 at last seized Rome, where he proclaimed Alexander pope. On May 18, King Rupert of Germany died. The archbishop-electors of Mainz and Cologne, who had supported Pisa, wrote to John XXIII, who had succeeded Alexander on the latter's death, saying that they intended to support Charles IV's son Sigismund for the Kingship.

On July 21, Sigismund was duly elected. Gregory recognized this action, but it was obvious that the new king would cleave to John. As king of

Hungary, the new German monarch had reformed that country's affairs so well that the kingdom would be able to resist the Turks for another century. Personally brave, Sigismund had rescued his queen from Hungarian nobles who had kidnaped her and had proved his mettle against the Turks in the Crusade of 1396, pushing them back into Serbia. He had inherited a great sense of the imperial office from his father, and this great man put all his considerable energy into the struggle for reuniting Christendom.

The wily John worked next to detach Naples from Gregory's allegiance. An able soldier before he became a cleric, the Pisan pope joined Louis II in his war against Ladislaus, being present as Louis won a crushing battle against Ladislaus in May of 1411. Rather than taking advantage of the opening, Louis returned to France to gather troops and money for further campaigns. John turned to Ladislaus and on October 16, 1412, he gave to the Neapolitan the title to the kingdom he occupied, the right to conquer Sicily, the title of standard-bearer of the Roman Church, and money. Ladislaus abandoned Gregory in return.

Ladislaus proved to be as tricky as John and seized Rome from him the next year. The Pisan pope was forced to seek refuge with Sigismund. John had called a Council at Rome the previous year, but it had accomplished little, apart from another condemnation of Wycliff. Now that John was in his power, Sigismund, who took his role as titular temporal head of Christendom most seriously, resolved to end the Schism himself. On October 30, 1413, the king invited Gregory XII and Benedict XIII to attend a General Council at Constance, which would open in a year's time. He then ordered John to officially convoke it because John had the largest number of adherents.

The death of Ladislaus on August 6, 1414, allowed John to return to Rome, while Gregory remained in the safety of Rimini. John and his nine cardinals entered Constance on October 28, 1414, and he officially opened the Council on November 5. Though the Pisan pope dominated at the beginning, Sigismund became the apparent leader. Because of John's immorality, among other faults, King Sigismund became convinced all three popes would have to abdicate to secure real reunion. Although he had promised to abdicate John fled, but he returned and abdicated at the Council's twelfth session.

Convinced that Sigismund was right, Gregory sent Malatesta and cardinal Dominici of Ragusa to represent him. On July 4, 1415, the Ragusan Cardinal read to the fifteenth session of the Council Gregory's bull solemnly convening it, and thus conferring legitimacy on its subsequent actions. Malatesta then read the pope's resignation. The Council accepted, making the former pope cardinal-bishop of Porto and legate for Ancona. Two years later, on October 18, 1417, before the cardinals elected a new pope, Gregory died.

# *Alexander V*

*Anti-Pope (June 26, 1409–May 3, 1410)*

Pietro Philarghi was born an orphan in Crete, around 1339. The island was at the time under Venetian rule, but the homeless lad felt no connection to his home island, let alone its distant overlords on the Adriatic. Taken under the wing of a Capuchin friar who recognized his intelligence, he was given an education and joined the friary in his native town of Candia. Because of his demonstrated academic talent, his order sent him to study in Italy, then to Oxford and Paris. The Great Schism broke out while he was teaching at the University of Paris. As a partisan of Urban VI, he was obliged to return to Italy, where he became tutor to the sons of the duke of Milan. Recognizing his abilities, the duke used him also as an ambassador and prevailed upon the pope to appoint him to various dioceses. Pietro became archbishop of Milan in 1402. Three years later, Innocent VII created him cardinal and legate for Lombardy.

From that time on, he became renowned for his zeal for reunion with Avignon and general reform. Pietro urged his brother cardinals to withdraw their allegiance from Gregory XII, and he convinced Henry IV of England and the archbishop of Canterbury to declare their neutrality in the Schism. Gregory stripped him of his titles and privileges, but Pietro was the leading light among the Avignon and Roman cardinals who assembled at Pisa and declared both popes deposed. He gave a blistering address at the opening, blamed both pontiffs for the continuing Schism, and called for its immediate end. Because of his purity of life, education, and administrative ability, coupled with a lack of family or nation to favor, he was the obvious choice as a successor pontiff. He was unanimously elected pope.

At first, prospects looked bright for Alexander. Only Scotland, Aragon, and a few Italian locales remained to Benedict's obedience—Gregory's consisted of the king of the Romans, Naples, and other Italian towns. But with these portions, both popes seemed content, and Christendom found it had three popes where there had been but two. Secular clergy and theology professors alike were upset with the privileges Alexander showered upon the orders of Friars. In 1410, Louis of Anjou captured Rome and Alexander was proclaimed pope there. The following year Avignon also fell to pro-Pisan forces. While staying with Baldassare Cardinal Cossa, in Bologna (who had come to dominate him), he died—Cossa's enemies claimed, of poison. Although Gregory XII has always been counted as the true pope, it is interesting that Alexander was never officially dubbed an anti-pope (the next pontiff to take the name numerated himself Alexander VI). Moreover, Alexander approved the foundation of the University of Leipzig.

# *John XXIII*

*Anti-Pope (May 17, 1410–May 29, 1415)*

Born Baldassare Cossa in 1379 to a poor but noble Neapolitan family, he early became a soldier. Feeling a calling to the priesthood (but not apparently any personal moral scruples), he joined the clerical profession. He became a doctor of law at Bologna, then entered the Curia. Boniface IX made him cardinal in 1402 and legate of Romagna the following year. From his seat at Bologna, he showed himself an able administrator, and in 1408 he joined the cardinals of Pisa. Helping to elect Alexander V, he became the dominant figure in the partnership and was elected to succeed him by the Pisan cardinals.

The main events of his career as anti-pope have been noted. Much of Constance was concerned with examining the many criminal charges against him, including the claim that he had poisoned Alexander V. After he abdicated, he was confined until the forty-second session, on December 28, 1417, after Martin V was elected. He made his submission to him, and in 1419 was created cardinal-bishop of Tusculum by the new pope. But he lived only a few months afterward. Dying on November 22, 1419, he was interred at the cathedral of Florence, where Cosimo di Medici erected him a beautiful monument that can still be seen today.

# Renewal and Renaissance

# Martin V

## (November 11, 1417–February 20, 1431)

With Gregory XII and John XXIII having abdicated, and Benedict XIII (refusing to follow his colleagues—which refusal cost him the support of St. Vincent Ferrer, heretofore his greatest ally) deposed, the Council of Constance was, in a real sense, the ultimate governing authority of the Church for a short period. The actions of King Sigismund in convoking it and securing the necessary abdications were properly in accord with the emperor's role of guardian of the Church. The symbolism was bolstered further when the Byzantine emperor Manuel II Paleologus arrived with a retinue of 20 Greek bishops. For a short period it seemed that everything was possible, in terms of reunion, reform, and defeat of the Turks. There was a cautious euphoria in the air (similar to that accompanying the fall of the Soviet Union in 1991).

However, a number of unpleasant realities remained. For example, the papacy had been tarnished severely by the behavior of its multiple holders, and the cardinals were blamed for the terrible state of affairs that had just ended. Moreover, the state of the clergy in Europe was very poor because of how supervision over them had been neglected during the Avignon papacy and the Great Schism. Added to this was the general unrest in Europe caused by civil war in various places, the Hundred Years' War in France, the innumerable struggles between Italian city states and factions, and, of course, the onset of the Turks.

Facing the Council were several problems: the election of a new pope; general reform; and the combating of heresy, which the virtual paralysis of Church government during the Schism had allowed to spread. Despite questions as to whether to address a new pope or reform first, the Council agreed in the end that a popeless Church was a monstrous thing. A decree passed early on that declared a general council superior to the pope, but it occurred before Gregory XII had legalized the proceedings and was ignored by most Catholics afterward.

This occasion proved that the cardinals could not be trusted to elect a pope by themselves. Therefore, a certain number of electors were chosen from the national delegations to the Council, and they, together with the college, set out to choose a new pope. Their choice fell on Oddone Cardinal Colonna. Born at Genazzano in the Campagna in 1368, he was a member of that famous (and infamous) family that had given many cardinals, but no popes, to the Church. A cardinal under Gregory XII, he had gone to Pisa and voted for Alexander V and John XXIII. Renowned for his purity and learning, Oddone was unanimously elected after a three-day conclave by the electors. A deacon at the time, he was ordained priest and consecrated bishop before his coronation on November 21, 1417 in the Episcopal palace of Constance. He took the name Martin after the saint upon whose day he had been elected.

The new pontiff now presided over the Council that had elected him. A large number of reform measures were passed. To enforce these, many of the Council Fathers wished to transform the institution of Ecumenical Councils into a sort of Parliament for the Church. To this end, the Council passed a decree requiring one every five years. In addition, the Council Fathers dealt with the question of Jan Hus, a Czech priest who was a disciple of Wycliff. His teachings were condemned, but he refused to recant. The Council remanded him to the secular authority, Sigismund, who was king of Bohemia as well. Hus was burned, but his followers, the Hussites, waged war against Sigismund and his successors for some years. (The Moravian Church of present day owes its origins to Hus, although in its present form it is the creation of the eighteenth-century Count Zinzendorf.)

After accomplishing these goals, on April 22, 1418, Martin closed the Council. This date reportedly may have ended the Middle Ages and begun the modern era. Martin remained in Constance a while longer, negotiating concordats with various sovereigns. The French asked him to return to Avignon, and Sigismund wanted him to take up residence in some German town, but he spurned all offers, determined to return to Rome. This was a mighty task, to be sure. The fourteenth century had been very unkind to both the city and the rest of the Papal States. Much of the former was in the hands of various mercenaries, and the latter's churches veered between neglect and abuse. Famine and sickness were the order of the day in Rome, and few people still lived there.

Martin brought the queen of Naples, who occupied the city, to his side, and on September 20, 1420, through various means of cowing the mercenary-lords, he returned to Rome. He immediately set to work rebuilding the ravaged metropolis, bringing in artists and architects from Florence to do so. After building almost a new city, Martin went about, with the help of his family—the powerful Colonnas—reducing the various mercenary-held towns of the Papal States to obedience. By 1428, the lands of St. Peter were again under the rule of his successor.

Another task facing Martin was dealing with Conciliarism—the teaching that councils are superior to popes. As agreed at Constance, he called another council at Pavia, which opened in April of 1423. But the plague forced the assembly to move to Siena in June. Poor attendance and dissension within the College of Cardinals allowed the pope to dissolve the Council on February 26, 1424, but Martin promised to hold another at Basel within seven years.

Restoring Rome and the Papal States took up most of his time. He did, however, manage to reform the clergy of St. Peter's. That was as far as his efforts went. In 1419, Martin approved the founding of the University of Rostock, and in 1425, that of Louvain. He preached a Crusade against the Hussites and negotiated with the Greek Church for reunion. Martin managed to reclaim certain rights from King Henry VI of England and to negotiate a favorable concordat with Charles VII of France in 1426. Though Martin left much important reform work undone, what he did accomplish was amazing, considering the limited resources at his disposal and the extent of the physical and spiritual damage he had to repair. At his death, Martin V was interred in St. John Lateran.

## Eugene IV
### (March 4, 1431–February 23, 1447)

Gabriel Condulmaro was born at Venice in 1383. His father came from a wealthy family—his mother was the sister of Gregory XII. Inheriting a fortune in his youth, Gabriel gave it all to the poor and entered the Augustinian monastery of San Giorgio, on the island of the same name in the Venetian lagoon. Gregory appointed him archbishop of Siena, but the young man resigned the diocese when the locals objected to his nationality. In 1408, Gregory appointed him cardinal-priest of San Clemente. For Martin V he acted as legate for Ancona and did great service in pacifying the territory and Bologna. He was elected on the first scrutiny at the conclave following Martin's death, after signing (with the others) a guarantee to split his revenues with the college after election and promising to consult the cardinals on all matters. On March 11, he was crowned Eugene at St. Peter's.

Though he was extremely holy, the new pope had a hatred of nepotism. This led to immediate conflicts with the Colonnas, whom Martin had given many offices as part of his campaign to reestablish pontifical control over the Papal States. That powerful family was ready for war, and only the intervention of Florence, Venice, and Naples convinced them to back down and surrender their castles to the pope. He then faced a greater difficulty. In accordance with Martin's orders, on July 31 the Council of Basel opened (with

poor attendance). Eugene did not trust those bishops who did arrive, thinking that they meant to take control of the Church. Using their few numbers as a pretext, he dissolved the Council on December 18, calling for a new one to open at Bologna eighteen months later. The prelates there assembled refused to disperse, believing that the pope was thereby attempting to prevent any reform of the Curia, and Church administration in general. All the kings of Europe supported them in their stance, and on April 29, 1432, they summoned the pope and his cardinals to appear at Basel within three months, or face punishment. An open break was, for the moment, averted by Sigismund. Sigismund had received the Iron Crown at Milan in 1431, and he now came to Rome to receive at long last the imperial coronation. Crowned by Eugene on May 31, the emperor convinced the pope to confirm the gathering at Basel as an Ecumenical Council, which the Pontiff did on December 15.

The following May, one of Rome's periodic revolutions drove Eugene from the city, and he took refuge at Florence at the Dominican House of Santa Maria Novella. The pope sent a legate to restore order in the Papal States and settled down in what was then arguably one of the most intellectually brilliant cities of Europe. Ruled by the Medici, it was a center of the new Humanist movement. The Humanists sought to base learning and culture upon the examples of Greece and Rome, and they looked down on the (by now primarily Aristotelian) Scholastic system. They thought of the intervening period between their own time and the fall of classical civilization as barbarous, and one wing clove particularly to pagan beliefs and morals. Another wing, however, sought to return Christian learning to the Platonic-Augustinian mode and to effect a thorough reform of Church abuses. It was a complex affair (such movements usually are). But the presence of the papal court at Florence helped expand Humanism's influence mightily.

Meanwhile, the Council fathers at Basel were working away mightily. They worked out a compromise with the more moderate Hussites, the so-called Calixtines. The Calixtines wished the cup given the laity. Their more radical brethren, the Taborites, held to Wycliff's teachings and refused any accord with the church. Against these, Basel heaped more anathemas. But in particular, many of the gathered prelates wanted to reduce the pope to a figurehead. Among other things, they wished to abolish all papal revenues. Against them, Eugene appealed to the crowned heads of Europe. The fight then crystallized around reunion with the Greeks—having solved the Western Schism, this seemed like the next logical step. But most of the Council Fathers wanted such a reunion council to be held in France or Germany. The pope wanted it in Italy, and John VIII Paleologus, the Byzantine emperor, and Patriarch Joseph II, of Constantinople, sided with Eugene. In response the radical prelates at Basel issued a decree against the pope on July 3, 1437. On September 18, the Pope sent a bull in reply, transferring the council to Ferrara. Many of the most able prelates went there, including Cardinal Nicholas of

Cusa, the leading Humanist. The Council of Ferrara officially opened on January 8, 1438.

The Fathers soon transferred to Florence. There, Eugene, the Byzantine emperor and his patriarch, and many of the greatest names in East and West labored successfully to bring about agreement on the Filioque (Lat., "and of the Son"), the use of leaven in bread, the ranking of the Patriarchates, and various other difficulties. These were resolved and the Act of Union was signed on July 5, 1439. Showing much pleasure by this reunion, the Council Fathers went on to reconcile with the Armenians on November 22, the Syrian Jacobites in 1443, and the Nestorians two years later. Powerful factions among each of these opposed the Union, but for the first time since Nestorius was anathematized the Christian body was at long last bound up together. Unfortunately, the saintly Joseph II died before the Council ended. On the night of his death he wrote a profession of Faith expressing belief in purgatory, the Filioque, and the primacy of the pope. The newly reunited Easterners asked the pope and Council for a definition of the scope and shape of the Church, which was duly granted in a bull:

> It [the Church] firmly believes, professes, and proclaims that none of those who are not within the Catholic Church, not only pagans, but also Jews and heretics and schismatics cannot become participants in eternal life, but will depart "into everlasting fire which was prepared for the devil and his angels" (Matt. 25:41), unless before the end of their life the same have been added to the flock; and that the unity of Ecclesiastical body is so strong that only to those remaining in it are the Sacraments of the Church of benefit for Salvation, and do fastings, almsgiving, and other functions of piety and exercises of Christian service produce eternal reward, and that no one, whatever almsgiving he has practiced, even if he has shed blood for the name of Christ, can be saved, unless he has remained in the bosom and unity of the Catholic Church. (Pope Eugene IV, the Bull Cantate domino, 1441, in Denzinger, Enchiridion Symbolorum, p. 714).

This unity would be severely tested. The Turks had recovered from the inroads of Tamerlane and were once again probing the Danube frontier and pressuring Constantinople. To relieve pressure on the city, another Crusade was preached and launched from Hungary. At first successful, the Crusaders suffered a crushing defeat at Varna, Bulgaria, in 1444.

Nor were the remaining prelates at Basel idle. Although their numbers were dropping, in 1438 they declared Eugene suspended, and the following year deposed. Having dwindled to one cardinal and eleven bishops, they elected Duke Amadeus VIII of Savoy as an anti-pope, under the name of Felix V.

Following the end of all major schisms East and West, the Church was not in a mood for another, and the effort went nowhere.

Politically, Eugene met with a great deal of success. His Italian position was secured by a treaty with King Alfonso of Aragon, whom he confirmed as ruler of Naples. As a result, on September 28, 1443, the pope was able to reenter Rome. Although he could convince King Charles VII of France to abrogate the so-called Pragmatic Sanction of Bourges (signed in 1438, which limited the rights of the Holy See in France), he did settle his relations with the Germans amicably by guaranteeing that a future council would be held in a German city. In 1443, he approved the charter of the University of Catania.

At his death, Eugene had accomplished much that scores of his predecessors had failed to do. For the moment, he had repaired Humpty-Dumpty. But human nature, alas, remained the same.

## *Felix V*

*Anti-Pope (February 5, 1440–1449)*

Amadeus VIII, count of Savoy, was born at Chambery on December 4, 1383. A wise and just ruler, he had presided over his hereditary lands in Savoy and Piedmont in an exemplary way. During the Great Schism, he looked after the Church in his dominions with paternal devotion. Emperor Sigismund was much impressed with him, and raised Savoy to a duchy in 1416, adding the county of Geneva to the Duke's domains in 1422. When Amadeus's wife, Mary of Burgundy, died, he withdrew to a life of meditation and prayer at the castle of Ripaille on Lake Geneva. He left the affairs of his duchy in the hands of his son, Louis. In his retreat, he formed his five knight-companions into an Order of St. Maurice (patron of his family) to sing the Divine Office and hear Mass with him.

After declaring Eugene IV deposed in 1439, the remaining prelates of the Council of Basel searched for a replacement. They turned to Amadeus, who had helped Sigismund with affairs at Constance (and thus could, they thought, be trusted as a conciliarist) and could bring money and power to the affair. The single cardinal, eleven bishops, seven abbots, five theologians, and nine canon lawyers who made up the Council by this point elected him as pope on October 30. On July 24, 1440, he agreed to accept the position, following his excommunication by Eugene IV the previous March (and completely renouncing his duchy). Until 1442, he boasted as his secretary the famed humanist, Aeneas Silvius Piccolomini.

Unfortunately, his election had the opposite effect from what the Basel fa-

thers intended—even the Nestorians had returned to the fold, so their schism looked silly. Switzerland and Savoy for the most part rallied to him, along with the dukes of Austria, Tyrol, and Bavaria, as well as the Teutonic Order and some orders and universities in Germany. But a number of those he appointed as cardinals refused to have anything to do with him, and Felix was soon fighting with the Council over money and prerogatives (which they would no more give him than Eugene). In 1442 Felix left Basel for Geneva, where he had taken over the diocese for the sake of funding. The last session of the Council ended on May 16 of the following year. For six years Felix soldiered on at Geneva, but in the end was reconciled to Nicholas V, who created him cardinal of St. Sabina and vicar general for the lands of the House of Savoy and various Swiss dioceses. He died at his retreat of Ripaille on January 7, 1451. Thus ended the last anti-pontificate. (One never knows what the future may bring, however.)

## Nicholas V

### (March 6, 1447–March 24, 1455)

The son of a poor doctor, Tommaso Parentucelli was born at Sarzana in Lugira, on November 15, 1397. The early death of his father meant that Tommaso's studies at Bologna had to be interrupted. Serving as tutor to the children of noble families in Florence, he became friendly with some of the leading Humanists of his time. Once his monetary situation was thereby solved, he returned to Bologna to finish his degrees, graduating in 1422 as a Master of Theology. He then entered the service of the holy Niccolo Cardinal Albergati, the archbishop of Bologna. For twenty years he was the prelate's right-hand man, refusing Eugene IV's offer of employment (Eugene had been much impressed by Tommaso's immense learning and administrative skill). When Cardinal Albergati, who had chaired the Council of Florence, died, Eugene appointed Tommaso his successor at Bologna. But the then-riotous city was impossible to enter, and so the pope used the new archbishop on various diplomatic missions. In 1446, Eugene appointed him cardinal, and he was elected pope on Eugene's death, taking the name Nicholas.

The new pontiff loved learning and all the arts. He resolved to make Rome a center of Humanism, of beauty, and of knowledge. To that end he invited scholars and artists from all over Christendom. (It is to him that we owe the

Vatican library, and the current appearance of the Papal Palace.) He built new aqueducts for the city, as well as new fortifications. Dismayed by the ruinous condition of St. Peter's (which was, after all, a millennium old and had endured much abuse) he began rebuilding it. Indeed, the plans he laid created modern Rome, although it would take many decades to complete. But so uncritical was Nicholas that many of the scholars and artists he attracted, though skilled in their fields, were far from the best of men. He thus unwittingly paved the way for a terrible reputation for the Papal Court. In 1451, he approved the charter of the University of Glasgow.

But he did much for the spiritual life of the Church. After calling a Jubilee Year for 1450, he concluded it by sending Cardinal d'Estouteville to France, Cardinal Nicholas of Cusa to northern Germany, and St. John Capistran (the Franciscan friar after whom the Mission in California, where the swallows return every year, was named) to southern Germany as his special legates. Concerned with bringing the graces of the Jubilee that thousands of pilgrims had sought at Rome, these men not only settled administrative affairs (d'Estouteville quashed the proceedings against St. Joan of Arc, thus paving the way for her eventual canonization), they also preached Mass to open air assemblies. In this way, countless people of all ages and classes in those regions returned to the practice of the Faith and reception of the Sacraments. The crowning achievement (quite literally) occurred on March 19, 1452, with the coronation of Emperor Frederick III of the house of Habsburg by Nicholas V. Three days earlier Frederick had married Leonora, daughter of the king of Portugal. This was the last imperial coronation at Rome.

Great as Nicholas's achievements were, they were overshadowed by events in the East. When the Eastern delegates returned to Constantinople, they found a population that was heavily anti-Western; many of the envoys recanted their adherence to the union, although neither the emperor, John VIII, nor his successor, Bl. Constantine XI, would do so. In 1449, at the Battle of Kosovo, the last of the Serbian nobility were crushed by the Turks on the same site where, back in 1389, St. Lazar, last independent king of Serbia, had also been defeated and killed. The Sultan, Mohammed II, was now master of the Balkans outside Constantinople. Constantine appealed for aid to the pope, who in turn called upon the Western ruler to help. Few replied, but in 1452 Nicholas sent Cardinal Isidore of Kiev, who had signed the Union on behalf of the Russians and been expelled upon his return home, to Constantinople. At the cathedral of Hagia Sophia, in the presence of the emperor, Isidore presided over a liturgy where both the pope and patriarch were prayed for. But Lucas Notaras, grand admiral of the empire, spoke for many of his fellow subjects when he said that he would prefer "the turban of the sultan to the tiara of the pope."

A fleet of ten papal galleys were sent to the city's relief, but they arrived too

late. On May 29, 1453, the Turks breached the walls of Constantinople. The emperor fell with his troops, fighting at the gate of St. Romanus. Those who sought refuge at Hagia Sophia were slaughtered, and Justinian's great church was turned into a mosque. As for Lucas Notaras, who had preferred the sultan's turban, he and his three handsome teenage sons were brought before Mohammed, who then demanded that the father give the boys to him as concubines. The admiral angrily refused, and the sultan ordered the trio murdered before their father's eyes, before ordering Lucas's death as well. Mohammed then chose Gennadios II as the new patriarch. He had been the leader of the anti-papal party among the Greek clergy. Chosen specifically to end the union, Gennadios was ironically a philosophical disciple of St. Thomas Aquinas—differing from his master both in rejecting papal primacy and in accepting the Immaculate Conception. Certainly, this was ironic in the light of subsequent Orthodox rejection of that dogma, when Pius IX defined it. Bl. Constantine's daughter had been married to the prince of Muscovy in far-off Russia and had brought with her the imperial throne in dowry. From this time on the Muscovite rulers called themselves "Tsar" (Emperor), used the imperial double eagle as their insignia, and functioned as the practical heads of Eastern Orthodoxy. "Rome fell to the barbarians," they declared, "and Constantinople, the New Rome, to the Turks. But Moscow is the Third Rome, and a fourth there will not be!" (Such was the animating idea of the Russian court ever after, until it too ended in 1917.)

Constantinople's fall affected the West as that of Acre had done in 1291. Many Greek refugees fled to safe havens in Europe—such as El Greco. Nicholas called immediately for a Crusade. Not only were the increasingly nationalistic countries of Europe unconcerned, some, such as Genoa and Venice, allied with the Turks for their own mercantile advantage. In this, as in so much else, the modern world was emerging. Nicholas V died, pleased with what he had done for Rome, but severely worried about the rest of Creation.

## Callixtus (Callistus) III

### (April 8, 1455–August 6, 1458)

Alfonso de Borja was born on December 31, 1378, near Valencia, Spain. Upon completion of his studies, he entered the service of Benedict XIII. When Alfonso V of Aragon decided to bring all of his subjects under Martin V, it was Alfonso who mediated and convinced Clement VIII to submit. Martin was so grateful he appointed Alfonso bishop of Valencia, and Eugene IV made him cardinal in 1444. Renowned for his penitential lifestyle and humble manner, as well as his zeal for the Crusade against the Turks, he was elected pope, taking the name Callixtus.

His first interest was to pursue the Crusade and free Constantinople. Envoys were sent all over Europe to beg the kings to forget their petty fights. In addition, missionaries were sent everywhere to preach the Crusade, and collectors were sent to raise money for it. Callixtus commanded the Faithful everywhere to pray for its success, and the bells all over Europe rang at noon to remind them. (This last custom, the Angelus bell, has continued to the present time.) Every country in Europe was busy, however, either fighting with its neighbors or indulging in succession disputes or civil war. Genoa sent a fleet, and thus was attacked by Aragon. On hearing this news, Portugal withdrew the ships her king had sent. Nevertheless, Crusaders did gather in Hungary, under the leadership of John Hunyadi and St. John Capistran. On July 22, 1457, these troops met and mastered the Turks at Belgrade, one of the few great defeats the Sultan suffered for the next century. But congratulations were the only reply Callixtus got from the kings who received the news, and John Hunyadi died of a fever shortly after his victory. An assembly of princes called by the pope later that year produced little effect. Only one other great captain emerged in the struggle against the Turks—Skanderbeg, leader of the Albanians. Adopting the double eagle of the empire as his banner, he managed to clear his country of the invader and was named captain of the Roman Church by Callixtus. Besides the pope, he received little aid, and after his death the Turks overwhelmed his countrymen.

(To this day the Albanians call themselves the "sons of Skanderbeg"; this is ironic, because most today are Muslim. Even more ironic is their struggle with the Serbs over Kosovo, given that nation's similar use of the double eagle and the region's sacredness to Serbia because of their double defeat there at the hands of the Turks. This quarrel doubtless gives much amusement to the Sultan's shade, in whatever region of the afterlife it might dwell.)

Callixtus came to realize that his work was a failure (and he became estranged as a result from his former sovereign, the king of Aragon), although the Angelus remains to remind us of the sincerity of his attention. One other act of his was to have lasting effects: the appointment of his nephew Rodrigo de Borja as cardinal. But these effects were certainly not what the upright old Spaniard had in mind.

## Pius II

### (August 19, 1458–August 14, 1464)

Aeneas Silvius Piccolomini was born at Cosigno, near Siena, on October 18, 1405. The eldest of eighteen children born to a poor noble family, he spent his youth helping his father cultivate their rundown estate. At the age of eighteen, he started at the University of Siena, where he studied freely and chased (and caught) women just as freely. In 1425 the preaching of St. Bernardine of Siena almost snagged him for the religious life, but his boon companions persuaded him otherwise. For two years he studied poetry and the classics at Florence, returning to Siena to study law. There, in 1432, he met Capranica, bishop of Fermo, who was on his way to Basel for the Council. The prelate hired Aeneas as his secretary, and the pair went to Basel to form part of the opposition to Eugene IV. Unable to continue his secretary's salary, Capranica released him to the service of several other bishops in succession, until he came to work for Cardinal Albergati. His new employer sent him on several diplomatic missions, finally sending him to Scotland. Aeneas arrived there after a frightening storm-tossed voyage, which led him to promise to walk barefoot to the nearest shrine of Our Lady, if she would grant him safe landing. He arrived and fulfilled his vow to walk ten miles to the shrine of Our Lady of Whitekirk. That unshod journey gave him the gout, which would afflict him the rest of his life. During his sojourn in that country, he also managed to father a child.

When he returned to Basel, Aeneas found his erstwhile employer reconciled to Eugene. But he stayed on, fulfilling various conciliar positions, fueling the opposition to the pope, and leading an extremely dissolute lifestyle. He retained his Faith, however, and as a result, he refused ordination—even to the deaconate, when the Fathers offered him a post as an elector for their attempted successor to Eugene. He served as Master of Ceremonies at the conclave that elected Felix V. Becoming secretary to the new anti-pope, he soon realized better than anyone how flimsy the Council's position really was. In 1442, he was sent to represent the prelates at the Diet of Frankfurt, when he switched sides.

At Frankfurt, Aeneas's literary abilities caught the attention of Frederick III, who engaged him as his secretary. The next year he became secretary to the imperial chancery at Vienna and gradually turned into an active partisan of Eugene IV. In 1445, he officially reconciled to the pope, who absolved him for his part in the Basel fiasco. But at the same time, his moral life improved, and he underwent a true conversion of life. Now no longer fearful of the clerical state, Aeneas was ordained a subdeacon in March 1446, after breaking up the Electors' League that was formed by certain princes in opposition to both Frederick and Eugene. While remaining in the emperor's service, Aeneas was consecrated bishop of Trieste in 1447 and translated to Siena three years later. Frederick brought him to Rome for his coronation, and Aeneas was made cardinal in 1456 by Callixtus III, whom he succeeded.

As Pius II, he made his predecessor's goal his own and bent all his efforts toward the Crusade. He called for an assembly of Europe's rulers to be held at Mantua on June 1, 1459, and founded Our Lady of Bethlehem, an order of knights, for the new Crusade. Few of the Monarchs showed, and all had excuses as to why they could do nothing. The Germans promised troops, however, and ordered a three-year war against the Turks—nothing developed. As Callixtus III had found, the personal and petty strife of Europe was more important to the continent's rulers than were their sworn obligations to the Church.

One rumor stated that the Sultan himself had lost faith in Islam. Pius sent an eloquent letter setting forth the Catholic faith, urging him to convert. Instead of converting, the Sultan assuaged his opposition to Islamic law by drinking.

Pius was also very reform minded, and appointed a commission to prescribe measures toward that end. In addition, he issued legislation tightening up monastic life. Whenever chided with his past immoral life and writings, he would reply, "Ignore Aeneas, but listen to Pius." He found time to write a great many things and to beautify Rome further. The day when a pope could summon the chivalry of Christendom to the field had passed. At last, despairing of action on the part of secular leaders, the pope himself went to Ancona, where Crusaders were gathering, determined to lead the venture. But death took the old pontiff before he could take ship, and the troops dispersed.

## Paul II

### (August 30, 1464–July 26, 1471)

Born Pietro Barbo at Venice in 1417, his mother was the sister of Eugene IV. Although trained in business, when his uncle became pope he entered the priesthood, becoming archbishop of Bologna, and was appointed cardinal in 1440. Nicholas IV and Callistus III relied on him greatly, but Pius II had little use for him. As a result, the cardinals, who had not been too happy with Pius, elected him. He took the name Paul, in honor of the Apostle.

Fond of festivity, he introduced elaborate carnival celebrations at Rome in imitation of his native Venice. As a resident he built the Palazzo San Marco, which after his death became the Palazzo Venezia, home of the Venetian ambassadors to the Holy See. (Years later, it would become the headquarters of Benito Mussolini, who used the pope's former bedroom as his office and made his many famous speeches from its terrace.) Paul gave all the cardinals (not just the cardinal-bishops as heretofore) the privilege of wearing the red biretta, and he suppressed the Roman Academy because of its rampant immorality. Nevertheless, he was in general a patron of Humanism. He also fought various Manichaean-style heretics in France, Italy, and Germany, as well as the pro-Hussite king George Podiebrad of Bohemia. On Christmas Eve, 1468, Frederick III, then at Rome, read the customary section of scripture that pertained to Caesar Augustus's ordering the census which brought the Holy Family to Bethlehem (the last time this ceremony was performed, although it remained in the Roman Ceremoniale until the 1960s). In 1470, he ordered that Jubilees be celebrated every twenty-five years (and they have been ever since). He also attempted negotiations with the Tsar of Russia for reunion—all of which proved fruitless.

The biggest failure of his pontificate was of course in regard to the Crusade, although he did win a hearing after the Venetian-held Island of Euboea fell to the Turks in 1470. But apart from getting much-needed funding to Skanderbeg and Hungary, he accomplished little against the Sultan.

## Sixtus IV
### (1471–August 12, 1484)

Francesco della Rovere was born near Abisola on July 21, 1414, to poverty-stricken parents. He entered the Franciscans while rather young and studied philosophy and theology at the University of Pavia. He became a lecturer at various Italian universities, attracting the great cardinal Bessarion as a student. Created cardinal himself in 1467 by Paul II, he gave himself up completely to theology, writing a treatise that attempted to prove that Aquinas and Duns Scotus, although the latter denied and the former promoted the Immaculate Conception, were in reality somehow agreed on the point. The conclave elected him pope after Paul's death, and he took the name Sixtus.

His first interest was of course, the Crusade. Although his legates preached the venture to crowds in France, Spain, Germany, Poland, and Hungary, little resulted. In addition, Sixtus continued negotiations with the Russian Orthodox. Although none of these efforts proved successful, his artistic attempts did; the Sistine Chapel was built by him, as well as the bridge across the Tiber and the Trevi fountain. Sixtus granted a charter to the University of Genoa in 1471. In 1472, he approved the founding of the University of Ingolstadt, which is today the University of Munich. In 1474, he followed suit with the University of Zaragoza, and two years later, Sixtus did the same for that of Mainz. In 1477 he approved the University of Uppsala, and in 1479 he similarly gave his approbation to the University of Copenhagen.

Nepotism became his only major vice. In 1478, his nephew, Rafael Cardinal Riario, was involved in the Pazzi conspiracy, which managed to assassinate one Medici brother, while leaving the other, Lorenzo, alive. The survivor wreaked a great vengeance on Cardinal Riario's party, and the Florentines rose against them. In response, the pope placed Florence under interdict, and a two-years' war with the city began. He then incited the Venetians to attack Ferrara, which he wanted to transform into a fief for another of his nephews. But Ercole d'Este, Ferrara's reigning duke, allied with most of the Italian states and forced the pope to make peace. This embarrassing affair not only tarnished Sixtus's reputation, it had the effect of helping to reduce the papacy in the popular mind to merely another petty Italian power. In any case, this defeat helped hasten Sixtus's death.

# Innocent VIII

## (August 29, 1484–July 25, 1492)

Giovanni Battista Cibo was born at Genoa in 1432, the son of the Roman senator Aran Cibo. In his youth he sowed his wild oats, fathering a son and daughter out of wedlock. But he repented of his ways, went into the priesthood, and entered the service of Cardinal Calandrini. Made bishop of Savona in 1467, he was translated to Molfetta five years later and created cardinal in 1473. At the Conclave after Sixtus IV's death (owing in part to the canvassing of Giuliano Cardinal della Rovere), he was elected pope, taking the name Innocent, in honor of Innocent IV who was a countryman.

He, too, was most interested in establishing peace in Europe to launch a Crusade. The struggle with King Ferrante of Naples inherited from his predecessors precluded this happy event, however. A younger brother of the Sultan was held prisoner at Rome, who promised to withdraw the Turks from Europe if restored, so it looked like a good time after all to take the Cross. In 1490, an assembly of princes met in Rome, but little resulted. Nevertheless, Innocent did live to see the fall of Granada the next year and the final accomplishment of the Reconquista. He granted in commemoration to the king of Spain the title of "Most Catholic Majesty" (which they bore proudly until it was renounced by Juan Carlos I on his accession to the throne of that country in 1975).

Politically, he confirmed the right of Henry VII of England and his heirs to occupy the throne after the defeat and death of Richard III at Bosworth Field in 1485, despite the fact that folk with closer claims to that crown still survived.

In other areas, Innocent did have more success. On December 5, 1484, he issued his celebrated bull against witchcraft. (Few topics have caused more upset in recent decades than the persecution of witches over the ages. Remember, however, the concept of the "witch," an individual who gives him or herself over to the powers of whatever the given culture or religion defines as spiritual evil, in return for preternatural abilities, is one common to all mankind.) Rather than being an invention of the Church, this notion may be found in earliest records (including the Hebrew scriptures). (Such people are put to death today in non-Christian areas, namely Africa and China.) During the Middle Ages, followers of various Manichaean sects who regarded the God of the Old Testament as evil, as noted earlier, sometimes worshiped Satan, defined in that book as God's enemy. Some of these were held to prac-

tice witchcraft, which was seen, like such heresy, as a threat not only to the well-being of individuals and communities, but the very foundations of Church and state. While Innocent VIII's bull is often seen as the beginning of prosecution for such folk, he was only the most famous of a long line of pontiffs and secular rulers who passed similar legislation. What made Innocent stand out was his official backing of the Dominican Fathers Kramer and Sprenger and their manual for witch-hunting, the Malleus Maleficarum. (A perusal of this book, and numerous other records, give the reader the impression that something strange and uncanny was up. This ought not surprise us—the scholar Chadwick Hansen assures us that something malefic was practiced at Salem, and accounts of modern Voodoo and Santeria imply the same thing. Certainly, modern wiccans, nature-worshiping adherents of a faith invented in the early twentieth century, have nothing to do with the medieval witch-cult, despite their own claims. The works of Montague Summers are recommended for those with further interest in the topic.)

During Innocent's reign, heresy per se also came under the gun. Not only did Innocent attack the Hussites and Waldenses, in December of 1486 he forbade the reading of the nine hundred theses that Pico della Mirandola posted publicly in the Eternal City. Mirandola (1463–1494), the handsome poster child for Humanism, made a number of startling points in theses, some of which came from his conviction that the Jewish Cabala could be a useful means of converting the Jews. As it happened, Innocent's successor declared Mirandola orthodox, and the young scholar died while working on an intense series of Catholic apologetic books.

In matters of security, Innocent was not so successful. Because he did not apply stiff enough penalties, robbery and other violent crimes flourished in the streets of Rome. He did crack down on forgers of papal bulls. But the crowning moment of his pontificate was the reception, May 31, 1492, of the biggest piece of the Holy Lance, which the Sultan surrendered to the Christians. However wild his youth had been, Innocent's age lived up to his name.

# Alexander VI

## (August 11, 1492–August 18, 1503)

Rodrigo de Borja was the nephew of Callixtus III, and born at Xativa, near Valencia, on January 1, 1431. His uncle brought him to Rome. Regardless of his lack of vocation, he was made a cardinal and eventually the dean of the Sacred College. In that position, Rodrigo was able to secure his election (whether by simony or not) in succession to Innocent VIII. Considered one of themselves by the people of Rome, they celebrated his election madly, with torchlight processions, bonfires, flowers, and the like. Upon his coronation at St. Peter's on August 26, he declared, "I shall be named after the unconquerable Alexander [the Great]." An odd hero for a pope to have, to be sure, but not inappropriate, as the new pontiff's subsequent career would show.

Alexander VI would rate in most people's minds as the worst of popes (though to this author, that dishonor belongs more properly to John XII or Benedict IX). Certainly, no one denies that as cardinal he had a married mistress who produced four children for him, most notably Cesare and Lucrezia. Whether he continued in that manner of life after he assumed the tiara is another question. Of course, the Renaissance in Italy was a time of easy virtue and easier morals (as is our own). But then (as now), a higher standard was expected of the priesthood. Thus, as Joseph de Maistre observed in Du Pape, "The vices lightly passed over in a Louis XIV become most offensive and scandalous in an Alexander VI." Perfectly true, but a major difference in Alexander's time was that even then there was public aspiration toward virtue, and Cardinal de Borja was denounced quite publicly for his lifestyle (apparently there was freedom of speech as well, given that such denunciations were not punished).

As with such figures as England's Richard III (and our own Benjamin Franklin), there are two radically different schools of thought. In Alexander's case, the majority of writers have denounced him not only for early but for ongoing immorality, for simony, and much else. The minority report (most notably as presented in A History of the Borgias, by the noted English eccentric Frederick Rolfe, Baron Corvo) holds that he lived an upright life after his election to the papacy, and was in fact, in Corvo's words, "a very great Prince, a very faithful Pastor, a very human Man." (But just as it is hard for those living at such a great distance in time to judge between the two Richard IIIs—evil nephew-murdering usurper or legitimacy-defending martyr—or the two

Benjamin Franklins—maxim-coining founding father or Hellfire Club member and British spy—so it must ever be with Alexander VI.)

Shortly after becoming pope he had to deal with the question of the New World that was discovered by Christopher Columbus in 1492 (as well as territories in the East found by Portugal). In a time that considered membership in the Church essential for salvation, Alexander had to decide how best to assure orderly evangelization of the natives, while keeping the Spanish and Portuguese from killing each other over the land. The solution was a division of the world into two parts. Alexander made the division, and as a result, the Portuguese colonized the East Indies and Brazil, while Spain looked after the rest of the New World and the Philippines. In a real sense, Alexander must be seen as one of the Fathers of the Church outside Europe (although any number of priests, religious, and lay folk did the actual legwork). And, of course, the cultural divide between Brazil and the rest of Latin America is thereby owed to him as well.

Alexander did restore order to Rome by cracking down heavily on street crime and murder. Dividing the city into four districts, each with a magistrate directly responsible for maintaining order and solving crime, he laid the foundation for modern Rome's police authority. This pope also built, rebuilt, and beautified any number of churches in the Eternal City. In addition, he installed the golden ceiling of Santa Maria Maggiore, using the precious metal brought back by Columbus and donated to the papacy by Ferdinand and Isabel. Alexander also expanded the noon bell-ringing order by his uncle Callixtus to three times a day, explicitly in honor of the Virgin. He passed a great deal of anti-witchcraft and anti–black magic legislation, but he exonerated Pico della Mirandola and other Cabalists of heresy. Alexander encouraged Humanism, and the theater in particular owes him a great debt. He was continually lampooned in print and cartoon for his past and possibly present lifestyle, and no one enjoyed reading these squibs more than he. Above all, he presided over an extremely successful Holy Year in 1500.

Conversely, against these accomplishments lay his political problems. A set of the cardinals, led by Giuliano della Rovere, sought and eventually succeeded in having Charles VIII of France invade Italy with the purpose of deposing the pope. The French king did indeed take Rome, but Alexander, holed up in the Castel Sant'Angelo, sat on his battlements and laughed at the invaders. Discouraged, the king left Rome to fight the Spaniards for control of Naples. A Holy League was formed against Charles that included the empire, Venice, and Spain. But the French-Spanish struggling over that kingdom effectively meant there would be no Crusade in this pontificate, a work whose prosecution Alexander had ardently desired. Instead, he set his son Cesare to work at reducing a number of the small tyrants who oppressed various towns nominally within the Papal States—this was done to secure a large duchy for Cesare. Because his importance did not outlast his father's pontificate, the

concrete result was to return these places to papal rule. Through successive marriages and other means (with or without poison, depending upon whom you read), daughter Lucrezia worked to help her father's policies as well.

During Alexander's time, the decadent heart of a new learning arose at Florence—the monk Savanarola. Like Alexander, this historical figure might as well be two men—saintly corrector of abuses, or fanatical enemy of culture. Whichever he was, Alexander at first reacted benignly to the monk's denunciations of his papacy. In time, however, both he and the people of Florence lost their patience, and Savanarola received excommunication and death by fire. Whether this was martyrdom or justice is another question that claims partisans on either side.

Rumor states that Alexander died of poison, but he actually died of the Roman marsh-fever. He was buried in the Spanish national parish of Santa Maria del Monserrato. Although he did leave a solid record of accomplishment behind him, he left a terrible reputation as well, which helped tarnish the papacy as a moral force in the minds of many.

## Pius III

### (September 22–October 18, 1503)

Francesco Todeschi Piccolomini was born at Siena on May 29, 1439. His mother was the sister of Pius II. He became an orphan at an early age, and his uncle took him in and gave him his name and arms. At the age of twenty-one, Pius II made him cardinal and archbishop of Siena, shortly afterward sending him as legate to the March of Ancona. Despite his youth, he impressed all there with his piety and administrative ability. Paul II sent him to Germany as legate, where he did very well thanks to his good knowledge of German. Disgusted by the moral tenor of Rome under Sixtus IV and Alexander VI, he stayed away as much as possible from the papal court. Because the conclave that followed the death of Alexander VI was hopelessly divided over cardinals della Rovere, d'Amboise, and Sforza, Francesco was eventually elected and took the name Pius in honor of his uncle.

Sadly, the new pope was quite ill, and the lengthy coronation ceremonies were too much for his waning strength. He died shortly thereafter. Initially interred in St. Peter's, he was later entombed beside his uncle in the church of Sant'Andrea del Valle.

# Julius II
## (November 1, 1503–February 21, 1513)

Born Giuliano della Rovere in 1443 of a distinguished noble family that had given many prelates to the Church, he was the nephew of Pope Sixtus IV (1471–1484). This favorable background allowed him to attain bishop of Carpentras, France, in 1461, at the age of eighteen. The same year he became cardinal, and as time passed he added various bishoprics, abbeys, and other positions to his portfolio. The seriousness with which he regarded his vocation may be seen by his three daughters.

When his uncle died, Giuliano lobbied strongly—reportedly with the help of bribes—for the election of the equally free-wheeling Giovanni Battista Cardinal Cibo as pope. This effort succeeded, and the new pontiff took the name Innocent VIII. For the next eight years, Giuliano enjoyed the lifestyle to which he had become accustomed.

Innocent was replaced by the Spanish Rodrigo Cardinal Borja y Borja, who took the name Alexander VI. As mentioned previously, historical opinion is sharply divided into two camps over Alexander. But whether he was saint or sinner, Alexander did not like Giuliano, who fled the Eternal City in 1494, fearful of Alexander arranging some mishap for him. While hiding in France, he attempted to interest King Charles VIII in a general council for the purpose of deposing Alexander. The effort failed, and until Alexander's death in 1503 Giuliano was forced to attend to his French dioceses in person.

The conclave after Alexander's death elected Pius III, who died almost immediately after his coronation. The next conclave elected Giuliano (who took the name Julius II)—again, not without suspicion of bribes.

Though not too pastoral, Julius II was an energetic pope. Three years after his election, he led a series of military campaigns in full armor to clear out of the Papal States the various small tyrants who had dominated so many cities nominally subject to the papacy. In 1508 in alliance with France, the Holy Roman Empire, and Spain, he trounced Venice, snatching several territories from the island republic. Fearing the French, however, he allied with the Venetians and recognized the claim of Ferdinand II of Aragon (of Ferdinand, Isabella, and Columbus fame) to Naples, despite the claim of the French king to that country's throne.

In 1511, the French invaded Italy and nearly captured Julius in battle. King Louis XII attempted to convene a council at Pisa on October of that year, with nine cardinals in attendance. The event was cosponsored by the

Holy Roman Emperor and culminated in a declaration deposing Julius. In reprisal, the "Council" Fathers were excommunicated and fled to Milan.

Meanwhile, Julius organized the "Holy League" to defend the rights of the papacy, uniting Spain, Venice, and—ironically, England's Henry VIII. The league drove the French from Italy and with them went the "Council," which eventually dissolved at Lyons. The Papal States had now reached their greatest extent in modern times, and even included Parma.

Although his work as a warrior was notable, Julius did perform some religious tasks as well. He established the first diocese in Latin America, declared that bribery nullified papal elections, and permitted Henry VIII to marry his brother's widow, Catherine of Aragon—a move designed to strengthen the Holy League. His contemporaries commented favorably on his strong-willed manner. Julius approved the foundation of the University of Compostela in 1504, that of Seville in 1505, of Madrid in 1509, and of St. John's College, Cambridge, in 1511. The following year, he convened the Council of Lateran V, which continued under his successor.

The art world remembers him as the patron of Michelangelo, Raphael, and Bramante. When he learned that the Constantinian basilica of St. Peter's was about to collapse, he oversaw the design and laid the cornerstone of the basilica that still stands today. Similarly, he commissioned Michelangelo's frescoes on the ceiling of the Sistine Chapel (as film buffs will recall from The Agony and The Ecstasy). Despite his warlike activities, he died not in battle, but of a fever.

# Northern Revolution

## Leo X
### (March 11, 1513–December 1, 1521)

Giovanni di Medici was born at Florence on December 1, 1475, the younger son of Lorenzo. From the beginning his vocation was the Church, and at his father's insistence Innocent VIII made him cardinal at age thirteen The pope insisted, however, on waiting for three years before bestowing the insignia of his rank on the boy. When this occurred, the Romans were pleasantly surprised by the maturity and learning of the boy, who had studied under some of the greatest Humanists of the day. Shortly thereafter, he attended the conclave that elected Alexander VI, whom he disliked intensely. His father's death that year called him back to Florence, and Giovanni stayed there until the revolution in 1494 that drove the Medicis from Florence. From then until his return to Rome in 1500, he traveled all over Europe, meeting the great scholars of his time. Giovanni's outstanding qualities were an unflagging cheerfulness, generosity to the point of bankruptcy, and a deep personal piety mixed with a love of secular amusements of all kinds—hunting to theater to the nascent ballet. Though he held strict morals, he tolerated in others flaws he rigorously repressed in himself. After his election to replace the short-lived Pius III, Leo remarked, "God has given us the papacy, now let us enjoy it."

Rome became a haven for artists, scholars, poets, musicians, and playwrights of all stripes, who could easily find money from the free-spending pontiff. Leo was fond of Carnival and all other festivities, as well as building and books. By 1515 he had emptied the treasury and fell back on that old standby of impecunious popes: creating offices and selling them. This move did not help much except to support Raphael and Michelangelo (and so we are indebted to him for that). Along with all of this activity, he found time to hear Mass and say his breviary every day and to fast three times a week. As cardinal he had kept a higher moral tone than his colleagues; as pope he continued to give a good personal example while tolerating all sorts of peccadilloes on the part of the writers, musicians, and artists who filled the Eternal City.

These qualities, though making Leo beloved in Rome and among the Humanists throughout Christendom, did not help him in other quarters. France and the empire alike wanted supremacy in Italy, but Leo thought a victory of

either would end the papacy's independence. He sided first with one, then the other—sometimes with both. Leo's diplomacy did prevent the triumph of either side, so Italy remained in turmoil, regarding the pope as just another shifty Italian prince. When at last he turned his mind to the Crusade, people refused to contribute, thinking (although in this case, he was sincere) it was just another means of raising cash.

The unrest of the past century and a half had now begun to take its toll on the life of the Church. To be sure, all over Christendom Masses were said and the sacraments continued to be confected. Pilgrims visited shrines and new saints were declared. Holy men and women continued to live in cloister and town. But priests were living in sin, in emulation of their ecclesiastical superiors, and clerics of all sorts were no longer wearing clerical garb. Many bishops held multiple dioceses, concerning themselves only with the revenue therefrom. The same was true for the many commendatory abbots, whose only role in their monasteries' lives was to collect money—from which monastic discipline suffered. Many places neglected catechetical teaching, and knowledge of Church dogma hardly existed. The vacuum created by this ignorance, superstition, and heresy caused witchcraft to flourish. Catholics everywhere were disgusted not only by this situation, but also by the feckless way in which Rome dealt with it (to say nothing of the corruption of the Roman curia and cardinals). But many of the secular lords who claimed to be scandalized by these situations were themselves partly responsible (a pattern most familiar in the early twenty-first century).

In this atmosphere the fathers of Lateran V soldiered on with Leo's permission. They legislated for five years against such concerns as the then popular notion among some of the educated that man has no soul or at least only one in common. They established pawn shops where the poor could get loans without usurious interest. In addition, they forbade the printing of books without an imprimatur, an idea first suggested by Alexander VI. (This was similar to the way the Federal Communications Commission functions with regard to broadcasting—the invention of the printing press had a similar effect on society to that of television or the Internet.) Finally, Lateran V issued all sorts of wholesome legislation against the disciplinary evils of the day. Nevertheless, the Council Fathers were all too aware that the pope and curia—for wildly different reasons—would sabotage the effectiveness of these decrees. In 1517 at the final session of the council, Gianfrancesco Pico della Mirandola (relation of the philosopher we met earlier) delivered a long oration on the evils facing the Church and the need for the pope to force reforms. If he did not, Mirandola warned, "God Himself will cut off the rotten limbs with fire and sword." It proved so indeed.

In that very year, an Augustinian monk named Martin Luther nailed his Ninety-five Theses upon the church door at Wittenberg, Saxony. (That such a

man was not only ordained, but rose high in his order, is proof that ecclesiastical affairs were poorly run.) Luther's initial annoyance with Church authorities was over the sale of indulgences, an abuse that had been protested against by many orthodox champions. This practice arose from a misapplication of a perfectly understandable Catholic practice (similar to the sale of marriage annulments in our own time). But, the corruption of the best is the worst!

Luther was excommunicated the next year by Leo X. Following his attack on the sale of indulgences, Luther went on to deny much more of Catholic teaching, including—perhaps as much to salve his own conscience—free will. He preached salvation through faith alone. "Sin, and sin boldly," he declared, "but believe more boldly still." For many in the Renaissance (given the lifestyles observed previously) this was a comforting notion. But his idea of private judgment—the Holy Spirit will tell each person what the Bible (for Luther the sole rule of faith) means—was to have a major effect in Western history. (The New Agers' admonition to "create your own reality!" is its logical conclusion and legitimate descendant.)

Luther and his disciples enjoyed tremendous success. By capturing Britain and Northern Europe, Protestant principles would dominate the creation of the United States (now the world's single remaining empire and superpower). But why did they succeed, when so many groups of heretics before them failed? The answer is simple. Though most of his predecessors were rebels to the State as well as the Church, Luther called on the princes to reform the Church by taking over complete control of it in their respective realms. Not merely in terms of government, discipline, and property (as among the Eastern Orthodox), but in doctrinal matters as well. Did the king of X want bishops? He could have them! Did his neighbor monarch think them unscriptural? Then away with them! And the reward for this was the Church's extensive properties. (Thus the Scandinavian countries and certain German districts have Lutheran State Churches; Scotland, the Netherlands, some of the Swiss Cantons, and certain other German districts have Calvinist ones; and England created a religion of its own, which, due to the growth of the British empire, is prominent in the United States, Canada, Australia, New Zealand, and South Africa, as well.)

But the notion of state control over the Church, as previously seen, was laid down by such men as William of Occam. Doctrinally, he and his colleagues were Catholic, but they were unable to see that deliverance of all ecclesiastical power into the hands of the prince would allow the prince to determine dogma as well. The Reformation merger of private judgment and complete state control would eventually develop into the modern system: anyone may believe what they like, so long as it is private, and the state maintains the absolute power to legislate right and wrong. In such an environment,

there is no question of an objective spiritual reality to which all—president or pauper—must conform themselves. The good of the state determines what truth is and religious beliefs are more or less a private fantasy.

Complete power over the Church enticed many monarchs to accept the stripe of Protestantism that pleased them, and then impose it violently on a more or less unwilling populace whose descendants would gradually accept it. (The violence and unpopularity of this process has been well established by historians of the school of Eamon Duffy.)

In Catholic countries, the Church was often forced to surrender powers of control over ecclesiastical appointments, which made the kings of France and Spain almost as much heads of their national churches as were their Protestant counterparts. The complete power of the papacy was destroyed in virtually all the nations of Europe—not merely in openly Protestant ones. Above all, Catholic rulers generally received the right to refuse to publish papal bulls in their respective nations—therefore, such bulls would have no effect on the national church.

What few if any of these monarchs realized was that such laying of violent hands upon the sacred could only, eventually, erode their own positions. If they themselves thus violate the altar, what would prevent others from so treating the throne? And so these monarchs began building up the state apparatus that would make the leading classes in such countries eventually realize that they could manipulate the machinery of government quite as well as (or better than) any king.

The year after Luther's excommunication, there was another imperial election. The three major contestants were Charles I of Spain (with Naples and Milan), Austria, and Burgundy; Francis I of France; and Henry VIII of England. Charles won, and, as Charles V, became ruler of the greatest empire ever seen up until that time. His possessions included the Spanish establishments in the West Indies.

From there, in 1519, Hernando Cortez began the conquest of Mexico, in the name of the emperor. Initially, the Aztecs believed that Cortez was their bearded white god Quetzalcoatl returned, because he arrived at precisely the time and place where that deity (believed by many scholars to have been a Norse or Irish priest) said he would make his reappearance. Once the Aztecs realized that they were mistaken, it was too late; their Indian subjects, tired of endless blood sacrifices of their lads and maidens, joined with the Spanish and ended the Aztec reign of cruelty. Thanks to the apparition of Our Lady of Guadalupe and devoted missionary work, most of the Mexicans would convert quickly, a pattern followed throughout Spanish America. Thus, at the very time that northern Europe was preparing to leave the Church, a whole New World was readying its entrance. In 1520, Leo created the title of Patriarch of the West Indies for the senior bishop in Spain. (Although Paul VI allowed it

to lapse when its last holder, the then-archbishop of Madrid, died, some have suggested that it ought to be revived and attached to the archdiocese of Santo Domingo as the oldest diocese in the Americas.)

So things stood when Leo X died of malaria. He was interred at Santa Maria Sopra Minerva.

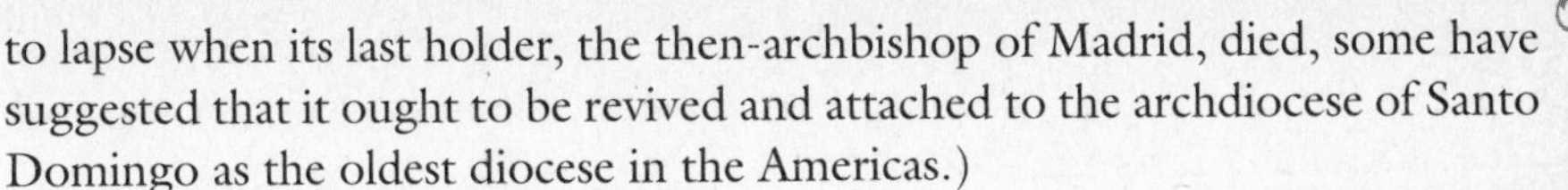

## Adrian VI
### (January 9, 1522–September 14, 1523)

Adrian Dedel was born at Utrecht on March 2, 1459. His father Florentius died when Adrian was still young, and his mother struggled successfully to keep him in school. He went to Zwolle to study with the Brothers of the Common Life (who also produced Thomas à Kempis), and then to the University of Louvain, where he studied theology, philosophy, and law, graduating as Doctor of Divinity in 1491. He rose to become vice-chancellor of the university and was quite popular among his students. His reputation was such that Emperor Maximilian I selected him as tutor to his grandson Charles, who grew up to become Emperor Charles V. With his charge he moved to Spain, where he became a close friend of Cardinal Ximenes, the grand inquisitor and regent of Spain. Because of this relationship with the emperor, and because of Adrian's great reputation for holiness at a time when all of Europe was denouncing the corruption of Rome, the cardinals unanimously elected him pope, and he left Spain for the Eternal City. He arrived on August 29, and was crowned ten days later, retaining his own name. He would be the last non-Italian pope elected until 1978.

Indeed, he had never been to Italy before; as a result, he was completely at sea after becoming pope. Announcing that the Church was "rotten in head and members," he immediately set to work to reform the curia. But knowing no one, and facing the sort of passive resistance that only a massive bureaucracy can muster, he made little headway. Unable to affect the curia, there was little he could do about the Protestant threat, save approve his former pupil's measures. But he could try to rally Christendom once more against the Turks, who again were on the move. Having taken Belgrade, the Sultan was preparing to move north of the Danube into Hungary. The Grand Turk was also preparing to snatch Rhodes from its knights. Adrian appealed to all the rulers of Christendom to come to their aid. They did nothing and that proud fortress fell to the Muslims on October 24, the news of which hastened the pope's demise. He was interred in the German church of Santa Maria dell'Anima.

## Clement VII
### (November 18, 1523–September 25, 1534)

Giulio de Medici was born at Florence in 1478, a few months after his father Giuliano was killed in the Pazzi conspiracy. He became a priest and a Knight of Rhodes, and when his cousin became Leo X, he moved to Rome and was made a cardinal. Giulio soon had a major voice in Leo's political policies. A typical Italian diplomat of his time, Giulio's own temper was extremely indecisive. He could not make a decision without immediately considering its opposite. Worst of all, the temper of his time and place were such as to cause the "wisest" to value honor and the given word lightly (yet another similarity between that time and present).

Nevertheless, he was able and personally of blameless life, so he did not lose all influence under the austere Adrian VI. He was eventually chosen pope after a long conclave and took the name Clement. At the time, Charles V was at war with Francis I. The emperor had every reason to expect the support of Clement because of the work he was doing to try to secure northern Germany for the Faith. Clement was uncontrollably shifty, however, and concluded a secret alliance with Francis. When Charles defeated and captured Francis at Pavia in 1525, he was in a position to wreak terrible revenge on Clement.

But the emperor took his position as nominal temporal head of Christendom very seriously. Seeing himself as indeed the successor of Charlemagne, he had plans even larger than his enormous empire. In addition to converting all the Americas, he wanted to reform the Church, conciliate the Lutherans and bring them back to the Faith, reunite with the Eastern Christians, and last, relaunch and prosecute the Crusade. To do all of this he would need the aid of the pope and the acquiescence of the king of France.

Thus, with Francis he signed the very moderate Treaty of Madrid in January of 1526, which the French king solemnly swore to uphold. But Francis broke his oath as soon as he was released, signing an alliance with Clement, Florence, and Venice at Cognac against Charles on May 22. This, in

addition to the growth of Lutheranism in the north (where prince after prince was joining the new religion and seizing the property of the old), was almost more than he could bear. Then, in August, the Turks overwhelmed the Hungarians at the Battle of Mohacs, and the Magyar king Louis II was killed. In the face of the Sultan's advance civil war broke out in that country, and in the end two-thirds of the nation passed under the crescent. Charles's patience with Clement was wearing quite thin. His unpaid German mercenaries in northern Italy (many of whom were Lutheran) took Rome on May 5, 1527, slaughtering the Swiss Guards who were defending the Vatican. The pope made his escape via a passage to the Castel Sant'Angelo, but the city was sacked. In a scene that was repeated all over the Protestant world, enemies devastated churches, desecrated the Blessed Sacrament, and destroyed priceless artwork. More horrific was the wholesale raping of nuns and the murder of clerics. Renaissance Rome paid for its sins, but the innocent suffered with the guilty.

After seven months the troops withdrew and Clement went to Orvieto, not returning to Rome until 1529 when he signed a treaty with Charles. Clement met Charles on February 24, 1530 and gave him the imperial coronation. This would be the last coronation performed by a pope. From then on, the holder of the office would be called emperor after his German coronation at Aachen (and later, at Frankfurt). But officially (and in the prayers of the Church) each would be called "emperor-elect." After that, Charles and Clement became allies, but not only was this accord too late to help, it led to complications elsewhere.

The Reformation was spreading beyond the imperial boundaries. In 1527, Gustavus Vasa, who had taken control of Sweden from the Danes, took control of the Church in his country as well. During his reign, he faced various risings of the Catholic peasantry, all of whom were duly slaughtered. His adaptation of Lutheranism was very superficial because he kept in office only those bishops who would go along with him (though he suppressed the monasteries). So Sweden (and Finland) boasted the only national churches on the continent that claimed the Apostolic Succession. Unlike the Church of England, which made the same boast, the Holy See never ruled definitely on the point. (For Catholics therefore, it remained an open question until the 1960s, when the Swedish government ordered their church to ordain women.)

England (whose king Henry VIII had been given by Leo X the title "Defender of the Faith" for his book, In Defense of the Seven Sacraments against Luther) was the next non-German to fall. Here the dispute was not doctrinal but biological. The king wanted to divorce his wife, Catherine of Aragon, with whom he had first been in love, but who had failed to bear a living male heir to him. He sought an annulment on the grounds that his wife had been married to his brother before (although he had had a dispensation, because that marriage had never been consummated). He desired to marry Anne Boleyn, which would have been impossible according to Church law at the time because her sister Mary had been Henry's mistress. At first Clement intimated that he would give the king his desire, but in the end he could not—partly because of his belief in the validity of Catherine's marriage, and partly because of her uncle, Charles V's displeasure should the pope do so. England left the Church, but the king did not alter its dogmas—that would come later. Like his Swedish counterpart, King Henry seized the abbeys and destroyed the shrines.

The interesting thing about the Reformation in Germany, Sweden, and elsewhere is the resistance to it. Peasants were slaughtered in droves, and more would follow. But this could be expected because peasants were conservative as a rule. Understandable, too, were the individual martyrs for the Faith—religious and lay—male and female—who were brought up in and believed the traditional teachings of the Church. But what is curious, because Humanism is always called a forerunner of the Reformation, is how few of the front rank of Humanists themselves sided with Luther. St. Thomas More in England is well known, of course. But Erasmus, Reuchlin (who was uncle to one of Luther's closest disciples), and many others rallied to the defense of the Church they had criticized so fiercely before 1517. Perhaps it is because their criticisms were based on a desire to build up rather than destroy (surely a novel notion in the present day).

Clement's reign was stormy; even his attempts to beautify Rome were somewhat stymied, though he did commission Michelangelo to do the famous last judgment for the Sistine Chapel. In addition, he employed Benevenuto Cellini, thus giving that artist his start. Moreover, he approved the formation of the Capuchin and Recollect Franciscans orders which would do much for the Church. Clement approved the foundation of the University of Granada in 1531, and that of Santo Domingo seven years later. At his death he was interred beside his cousin Leo X at Santa Maria Sopra Minerva.

# Paul III

## (October 12, 1534–November 10, 1549)

Alessandro Farnese was born at Rome on February 29, 1468. His family was one of the most notable of the Roman nobility, and his ancestors had performed many services for the Church. During a brilliant education at the Florence of Lorenzo di Medici, he made the friendship of the future Leo X. On September 20, 1493, Alexander VI made him a cardinal. He occupied this office for more than forty years, maintaining his popularity with all parties and the people of Rome. Part of this latter was because of the way he freely spent the money that came to him from many different benefices. This together with his piety and zeal made him the obvious candidate at Clement VII's death.

The new pontiff was extremely popular with the Romans, being the first native of the city to wear the tiara since Martin V. But the city he now presided over suffered much by the sack of 1527. Unlike Adrian VI, he faced little opposition to the reform program he quickly put into place. All sorts of abuses were ended, and he placed supervisorial machinery in action.

The Protestant revolt continued, and seemingly every month arrived with news of another defection on the usual pattern, such as Christian III of Denmark in 1536. On June 2 of that year, the pope summoned a general council to be held at Mantua in May of 1537. The Protestant princes refused to attend, and the Duke of Mantua would take no responsibility. Paul tried again, calling for another council at Vicenza for May 1, 1538. But renewed warfare between Charles V and Francis I prevented it. The pope then prevailed on both successors of Charlemagne to meet with him and negotiated a truce for ten years between them.

But Francis was not in favor of a General Council, because, if successful, it would reunite Germany under Charles. So, while he persecuted the Protestants (Huguenots) in his own realm so harshly that Paul begged him to show mercy, the king of France allied with the Smalkald League of Protestant German princes. For his part, Charles did not want the proposed council to define dogmas clearly; rather, like the emperors faced with Arianism, Nestorianism, and Monophysitism, he hoped for doctrinal formulae vague enough for all parties to subscribe to. Paul, on the other hand, wanted to reaffirm the Church's teachings as clearly as possible.

After Francis and Charles made yet another treaty at Crespi on September 21, 1544, Paul set down in earnest to convene the Council. The Protestant

princes would not recognize any such council presided over by a pope, so Charles declared himself in favor of defeating them before convening the assembly. Moreover, he asked Paul to confine the Council's work to disciplinary measures in order to hold open the possibility of doctrinal conciliation. Paul refused. On December 13, 1545, the Council at last opened at Trent. In seven sessions, ending on March 3, 1547, the Council Fathers defined once and for all the Catholic teaching on Scriptures, the Sacraments, salvation, and much else that had been called into question by the Protestants. An outbreak of the plague forced the Council to close, however, and all save fifteen Fathers (subjects of Charles V) moved on to Bologna. They had Paul's permission to do so, but Charles insisted that they reconvene somewhere within his dominions. Rather than face a schism, Paul suspended the Council indefinitely. Charles, in the meantime, issued on his own authority a doctrinal interim that was rejected by both sides. For the few years remaining to him, the pope and the emperor were estranged.

Moreover, having made one of his relations duke of Parma and Piacenza (which duchies belonged to the Papal States), Paul tried to get them back. But Charles backed up the erring relation (a grandson, as it happened), and they remained permanently out of papal hands. The pontiff's death was hastened by this defection. Paul's lasting legacy is not only the Council of Trent, but the art of Titian, whom he patronized. He also approved many new orders who would speed the work of Catholic reform, such as the Jesuits, Theatines, and Ursulines. In addition, he gave a charter to the University of Macerata.

## Julius III
### (February 7, 1550–March 23, 1555)

Giammaria Ciocchi del Monte was born at Rome on September 10, 1487, the son of a noted lawyer. He followed his uncle Antonio into the priesthood and succeeded him as archbishop of Siponto in 1512, and as bishop of Pavia in 1520. Giammaria was prefect of Rome under Clement VII and was taken hostage by the German troops. Made a cardinal by Paul III, he presided over the first sessions of the Council of Trent and transferred it to Bologna because of the plague. When Paul died, the forty-eight cardinals of the conclave were divided into French, Imperial, and Farnese factions. The first and second cooperated to elect Giammaria, and he took the name Julius.

One of the new pope's first acts was to confirm Ottavio Farnese in control of Parma. Farnese, however, declared himself an ally of the French. Julius allied with the emperor and so the pair were at war. At first zealous for reform, the pope reconvened the Council and sent it back to Trent, ordering its sessions to resume on May 1, 1551. The approach of French troops (as well as the refusal of that country's bishops to attend) caused Julius to prorogue it once more. The emperor fled to Innsbruck, and the pope was forced to make peace with the French on April 29, 1552.

Julius then withdrew from the political affairs of Italy, withdrawing likewise to his luxurious villa, the Villa Giulia, near the Porto del Popolo. There, together with his favorite, Innocenzo del Monte, a teenager he had picked up in the streets of Parma and made a cardinal shortly after his coronation, he "participat[ed] in entertainments of a questionable character" (in the coy words of the 1911 Britannica). The villa was a byword for decadence and ostentation, and the last few years of his pontificate led many to wonder if the bad old days were back. (Certainly, the stories told of the Villa Giulia remind us of some clerical establishments of our time.)

Despite the unusual festivities of the papal villa, the reform's momentum had taken hold. The Jesuits flourished, the Church founded the Collegium Germanicum for the education of German priests in Rome, and the accession of Queen Mary in 1553 brought England back to the Catholic faith. Two years before, Julius had approved the founding of the universities of Mexico City and Lima. A more worthy holder of the papal office seemed all that was needed, and in a short time the chair became vacant once more.

## Marcellus II

### (April 8–May 6, 1555)

Born Marcello Cervini degli Spannochi May 6, 1501, at Montepulciano, his father Ricardo had been apostolic treasurer in the March of Ancona. Young Marcello thus had an in to the papal bureaucracy. Studying at Rome after 1528, he was soon renowned for his love of piety and learning. Paul III promoted him through several positions, making him at last a cardinal in 1539. He employed Marcello on a number of diplomatic errands, and at one point Marcello served as president of the Council of Trent. Under Julius III's pontificate, he withdrew from public life. Marcello's learning, piety, and zeal for reform were so well respected that at the conclave following Julius's

death, even the imperial cardinals, who had been instructed by Charles V to oppose him, supported his election. He chose to retain his baptismal name.

Because he was elected during Lent, the new pope chose to keep the coronation festivities to a minimum. But the Holy Week ceremonies were celebrated by Marcellus with such fervor that he died of a fever resulting from the strain. Palestrina composed a Mass in his honor, and St. Ignatius always referred to him as "Good Pope Marcellus."

## Paul IV
### (May 23, 1555–August 18, 1559)

Giovanni Pietro Caraffa was born on June 28, 1476, into one of the most famous Neapolitan noble families. He was educated by his uncle, Oliviero Cardinal Caraffa, who introduced him in 1494 into the papal court. His uncle further resigned to him the diocese of Chieti (Theate in Latin). Leo X used him on various diplomatic missions, but driven by a desire for religious life, in 1524 he resigned all his offices to enter either the Dominicans or the Camaldolese. In the event, he joined the order of Clerks Regular founded by St. Cajetan (they are commonly known as Theatines, in honor of Giovanni, who was elected their first General). Three years later, the young congregation was severely devastated in numbers by the sack of Rome and its members fled to Venice. Paul III, knowing Giovanni's value, summoned him back to Rome to serve on his commission for reform of the Roman curia. The pope put him at the head of every effort he made to tighten discipline. Giovanni reorganized the Inquisition in Italy, but despite his knowledge of it, he was an enemy of Humanism—among those he despised at Rome was Reginald Cardinal Pole, the English refugee, a disciple of St. Thomas More. No one was more surprised than he when he was elected pope, and he probably would have refused the honor had not Charles V insisted that he not be pope. That was enough to force him to accept, taking the name Paul.

Though his Italian nationalism was understandable, his hatred of the Habsburgs led them to ignore him in important questions: The pope was not consulted about the religious peace of Augsburg, nor about Charles V's decision to leave Austria and the Empire to his pro-Protestant brother Maximilian, rather than his orthodox son, Philip II (to whom he did, however, leave Spain and its Italian and American possessions). Paul's dislike of Philip

in turn poisoned his relationship with Mary I of England, his wife, who had appointed Paul's other enemy, Cardinal Pole, to be archbishop of Canterbury. Pole, realizing that a large piece of support for Protestantism in England would dissipate if those to whom Henry VIII had given the stolen monastic lands were allowed to keep them, negotiated a treaty to that effect. Paul relieved Pole of his position and summoned him to Rome to face the Inquisition. When Mary died, she had guaranteed Elizabeth the throne, providing she promised to keep England Catholic. Paul refused to recognize Elizabeth as legitimate, however, which influenced her decision to recreate the Anglican Church. (This body owes its present nature to her, rather than her father.) Papal recognition might not have stopped the "Virgin Queen" from pursuing this course, but perhaps it might have.

On a more positive note, he did continue the work of reform; moreover, he established the hierarchy of bishops in the Netherlands and the Portuguese possessions in the East Indies. Thus, the Church in India, Pakistan, Bangladesh, Sri Lanka, Burma, Malaysia, and Indonesia partly owes its origins to him.

Unfortunately, as pope he showed a nepotism that he had never shown as cardinal. As was often the case with popes, he was under the mistaken impression that relatives could be relied on more than others—an understandable mistake. Due to his economical ways and increasingly morose demeanor, he was not excessively mourned by the Romans.

## Pius IV

### (December 26, 1559–December 9, 1565)

Giovanni Angelo Medici was born in Milan on March 31, 1499, to a poor branch of the Florentine dynasty. His brother, Giangiacomo, became a mercenary and was eventually created Marquis of Marignano for his bravery. Giovanni's fortune came through scholarship. He became renowned for his learning and in 1527 joined the clerical state and immigrated to Rome. Clement VII made him a protonotary, and Paul III was impressed with his abilities and asked him to govern different cities. Next, he appointed him cardinal. Julius III made him legate in Romagna and captain of the papal armies. But Paul IV had little use for him, a sentiment roundly returned. On the conclave following Paul's death, neither the French nor Spanish-Austrian factions

could elect a candidate; after three months, Giovanni was elected by affirmation, and was crowned on January 6, 1560, taking the name Pius.

As his first act, he purged the Caraffa relations from the papal administration. Those whom Paul had executed or expropriated for political reasons, Pius rehabilitated. He then turned his attention to the stalled Council of Trent. Fortunately for the Church, the nephew whom the pope elevated to the cardinalate to help him, St. Charles Borromeo, really was worthy of his trust. Under his guidance, the Council completed its labors, having passed measures for the reform of every aspect of Catholic life. It also requested that the pope issue a creed summing up the Catholic faith.

The bull doing this, Injunctum nobi, was sent out by Pius IV on November 13, 1564. The profession of Faith contained in this bull summarizes the doctrines Catholics must believe. (Until after Vatican II, all clerics had to subscribe to it upon taking any sort of office, and all converts had to do the same.)

Paul accomplished a number of other important acts. He founded the Polyglot Press in Rome for printing books in all known languages. His improvements to the city were legion, and he contributed a great deal of money to fighting the Turks in Hungary. When Pius lay dying, he was attended by two great saints—Charles Borromeo and Philip Neri. Initially buried in St. Peter's, in 1583 Pius was reinterred at Santa Maria degli Angeli, designed by Michelangelo at Pius's request.

## St. Pius V

### (January 7, 1566–May 1, 1572)

Michele Ghisleri was born in 1504 at Bosco, in Piedmont, of a noble Bolognese family. At fourteen he became a Dominican, then taught philosophy and theology at Voghera for sixteen years. In 1556 he was chosen bishop of Sutri and inquisitor for Lombardy. He was made a cardinal the following year. Translated to Mondovi, Piedmont, he worked very closely with St. Charles Borromeo, helping with the spread of the liturgical reform. He was an obvious choice for election to the papacy.

Because of his status as a Dominican, Pius continued to wear the white habit of his order (the popes have worn white ever since). The new pope's first work was to reaffirm the supremacy of the Church over secular power. His efforts were always aimed against the Protestants and the Turks. After

Elizabeth I of England recreated the Church of England, Pius declared her excommunicated and deposed. This bore little fruit, however, except to have Catholics declared traitors—many became Anglican as a result, either out of fear or misplaced patriotism. The pope, however, supported Mary Stuart, Queen of Scots, as the rightful heiress to the English throne. He also supported the Catholic League in France and the Spanish in the Netherlands.

The Turks, too, were on the prowl. Despite their being slowed in northern Hungary, their fleets threatened to turn the Mediterranean into a Muslim lake. Pius organized the Holy League, uniting his own fleet, Venice's, and Spain's. This was put under the command of Don Juan of Austria, illegitimate son of Charles V, and half brother of Philip II. The pope organized a network of prayer throughout Catholic Europe to offer rosaries on behalf of the Christian fleet. On October 7, 1571, when the two forces met off Lepanto, Greece, Don Juan's forces were heavily outnumbered. But invoking the Virgin (Juan had an image of the Mexican Virgin of Guadalupe placed prominently on his ship), the Christians broke the Turkish fleet. Pius had a vision of the victory, and the details were confirmed by the messengers who arrived weeks later. He made October 7 the feast of Our Lady of Victory, changed later to Our Lady of the Rosary. G. K. Chesterton wrote his stirring poem Lepanto in commemoration.

Pius carried out the reforms decreed by Trent in every particular. In 1566, he issued the Catechism of Trent, still the most complete work of its kind in existence. Two years later he brought out a reformed breviary, and in 1570 by the bull Quo Primum, a revised Missal. The order of Mass contained therein, the so-called Tridentine Mass, was no great departure from what had gone before. Rather, during the past two centuries, liturgical usages had become so chaotic and diverse, varying wildly from place to place, that the Council had seen uniformity as an antidote to abuse. Though Pius ordered almost all Western-rite priests to use this missal, he expressly exempted all rites two hundred or more years old. Thus the rites of Sarum in England, Lyon in France, the Mozarabic in Spain, Braga in Portugal, and the Ambrosian in Milan were allowed to continue, as well as the rites peculiar to the Dominicans, Carmelites, and Carthusians. The Tridentine rite was a codification, rather than a radical change, because liturgical development had always been gradual rather than radical or arbitrary. So it would remain after 1570 for exactly four centuries.

Pius's reforms extended to the curia, where he reorganized the Sacred Penitentiaria and in 1571 founded the Congregation of the Index to monitor writing. He avoided any sort of nepotism and inspired the populace by his personal piety. Pius also granted a charter to the University of Urbino in 1566.

Some scholors say Pius launched the Counter-Reformation, a movement spearheaded by the Jesuits and other orders that involved both reforming and

purifying the Church to reorient her toward the salvation of souls, along with a coordinated missionary effort both abroad and in the lost lands of northern Europe. Preaching and doctrinally rich hymns became a major priority, and ultimately a new sort of architecture would develop alongside it—the baroque.

Pius V was beatified in 1672 and canonized in 1712. His feast day is May 5 and his relics are at Santa Maria Maggiore.

## Gregory XIII
### (May 13, 1572–April 10, 1585)

Born Ugo Buoncompagni at Bologna on January 7, 1502, he studied and taught law at that university. He fathered a child out of wedlock, but was the teacher of many prominent churchmen. As a result, in 1539 he came to Rome, where Paul III appointed him a judge. Holding various positions and carrying out diplomatic and other missions for the succeeding pontiffs, Ugo became quite well known in the curia and was elected in succession to Pope St. Pius V, taking the name Gregory.

He was hailed by all the Catholic rulers at his accession, but he was unable throughout his pontificate to rally them for the Crusade. His major goals were to combat the spread of Protestantism, to reconvert those nations already fallen to it, and to evangelize the new territories in the Americas, Asia, and Africa. He was the first pope to receive envoys from Japan and mediated between Russia and Poland. Gregory founded more than twenty-three institutions of learning in Rome and around Europe to produce clerics capable of furthering these goals.

In Rome itself he furthered the work of reform in the Church structures, although he was unable to combat the rising tide of banditry throughout the Papal States. His appetite for reform included the calendar. Owing to slight errors in the Julian calendar the seasons were becoming out of sync with the months, a great problem for farmers and others. Gregory appointed a commission to correct it, creating the Gregorian calendar that is used by the entire world today. In 1579 this pope also approved the creation of the University of Vilnius. In addition he built a great deal in Rome, including the Quirinal Palace—at first a papal residence, after 1870 the Royal Palace, and now the home of the president of Italy.

# Sixtus V

## (April 24, 1585–August 27, 1590)

Felice Perreti was born at Grottamare, near Montalto, on December 13, 1521. He joined the Franciscans at a young age, and his preaching at Rome in Lent, 1552, brought him to the notice of the curia. In 1557, Pius IV made him inquisitor at Venice, where he became so unpopular with the government that they demanded and got his recall three years later. Sent with Cardinal Buoncampagni to Spain in 1565 to look into charges of heresy against Archbishop Carranza of Toledo, he came to dislike his companion very much. In 1570 St. Pius V made him both cardinal and his confessor, but the election of Buoncampagni as Gregory XIII sent Felice into private life. Four days after his enemy's death, he was elected as pope, and at his coronation May 1, took the name Sixtus.

His first interest was to suppress the brigandage that under Gregory had assumed epidemic proportions. Sixtus went to work with a will, punishing severely, organizing troops, and vigorously rooting out the bandits. In two years, the Papal States were the safest nation of Europe.

Sixtus made many improvements in the Roman infrastructure and building. Above all, he organized the system of Congregations, which govern the Church today. Prior to this time, the pope had ruled the Church in concert with the cardinals; afterward, it would be up to the various congregations to do so, subject to the pope's approval.

Sixtus was extremely worried about France. Supporting the Catholic League, he excommunicated Henry of Navarre, the Protestant heir to the French throne. Much concerned with the Counter-Reformation, he assisted it in many ways. Though he supported the Jesuits, he wished to alter their name and rules. They prayed that he would not do so, and in fact he died before signing the order.

# Urban VII

## (September 15–27, 1590)

Giambattista Castagna was born at Rome on August 4, 1521, to a Genoese nobleman and his Roman wife. Nephew of a cardinal, he studied civil and canon law at various Italian universities, receiving his doctorate at Bologna. Assisting his uncle, he entered the curia under Julius III and served under the succeeding popes in increasingly important and sensitive administrative and diplomatic roles. In 1583 he was appointed a cardinal by Gregory XIII, and Giambattista was made inquisitor-general by Sixtus V three years later—a role he filled with scrupulous fairness and probity. As a result, when the news came that the conclave had elected him, the city broke out in universal rejoicing.

He took the name Urban ("kind" in Latin) to remind himself to be kind to all his subjects. He ordered that a list of all the poor in Rome be made up, in order to relieve them, and redeemed all pawn tickets out of his own money. He further ordered bakers to make their loaves bigger and cheaper, making up the difference himself. In addition, Urban required economies in his own entourage to pay for these expenses, banishing silk from his courtiers' dress. Sadly, a few days later, he became ill. Processions, expositions of the Blessed Sacrament, and much public prayer took place for his recovery, and Urban received communion and confessed every day. The pope wished to leave the Vatican for the healthier air of the Quirinal, but this was not permitted before the coronation. Unfortunately, Urban died before that could take place, leaving all his money to the Archconfraternity of the Assumption to provide dowries for poor girls. Initially buried at St. Peter's, his remains were moved in 1606 to the church of Santa Maria Sopra Minerva to rest under a splendid monument erected by subscription of the people of Rome.

# Gregory XIV
## (December 5, 1590–October 15, 1591)

Niccolo Sfondrati was born to a Milanese senator on February 11, 1535. Following his wife's death, Niccolo's father joined the priesthood and was made cardinal by Pope Paul III in 1544. After studying at Perugia and Padua, the cardinal's son was ordained priest, and then consecrated bishop of Cremona in 1560. A participant at the Council of Trent, in 1583 Niccolo was himself created a cardinal by Gregory XIII. From his youth, Niccolo had been known for piety, and the great companion of his youth was St. Charles Borromeo. During his cardinalate he was a great friend of St. Philip Neri. After a long and divided conclave, the cardinals elected him pope. He greeted the news with tears, exclaiming "God forgive you! What have you done?"

Gregory's major concern was the situation in France, where in 1589 Henry of Navarre had promised that he would become a Catholic. Contrary to popular belief, Henry did not say of his conversion, "Paris is worth a Mass." Rather, after consulting Huguenot theologians who assured him that he could save his soul as a Catholic, and Catholic theologians (some of whom were themselves converts) that he could not do so as a Protestant, he replied, "I take the surer course." But by Gregory's accession, Henry had not yet done so, and the new pontiff doubted that he would. Given this circumstance, he supported the Catholic League in France in their continued resistance and sent money to Philip II of Spain for this purpose. On March 1, 1591, he renewed the excommunication against Henry and called upon all the French to reject him.

Gregory's attention was directed elsewhere. He confirmed the charter of the Clerks of St. Camillus de Lelis, called the Fathers of a Good Death, whose special vocation was (and is) to assist the dying. The pope forbade, under pain of excommunication, betting on papal elections. Above all, on April 18, 1591, Gregory issued a bull that ordered the freedom of all slaves made by the Spanish in the Philippines and reparation to be made to them. (Gregory is in no small part responsible for that country's current status as a Catholic nation.)

Gregory XIV's demise was as mourned as it was unexpected.

## Innocent IX
### (October 29–December 30, 1591)

Born Giovanni Antonio Facchinetti at Bologna, on July 22, 1519, he studied law at the university in his hometown, receiving his doctorate in 1544. Going to Rome at that point, he became a cardinal's secretary and later worked for Allesandro Cardinal Farnese, who had him manage first his archdiocese of Avignon and then the duchy of Parma. In 1560, Giovanni became bishop of Nicastro in Calabria, and two years later he attended the Council of Trent. As Nuncio to Venice in 1566, he helped bring about the alliance that fought the Battle of Lepanto. In 1575, he was made Latin patriarch of Jerusalem and in 1583 was made cardinal-priest of the Quattro coronati (borne in present day, as previously mentioned, by Roger Cardinal Mahony of Los Angeles). Giovanni actually carried on the burden of day-to-day administration under Gregory XIV, so it was little surprise when he was elected pope after his patron's death, with the assistance of the Spanish party among the cardinals.

During his short pontificate, he supported Philip II and the Catholic League against Henry of Navarre, and he laid many plans for the financial future of the Holy See. Among his many writings was an attack on Machiavelli's idea of pragmatism.

## Clement VIII
### (January 30, 1592–March 5, 1605)

Ippolito Aldobrandini was born at Fano in March of 1536, of a noble Florentine family. Known for personal holiness, for thirty years before his ascension to the papacy he was a disciple of St. Philip Neri. His lawyer-father guided his rise through the ranks of the ecclesiastical justice system, and in 1585 Sixtus V appointed him cardinal and made him grand penitentiary. During his time as legate to Poland, he negotiated the release of Archduke Maximilian, who had unsuccessfully attempted to win the Polish throne, thus gaining the undying gratitude of the Habsburgs. Nevertheless, at the death of

Innocent XI, Ippolito was the candidate of those cardinals who wished for Italian independence from Spain. Against his will they mustered the votes to elect him.

Despite the political problems that faced him, Clement turned his attention first to religious ones. He immediately began visiting all the churches, hospitals, and charitable and educational institutions of Rome. He founded the Scots College and the Collegio Clementina, issued a bull against dueling, and instituted the "Forty Hours Devotion," whereby Catholics adore the Blessed Sacrament for that length of time in reparation for any and all excesses performed by others during Mardi Gras. (Until the advent of sinlessness in the 1960s, it was quite popular, and is still seen in some places. In 1598, Clement issued new editions of the Missal, Breviary, Vulgate, Pontifical, and Caeremoniale.

But Clement could not ignore politics, either. When Henry of Navarre (Henry IV of France) finally entered the Church on July 25, 1593, the pope immediately began looking into the sincerity of the king's conversion. Despite the displeasure of Philip II, once satisfied, Clement two years later absolved Henry of all ecclesiastical penalties, welcomed him to the family of Catholic rulers, and called upon all the French to rally to him. In 1598 Clement negotiated a peace between France on one hand and Spain and Savoy on the other. The pope also sent needed money to help the emperor fight the Turks in Hungary. Though defeated at sea, the Sultan remained a formidable foe on land.

In 1595 another triumph had already occurred with the union of Brest. The kingdom of Poland was united with the grand duchy of Lithuania, consisting roughly of the country of that name, Belarus, and Ukraine. Many of the inhabitants of the grand duchy were Orthodox. By the union they accepted once again the primacy of the pope, and from this accord come those Eastern Rites of the Church referred to as Ruthenian, Ukrainian, and Belarusan. Equally faithful to the popes and their Byzantine traditions, they and their descendants underwent enormous persecution at different times by successive Russian and Soviet governments. (Even today they receive a certain amount of discrimination on the part of the current Russian, Ukrainian, and Belarusan governments, although—in the first two countries particularly—their situation is far better than it was under the Communists. National authorities, who still tend to identify their nationality with Orthodoxy exclusively, consider their loyalty suspect. In America, despite nineteenth-century treatment at the hands of Latin churchmen, which led some to go into schism, they have not only preserved their own traditions but provided a haven for many of their Latin brethren disgusted with developments in their own rite.)

Clement also ruthlessly fought brigandage and the lawless Roman nobility, once again restoring order in the Papal States. On February 17, 1600, the pope had Giordano Bruno burned at the stake. That year also witnessed a Holy Year, wherein three million pilgrims descended upon Rome. Clement mediated between the Jesuits and Dominicans, who were fighting each other on the insoluble problem of grace and free will. At his death, he was laid to rest in Santa Maria Maggiore.

## Leo XI
### (April 1-April 27, 1605)

Alessandro Ottaviano de Medici was born at Florence in 1535 and was a cousin of the grand duke. Although he had wished to enter the priesthood, he had to wait until his mother's death. When she died, his cousin Cosimo sent him as ambassador to the court of St. Pius V, where he stayed fifteen years, making the acquaintance of St. Philip Neri (who predicted that he would one day be pope). Gregory XIII made him bishop of Pistoia in 1573, archbishop of Florence the next year, and cardinal in 1583. In 1596 Alessandro was sent by Clement VIII as legate to France, where he worked successfully to reduce Huguenot influence at the court of Henry IV. At the conclave following Clement's death, the sixty-two cardinals were divided into three parties—Spanish, French, and Italian. The last two united behind Alessandro and secured his election, despite the wishes of Philip III of Spain.

Taking the name Leo, the new pope fell sick immediately after his election. Although many of the cardinals and foreign ambassadors wished for him to give one of his nephews the Red Hat, he so hated nepotism that he refused. When even his confessor joined the chorus, the dying pontiff dismissed him and took a new one to prepare him for death.

# Paul V

## (May 16, 1605–January 28, 1621)

Camillo Borghese was born at Rome on September 17, 1550, to a Sienese noble family (related to St. Catherine) who had long been established in the Eternal City. Studying law at Perugia and Parma, he rose through the ranks of the papal bureaucracy, and in 1596 was appointed cardinal by Clement VIII, then cardinal-vicar of Rome. A lawyer rather than a diplomat, he belonged to no party and had little care for the interests of foreign nations, although he had much zeal for the rights of the Holy See. As a result, the faction-ridden conclave held after the death of Leo XI elected him easily, despite his making no commitments to any of the three sides.

Paul's first act was to send back to their dioceses all prelates and cardinals who possessed such while living at Rome, whatever their interests or offices there, in accordance with decrees of Trent.

The new pope's first foreign challenge came from Venice, which, in contradiction to canon law had passed two measures forbidding clerics to acquire property, and requiring the republic's permission for building new churches. About that time, two Venetian priests were sentenced to prison by a secular court. Paul demanded that the two laws be repealed and the priests remanded to an ecclesiastical court; otherwise, the penalty would be an interdict. Controversy ensued, between cardinals Baronius and St. Robert Bellarmine on the papal side, and the renegade Servite Paolo Sarpi on the Venetian. At last, on April 17, 1606, the pope excommunicated the doge, senate, and government of Venice, and a short time later he imposed the interdict. Except for the Jesuits, Theatines, and Capuchins, who were all expelled, the secular and religious clergy of Venice ignored the interdict. Corpus Christi was celebrated with more than usual splendor, and even the unbelieving Sarpi took to saying Mass again, in spite. After a year's standoff, a compromise was affected by France and Spain. Venice would retain the laws, but not enforce them.

England proved more difficult. Elizabeth I died in 1603 and was succeeded by Mary Stuart's son (who had been raised as a Calvinist), James I. On July 9, 1606, Paul wrote the king and congratulated him on his accession and his survival of the Guy Fawkes plot, but he asked him not to punish the many for the few. The pope promised that he would exhort the Catholic English to obey their king in all things not violating their religion. But James ordered all his subjects to take an oath that, among other things, renounced Transubstantiation. Paul condemned the oath in 1607 and forbade Catholics to take

it. This led to an internal fight among the remaining Faithful in the country and helped weaken the Church in England even more.

In the empire, the pope seconded the efforts of Ferdinand II and the Catholic League to consolidate the position of the Church there. Although a Catholicizing element appeared in Lutheranism (epitomized by such as Johann Arndt and later by Georg Calixtus), which looked to the Church Fathers and early Middle Ages for inspiration, it was studiously ignored by Catholic authorities. A new problem emerged with a number of Protestant princes switching from Lutheranism to Calvinism, thus upsetting the intra-Protestant balance. One of the most prominent of these was Frederick, elector of the palatinate and married to Elizabeth, daughter of James I. In 1618, he was elected king of Bohemia in opposition to Ferdinand. A year later, at the Battle of White Mountain, the Habsburgs crushed Bohemian resistance and drove Frederick "the Winter King" and his queen into exile. Bohemia was retaken for the Faith, but war erupted between the emperor and the Catholic princes on one side, and the Protestant princes on the other. Spain supported the former, and successively Denmark, Sweden, and France (despite her religion) aided the latter. The result was the long and bloody Thirty Years' War, which devastated Germany and made the Holy Empire, already vitiated by the Reformation, ever more a phantom.

But in Rome, Paul had a happy and fulfilling pontificate. Although guilty of nepotism, he was fortunate that his nephews were able men of good character. He finished the rebuilding of St. Peter's and enriched the Vatican Library. In 1607 he granted a charter to the University of Cagliari, and in 1619 he approved the founding of the University of Chile, in Santiago. At his death, he was interred in Santa Maria Maggiore.

## Gregory XV

### (February 9, 1621–July 8, 1623)

Ludovico Ludovisi was born at Bologna in 1554. He studied philosophy and theology at Rome and law in his native city's university, and he returned to Rome and was appointed a judge by Clement VIII. In 1612, Paul V appointed him archbishop of Bologna and Nuncio to Savoy, creating him a cardinal in 1616. He stayed in Bologna after that, only coming to Rome for the conclave that elected him as pope.

The new pope's first interest was to end, so far as he could, outside manipulation of papal elections. In two bulls he outlined precisely how to conduct conclaves, what ceremonies to perform, and above all, the secrecy that was to envelop the operation. From his time until that of Paul VI, the methodology would remain basically untouched.

Gregory was keenly interested in the foreign missions, which, under the French, Spanish, and Portuguese were bringing the Faith to ever farther flung places. Such activity was hard to supervise; up until now, various ad hoc committees of cardinals had sufficed. But on January 6, 1622 (the Feast of the Epiphany, selected for its commemorating the first coming of gentiles to Christ), Gregory founded the Sacred Congregation for the Propagation of the Faith, the Propaganda fide. This congregation (from that day to our own) had jurisdiction over all mission territories and was considered a mark of a national church's coming of age when it moved from the Propaganda's supervision to that of the Congregation for Bishops (as the United States did in 1908, although recent events have led some commentators to ask if this move was not premature). In keeping with his missionary concern, he approved the founding of the Universities of Cordoba, Argentina; Quito, Ecuador; and Xavier University, in Bogota, Colombia, in 1621, acts confirmed the next year by Philip IV of Spain. Among the saints Gregory canonized were Francis Xavier, Ignatius Loyola, Albertus Magnus, and Teresa of Avila. He also confirmed a number of new religious orders.

Gregory sent missionaries to Bohemia and Moravia to assist Ferdinand II in the reconversion of those provinces. Additionally, the pope sent the emperor a great deal of money to help prosecute the war against the Protestants. In January 1623, at the Diet of Regensburg, Gregory's influence helped the transfer of the electoral dignity from Frederick of the Palatinate to his Catholic cousin Maximilian of Bavaria. Moreover, relations with England improved considerably as James I sought the hand of a Spanish princess for his son Charles and allowed his Catholic subjects to breathe freely. Gregory helped Louis XIII with the conversion of Huguenots. Even in the Netherlands, despite the persecution of the Church and her clergy by the House of Orange, the Faith began once more to spread.

By pursuing a friendly policy of neutrality toward intra-Catholic squabbles, and supporting all the Catholic princes of Europe equally, Gregory gained a respect that not all of his successors would preserve.

## Urban VIII
### (August 6, 1623–July 29, 1644)

Maffeo Barberini was born in 1568 to wealthy parents. A career curia man, he made cardinal in 1606. Occupying several high offices, he finally made prefect of the Signatura of Justice (the Church's equivalent of the American Chief Justice). Elected pope on August 6, he was crowned on September 23.

Urban found positions for his many brothers and nephews in the Church's bureaucracy. Care of family aside, his record was extremely mixed. A great builder, he refortified Castel Sant'Angelo and the town of Civitavecchia. More important, the new St. Peter's was completed during his reign and he consecrated it on November 18, 1626. Urban hired Bernini and many other artists and architects to beautify the new basilica and many other churches, streets, and piazzas in Rome.

In liturgical affairs, he revised the Roman Missal and Pontifical and dropped the number of Holy Days of Obligation to 34. Under the influence of "classicists" he ordered the revision of the Breviary, including the hymns of the Divine Office. Subsequent historians felt this was not a good decision, and the Benedictines were given permission by subsequent popes to return to the historic hymns. Side-by-side comparison of the two versions shows the easy grace of the earlier mode and the stilted artificiality of the later.

In 1627 he founded the Urban College of Propaganda to train missionaries and a polyglot press to print material for them to use. Urban's fascination with the non-European world led him to send more missionaries to the Far East, and on April 22, 1639, he forbade the use of American Indians as slaves. He approved the Vincentian Order of St. Vincent de Paul, and the Sisters of the Visitation, founded by SS. Francis de Sales and Jane Frances de Chantal. Additionally, Urban ordered bishops to live in their dioceses.

He condemned his close friend Galileo a second time for pushing the Copernican system (after Galileo had promised not to)—Galileo's theories were at the time unproved and unprovable, and the great majority of European scientists of that era disagreed with them. Galileo's responses to his colleagues in the scientific community were abusive, especially since the bans on his teaching were made at their request. It was in fact because Paul V and Urban VIII did respect the opinions of contemporary science that they condemned Galileo. The Copernican theory had little effect on Church dogma; the focus of science was on the purely physical, and the sheer changeability of scientific theory precludes its "disproving" Catholic doctrine. (Ironically, however,

under the influence of the New Physics, some mavericks are exploring a new sort of Geocentrism!)

Though the rest of his record is a mixture of successes and failures, Urban's foreign policy was an unmitigated disaster. In 1618, the Thirty Years' War began in Germany. The conflict pitted the Holy Roman Empire, Spain, and the Catholic German states against the Protestant ones. The goal on the Catholic side was the defeat of political Protestantism, the eventual reconversion of northern Germany, and the restoration of the unity of the empire. The Protestant princes, understandably, wished to prevent these from happening.

Lutheran Denmark and Lutheran Sweden were allies to the Protestants, but both were defeated eventually by Emperor Ferdinand II. Fearing Habsburg dominance, Urban plotted with the Swedes against the Catholic side. The Roman mob began to say, "The king of Sweden has more zeal for his Lutheranism than our Holy Father has for the Catholic Church, which alone can save us."

Following Gustavus Adolphus's death, the pope encouraged King Louis XIII of France and his counselor Cardinal Richelieu to intervene in the war on the Protestant side. They did, frustrating the imperial cause and ending the Counter-Reformation. Four years after Urban's death, at the Treaty of Westphalia, the action of the peacemakers in ignoring the papacy's directives underlined the fact that Urban's action had made the Holy See nearly irrelevant in European power politics.

Urban had done almost as much to the papacy's position in Italy itself. His nephews, ever in search of more cash, prevailed upon the pope to seize a papal fief for their benefit. The lord of said fief, the town of Castro, felt ill-used and called in allies—Venice, Tuscany, and Modena. These three trounced the pope's army, despite his extracting the bronze from various Roman monuments to make into weapons. Although this measure did not win the war, it caused the people of Rome to quip, "What the barbarians did not do, the Barberini did." Urban was accused of conducting magical ceremonies in his apartments; therefore subjects were quite pleased when he died.

# Innocent X
## (September 15, 1644–January 7, 1655)

Born Giambatista Pamfili at Rome on May 6, 1574, he graduated from the Colegio Romano at age twenty and was appointed an auditor of the Rota by Clement VIII shortly thereafter. Under Gregory XV, he became nuncio to Naples, and Urban VIII appointed him Latin Patriarch of Antioch, nuncio at Madrid, and cardinal. He held positions in several congregations and was skilled in administration when the conclave opened on August 9, 1644, after Urban's death. Giambatista, though sympathetic to Spain (important due to Urban's discredited policies) was no enemy to France. Thus he emerged as a compromise candidate.

After his accession, Innocent found it necessary to prosecute Urban VIII's nephews for misappropriation of funds. The cardinals Barberini thereupon fled to France, seeking refuge with Cardinal Mazarin. The pope confiscated their property and decreed that if they would not return within six months, they would be deprived of their dioceses and eventually their red hats. Mazarin was grateful for the essential support their uncle had given the French and prepared to mount an expedition against Rome, at which Innocent relented.

The pope became very friendly with Venice and provided funds to assist their attempt to hold Crete. They in turn returned the right of appointment to diocese to the pope. Innocent also recognized the independence of Portugal, which had regained its freedom from Spain—something neither of his two predecessors was willing to do. As a result, the pope was able to fill all the vacant dioceses in that country (only one bishop remained at the time).

Unfortunately for Innocent, Urban VIII's policy caused the papacy to be ignored at the Peace of Westphalia that ended at last the incredibly bloody Thirty Years' War. Among the sections of the treaties that were objectionable were the granting of equal status within the empire to Calvinism, Lutheranism, and Catholicism; the leaving up to each prince the religion of his territory and people; and the turning over of certain dioceses and archdioceses (like Bremen) to the Protestants. It was even decided that the diocese of Osnabruck would rotate between Catholic and Protestant bishops (the latter being purely territorial princes). Innocent issued the bull Zelo domus Dei, in which he condemned as null those provisions of the peace that were contrary to the Catholic religion. But none of the powers took notice. This peace would have several (from the Catholic view) baleful effects. Switzerland and the Netherlands were henceforth independent of the empire—the practical effect

of this was also to end any real imperial involvement in Italy, although the Duke of Savoy received the meaningless title "Perpetual Vicar of the Empire in Italy." (Those dukes and the kings of Sardinia and Italy who succeeded them retained this title until Humberto II was deposed in a rigged referendum in 1946.) The empire itself became ever more wraithlike, with the emperors having no real control outside of the Habsburg domains and the Imperial Free Cities. This allowed Brandenburg-Prussia to develop as a counterweight to Habsburg and Catholic interests. More important, the institutionalization of the rent in Christendom would be accepted as an unchangeable fact—first by secular authorities and at last by Churchmen. Many unfortunate consequences resulted, not least of which the growth of disbelief in any Christianity at all.

Another setback to the Church that the pope had even less of a say in was the defeat of Charles I and his beheading in the English Civil War. Charles, whose mother and wife were both Catholic, was generally much friendlier to the Faith than his father had been. Moreover, he encouraged his archbishop of Canterbury, William Laud, to reorient the Church of England in a more Catholic direction. The King even negotiated reunion terms. But all of this ended with the triumph of the Puritan Oliver Cromwell and the king's judicial murder in 1649.

Innocent condemned Jansenism, a sort of Catholic Calvinism that emphasized the justice of God to the exclusion of His mercy. Above all, it turned the Sacraments from a medicine for the sinful into a reward for the virtuous and denigrated the corporal works of mercy. Not surprisingly, its biggest foe in France was St. Vincent de Paul. But it had strong allies there too, and they were in some of the highest positions in the realm. In 1645, Innocent approved the founding of the University of Santo Tomas in Manila.

Innocent was rather irresolute and much under the dominance of his elder brother, and—after his death—of his sister-in-law. That there was nothing immoral going on between the pope and the widow made his reliance on her all the more ridiculous in contemporary Italian eyes. He was nevertheless much more mourned than Urban VIII had been.

# Watching and Waiting

## Alexander VII

### (April 7, 1655–May 22, 1667)

Fabio Chigi was born at Siena on February 13, 1599, the scion of an ancient and noble family. Frail as a youth, he was taught by his mother and private tutors until able to go to the university, graduating from Siena at age twenty-seven with doctorates in philosophy, theology, and law. Occupying various diplomatic posts, he was appointed as envoy to the Peace of Westphalia by Innocent X, where his efforts often brought him into conflict with the French and Cardinal Mazarin, their prime minister. In 1652, he was named cardinal by Innocent, who had made him secretary of state a year previously. Three years later, at that pope's demise, the conclave was so ridden with faction that it lasted eighty days. At last, Fabio was elected unanimously as a compromise candidate and took the name Alexander VII.

Though he rejected nepotism at first, he later came to rely on nephews and friends as an alternative to dealing with cardinals, most of whom came from powerful families (and who had furnished past pontiffs) and were quite nepotic themselves. A great deal of Alexander's time was spent in literary pursuits, which he found calming.

It was good that he had an outlet. One major problem of his reign was his relationship with France. Mazarin disliked him intensely because of Alexander's resistance to him at the peace treaty. Although he accepted the new pope's election, he refused to allow the young Louis XIV to send the usual embassy of submission. In addition, he refused to send an ambassador to Rome, leaving diplomatic relations with the Holy See in the hands of a cardinal protector. Understandably, when Louis came of age, he also treated Alexander with contempt. When a scuffle occurred between servants of the finally appointed French ambassador and the pope's Corsican guard (a unit recruited in memory of Corsica's status as a nominal papal fief), the king demanded an abject apology even though he acknowledged that it was not an important affair. When the pope refused, Louis occupied Avignon until the apology was presented. The Jansenists in France, seeing this climate as an opportunity, redoubled their anti-papal agitation.

France was not the only difficulty Alexander faced, however. Troubles be-

tween Portugal and Spain evaded his mediation, and the Venetians continued to fight their battle for Crete against the Turks; Alexander continued to aid them.

But there were consolations. Queen Christina of Sweden converted and fled her native realm for Rome (portrayed in the touching movie about her, "Queen Christina," where the queen is played by Greta Garbo), finding refuge with Alexander who became her friend and protector. She is buried today in St. Peter's. Moreover, Charles II of England was restored to his father's throne and married a Catholic princess from Portugal—a hopeful sign, as it seemed at the time.

Alexander was a great patron of art, and among many other things we owe him is the colonnade of St. Peter's. Built by Bernini—of whom Alexander was the great benefactor—it was also fitting that Bernini design his tomb.

## Clement IX

### (June 20, 1667–December 9, 1669)

Giulio Rospigliosi was born on January 28, 1600, at Pistoia, to a Lombard family that had lived there many years. Studying at the Roman Seminary, he graduated from the University of Pisa at twenty-three. He taught philosophy there and became a favorite of Urban VIII, who made him titular archbishop of Tarsus and nuncio to Madrid. Although he withdrew from public life during Innocent X's pontificate (who hated the Barberini and their friends), he was brought back into government by Alexander VII. In 1657, Alexander created Giulio a cardinal, and a decade later he was unanimously elected pope, taking the name Clement.

The Roman people were overjoyed at his election because he had proven to be both charitable and approachable while cardinal. The new pope bought off the grain monopoly, allowing bread prices to fall rapidly. Two days each week he occupied a confessional at St. Peter's. He delighted in visiting hospitals and giving alms, and he refused to allow his name to be placed on any of the buildings he had erected. Clement beatified Rose of Lima, who would be the first saint born in the Americas.

The pope negotiated a compromise formula with the Jansenists, which brought a temporary peace to the French Church; moreover, he negotiated a treaty between France and Spain, ending the war that had begun between them. But he warned Louis XIV quite severely of the problems his warlike temper would bring him.

Through many economies he straightened out the papal finances, and thereby was able to continue funding the Venetians in their twenty-year defense of Crete. His appeal to the Catholic powers to break the Turkish siege fell on deaf ears, however, and the island fell, perhaps hastening the pope's death. He was interred in Santa Maria Maggiore.

## Clement X

### (April 29, 1670–July 22, 1676)

Emilio Altieri was born at Rome on July 13, 1590, to an old Roman noble family. Early destined for the Church he had held various high offices under successive popes (managing to stay friendly with allies and foes of the Barberini, because of his obvious preference for prayer to politics). Following the death of Clement IX, who had made Emilio a cardinal, the divided cardinals at the conclave elected him because of his age and piety. He took the name Clement as a tribute to his predecessor.

Canonizing a number of saints, including the martyrs of Gorkum who had been killed by the Dutch Protestants (and who included in their number a Danish refugee), he continued to prefer prayer to politics. Nevertheless he struggled with Louis XIV over the regalia and the revenue of vacant dioceses and abbeys, and he attempted to persuade him to maintain the peace. Clement supported the Poles financially in their war with the Turks. He beautified Rome, among other things adding the two fountains to the Piazza San Pietro so admired today. He was buried in St. Peter's.

# Bl. Innocent XI

## (September 21, 1676–August 11, 1689)

Benedetto Odescalchi was born at Como on May 16, 1611. He was educated by the Jesuits there and studied law at Rome and Naples. After Urban VIII appointed him to various judicial positions, Innocent X made him a cardinal in 1645. Benedetto was pious, charitable, and devout, and Innocent sent him to Ferrara when that city was plagued with famine. Next he was appointed to the diocese of Novara, which he administered in an exemplary way until resigning it in 1656 to return to Rome and work with various congregations. Although Benedetto was a favored candidate after Clement X's death, Louis XIV had instructed the French cardinals to vote against him. But so popular was he by the time of Clement XI's demise that the French king thought it prudent not to interfere. At this conclave, in addition to the national parties among the cardinals, the Zelanti emerged, a party who swore to vote for a candidate based not on political or earthly consideration—only spiritual. He was elected after a two-month conclave and took the name Innocent.

His first interest was reform of the curia. Innocent lived frugally and he ordered the cardinals to do the same. In addition, he decreed heavy penalties against nepotism among the cardinals. His greatest struggle, however, was with Louis XIV.

The king expanded the rights of regalia to the provinces of Languedoc, Dauphine, Guienne. Furthermore, he gave the rights to Provence, where it had never existed. This was in violation of the Council of Lyons, which in 1274 had permitted the custom where it was in place, but excommunicated those who would expand it. Two French bishops who protested were persecuted, and Innocent's efforts to persuade Louis to desist were in vain. Moreover, the king called an assembly of the French clergy, who passed the following four articles.

1. St. Peter and his successors had received no power from God over temporal matters, and no power of deposition.
2. Ecumenical Councils are superior to the pope.
3. The customs of local churches are valid in their own right.
4. The pope has principal share in all questions of Faith and he may issue decrees for local churches, but his judgment is not irreformable without the consent of the whole Church.

Innocent annulled these articles in 1682 and declared that he would not approve any Episcopal candidate who had subscribed to them.

Louis wished to regain the Pope's favor and began to work more strongly for the Faith. In 1685, he revoked the Edict of Nantes, which had given the Huguenots the status of a state within a state. He did so with such rigor and occasional cruelty that he earned a rebuke from Innocent. Moreover, the pope abolished the right of asylum for foreign embassies at Rome, by which they had been able to harbor all sorts of riffraff. Next, he informed Louis that his ambassador would not be in control of the Palazzo Farnese, the residence in Rome, unless he renounced this right. Louis refused, and the French envoy Lavardin occupied the palace by force in November 1687. Innocent excommunicated Lavardin and placed the Church of San Luigi di Francesi, where he attended Midnight Mass the following Christmas Eve, under interdict.

Things became worse the next year, when the archdiocese of Cologne fell vacant. There were two candidates—one pro-French, one pro-imperial. At the election held in July 1688, the canons of Cologne Cathedral were unable to produce enough votes for either one, and so the decision fell to Innocent. He chose the pro-imperial candidate. Louis XIV retaliated by again seizing Avignon, imprisoning the nuncio at Paris, and appealing to a general council. The king even intimated that he intended a schism, but Innocent refused to back down.

That things should have come to such a pass between the pope and the most powerful Catholic king in Europe was not only a tragedy for the two principals—others suffered as well. James II succeeded his brother Charles II (who had converted to Catholicism on his deathbed) in 1685. James too was a convert to Catholicism and a friend and ally of Louis XIV, who aided him financially. James submitted the coronation service to the pope for approval; thus (except for the communion service and the later oath to maintain Protestantism), the English ceremony is the only Protestant one that has papal approval. Once on the throne, James favored his co-religionists and did his best to bring his kingdom back to the Faith. Whether or not he would have succeeded in doing so is problematic, but he used bloodless means, unlike Elizabeth when she protestantized her realm.

Because of his alliance with Louis, which was vital to maintaining his throne, Innocent gave James no support. Moreover, the pope was pleased when James's Protestant son-in-law, William of Orange, conducted the last successful invasion of England and drove James from the throne. Of course, his pleasure was not at the defeat of the Catholic cause in Britain per se, but in the way this weakened Louis's position in Europe. He could not foresee the disastrous results this would have later.

In more positive developments to the east, when the Turks besieged Vienna in 1683, the apogee of their advance in Europe, it was the pope who inspired so many foreign soldiers to assist the Emperor and his captain, Eugene of Savoy; it was also the pope who persuaded John Sobieski, king of Poland, to ride all unlooked for from out of the north and break the siege. As a reward, Innocent granted the kings of Poland the title "Most Orthodox Majesty." The fleeing Turks left behind cases of coffee (it is to this captured booty that we owe the Viennese coffee houses that are still famous today and forerunners of all the others, from Paris to Seattle). Innocent lived long enough to see the imperial forces push the Turks entirely out of Hungary and seal their victory with the capture of Belgrade in 1688.

Innocent was just as strict with others as he was with himself, and he passed all sorts of decrees for the propagation of morals in Rome—outlawing immodest dress in women and shutting down gambling houses. He also attacked Quietism and Laxism, heretical notions that were the opposite of Jansenism (teaching that if one quieted one's own will, and completely subordinated it to God, he would be incapable of sin no matter what he physically did)—thus illustrating the old truth that one heresy begets its seeming opposite. Innocent confirmed the charters of the universities of Innsbruck and Guatemala. Interred in St. Peter's, Innocent was beatified in 1956 by Pius XII.

## Alexander VIII

### (October 5, 1689–February 1, 1691)

Pietro Ottoboni was born at Venice, in April of 1610. His father was Marco Ottoboni, chancellor of Venice and a member of one of the noble families to whom public office in that republic was restricted. In 1627 the young aristocrat took his doctorate in law from the University of Padua and went to Rome under Urban VIII. Successively governor of several cities in the Papal States, he then became an auditor of the Rota before being created cardinal in 1652 by Innocent X at the request of the Venetian government. His best years were spent as bishop of Brescia, although he was appointed Cardinal Datary by Clement IX. As is customary when cardinals cannot agree, he was elected because of his extreme age—not in spite of it.

Louis XIV took advantage of his accession to evacuate Avignon and renounce the right of asylum. But Alexander declared once more that the Gallican articles were invalid. When the news came of the defeat of Louis's ally James II, by William of Orange at the Battle of the Boyne, the pope or-

dered the Te Deum sung (something Protestant and Catholics alike should think about on the twelfth of July, as well as those who think that popes know all, given what would befall Ireland in the wake of James's defeat). He assisted his native country in its war with the Turks, and bought the library of Queen Christina for the Vatican. Although Alexander lowered taxes, he allowed his nephews to make as much money as they could, which revived the practice of selling offices that had been banned by Bl. Innocent XI.

## Innocent XII
### (July 12, 1691–September 27, 1700)

Antonio Pignatelli was born near Naples on March 13, 1615, to a Neapolitan noble family. He entered the curia at age twenty and was appointed nuncio to Tuscany by Innocent X, and in the same capacity to Poland by Alexander VII. In 1682, Innocent XI created him cardinal and bishop of Faenza. Five years later this pontiff translated him to the archdiocese of Naples. When Alexander VIII died, the French and Habsburg factions among the cardinals could not agree, until at last Antonio was elected as a compromise. He took the name Innocent after the pontiff who had raised him to the purple.

One of his first moves was to decree that no pope could appoint more than one of his nephews as a cardinal. Calling the poor his "nephews," he was lavish in alms giving. Innocent built a number of charitable and educational buildings, as well as the palace currently occupied by the Italian lower house of Parliament. Innocent recondemned Jansenism and Quietism.

Papal relations with Louis XIV smoothed considerably when the king withdrew the four propositions (see Clement X); the bishops who had signed it sent a written recantation to Rome, whereupon Innocent confirmed in their Sees those bishops who the popes had not confirmed because of their signing the condemned propositions. But Innocent's relationship with Emperor Leopold I suffered when the imperial ambassador Count Martinitz insisted upon the right of asylum. As a result, Innocent advised the childless Charles II of Spain to leave his realm not to his cousin, the Holy Roman Emperor, but to his nephew and Louis's grandson, Philip, the Duke of Anjou. This would precipitate the War of Spanish Succession, which would help to ruin Spain, France, and the empire alike, and benefit only the Protestant powers of Britain and Prussia. (But as we have seen, of such pettiness and short-sightedness are human affairs made up—now as then.)

# Clement XI

## (November 23, 1700–March 19, 1721)

Giovanni Francesco Albani was born at Urbino on July 23, 1649, to an Umbrian noble family. Destined for the Church at an early age, and coming from a house that had given many members to the papal service, he studied at the Collegio Romano, and by the age of eighteen was known for his writing. He was a member of the glittering circle around Queen Christina of Sweden, and he was as renowned for piety as wit. He held a succession of important offices under various pontiffs and was made cardinal under Innocent XII, assisting that pope in drafting his anti-nepotism legislation. In addition, he formulated the suggestion to Charles II of Spain that he leave his territories to Philip of Anjou, rather than to his cousin, Emperor Leopold I. At the conclave that followed Innocent's death, the favored candidate, Cardinal Mariscotti, was vetoed by the king of France. After forty-six days the cardinals settled on Giovanni, who, despite being relatively young at fifty-one, was so well known for his abilities and piety that all parties at the conclave were pleased with him. Being aware of the difficulties he would face (the emperor would have vetoed his election had he known of Giovanni's part in Charles II's will), it took three days to persuade him after the vote to accept the papacy. Consecrated a priest on November 30, he was crowned on December 8.

As had been the case all through his career, Clement combined industry with piety, looking after every detail of every brief issued in his name, as well as saying Mass and confessing daily. Sleeping and eating little, he threw himself into the temporal administration of the Papal States and the spiritual governance of the Church at large. In the one area, he reformed prison administration, pioneered public works, and distributed vast amounts of charity. With regard to the second, Clement organized the hierarchy of the Philippines, made the archdiocese of Lisbon a patriarchate, declared the feast of the Conception of the Virgin a holy day of obligation, and composed the Breviary office of St. Joseph, which was used until after Vatican II. Among others, he canonized Pius V and Andrew of Avellino, and he issued another condemnation of Jansenism.

Though his spiritual activities were his most favored, the tenor of Clement's times ensured that he would have to devote more time and energy to politics. The pope officially protested the assumption in 1701 by the elector of Brandenburg of the title "King of Prussia" for two reasons: first, because the elevation of a land into a kingdom was a prerogative of the pope; and second, because Prussia itself still belonged de jure to the Teutonic order. His

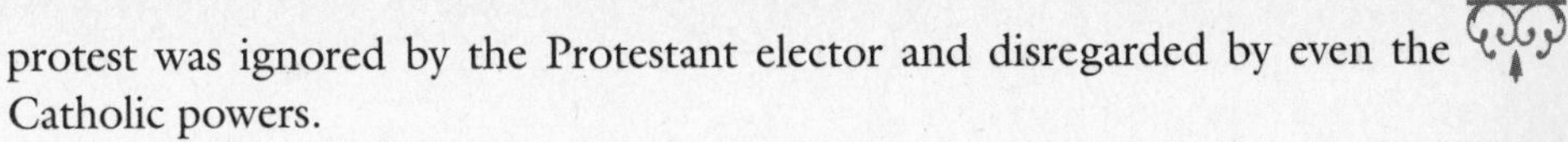

protest was ignored by the Protestant elector and disregarded by even the Catholic powers.

Far worse was to come. At first, Clement attempted to remain neutral in the War of Spanish Succession, despite his part in setting the stage for it. But when the duke of Anjou was hailed as Philip V in Madrid, the pope recognized the action (which was popular in all Spain except Catalonia). Clement was publicly elated by the march of the Franco-Bavarian army toward Vienna; however, this column was trounced by the British and Austrians at Blenheim. Leopold would have his revenge—the Austrian army followed up Blenheim by conquering Piedmont, so placing Italy at the emperor's mercy. Leopold then died and was replaced by his son Joseph I.

The new emperor had even less regard for the papacy than had Leopold. Demanding the right to appoint bishops to vacant dioceses, his army seized Parma and Piacenza and laid siege to the city of Ferrara in the Papal States. Unaided by outside forces, Clement was forced to sue for peace, recognizing Joseph's brother, Archduke Charles, as King Charles III of Spain on January 15, 1709—with the caveat "without detriment to the rights of another." Nevertheless, the two Bourbon courts were quite annoyed with Clement. At the Treaty of Utrecht in 1713, which ended the war, the papal envoy was ignored, and the Papal feudatories were given away without consulting him—Naples and Sardinia to Austria, and Sicily to Savoy. This last was particularly galling. Victor Amadeus II of Savoy had from the day of his accession quarreled with the Holy See in regard to Episcopal appointments in his country. As King of Sicily (a title he now assumed) he claimed all the rights of the medieval Sicilian kings over the Church. The problem was not solved until 1718, when Victor Amadeus traded Sicily to the Spanish for Sardinia; he then proclaimed himself king of that island, again without consulting the pope.

The Turks took advantage of the strife between the Christian powers to swarm over the Danube. Despite earlier difficulties, Clement sent major funding to Joseph's brother who had ascended the imperial throne as Charles VI. The result was that the imperial general Eugene of Savoy crushed the Turks at the battle of Temesvar, putting an end to the Sultan's military threat. As a reward, the pope sent Eugene the blessed Berettone and Stocco (hat and sword), which up until the twentieth century were consecrated every Christmas by the pope and sent to a prominent Catholic soldier. Even Philip V sent a fleet to assist in the Crusade. But the wily cardinal Alberoni, at the time Philip's chief minister, diverted the ships to attack Sardinia.

One requirement of the Treaty of Utrecht was that James III, son of the exiled James II of England, leave French soil. After James's disastrous attempt to regain his three realms in 1715, Clement offered him asylum at Rome and a pension, and assisted the exiled king in procuring a worthy consort. This came to pass with the wedding of James to Clementine Sobieska, daughter of the former king of Poland. Spiritual man though he was, Clement's pontifi-

cate had been disastrous for the Holy See in terms of foreign policy—often for reasons beyond his control.

## Innocent XIII
### (May 8, 1721–March 7, 1724)

Born Michelangelo dei Conti, May 13, 1655, at Rome, he was the son of Charles II, the Duke of Poli, and studied at the Collegio Romano. Brought into the curia by Alexander VIII, he was sent in 1690 to bring the berettone and stocco to the Doge of Venice, Morosini. After serving as nuncio at Lucerne and Lisbon, Michelangelo was created a cardinal by Clement XI in 1706. That pope appointed him to the diocese of Viterbo in 1712, but he resigned because of sickness seven years later. He was elected by a thoroughly divided conclave, and he took the name after Innocent III, a member of his family.

Much had changed since the days of his great relative, however. Although Charles VI received Sicily from Innocent and took the oath of allegiance to the pope (having traded it with the Duke of Savoy for Sardinia) in accordance with ancient custom, the emperor then gave the Spanish prince Charles the duchies of Parma and Piacenza a year later. Innocent protested, for the two duchies also were feudatories of the Holy See—but the emperor ignored him.

As had his predecessor, Innocent hosted James III at Rome and gave him a pension, offering still more money if the king made another attempt to regain his thrones. Additionally, the pope tried to rally the Catholic powers behind James, rightly seeing that such a restoration would benefit the Faith throughout Europe. But Habsburg and Bourbon would not be reconciled. The pope continued to assist the Venetians in their struggle with the Turks.

Unfortunately, Innocent sided with the Dominicans against the Jesuits in the question of the Chinese Rites—practices involving, among other things, veneration of the ancestors and Confucius. The Jesuits maintained that they were permissible, because not religious (that is, pagan); the Dominicans took the opposite view. But he renewed the condemnation against the Jansenists, although part of the price for the French Crown's cooperation was the elevation of the worthless prime minister, Du Bois, to the cardinalate. To be sure, Innocent did what he could with the ever more limited prestige at his disposal. In 1721, he cofounded with Phillip V of Spain the universities of Havana and Caracas.

## Benedict XIII

### (May 29, 1724–February 23, 1730)

Pietro Francesco Orsini, scion of the great Roman princely family, was born February 2, 1649. His family wished for him to play his part as a great noble, but instead he joined the Dominican order at an early age. In the end, they came to accept his decision. His learning, piety, and connections ensured his ecclesiastical advancement, but he was not pleased with it. At last, in 1672, his kinsman, Clement X, created him cardinal—an honor he refused until compelled to accept it by the master general of the Dominicans. Not surprisingly, Pietro took his place among the Zelanti at the conclave of 1676, and all he attended thereafter. At Innocent's XIII's death, the conclave assembled on March 20. By May 25 the deeply divided college had been unable to come up with a new pope. On that day, Pietro began a novena to St. Philip Neri to allow the cardinals to vote successfully. His chagrin was great when the choice fell on him. He refused, only to be compelled once again by the master general of the Dominicans. He took the name Benedict after Benedict XI, who had also been a Dominican.

The new pope went to work immediately to abolish worldly pomp and luxury among the cardinals. He founded the Congregation of Seminaries to supervise clerical education throughout the world and to bring it into accord with the decrees of Trent. In addition, Benedict renewed the ban on Jansenism, compelling even the haughty Cardinal de Noailles of Paris to condemn it. The election of Cyril Tanas, Greek Orthodox patriarch of Antioch, precipitated a split in that body. Many of his followers followed him into reunion with the Holy See, but many refused. Nevertheless, as an organized body, the Melkite Rite of the Church dates from this time.

Unfortunately, Benedict's choice of subordinates was unwise. Most had served him well in the archdiocese of Benevento, but they were greedy and rapacious and took cash wherever they could from the papal treasury.

The diplomatic side of the pontificate was not so dramatic as his immediate precedessors' had been. He granted the kings of the Two Sicilies (Habsburg, for the moment) the right to appoint a judge for ecclesiastical affairs, but reserved the most important cases to the Holy See. John V of Portugal demanded the right, held by other Catholic kings, to nominate cardinals in his own land. Benedict refused. In response, John called all Portuguese in Rome back to their motherland, broke off diplomatic relations with the Holy See, and attempted to withhold any money destined from the Portuguese people to Rome. In 1728, he extended to the Universal Church the office of

St. Gregory VII, with its account of Emperor Henry IV's excommunication and deposition. This annoyed Protestants, Gallicans, and Regalists of all stripes.

All in all, Benedict attempted to bring peace between the Catholic sovereigns. But like so many other popes, he was unsuccessful.

## Clement XII
### (July 12, 1730–February 6, 1740)

Lorenzo Corsini was born at Florence on April 7, 1652. His noble line had produced many great men, including St. Andrew Corsini. Educated at the Collegio Romano and the University of Pisa, after the death of his father and his cardinal uncle in 1685, he entered the clerical state himself, resigning his rights as eldest son. In 1691 Alexander VIII appointed him nuncio to Vienna, a post he did not take up because of Leopold I's insisting he be able to choose the nuncio himself. Five years later, Lorenzo was appointed governor of Castel Sant'Angelo. Clement XII made him papal treasurer (creating him cardinal in 1706), and Benedict XIII elevated him to headship of the Holy Office of the Inquisition. Despite his age and infirmity (Lorenzo was going slowly blind), his financial abilities recommended him to the other cardinals, given the state of the papal treasury. They elected him, and he took the name Clement in honor of his benefactor, Clement XI.

He immediately went to work clearing up the financial problems Benedict XIII had left, forcing that pope's wayward assistants to repay the monies they had taken and imprisoning the most prominent. Clement relaunched the lottery that Benedict had abolished, thus filling the treasury. In addition, he imposed many economies, although public works of every sort were executed. He drained marshes and built aqueducts—his harbor at Ancona became the envy of the Adriatic. But in his second year he became totally blind and bedridden. This did not prevent Clement from keeping up the same volume of work until his last illness.

The pope worked hard to restore the then low moral tone of many of the cloisters, and he approved and assisted the new order of the Passionists with their emphasis on preparation for death and their devotion to the sacrifice of Jesus. He also issued the first of many papal condemnations of the Freemasons, owing to the essentially materialist nature of their creed and the language of their oaths of secrecy. Clement canonized, among others, St. Vincent de Paul. Moreover, he was very concerned with reunion with the

East. Sending a legate to preside over a synod of the Maronites in Syria (the only Rite without a non-Catholic equivalent), he also founded a college for Melkite students in Calabria and gave them the church of Santa Maria in Domenica in Rome. In Egypt, ten thousand Copts, with their Patriarch, entered into union with Rome (wherein comes today's Coptic Catholic Church). The Armenian Catholicos removed the anathemas from their liturgy against St. Leo I and the Council of Chalcedon.

For the most part, Clement was able to stay on good terms with the empire, France, Spain, Portugal, Sardinia, Poland, and Bavaria. When his legate, Cardinal Alberoni, annexed the tiny republic of San Marino, he immediately repudiated the envoy's action and guaranteed the little state's independence—which it has retained to the present.

Although reliant on his nephew for a great deal of his pontificate, he refused to allow his family to enrich itself. Altogether, it is amazing what Clement XII accomplished from his bedside.

## Benedict XIV
### (August 17, 1740–May 3, 1758)

Prospero Lorenzo Lambertini was born at Bologna on March 31, 1675. In 1694, he was graduated as a Doctor of Theology and Law from the Collegium Clementinum at Rome. Holding a succession of curial offices, he was made bishop of Ancona in 1727 and translated to the archdiocese of Bologna in 1731. After a divisive conclave of six months, Lambertini was elected as much for his honesty as his reputation. He took the name Benedict in honor of his friend and patron Benedict XIII.

The reputation of the new pope was indeed extraordinary, for he was as truly a Renaissance man (in the best sense of that term) as any who ever graced the throne of St. Peter. A deeply prayerful master of theology, he was also up-to-date in his knowledge of all branches of learning at that time. Married to a deep personal piety was a cutting wit that even Voltaire was forced to admire. He did not fear the so-called Enlightenment, which was the latest intellectual fad. He recognized its admirable elements and laughed to scorn the rest. Benedict was a prodigious writer, producing published works that filled twelve folio volumes. He was interested in every facet of Church and civil life and did not fear to work for reform in any of them. Benedict was amiable, but he could be intimidating when circumstances called for it.

Voltaire dedicated his poem "Mohammed" to him, writing, "To the head of the true religion, a writing against the founder of a false and barbarous religion." Rather an extraordinary comment from the old unbeliever, to be sure. Given the nature of the times, however, Benedict would need every scrap of charm and wit at his disposal.

In spiritual matters, he applied his vast store of learning to revision of the calendar and martyrology. The pope laid down a number of guidelines on beatification and canonization and found against St. Thomas Aquinas in the question of relics of Christ's blood (which Aquinas declared could not be authentic). He originated the current "encyclical," the letters by which he and subsequent popes normally communicate matters of concern to the faithful. Benedict approached the question of mixed marriages (which, since the lessening of Protestant-Catholic tensions began to become common) in a prudent manner, ruling that though they were valid, the Church could not approve of them because of the danger the lack of unanimity of faith would bring to the Catholic partner and resulting children. (From his time until the 1960s, such marriages would require an oath on the part of the non-Catholic partner that their children would be raised in the Faith, and moreover prescribed that such weddings could not take place with the full nuptial ceremonial. Because the couple could not receive communion together, this made sense.)

Benedict, too, was very concerned with reunion with the East. He sent the pallium to the reconciled patriarch of Antioch and passed a number of measures to prevent Eastern rite-members from being brought into the Latin rite by missionaries, and in everything he decreed he emphasized the equality between the liturgies of the Church.

His good sense and affability reduced diplomatic problems to a minimum. He recognized the title of the King of Prussia, for which Frederick the Great granted freedom to his Catholic subjects (important since his seizure of Silesia in the War of Austrian Succession) and built St. Hedwig's Cathedral in Berlin. The atheistic monarch even permitted the Jesuits in his realm. In 1740, the pope gave Portugal's John V the right of presentation to all dioceses and abbeys in his kingdom and eight years later bestowed on him and his successors the title of "Most Faithful Majesty," in token of that monarch's ongoing fight against the Barbary pirates, who were taking slaves as far away as Ireland and Iceland. For the same purpose, in 1754 Benedict permitted the Spanish king to collect all ecclesiastical revenues to fight the same foe. The pope witnessed the War of Austrian Succession, in which Prussia, Bavaria, and France joined to deprive Maria Theresia (daughter of the sonless Charles VI) of her possessions. He was overjoyed when that queen (of Hungary) was able to keep most of territories intact and oversee the elevation of her consort, Francis, Duke of Lorraine, to the throne of the Holy Roman Empire. Far less joyful was the defeat of Prince Charles Edward Stuart, "Bonnie Prince Charlie," in his attempt to regain the thrones of England, Scotland, and Ireland, for his father, James III. The battle of Culloden in 1746 signaled the end of Catholicism as a political force in Britain until the nineteenth century, and of the dream of a Catholic king in London.

But his final years were cheered by the marriage of Louis, heir to the throne of France, and Maria Antonia, daughter of Francis I and Maria Theresia. Here at last was the reconciliation of France and the empire that so many pontiffs had sought. It was, however, very late. Had it occurred two centuries before, then the scandalous spectacle of Catholic kings conspiring with Protestants and Turks against each other would have been avoided. As it was, this long-sought reunion would do little to avoid the catastrophe that unbelief would bring to Europe. Benedict's immediate successors would lack both his charm and his good fortune.

## Clement XIII

### (July 6, 1758–February 2, 1769)

Carlo Della Torre Rezzonico was born at Venice on March 7, 1693. Educated by the Jesuits at Bologna, he graduated in law at Padua and in 1716 entered the Roman Curia. He held ever more responsible offices, until at last Benedict XIV made him bishop of Padua in 1743 and created him cardinal in 1747. Noted for personal holiness and public charity and zeal, he ran his diocese very well, indeed. Well aware of the anti-Catholic and materialistic tendencies that Benedict had kept in check, he burst into tears when elected pope—he knew all too well what lay ahead.

Two strains had united in Catholic Europe by this time: Regalism, which as noted earlier, in various forms had plagued the Church since Constantine; and the Enlightenment. The first saw a force in the Church that must be subordinated to the secular power for the good of the state; the second measured all things by human reason, and dismissed as superstition all that either was old or else could not be easily understood by those who deemed themselves reasonable. The practical effect of this union was to create in Catholic Europe ruling classes that looked with envy to the complete power Protestant princes exercised over their pet clergy. Moreover, they sought to purge the Church of anything that seemed to them to be repellent to the spirit of the age, as represented by themselves. Thus, folk who themselves were personally immoral sought to reduce to mere moral precepts the Church's teaching, purging so

far as might be done any supernatural element. Devotions to the saints and relics, pilgrimages, monastic orders, Latin in the liturgy—all must be eliminated. Ecclesiastical appointments must be solely in the gift of the civil power (and made to like-minded clerics), and the authority of the Holy See restricted so far as possible. They further frowned on any evangelizing of non-Catholic Christians because they believed in universal salvation—or at least, salvation purely through conduct, rather than creed. Some of the more extreme discouraged converting non-Christians. In any case, to be fair, many of these folk sincerely saw in such measures a method of saving the Church by keeping her relevant in what they saw as the first truly civilized era—and many who held these notions were themselves priests and bishops. There are none so superstitious as the educated, for they often see in their own time—as an article of faith unsubstantiated by experience—the final end of human progress. No class of people are so sad to study in retrospect (for we know—as they could not—the consequences of their thought and action, and so we may smugly pat ourselves on the back for our own superiority—one at which our own descendants doubtless will smile or sneer at, depending on their level of charity and self-knowledge). The uneducated rarely suffer from this failing, although they have others to suffer from.

Regardless, the major counterweight to this point of view in the middle of the eighteenth century was the Society of Jesus. Given by their founder, St. Ignatius Loyola, a complete loyalty to the pope, and a military organization that paradoxically utilized to the fullest extent the individual personalities and talents of their members, the Jesuits had spread all over the world. With a strong community spirit, coupled with training designed to permit individual Jesuits the ability to carry on their mission alone for decades at a time, they had pioneered a network of institutions across the globe. In Europe, their preaching had regained large sections from Protestantism, and their colleges educated the elite. Jesuit missionaries were everywhere in the new regions. They evangelized Canada and Maryland and staffed large stretches of Latin America—Padre Kino introduced the Faith to Baja California and Arizona. But the gem in the Jesuit crown was certainly the mission-state of Paraguay.

Their success there, however, was their downfall. Paraguay in particular excited envy from the colonial authorities. When the Indians there fought against Portuguese slavers, it was considered a rebellion. Moreover, when the husband of one of King Joseph I's mistresses shot at him at the opera, the king's minister, Pombal, convinced his nominal master that the Jesuits were behind it. Pombal was of the ranks of "advanced" folk previously described. Despite papal protests, in 1759, except for the imprisoned superiors, the Jesuits were expelled. Next it was the turn of the French Jesuits, who were accused of financial improprieties by the heavily Jansenist Parlement of Paris. At first, Louis XV resisted moves against them. His mistress, Mme. de Pompadour, was both dead set against the Jesuits and had the ear of the king, so

Louis's resistance eventually crumbled. In 1764, the order was expelled from France and its possessions. Although Clement published a bull in defense of the Jesuits the next year, their turn in Spain and its empire came when they were expelled in 1767. A year later, they were exiled from Naples and Parma, both under young Bourbon princes whose regent was Charles III of Spain. At last, the French, Spanish, and Neapolitan ambassadors presented demands to Clement to suppress the Jesuits. This action, striking Clement as betrayal, killed him.

He was able to show independence in one area, however. In 1766 James III died and was succeeded by his elder son (according to their adherents) as Charles III. But Clement, desirous of forging good relations with Great Britain as a counterweight to the erring Bourbon powers, took the opportunity to recognize George III as king of Great Britain. Much to the pope's embarrassment, when Charles visited Rome, although denied royal honors by the papal government, he was greeted as king by the large expatriate community there, including the priests in charge of the English, Scots, and Irish colleges. Clement sacked all three in reprisal.

## Clement XIV
### (May 28, 1769–September 22, 1774)

Born in 1705, Giovanni Ganganelli became a Franciscan friar. A learned and spiritual man, he held various academic positions in his order and in 1759 was made a cardinal by Clement XIII. Ten years later, he succeeded to the throne after a conclave dominated by the Jesuit question. The Catholic powers (Spain, Portugal, France, Naples, and Parma) all favored suppression of the Jesuits throughout the world, having done so on their own soil over the previous five years. A certain number of cardinals were in their corner. Another faction opposed the suppression as an attack on the Church, yet a third faction cared little either way. Cardinal Ganganelli, the only member of the conclave who was a member of a religious order, was seen as a compromise candidate despite his friendliness to the Jesuits. He was elected, consecrated a bishop on May 28, and crowned pope on June 4.

For four years, Clement XIV tolerated both the suppression of the Jesuits in those countries that had exiled them and their continuance in those which had not. But both Naples and France had occupied papal territories, which they would not restore without a total end of the Society of Jesus. In the end,

citing merely that their existence was a cause of strife, the pope suppressed the Jesuits throughout the world and imprisoned their leaders for questioning the decree. The suffering of the Fathers and Brothers of the Jesuits was often extreme. But in Protestant Prussia and Orthodox Russia, because those countries' non-Catholic rulers would not allow the bull of suppression to be published, the Jesuits there continued their work. It was a well-disguised defeat for the Catholic monarchies, however. The Jesuits had steadily preached loyalty to the sovereigns, and their ill-treatment severely eroded respect for the kings among the people. Moreover, in Latin America, it created a manpower shortage in the ranks of the clergy that could not be filled, much as the Franciscans and Dominicans scrambled to (staffing their Baja missions was what brought Bl. Junipero Serra to California). In many ways, the suppression contributed not merely to the revolutionary storm that would soon break out in Europe, but also to the Independence movement in Latin America.

The other major diplomatic problem facing the Holy See was the upcoming partition of Catholic Poland between Russia, Prussia, and Austria. Here too, Clement's efforts were in vain. The year following his death choice portions of Polish land were snatched by the three powers, foreshadowing two further ones in 1793 and 1795, which would snuff the country out completely.

Clement died in deep depression over the state of Europe, which he saw plummeting rapidly toward a great conflagration. He was, at least, fortunate enough not to see it. Moreover, he was attended on his death bed by St. Alphonsus Liguori. It is reported that the saint, although seen by many at Clement's side, also was seen by a great crowd at the same time in his cathedral at Sant'Agata dei Goti, near Naples. It is one of the best accounts of bilocation on record.

# Revolution and Despair

# Pius VI

## (February 15, 1775–August 29, 1799)

Giovanni Angelico Braschi was born at Cesena to an impoverished noble family on December 27, 1717. He was educated at the Jesuit college of Cesena and studied law at Ferrara. Appointed papal secretary in 1755, Clement XIII appointed him treasurer of the Roman Church in 1766 and Clement XIV created him cardinal a few years later. On his elevation he retired to the monastery of Subiaco. At the conclave following the death of Clement XIV, his candidacy was at first opposed by France, Spain, and Portugal because of his support of the Jesuits—but the powers relented. It appeared as though the Bourbon states wanted to create national churches independent of Rome, but in this they could not compare with Joseph II, who was the son of Maria Theresia and the Holy Roman Emperor.

Keen to regulate the life of the Church along the lines mentioned earlier, the emperor imposed a new order on the Church in the Habsburg possessions. He limited rights of the pope in Austria, his ultimate goal being a national church independent of Rome. He dissolved seven hundred to eight hundred Catholic and Orthodox monasteries under the pretext that they were neither charitable nor educational—their fortune was confiscated by the state. The Orthodox faithful in Galicia, Bukovina, and Transylvania, who venerated their monks, were permanently alienated from the Habsburgs—something that would bear bitter fruit in the late nineteenth and early twentieth centuries. The seminary training was henceforth to be regulated by the state. It was to be the express goal of the priests to make not only believers but good subjects. Moreover, a network of parish churches was to be built so that no one would be more than a half hour from a church.

But Joseph's interest in change was not restricted to Church government and administration—he had a mania for organizing the internal life of the Church to his liking as well. The government published guidelines for the liturgy and preaching: Latin hymns sung by a choir were replaced by German songs performed by the congregation; processions and pilgrimages were limited; and a new, cheaper funeral order was introduced, forcibly. Joseph even regulated the number of altars and candlesticks each church could have, caus-

ing Frederick the Great, in whose Protestant realm the Church was freer, to derisively call Joseph, "my cousin, the sacristan." In 1781, Joseph issued the "Patent of Toleration," which allowed Protestants freedom of worship, although they were not to proselytize or have identifiable churches. This "Josephinism" was to be echoed in the rest of Catholic Germany by "Febronianism," a movement among the higher clergy led by a bishop who wrote under the name Febronius.

Pius resolved on an unheard of step—he would go to visit Joseph himself. Leaving Rome on February 27, 1782, he arrived at Vienna on March 22. Although received courteously by the emperor, the chief minister, von Kaunitz, was extremely rude. Remaining a month in the Imperial City, the pope lodged with the Capuchins, who ironically were and are the custodians of the imperial crypt. (The side altar at which the pope said Mass is still preserved and it is in fact one of the few places in Vienna today [2003] where the Tridentine Mass is offered on a daily basis.) But all that Pius could extract from Joseph before he left on April 22 was the emperor's promise that none of his alterations would conflict with Catholic dogma, or compromise the "dignity" of the pope. Joseph accompanied Pius as far as the monastery of Mariabrunn, and a few hours after the pope was out of sight, the emperor suppressed the abbey. Joseph then decided to fill the vacant archdiocese of Milan on his own authority, and the pope threatened solemn excommunication. This threat did get the emperor's attention, who appeared in Rome on December 23, 1783, as a surprise. Maintaining that it was a strictly personal visit to Pius, he refused any of the rich ceremonial formerly given by Rome to its titular emperor. He confessed to the Spanish ambassador that he intended to set up a separate Church independent of Rome, but the diplomat convinced him that this would be unwise, as his subjects were already restive. To assuage his ambition, the pope in 1784 gave Joseph the right to nominate bishops in the duchies of Milan and Mantua.

The emperor's brother, the Grand Duke Leopold II of Tuscany, followed Joseph's example by encouraging his bishops to hold the synod of Pistoia. This gathering ended papal supremacy in Tuscany, endorsed Jansenism, condemned the doctrine of Limbo, and in effect created a separate Tuscan church. In Germany, the three archbishop-electors and the archbishop of Salzburg held a conference at Ems and agreed to unite against Rome and to introduce Joseph's measures into their own territories—measures bitterly resented and resisted by those common folk whom they were supposed to be for.

Although Spain, Sardinia, and Venice also carried out parts of Joseph's pattern, they were far excelled by Naples. Her Bourbon king, Francis IV, refused to allow any papal briefs to be published without royal approval, and he insisted on appointing bishops, which Pius would not permit—the Episcopal vacancies began piling up. As seen previously, Sicily was supposed to be a papal fief; from time immemorial, on the feast of SS. Peter and Paul (January

29), the king would send the pope a white horse in token of his feudal submission. In 1787, Francis announced that he would send Pius the cost of a horse, but he would never again provide tribute.

On a happier note, Portugal, where the Jesuit difficulties had begun, received a pious queen when Maria I came to the throne in 1787. In 1788 she settled all the questions at issue with a favorable concordat, which was a great consolation to the pope.

Another event occurred during this pontificate that, at the time, seemed minor—the independence of the United States. George III was the first British king since the deposition of James II (with the partial exception of Queen Anne) to show any favor at all to Catholics. He received them at court, and in 1774 passed the Quebec Act, which gave the Catholics of Canada freedom from British penal laws. This in turn was one of the outrages that so upset the colonists and is duly mentioned in Orwellian terms (the king is accused of abolishing "the free system of English laws in a neighboring province") in the Declaration of Independence. The conflict broke out in 1775, and owing to the large number of Loyalists, acquired the nature of a civil war. The Continental Congress early on sent letters to the people of Quebec, urging them to put aside religious differences and join with the rebels; and to the people of England, in which the king was once more attacked for favoring Catholicism in Quebec. Father John Carroll, of a prominent Maryland Catholic family, and Benjamin Franklin were dispatched to Quebec to persuade the inhabitants to join the rebellion. Unfortunately for their mission, Bishop Briand had copies of both letters, published them, and threatened with suspension any priest who would have anything to with Carroll.

The mission was a failure, but it forged a strong friendship between the quasi-Unitarian Franklin and the Catholic priest, who, in common with the contemporary educated opinion of his class, wished to have papal authority limited, the liturgy in the vernacular, elected bishops, and so forth. After the war ended and independence was granted in 1783, the Catholic organization needed revamping; such as there was depended upon the Vicar-Apostolic of London. Ecclesiastical appointments in the English-speaking world were usually vetted by Henry Maria Stuart, Cardinal York, who was the younger brother of Britain's claimant, Charles III. But the Federal government was leery of him. In 1788 his brother died, and the cardinal legally became Henry IX of England, Scotland, and Ireland. American authorities made it clear that they would look with disfavor on his making appointments in the new country. So Pius turned to the most famous American of his day for advice—Benjamin Franklin. He in turn suggested his old friend Carroll, who in 1789 duly became the first bishop of Baltimore. It was a fateful choice.

In that same year the French Revolution began. Ironically this conflict began in what was the wealthiest country in Europe. It is not within the scope of this book to go into the details of the conflict, but it is important to note

that after 1774, when Louis XVI and his Austrian queen Marie Antoinette ascended the throne, the country's polices became much less anti-papal. The king tried to make decent appointments to the episcopate, but was hampered by low standards in faith and morals among the higher clergy (when a friend remonstrated with him about one such appointment, known for his immorality, Louis replied, "Yes, I know. But what have I to choose from? At least this one believes in the Trinity!"). His reforms of the armed forces and in other areas made possible the French victory in the American War—the first such won by France over Britain in a century. But it bankrupted the country, thus contributing mightily to France's own revolution.

When that blow struck against the institution of monarchy, all desire for national churches and regulating altar cloths went out the window. Suddenly, the "Enlightened Despots" came to a harsh realization: if the altar was not sacred, neither was the throne. The Revolutionaries took full control of France in 1791 and passed the Civil Constitution of the Clergy, which in a nutshell separated the French Church from Rome in all except name. Pius condemned it, and those priests who refused to sign it were either expelled, murdered, or went into hiding. The pope provided for the exiles as well as he could. In January of 1793, Louis XVI was beheaded by the new regime. Pius VI said in his allocution of July 17, 1793, Pourquoi Notre Voix:

> The most Christian King, Louis XVI, was condemned to death by an impious conspiracy and this judgment was carried out. We shall recall to you in a few words the ordering and motives of this sentence. The National Convention had no right or authority to pronounce it. In fact, after having abolished the monarchy, the best of all governments, it had transferred all the public power to the people—the people which, guided neither by reason nor by counsels, forms just ideas on no point whatsoever; assesses few things in accordance with the truth and evaluates a great many according to mere opinion, which is ever fickle, and ever easy to deceive and to lead into every excess, ungrateful, arrogant, and cruel. (Acta Apostolicae Sedis, cap. 2)

He was about to find out how cruel the revolutionaries could be. In response to this allocution, the republic seized Avignon and set up their guillotine to introduce the inhabitants to the new life. The Papal States joined the Allies against the French and in 1796 were defeated by Bonaparte. As part of the peace, all prisoners in the Papal States were freed, the harbors were opened to French shipping, and the Romagna ceded to the French. Two years later, a French general who attempted to start a revolution in Rome was shot—retribution was swift. The French took Rome on February 10, 1798 (troops entered the Quirinal, took Pius prisoner, and snatched the papal ring off his finger), and five days later proclaimed a republic. Pius refused to recognize any of this, and so was taken away to France, where he was confined in the town of Valence. He died there. His body was taken from its exile and buried at St. Peter's in 1802.

## Pius VII
### (March 14, 1800–August 20, 1823)

Barnaba Chiaramonti was born at Cesena to a noble family on August 14, 1740. Raised in a pious atmosphere (his mother became a Carmelite nun when he was twenty-three, following his father's death), Barnaba was educated at the College for Nobles in Ravenna, and at the age of sixteen he joined the Benedictines. Pius VI, who was a friend of his family, made him an abbot and eventually bishop of Imola. He was created cardinal by that pope in 1785. In 1797, the French detached Romagna from the Papal States, merging it into their Cisalpine Republic, which included Lombardy (in time it would grow into the kingdom of Italy, of which Bonaparte would be king). Barnaba preached submission to the new authorities by this people, many of whom were disgusted by this action. But when neighboring Lugo resisted, it was pillaged, and saved from final destruction only by Barnaba literally throwing himself on his knees before the French commander.

The Treaty of Campo Formio in 1797 between France and Austria had given Venice to the latter power. The new emperor, Francis II, was a very different man from his uncle Joseph II and his father Leopold II. Convinced that their Church policies had helped pave the way for the Revolution, and of a pious nature in any case, Francis offered refuge to many refugee cardinals in Venice. Since, foreseeing that Rome might be in enemy hands when the time came, Pius VI had issued a bull in 1798 allowing the conclave to be held wherever the largest number of cardinals were gathered. After he died, the conclave was held in Venice under Austrian protection at the island monastery of San Giorgio, as arranged by Henry IX, Cardinal York. Because the cardinals wanted a pope independent from Habsburg influence, and since the emperor vetoed the front runner he considered too independent, Barnaba was elected as a compromise, crowned as Pius VII on March 21, and returned to Rome on an Austrian warship.

Once established in the Eternal City, Pius named Ercole Cardinal Consalvi secretary of state. Consalvi became one of the most able diplomats of his time

and would act as Pius's right-hand man for the entirety of his pontificate. The first problem was that of Bonaparte and the new French government.

As a measure for national unity, Bonaparte was anxious to reconcile his country with the Church. His many victories and a coup or two had elevated him to the status of Consul for Life. He negotiated a concordat with Consalvi, which on the one hand allowed those who had bought Church property to keep it, recognized the absorption of Avignon by France, and confirmed as permanent much of what the Revolution had inflicted on diocesan organization. But on the other hand, it also recognized Catholicism as the religion of the state (which would pay for clerical salaries and for church buildings) and gave the Church a certain amount of control over education, social services, and the like. After the Concordat's passage in 1801, the most conservative of French Catholics, many of whom had lost relatives in defense of the monarchy and some of the privileges being given up, refused to accept it. Excommunicated and loaded down with heavy civil penalties, these formed the so-called Petite Eglise. Their last priest had died in 1832, and ever since had existed in a priestless limbo until Pius XII lifted all censures. (Even so, in 2003 a few still refuse to return to communion on the one hand, or to join non-Catholic groups on the other.)

The same year as the Concordat was signed, however, another of Bonaparte's actions precipitated difficulties in Germany. By the treaty of Luneville, the imperial princes on the left bank of the Rhine had lost their lands to France, but the same treaty declared that they might seek compensation elsewhere in Germany. Not just theirs, but many sets of greedy eyes looked upon the imperial free cities, the estates of the imperial knights, and the lands of the independent bishops and abbots across the empire. Pius ordered Dalberg who was the archbishop-elector of Mainz to watch over the interests of the Church. But the wily Dalberg had already joined Bonaparte's camp; in 1803, the imperial deputation at Regensburg, through the fiction that the emperor was simply consolidating his feudatories, allowed the smaller states, free cities (save six), and knightly estates to be gobbled up by the larger ones. As far as Church territories were concerned, this process was simply called "secularization." These small countries had been for the past two centuries the greatest supporters of imperial rule (under whom their independence was safeguarded); therefore, the empire itself had been badly weakened by this development, superintended as it was by France. In 1804, Bonaparte brought Pius to Paris to crown him as "Napoleon I, Emperor of the French" (although, in the event, the new monarch crowned himself). Seeing the writing on the wall, Francis II took the new title "Hereditary Emperor of Austria." The next year Napoleon constructed the "Confederation of the Rhine"—all the German states outside of Prussia and Austria of which he was to be "protector" and Dalberg chancellor. Under French pressure Francis abdicated the Holy Roman throne in 1806 and was known henceforth as "Francis I, Emperor of

Austria." This is commonly quoted as the year of the empire's end, but neither Great Britain nor Pius would recognize this, and legal scholars, pointing out that offices do not end because their incumbent quits, have maintained that the empire subsists as a sort of legal phantom. Certainly the Imperial offices in Vienna kept functioning, the prayers in the Missal for the emperor continued to be recited in Austria, and the king of Sardinia happily retained his title as Perpetual Vicar for the now-vacant empire in Italy.

Pius's relationship with Napoleon was doomed to sour. The emperor wished to be the successor of Charlemagne and run Europe as one nation. As far as he was concerned, Pius was to be his chaplain. The pope had other ideas, however; he maintained diplomatic relations with Catholic countries at war with France during the bloody years of 1806, 1807, and 1808. He protested the presence of the French navy at Ancona and chided Napoleon for various infractions of the canons. At last, an infuriated Napoleon annexed Rome and took Pius prisoner to Savona. But the pope would not give in to Napoleon on any point. After four years of this resistance Bonaparte sent Pius to Fontainbleau. He remained there until Napoleon's fall, then he triumphantly returned to Rome.

The Congress of Vienna followed Napoleon's defeat and exile as an extraordinary attempt to put Humpty-Dumpty back together again. Of the big five powers, Austria was ruled by Francis I, a friend of Pius; France by Louis XVIII (who unlike his older and younger brothers was not much of a believer, but was committed to restoring the Church's role in his country); and Russia by Alexander I, perhaps the best friend Catholicism has ever had among the Tsars. Great Britain was far less antagonistic to the Church than formerly because of the large numbers of French Catholic refugees who refamiliarized many English with a religion that had become completely foreign to them and won their sympathy by their loyalty to their exiled king. This state of affairs strengthened the papacy's hand tremendously at the Congress. Although Cardinal Consalvi failed to restore the Holy Roman Empire or to make Germany surrender Church lands, he did restore the Papal States, almost in their entirety. Another singular success was to have the Congress (which also regulated diplomatic protocol from that time to this) declare that the papal nuncio in Catholic countries would function as dean of the Diplomatic Corps (in present day, a few primarily non-Catholic countries, like New Zealand, have also adopted this measure).

Pius was very kind toward Napoleon's family, despite his abuse at the fallen emperor's hands, giving asylum to Napoleon's mother, uncle, and brother. When news came that Bonaparte wished to be reconciled with the Church, Pius dispatched a chaplain to St. Helena, who ensured that the pope's former foe died a good death.

Pius spent much of his remaining life reorganizing the shattered Church in Europe. This task was made far easier by the wave of piety that swept Catholic

Europe, starting about the turn of the eighteenth century. Partly fueled by the Romantic movement, spearheaded by writers like Chateaubriand (who emphasized in his Genius of Christianity that Catholicism is beautiful as well as true) and Novalis (who argued in his Christendom or Europe? that the medieval unity under the Church was far preferable to what succeeded it after the Reformation), it led to a tremendous rise in faith on the part of a generation who had come to believe that the disbelief of the Enlightenment had been the direct cause of the horrors of the Reformation. Such writers as De Maistre and de Bonald in France called for the closest possible cooperation between "altar" and "throne." In this atmosphere, the work of restoration proceeded along apace.

But there were other problems. The occupation of Spain by the French and the imprisonment of Ferdinand VII had led to rebellions in Latin America; the Church in those countries was closely tied to the Spanish crown by the Patronato. In Spain itself, a liberal revolt in 1820 led to a rupture of relations between the Holy See and that country, as the new government seized Church property, closed abbeys, and prepared to form a national church. It was crushed by the French in 1823, however.

The United States saw a great growth in her Catholic population; by the time of Pius's death, there were seven dioceses under the archdiocese of Baltimore.

Pius reorganized the administration of the Papal States, retaining some of the French reforms and confirming the abolition of feudalism and municipal liberties that the revolutionaries had pushed through. This did breed resentment in such quarters. At this time, the Carbonari, a secret society dedicated to founding a united republic of Italy, came into being. Outside Pius's dominions, the Italian states were the Two Sicilies and Parma, under two branches of the House of Bourbon; Tuscany and Modena, under two branches of the House of Habsburg; the Lombardo-Venetian Kingdom directly under Austria; and the Kingdom of Sicily, belonging to the House of Savoy.

In this period, a large number of artists came to Rome, such as the German Nazarene group and the Dane Thorwaldsen, who converted. But as Pius VII lay dying, St. Paul Outside the Walls, built originally by Constantine, burned down. His attendants did not tell the dying pope.

# Leo XII
## (September 28, 1823–February 10, 1829)

Annibale della Genga was born at the Castello della Genga near Spoleto, on August 22, 1760, of a family ennobled by Leo XI in 1605. Graduating from the College of Noble Ecclesiastics in 1783, he was ordained a deacon. Made a priest two months later, he came to the notice of Pius VI who made him a papal chamberlain. In 1790, he was selected to preach the funeral oration on Joseph II. Annibale managed to do so without either offending the Austrians or derogating from papal authority. Successively nuncio at Lucerne and Cologne, Pius VII sent him to the Diet at Regensburg in 1805. He was unpopular with Bonaparte and did not do well representing the papacy in France. When the pope was imprisoned in 1808, Annibale withdrew to a remote monastery. When Pius was restored to Rome in 1814, he dispatched Annibale to Paris to congratulate Louis XVIII on his return to power. Pius created him a cardinal in 1820 and made him vicar-general of Rome that same year. When the Pope died three years later and the cardinals went into Conclave on September 2 at the Quirinal, there were two parties among them—the Zelanti and the "Moderates," who wished to keep the favor of the Great Powers. The Zelanti candidate looked as though he would win; thus, the Austrian emperor cast his veto against him. The Zelanto then urged his supporters to vote for della Genga, and so he was elected. Crowned on October 5, he took the name Leo in honor of his family's patron.

Among other measures, Leo tried with little success to stamp out brigandage. He did manage to rein in the curia officials who had become very venal and bribable during Pius VII's dramatic pontificate. The new pope worked very hard to prevent Protestant proselytizing and the spread of the Carbonari in the Papal States—this last effort he put in the hands of the stern Cardinal Rivarola. The work of rebuilding St. Paul's Outside the Walls was begun, and Alexander I of Russia contributed the beautiful malachite columns (seen in the nave today). A Holy Year was called for 1825, and Rome became filled with pilgrims.

Politically, the pope supported Daniel O'Connell's work for Catholic Emancipation in the British Isles, which eventually bore fruit in the first of several Catholic relief acts in 1829; anti-Catholic activity in the Netherlands was also faced and overcome, although the government's policy there would soon bear fruit in the Belgian revolt. Leo also supported the efforts of the powers to repress revolutionary activity in their countries and colonies and

had the joy of the pious Charles X receiving a traditional coronation at Rheims in 1825. This pope's last illness came about suddenly, but he did receive the Last Rites before his death.

## Pius VIII

### (March 31, 1829–December 1, 1830)

Francesco Xaverio Castiglione was born at Cingoli on November 20, 1761. Born into a noble family, he was educated by the Jesuits and studied at Rome and Bologna. In 1800 he was made bishop of Montalto by Pius VIII. Imprisoned by the French for refusing to take the oath to Napoleon as king of Italy, Francesco was made a cardinal in 1816 by Pius after his release. He was the favored candidate of the Moderated in the 1823 conclave. Favored both by Charles X of France and by Francis I of Austria, he was elected after five weeks, taking the name Pius after the pope who had given him the Red Hat.

Although he reigned but a short time, Pius lived to see the passage of the Catholic Emancipation Bill in England. He also decreed that priests could bless mixed marriages only when the non-Catholic partner promised to raise the children as Catholic.

But Pius's last months were filled with apprehension. In July, Charles X was overthrown and his liberal cousin was made "king of the French"; revolts also broke out in Belgium and Poland. A Carbonari cell was discovered in Rome, and revolt broke out in the Eternal City after Pius's death.

# Gregory XVI

(February 2, 1831–June 9, 1846)

Bartolomeo Alberto Cappellari was born to a family of the minor nobility of Belluno on September 8, 1765. Professed into the rigorous Camaldolese order as Mauro, he became renowned for his learning and was a teacher to his brethren. Mauro eventually ended up at his order's great monastery of San Gregorio al Celio, formerly the abbey of St. Gregory the Great. He was there in 1798 when Pius VI was kidnaped by the French. The year following Pius's death, Mauro's book, Il Trionfo della Santa Sede, in which the earnest young monk argued for the temporal sovereignty of the pope and papal infallibility, appeared. After Pius VII was taken prisoner, Mauro went to the house of his order at Venice. After it was closed by the French authorities in 1813, he left for Padua, returning to Rome when the pope did. Pius employed Mauro in a number of capacities, and Leo XII made the Camaldolese a cardinal in 1825. In 1827 Mauro negotiated an accord between the king of the Netherlands and his Catholic subjects n Belgium, and in 1829 one between the Armenian Catholics and the Turkish Sultan. At the conclave following the death of Pius VIII, Spain vetoed the front-runner, and Mauro was elected as compromise. He took the name Gregory in honor of the pope who founded the monastery where he had been abbot.

Revolution broke out in northern Italy, however, before Gregory could be crowned. Spreading from Modena to the papal city of Bologna, the Italian tricolor was raised there on February 4. Soon, virtually all the Papal States were in arms, and Gregory appealed to Austria for aid. The emperor's troops quelled the revolt in a month, but at this point representatives of the powers—Britain, Austria, France, Russia, and Prussia—met at Rome on May 31 and drafted a proposal of "reforms" to the papal government. Among other things, they demanded lay participation in the administration. Gregory XVI rejected this and instead overhauled the government of the Papal States entirely on his own. Rebellion broke out again, but the Austrians again suppressed it and the French occupied Ancona as a counterweight to the Habsburgs. Finally, both states withdrew in 1838.

Meanwhile, the revolutions in France and Belgium were difficult, because both sides in both countries demanded papal support. In 1831, Gregory declared the papacy's neutrality in all strictly dynastic matters.

In November of that year, the priest La Mennais and his followers, who declared that the Church must line up behind "the people" and "democracy," had been condemned by French bishops and came to Rome to appeal directly

to the Pope. Though Gregory was kind to them, he intimated that their appeal would not do well if he were forced to make a decision. They did press their suit, and the result was Gregory's encyclical, Mirari vos, which condemned democracy, separation of Church and state, divorce, and clerical marriage. (As a result of these and other writings, Gregory has been attacked by "progressive" opinion from his day to ours.) He thought that what was called "democracy" would inevitably degenerate into oligarchy—rule by a monied elite with no real roots in the given country's society, culture, or history. (Given in 2003 that the majority of U.S. senators of both parties are millionaires, it may well be that he had a point.)

There were other problems facing him too. Even as the house of Bourbon in France had split into a conservative elder and a liberal junior branch, so too did the Bourbons of Spain and the Braganzas of Portugal. Civil war broke out in both countries and the younger lines triumphed. They took revenge upon the Church, by abolishing monasteries and religious orders (and, of course, seizing their property), expelling the nuncio, and the like. In Prussia, a fight with King Frederick William III broke out over the Church's refusal to bless mixed marriages, which resulted in an archbishop and a priest being imprisoned or expelled. Poland had revolted in 1830; when Tsar Nicholas I suppressed the revolt the next year, despite the exhortations of the pope to be loyal to him as their sovereign, he too took his frustration out on the Church. Among other things, he suppressed the Union of Brest in what are present-day Belarus and eastern Ukraine in quite a bloody manner. The actions of anti-Catholic Bible societies in spreading their propaganda throughout Italy also had to be combated. In the midst of all of these events, Gregory simply reiterated his principles and refused to compromise. At his death, however, the tide of what was called "liberal opinion" was rising through all Italy and Europe.

## Bl. Pius IX

### (June 16, 1846–February 7, 1878)

Giovanni Mastai-Ferretti was born at Sinigaglia to a noble family on May 13, 1792. He began his education at the Piarist College at Volterra when he was ten years old, and in 1814 he asked to be admitted to the Papal Noble Guard; his epilepsy kept him out of the service. That year he began his studies at Collegio Romano. He was ordained a priest in 1819 and was sent by Pius VII to Chile in 1823 to assist the nuncio. The Freemasons claim that he was initi-

ated into one of their lodges there. Whether or not that is true, upon his return he began to acquire a reputation for liberalism. Leo XII made him archbishop of Spoleto in 1827, and he was instrumental in getting a large band of revolutionaries to lay down their arms four years later. In 1832 Gregory XVI translated Giovanni to Imola and created him a cardinal in 1840. On June 14, the conclave was divided between conservatives who wished to continue the policies of Gregory, and liberals who wanted to open up the administration of the Papal States to laymen. The latter had a majority, and on the fourth scrutiny elected Giovanni, who took the name Pius in honor of Pius VII.

The people of Rome greeted his accession with joy, for he was known for wit and amiability. The liberals did so as well, for they believed that one of their own was in power. Although Pius initially formed a lay council of state and appointed a lay prime minister (Count Rossi), he found that rather than reduce the plotting on the part of such as "Young Italy," every concession simply increased demands by the agitators. Finally, in the revolution year of 1848 when governments toppled throughout Europe—from France through Prussia to Austria, Hungary, and Italy—the revolutionaries in Rome demanded that Pius declare war on Austria. The pope refused to do so and his prime minister was murdered and he was at last forced to flee from the city in disguise to Gaeta. There, under the protection of the Neapolitan king, he appealed to the powers to regain the Papal States for him. A Roman republic was proclaimed, which initiated its own junior reign of terror. On June 29, 1849, French troops entered Rome and the pope returned the next year.

Why did the popes up to and including Pius IX feel such a need to cling to the temporal possessions of the Holy See? There were several reasons. The most obvious is that since Constantine Catholic monarchs had often been at cross-purposes with each other. To maintain his spiritual mission as father of all, the pope had to have sufficient territory to maintain his neutrality. Never have secular rulers—whose temporal roles the popes have usually been the first to uphold—scrupled to try to use the papacy as they could. This too is understandable, given the amount of prestige a pope can bring to a given political cause. Such causes do not last long. The pope, therefore, must think in terms of centuries if he is to be true to his trust. Another question is that of sacrilege. Because they were donated to the Holy See, the Papal States were seen to be sacred. Allowing annexation by a temporal ruler would be like allowing a Mass-chalice to be used for cocktails. (Obviously, a country dedicated to a given religion will always have strains peculiar to it—Israel is a good example; just as the secular and religious requirements of the Jewish state often come into conflict, so it was with the Papal States.)

Because of the insecurity of the Italian situation and the ever clearer resolution of Sardinia under its chief minister, Cavour, to annex the entire peninsula, something had to be done about the Papal army. It was reorganized and expanded and volunteers worldwide flocked to join the "Pontifical Zouaves"—

from France, Quebec, Belgium, the Netherlands, and Germany. This was seen as even more necessary owing to the impending quarrel between Austria and the France of Napoleon III, upon both of whom the Papal States were militarily dependent.

The war broke out in 1859. The Austrians were trounced by the French, who demanded Lombardy for their victory. They in turn exchanged that province to Sardinia for Savoy. Although they held on to Venice, the Austrians were out of the Italian game. In 1860, the Sardinians annexed Tuscany, Parma, Modena, and Romagna; they then invaded the remainder of the Papal States. The Zouaves were defeated at the battle of Castelfidardo. But the French occupied Rome, saving it for Pius. Garibaldi then invaded the kingdom of the Two Sicilies, conquered it, and turned it over to Sardinia. Six years later, Austria was defeated by Prussia, who then took over direction of the rest of Germany, excising the Habsburg influence. The Italians attacked at the same time, but were roundly defeated—still Bismarck insisted that Austria cede Venice to Italy. In 1870, the Franco-Prussian War erupted; Napoleon III withdrew his troops, and the Italians invaded. To spare bloodshed, Pius bade his Zouaves to lay down their arms. He refused to accept this action as legal, and the pope fled the Quirinal, shutting himself up in the Vatican. The king of Italy transformed the Quirinal into his royal palace.

Pius forbade Catholics to participate in the political life of the new country. Moreover, the Roman nobility split—the White nobility accepted the new order of things and took service under the king of Italy; the Black nobility refused to. In their city palaces, the thrones reserved for the pope when he came to call on them were turned against the wall, or the reception room locked up. Refusing to take the oath to the king, the Black sacrificed the sorts of careers in the military, diplomatic corps, and administration they had been used to—both for themselves and for their children. It was a heroic sacrifice in many ways. In any case, the career of the popes as temporal princes had come, for the moment, to an end.

The spiritual side of the papal office continued. Indeed, before 1870 as after, Pius faced many challenges. In 1854, he had defined the Immaculate Conception of the Virgin Mary at long last. The Eastern Orthodox greeted this with an angry denial. The fact that they had believed it heretofore meant little to their religious leaders apparently. In 1864 Pius published the encyclical Quanta cura, with the famed "Syllabus of Errors," condemning many "modern" beliefs then in circulation. It was argued at the time as to how binding it was, and whether it was infallible. (It remains a good standard for Catholics wherewith to evaluate the world around them, considering that most of the condemned propositions have become maxims of everyday life.)

Most important was the convening of Vatican I in 1869. The fathers of this council defined papal infallibility after carefully examining the many papal failures throughout history. They declared papal infallibility a gift of the Holy

Spirit, whereby, when speaking solemnly from the "Throne of St. Peter" (ex cathedra), on a matter of faith and morals, and intending to bind the whole Church, the pope will be prevented by God from defining error. Obviously, this covers only a small piece of papal pronouncements. But this definition sparked a firestorm of disapproval, even after the fall of Rome in 1870 broke up the council.

In Germany, Austria, and Switzerland, small groups calling themselves "Old Catholics" rejected Infallibility as an innovation. Uniting with a surviving group of Jansenists (with valid orders) in the Netherlands, they proposed a "continuing" Church. But having got their start as supposed Conservatives, by 1922 each of their national groups had jettisoned Latin and clerical celibacy (a few years ago, several began ordaining women). A network of "liberal Catholics" grew up, who, without wanting to break openly with the church as the Old Catholics had, nevertheless wanted to reinterpret many of her doctrines, downplay miracles, renounce the Temporal Power, and so forth.

But Pius's spiritual activities went far beyond these actions—he extended the feast of the Sacred Heart to the Universal Church and consecrated the world to it. Despite much protest, he reestablished the hierarchy in England and Scotland. During his pontificate he established twenty-six new dioceses in the United States, whose Catholic population had been greatly expanded by immigration.

At his death in 1878, he had been on the pontifical throne longer than anyone else—two years longer than St. Peter. His record has still not been excelled. Interred at St. Lawrence Outside the Walls, he was beatified on September 3, 2000, by Pope John Paul II.

## Leo XIII

### (February 20, 1878–July 20, 1903)

Gioacchino Pecci was born on March 2, 1810, at Carpineto, to the family of the Counts Pecci. He obtained his doctorate in theology and in 1832 entered the College of Noble Ecclesiastics and began studies at the University of Rome. Gioacchino entered the curia and was ordained five years later. In 1838, Gregory XVI sent him off as legate for Benevento, a papal city surrounded by Neapolitan territory and almost overwhelmed by brigandage and other evils. Within three years he had so improved conditions that the place was unrecognizable. Pleased by his work, Gregory sent him to Perugia in Umbria to work similar miracles. In two years, after establishing cooperatives and credit unions, he revolutionized the local economy. The pope then dispatched him to Brussels as nuncio. He was so successful there, he completely altered the political situation in favor of the Catholic Party. In 1844, Gregory appointed him bishop of Perugia. He remained there for thirty-six years through various political upsets. His unswerving devotion to his spiritual office, plus his tact and wit in dealing with the new authorities after 1860, made the transition in Perugia far less difficult than it might have been. Pius IX brought him to Rome in 1877, and appointed him Cardinal Camerlengo, the second most powerful position at Rome. Although, when Pius died, the cardinals feared the interference of the Italian government (which that body had promised), the death of King Victor Emmanuel II at the same time, and the eruption of war between Turkey and Russia gave them other things to think about. The cardinal camerlengo was himself elected, and he took the name Leo.

The Holy See the new pope ascended to was at once stronger and weaker than Pius IX had found it in 1846. Spiritually, the stock of the papacy had not perhaps been so high since before Leo X. New orders and new devotions were growing, and there were hopeful signs everywhere. Dom Prosper Gueranger had revived the Benedictines in France and launched the liturgical movement with his writings—as well as revived Gregorian chant. In every Catholic country new orders were being founded and devotions spreading. Politically, however, the Holy See had not been so weak since the days of Napoleon. True, there were Catholic parties in Germany, Austria, Belgium, Switzerland, and the Netherlands, which fought hard for the Church's interests. But in France, the new republican government had been anti-clerical since 1878. Bismarck had unleashed the Kulturkampf against the Church, and the situations in Ireland and Poland were not good. In all three countries, the loyalty a good Catholic owes his sovereign was being severely tested by persecution or other malfeasance. In Italy, things were particularly precarious.

But there was a greater problem underlying the political—one which the smug liberal politicians were overlooking: the social. The great fact of nineteenth-century Europe was the Industrial Revolution—and with it the creation of a great underclass of workers who lived in abysmal poverty. Moreover, being in many cases cut off from the religion and traditions of their ancestors, people were looking for something to believe in. Differing groups of socialists and anarchists were filling this ideological vacuum by offering hope of secular salvation through the sacrament of revolution. What Leo saw (and the anti-clerical politicians most often did not) was that the reintegration of the proletariat into society was the burning issue of the day.

Leo had a great affection for France and feared that the republican government would make use of the fact that most Catholics in that country were

Royalists to end the Concordat. Advised by his liberal secretary of state, Cardinal Rampolla, Leo ordered the Catholics of France to "rally to the republic." This proved to be a major mistake. For French Catholics it appeared that they were being ordered either to betray their king for their Faith, or else to defy their pope for basic loyalty. Different Frenchmen reacted differently, but the "ralliement" split the French Church and destroyed her as a political force at the worst possible moment.

In Germany, however, things went better. Due to the skillful work of the Catholic Center party, Bismarck came to realize his need for the Catholic vote and ended the Kulturkampf. When Germany and Spain disputed the Caroline Islands in the Pacific, Leo was asked to arbitrate. The pope's relationship with Kaiser William II became particularly warm after his accession to the throne in 1888.

Leo's interest in English affairs was particularly acute. After the Napoleonic Wars ended, the Romantic movement in Britain had inspired a great interest in things medieval. From this had arisen the Oxford Movement, which sought to make the Church of England Catholic in faith and life (while claiming that in some sense it always had been). One of the leaders of this group was John Henry Newman. At length, convinced that Anglicanism was a dead end, Newman had converted and become a priest. This unleashed a floodgate of conversions—it seemed that England might well return to the Faith. Leo made Newman a cardinal. In addition, he became a friend of Edward VII, who visited him in 1903 (five years later, the king would attend the requiem Mass of the murdered king of Portugal—the first British monarch to do so since James II—and convert on his deathbed). Most annoying to the Anglicans, however, was Leo's extensively reasoned authoritative declaration that Anglican orders are invalid. They denied this, but then began having their bishops co-consecrated by Old Catholics.

The United States also consumed a great deal of Leo's interest. A great deal of tension had developed there between certain segments of the primarily Irish hierarchy, led by Cardinal Gibbons of Baltimore and Archbishop Ireland of St. Paul—two men of the Archbishop Carroll stamp—and the more Roman-oriented faction, led by the archbishops of New York and Rochester. The question was exacerbated by the mistreatment at the hands of the former clique of Catholics of French-Canadian, German, Polish, and Ruthenian derivation. The Gibbons-Ireland group was called the "Americanists," after their belief that the United States were divinely ordained to alter and advance the world. Thusly, they reasoned, the Church in America ought to be different from that of the rest of the world, and their country's example of freedom and practicality should be the Catholic pattern. They emphasized the so-called active virtues over the "passive" ones of prayer and evangelization. Further, they believed that all immigrants should be assimilated as quickly as possible into American culture. Cardinal Rampolla was their great

ally in Rome and prevailed upon Leo to tone down his decree against "Americanism" in a doctrinal sense and to avoid naming specific holders of it. Above all, he managed to persuade the pope not to take any specific action against it.

The European nations expanded their empires all over the globe in Leo's time, and he ensured that missionaries would accompany the colonizers—not only to spread the Faith, but to try to protect the locals against exploitation. Moreover, he favored Catholic social action to assist the proletariat. His encyclical Rerum novarum spelled out a concrete program for dealing with the social question. It was, of course, too conservative for the rising socialist parties, and too communalist for the liberals (as the word was used in Europe and Latin America; in the United States they would be called conservatives—what was classically called conservative in those places does not exist as an organized body in the United States). In recognition of the growth of the Church in Asia, Leo granted the archbishop of Goa, India, the oldest diocese in colonial Asia, the title "Patriarch of the East Indies," which is still attached to it.

With regard to Italy, Leo maintained Pius IX's stand of non-recognition. He believed that Catholic abstention from elections would lead to a growth of strength for the socialists and eventually bring the Italian government to the bargaining table. Umberto I, Victor Emmanuel's successor, was himself very pious, but was unable as a constitutional monarch to force his ministers to deal with the question. But his status as an excommunicate was very painful to him—he feared for his soul. Leo arranged that, though still excommunicate as king of Italy, he and his wife were reconciled as private individuals. So while they did not attend High Mass or the Holy Days in public, as did (and do) other Catholic sovereigns, they nevertheless were able to attend low Masses in private.

Extremely industrious, in his long pontificate Leo intervened in every aspect of Catholic life—and in every nation. He was confined to the Vatican and yet operated worldwide—the first modern pope.

## St. Pius X
### (August 4, 1903–August 20, 1914)

Giuseppe Sarto was born on June 2, 1835, to a postman and his wife at Riese, near Venice. Studying at the seminary of Padua, he was ordained in 1858. He held a number of pastoral positions in the diocese of Treviso and became concerned both with the devotional and with the educational lives of the people, as well as the social question. In 1884, Leo XIII made Giuseppe bishop of Mantua, where poverty and anti-clericalism were rife. His work was so effective in reforming the place that in 1893 the pope created him a cardinal and patriarch of Venice. But the Italian government claimed the same right of approval over the patriarchs of Venice that had been exercised by the Austrian emperor. Leo refused to grant it and Giuseppe had to wait eighteen months before taking possession of his patriarchate. Once ensconced, he addressed the same concerns that had characterized his priesthood and early episcopate—catechetics, administration of the Sacraments, use of Gregorian chant, and amelioration of poverty. He founded rural parochial banks and other social organizations, and he discouraged the growth of socialism among his flock. When Leo XIII died, the front-runner among the cardinals was Rampolla, the secretary of state. He was quite liberal, however, and friendly to both the French republican politicians and the Americanists. Some quarters rumored that he was a Freemason. Whether true or not, the cardinal of Cracow presented the emperor of Austria's veto against him. Sarto was elected instead, taking the name Pius on his coronation on August 9.

The new pope's first interest was to spread devotion—especially Eucharistic devotion—among the faithful. At this time, reception of Holy Communion was a rare thing. Many Catholics received only around Easter, which was the bare minimum required. But Pius began a campaign to revive frequent communion—daily if possible—and with it frequent confession in order to receive the Sacrament worthily. (Today most receive at every Mass, though few still confess their sins—a frightening thing from the perspective of Catholic theology.) Moreover, young people generally made their First Communion only after being confirmed. Pius changed the law, urging children as young as seven (the age of reason) to receive.

On November 22 (St. Cecilia's day), 1907, Pius issued a decree on Church music, which gave Gregorian chant pride of place and banished from churches most theatrical and secular music. Additionally, he encouraged devotions to the Virgin Mary. Pius created regional seminaries in Italy, began the codification of a new code of Canon Law, put through a restructuring of the Roman

Curia, and revised the breviary and calendar. Among the feasts he eliminated were those of the Guardians Angels of the various Latin American countries (perhaps not that well advised, given their subsequent history).

But the major spiritual problem of his pontificate was the struggle with Modernism. This was the notion that not only the Church's government and practices (as Liberals and Americanists believed) but her very doctrines had to evolve along with the ever-upward movement of mankind toward the great wonderful future. Doctrinal formulations are, for the Modernist, not true, per se, but symbolic of some greater truth—whatever that means. Thus, from Transubstantiation to the Trinity, the Church's teaching, while doubtless literally understood by those who first formulated them, are simply stages in the growth of human consciousness, and are not to be taken literally. As might be guessed, these ideas were very popular with many clerics (and a few laymen) who liked to think of themselves as thinkers. It was in reality an insidious thing, which would empty Catholic dogma of all real meaning. In 1907, Pius issued Lamentabili, a syllabus of Modernist errors. Shortly afterward, he issued Pascendi, an encyclical that analyzed Modernist methodology in detail. (To the current—2003—reader, these documents are amazing for their clear description of much of what passes for Catholic theological writing today.) Like Arianism, Modernism has outlived its condemnation and prospered. But Pius dealt the thing a strong blow. He identified the clandestine and semi-organized nature of Modernism, and he organized a sort of secret service, the Sodalitium Pianum, to neutralize it, placing it under the direction of Monsignor Umberto Benigni.

In the political arena, Pius encouraged the founding of Catholic labor unions. The French government, despite Leo XIII's attempts, did indeed break the concordat. They expelled the religious orders and seized all Church property—hence churches built before 1905 in France all belong to the local government. Although this action was condemned by Catholics at the time—to say nothing of Pius himself—it had, years later, unexpected results. For in the 1960s, when the French clergy (as with many priests everywhere) were keen on emptying out their churches of every statue, altar, communion rail, and other things of beauty, many communist mayors, the nominal owners of these buildings, refused to allow them the out of anti-clericalism. At the same time, many conservative religious mayors allowed their clerics to indulge in the sort of iconoclasm not seen in those parts since the Revolution.

Pius's relations with Italy were dominated by the question of the violated temporal rights of the Church. He allowed Catholics to vote in local elections if this would improve the general welfare. Revolution in Portugal introduced a fanatically anti-clerical republic there, and persecution broke out. Ecuador, Spain, and Bolivia were also host to anti-Catholic developments.

Witness to the growth of Modernism in the Church, of warlike attitudes among the European nations, of Socialist class hatred, of the drop in public

and private morals, and of the general materialization of life, Pius feared a great conflict—an Armageddon. He wrote that he was afraid that the anti-Christ was already on earth. When Archduke Franz Ferdinand was assassinated at Sarajevo, Pius was sure that the end was beginning. On August 2 he wrote an appeal to the European powers not to plunge their peoples into war. His appeal was ignored. Eighteen days later he was dead, having escaped the horror he could not prevent.

## Benedict XV
### (September 3, 1914–January 22, 1922)

Born in 1854 to a noble family, Giacomo della Chiesa had a number of slight birth defects—half his face and one shoulder were higher than the other, and he had a limp. He studied at the Vatican's diplomatic school, the College of Noble Ecclesiatics, and he became secretary to Cardinal Rampolla in 1883, who became secretary of state in 1887. Della Chiesa became undersecretary in 1901 and in 1907 was appointed archbishop of Bologna by St. Pius X.

The reason for his transfer from the diplomatic service to diocesan ministry was his association with Cardinal Rampolla, suspected by St. Pius X and his secretary of state Merry del Val of Modernist leanings. Nevertheless, in May of 1914, St. Pius X named him a cardinal. Three months later, the pope was dead, Europe was at war, and Giacomo della Chiesa was elected Benedict XV.

Although the war had broken out, another problem claimed the new pontiff's attention. Even though the most radical Modernists, who believed that Church doctrine, rather than being delivered by Christ had to be revised by each generation, and had been excommunicated, many more had not. As noticed under St. Pius X, those who had gone underground in hopes of pursuing their agenda quietly were pursued by those who feared them as subversives. The opponents of the Modernists often called themselves "Integral Catholics," or "Integrists." In his first encyclical, Ad beatissimmi Apostolorum, November 1, 1914, he forbade the use of such party names among Catholics. He also officially disbanded the Sodalitium Pianum.

World War I of necessity took up the largest part of the new Pope's time. Benedict was crowned in a low-key ceremony in the Sistine Chapel, not thinking it appropriate to carry out the full range of jubilant ceremony when so many of his children were fighting one another. He sent huge sums of war relief to the afflicted on both sides and maintained a studious neutrality. On

August 1, 1917, he proposed a seven-point peace plan, which included return of all occupied territories, renunciation of indemnities, and the restoration of Polish independence.

It was denounced by all sides, owing to its reasonableness. Only the emperor of Austria, Charles I, accepted it (he himself is now a candidate for sainthood, and his body is incorrupt). The result was that Woodrow Wilson insisted on Benedict being excluded from the treaty process after the war. But Wilson did have his way—Charles was deposed and the last vestige of the Roman Empire in the West vanished.

But the war and the following Russian and other revolutions led to new challenges for the Church, which Benedict attempted to tackle. (The Revolution in Russia in 1917 deposed Tsar Nicholas II, the other guardian of imperial tradition.) He founded a special college for Russian priests and ordered that missionary training be improved. Moreover, he forbade missionaries to act as agents of their countries of origin in the mission field.

It was also in 1917 that three Portuguese shepherd children claimed to have a vision of Our Lady at Fatima. Apart from the miracle of the sun (witnessed by thousands) the Fatima event is noteworthy for the Virgin's predictions, which included notice of another and larger war, "which will break out in the reign of Pope Pius XI."

On the diplomatic front, he exchanged ambassadors with Great Britain and France (relations with the one having been broken in the seventeenth century after the deposition of James II, and with the other after the French government seized the churches of their country in 1904). He allowed Catholics in Italy to take part in politics as a counter to the growth of Communism there, and he initiated talks with Mussolini to end the division resulting from the seizure of the Papal States in the nineteenth century.

His short pontificate was one of the most eventful in history, and he was much missed when he died rather suddenly after contracting pneumonia.

# Pius XI

## (February 6, 1922–February 10, 1939)

Achille Ratti was born at Desio near Milan on May 31, 1857. He was ordained in 1879 and studied at the Gregorian University, becoming a professor at Milan's major seminary three years later. In 1888 he was named to a staff position at the Ambrosian Library in Milan, becoming director in 1907. His work there attracted the attention of St. Pius X, who placed him in the Vatican Library in 1911. Three years later, he was appointed prefect of the establishment. Benedict XV appointed Achille first as Visitator Apostolic to the new Polish republic and the next year designated him as nuncio to that country and the new Baltic states of Latvia, Lithuania, and Estonia. But tensions over the Upper Silesian plebiscite area, where Achille openly favored Poland over Germany led to his withdrawal. Benedict appointed him archbishop of Milan and cardinal. In the conclave after Benedict's death, Achille was elected on the fourteenth ballot, taking the name Pius after St. Pius X who had brought him to Rome.

The new pope faced a number of enormous problems brought about by the course of World War I; for the first time since Constantine, there were no Christian emperors—indeed, there was no great power at all with a professedly Christian outlook. Moreover, Russia was actively exporting revolution (although the first Communist attempts after 1917 outside Russia—Hungary, Finland, Bavaria, and Slovakia—were dismal failures). Moreover, the defeat of Greece by Turkey in 1922 resulted in virtually the entire Armenian and Greek population of Asia Minor being driven out of Asia Minor (or killed). Thus, for the first time since St. Paul of Tarsus, a region once as Christian as Italy or Spain was almost totally bereft of the faithful. The human cost in Europe, in terms of bloodshed, starvation, and disease during World War I and its aftermath were without equal in the history of the world (up until that time). If relief efforts (simply to save as many of the starving as possible) were successful to a great degree, the social and political problems of the pre-1914 world were joined by a host of new ones. The construction of a power vacuum by the destruction of the Austro-Hungarian Empire and the creation of the Weimar Republic boded badly for continued peace in Europe. The initial replacement of the "autocratic" Central European regimes with poorly established "democratic ones" would indeed be followed up by true totalitarian ones.

Moreover, the social tone of Europe had suffered greatly because of the war, as it usually does with such conflicts. Two great evils, from the Catholic

point of view, began to acquire acceptance after World War I in European society; they would dominate with ever greater strength the Church's relationship with the secular world in the twentieth century—abortion and artificial contraception. Remember that the Catholic view was, for the most part, the universal view of these matters for a very long time. The first country to legalize abortion was the Soviet Union in 1918, in keeping with their unique view that the disposition of the human individual is at the behest of the Party. Prior to this time it had been murder, as may be witnessed by the Hippocratic Oath taken by physicians everywhere and originated in classical times: "I will procure no abortion" is one of the clauses. Giving potions designed to cause abortion was one of the frequent charges against "wise women" in the Middle Ages. Most anti-abortion laws in Britain and America were imposed by Protestants during the nineteenth century; despite the Soviet legalization, during Pius XI's reign, most Europeans and Americans viewed abortion with horror. (It is instructive to view pre-1973 crime shows like Ironside, where abortionists appear as criminals, pure and simple.)

Contraception was another question. Genesis had condemned it with the story of Onan, who "spilled his seed upon the ground" (Gen. 38:8-10) and was struck dead for his trouble. The medieval teaching on the topic was extremely severe. Geoffrey Chaucer has his Parson declare, "When a man interrupts the conception of a child and makes a woman either barren by drinking harmful herbs so that she may not conceive, or slays a child by drinking willfully, or else put certain things in her secret places to kill the child, or else does unnatural sin by which man or woman diffuses their nature in a way or a place so that a child may not be conceived . . . that is homicide." By 1922, however, women like Margaret Sanger, the founder of Planned Parenthood, were stepping up pro-contraception propaganda. Though Mrs. Sanger's agitation was primarily to limit the number of births among "inferior" peoples, such as blacks and mulattoes (not an unpopular message in some eugenics-crazed quarters in the 1920s), it was obvious to religious leaders of many kinds that the result of such activity would be to spread what Christians of all types considered then to be "immoral" activity. Thus, in 1920, the Lambeth Conference of Anglican Bishops condemned contraception in no uncertain terms. But so great was the rise in propaganda for the practice that ten years later the Anglican Churches reversed themselves.

In common with these developments was a general lowering of standards of modesty in female (and male) dress; the "Lost Generation" who had been through so much in World War I often considered chastity to be at best quaint, at worst repressive. At the same time, Sigmund Freud's works, linking virtually every human endeavor—including religion—to repressed sexuality, became popular. This message was repeated in novel after novel, magazine after magazine. The new media of movies and radio often spread the same message.

The social issue had not been improved by the war—quite the contrary. With the added ingredient of communism, an equitable solution to the problems of labor and capital became paramount. One answer that was offered by such leaders as Benito Mussolini in Italy and elsewhere was to insist that both sides must be straitjacketed into working for the greater good, as decided by the state.

In foreign affairs, the horrors of the last war made Europeans and Americans extremely frightened of another one, given the ever-rising level of munitions technology. The League of Nations was created to prevent such an occurrence; but as the years went by, it became ever less credible as a force for peace. Moreover, the rise of nationalism in Europe and elsewhere, as well as the exaltation of war itself by Fascist-minded regimes and the threat of Communist revolution, increased fears of another conflagration, particularly as the short period of prosperity in the 1920s made way for the Depression in the "dirty thirties."

There were, however, opportunities as well. The rift with the French government had been partly healed by the Union Sacree, which had brought Catholics and republicans together to prosecute World War I. As a result, the religious orders had been allowed to return. All over the Catholic world there was a literary revival, which saw practically every country where Catholics lived (and some where they were small minorities) produce great writers anxious to spread the Faith. A great growth occurred both in public devotion among Catholics and in evangelization in mission countries.

Pius's tactic for dealing with new conditions was several-fold. First, as regarded relations between states and classes in general, he called for general recognition of the Kingship of Christ over peoples and individuals, in his 1926 encyclical, Quas primas. To further ingrain this teaching in Catholic life, he inaugurated the feast of Christ the King, on the last Sunday in October. Three years later, Pius issued another encyclical, Divini illius magistri, on Christian education of children. In this document he declared against the Fascists and Communists that parents had the primary role in education, followed by the Church, and only lastly by the state. He followed in 1930 with Casti connubii, which dealt with the family and such evils as divorce, contraception, abortion, and what was vulgarly called, "shacking up." The following year he wrote Quadragesimo anno to commemorate Rerum novarum of Leo XIII, and he dealt with the Church's reaction to current questions of economic organization; the Pope advocated a "third way" between socialism and capitalism.

After he addressed what was needed for societal happiness, as things then stood, Pius next attacked the open enemies of good order: Non Abbiamo Bisogno, in 1931 attacked Italian Fascism; Nazism felt the lash next, in 1937, with Mit brennender Sorge; and the same year saw Divini redemptoris, which

took on communism. (If one wants a crash course on Catholic social teaching, these seven short encyclicals lay it all out quite well.)

But stirring as his writings were, Pius's practical efforts had decidedly mixed results. From the beginning of his pontificate, he wished the Church and the Holy See to be not a political player, but, as it were, the conscience of the world. He originated Catholic Action, an international body that attempted to guide laymen in spreading the Faith through prayer, example, and evangelization wherever their given walk of life took them. To this end, CA was organized worldwide and received papal patronage.

At the same time, Pius wished to end the role of the Catholic political parties that had fought for the Church's interests in various countries. So, when Catholics were allowed to vote in Italian elections by Benedict XV, a Catholic Party was organized—the Popolari—under Don Luigi Sturzo. In return for a Concordat and the ending of the Roman Question on a favorable basis, Pius directed the Popolari to dissolve. Much the same thing happened with the Catholic Center Party in Germany after Hitler signed a Concordat with the Vatican. In Mexico, where the anti-clerical government had become so oppressive, the Catholics rose in revolt and the pope supported the Cristeros, as they were called. When victory appeared possible for the Cristeros, however, the Mexican government asked Pius to tell the rebels to lay down their arms in return for a lightening of the laws. Pius did, and the Mexican government slaughtered the Cristeros and broke their promises. In 1926, in pursuance of rapprochement with the French republican officials, Pius condemned the Action Francaise, a French Royalist organization, on the grounds that its founder and leader, Charles Maurras, was a neo-pagan and atheist. Because its members were many of the most zealous Catholics in France, a drama akin to that of Leo XIII's rally was played out—with as little benefit to the Church.

Another ominous sign was the terrible state of the Holy See's finances. In 1928 the papacy was on the verge of bankruptcy and was bailed out only in the eleventh hour by loans from American banks negotiated by Cardinal Mundelein of Chicago. Though the cash given by the Italian government the next year by the terms of the Lateran treaty ended the immediate crisis, the importance of the United States in Church affairs was underlined (a dangerous importance, perhaps, given the non-Roman tendencies of many of her most influential Churchmen).

Pius encouraged the Eucharistic Congresses that underlined reverence to the Blessed Sacrament, and he oversaw the erection of native hierarchies in the mission countries. He also helped with the building of Eastern Rite seminaries and colleges and Catholic universities in general. Until 1924 Pius continued the conversations on reunion at Malines between Cardinal Mercier on the Catholic side, and Charles Wood, Lord Halifax, on the Anglican side. Following Cardinal Mercier's death, however, the talks were suspended. Although His Lordship was an influential churchman in England, he in reality

represented only the Anglo-Catholic wing of the Church of England; sincere as he was in faith, he could not speak for any other segment of his church. Pius issued Mortalium animos, which forbade interfaith activities.

The pope's greatest accomplishment was the conclusion of the 1929 Lateran Treaty with the Italian government. In return for ceding all rights to the Papal States (save Vatican City, Castel Gandolfo's Papal Villa, certain buildings in Rome, and a patch of territory outside the city where Vatican Radio is located) Catholicism was recognized as the religion of the state. The government undertook to pay clerical salaries and the upkeep of churches and other institutions, and marital and others laws were brought into accord with Catholic teaching. The Black Nobility, in token of their loyalty to the popes and their sacrifices for them, were given dual citizenship, Italian and Vatican. Although Mussolini's motives were cynical, after his fall in 1943, the accords were endorsed by subsequent royal and republican governments. The Black Nobility were now free to enter public service; the Noble Guard, heretofore open only to nobility from the former Papal States, was now accessible to Italian nobles from all over the country. In 1931, Alfonso XIII of Spain petitioned Pius to open its ranks to nobles from all Catholic countries, but the pope refused.

The last years of his life were shadowed by the growth of Nazism and the countdown to World War II. Particularly vexing were events in Spain, starting with the departure of Alfonso and culminating in the Civil War. Similarly, Pius was pained by the absorption of Austria by Nazi Germany in 1938. But he was spared the actual invasion of Poland by his early demise.

## Pius XII

### (March 2, 1939–October 9, 1958)

Eugenio Pacelli was born in Rome on March 2, 1876, to Filippo Pacelli, a lawyer, and his wife Virginia. He studied at the Lateran University and he was ordained in 1899. He received his doctorate in canon law four years later. He joined the papal secretariat of state in 1902, becoming the collaborator of the secretary, Cardinal Gaspari, in the revision of canon law. Eugenio was professor of ecclesiastical diplomacy at the College of Noble Ecclesiastics from 1909 to 1914, and he held a number of posts before being named nuncio to Bavaria in 1917. This put him in charge of papal peace negotiations there, although, as previously seen, only Austria-Hungary responded favor-

ably. Kaiser William II was sympathetic, but by that time no longer in charge of German policy. Eugenio was created Cardinal in 1929 and named secretary of state the following year. In 1933, Eugenio signed the Concordat with Hitler's government (as will be noticed, this has since contributed to the growth of a body of folklore labeling him as a pro-Nazi, but considering the context of the time, this is rather like saying the succession of American presidents who granted Most Favored Nation status to mainland China endorsed that country's bloody-handed repression—which continues until today). From then until 1937, when Pius XI issued his anti-Nazi encyclical, the secretary of state struggled unsuccessfully to persuade Hitler to abide by the Concordat. Among other tasks, Eugenio visited the United States in 1936, dining with President Franklin Roosevelt at Hyde Park. On this trip he became very impressed with America and its strength. At the pope's death, Eugenio was the obvious choice. He was crowned on March 12, taking the name Pius.

His most obvious task was to attempt to mediate between Germany, Poland, France, Italy, and Britain, and he immediately suggested a conference among these powers. This was rejected on all sides. From then until the end of World War II he issued a never-ending flow of requests for peace; these, of course, fell on deaf ears. During the course of the war, he directed certain Churchmen to collaborate with American O.S.S.; indeed, his lack of neutrality was as well known in Berlin as Washington. Pius threw open the Vatican and annexed buildings to Jewish refugees, and he ordered monasteries and abbeys to take them in. Moreover, he recruited Jews for the Palatine Guard of Honor, the papal military unit manned by Romans. Pius directed Catholic agencies to smuggle Jews out of Europe and spent 4 million 1939 dollars in this pursuit. In his Christmas broadcast of 1942, the pope condemned the extermination of the Jews, a condemnation he repeated during a consistory (June 2, 1943). So impressed with his work in this area was Grand Rabbi of Rome Satolli that he converted after the war, taking the name Eugenio in tribute to the pope. Numerous Jewish leaders, including Albert Einstein, Israeli prime ministers Golda Meir and Moshe Sharett, and Chief Rabbi Isaac Herzog, expressed their public gratitude to Pius XII, praising him as a "righteous gentile" who had saved thousands of Jews during the Holocaust. But in 1963, a leftist Protestant German playwright, Rolf Hochmuth, released a play called The Deputy, in which he attacked the pope as a collaborator. Since then, such condemnations have become a cottage industry on the part of many with no direct experience of the event. (Still, as it has earned a number of writers a living, it would be unkind to condemn this sort of myth-making.)

The war ended, and in accordance with Roosevelt's agreement with his ally, Josef Stalin, at Yalta, Eastern Europe was gobbled up by the Soviets. This was followed by the fall of China to the Communists. Incredible sufferings were the lot of the Catholics and other Christians in those countries, as they

remained in China. (This seems to have been forgotten—especially the ongoing persecutions in the last-named country. Memory is indeed a flexible thing.) As Pius had labored for the Jews and other victims of the Nazis, so he did for those persecuted by the Communists. Moreover, seeing in the United States the sole protector of the "Free World" against the Soviets and their minions, he wholeheartedly supported American foreign policy for the rest of his reign. This concern for American opinion was compounded by the fact that, with the ruin of traditional European sources of funding for the Church and the Holy See, the Church in the United States became the financial heartland of the Church Universal. (This dependence upon the American Church has lasted until present day.)

In doctrinal matters, Pius was extremely concerned about the so-called new school of theologians, exemplified by such as the Jesuit duo, Karl Rahner and Pierre Teilhard de Chardin—whom St.Pius X would have dubbed "Modernists." Their basic ideas include the notions that dogmas are merely attempts to describe the indescribable to the best of each generation's ability, and so are open to revision; the same is true for morals; the world and humanity are constantly evolving toward some sort of natural paradise; and the Church and her sacraments are, ultimately, not necessary for salvation. In his 1943 encyclical, Mystici corporis, Pius reendorsed the teaching of Boniface VIII in Unam sanctam and expounded upon the nature of the Church as the Mystical Body of Christ. But the influence of the new school continued to grow and to find favor—in particular in the United States. On August 12, 1950, Pius therefore issued another encyclical, Humani generis. Among other erroneous points spreading in clerical circles, Pius condemned the following:

> 25. It is not surprising that novelties of this kind have already borne their deadly fruit in almost all branches of theology. It is now doubted that human reason, without divine revelation and the help of divine grace, can, by arguments drawn from the created universe, prove the existence of a personal God; it is denied that the world had a beginning; it is argued that the creation of the world is necessary, since it proceeds from the necessary liberality of divine love; it is denied that God has eternal and infallible foreknowledge of the free actions of men—all this in contradiction to the decrees of the Vatican Council.
>
> 26. Some also question whether angels are personal beings, and whether matter and spirit differ essentially. Others destroy the gratuity of the supernatural order, since God, they say, cannot create intellectual beings without ordering and calling them to the beatific vision. Nor is this all. Disregarding the Council of Trent, some pervert the very concept of Original Sin, along with the concept of sin

> in general as an offense against God, as well as the idea of satisfaction performed for us by Christ. Some even say that the doctrine of Transubstantiation, based on an antiquated philosophic notion of substance, should be so modified that the Real Presence of Christ in the Holy Eucharist be reduced to a kind of symbolism, whereby the consecrated species would be merely efficacious signs of the spiritual presence of Christ and of His intimate union with the faithful members of His Mystical Body.
>
> 27. Some say they are not bound by the doctrine, explained in Our Encyclical Letter of a few years ago, and based on the Sources of Revelation, which teaches that the Mystical Body of Christ and the Roman Catholic Church are one and the same thing. Some reduce to a meaningless formula the necessity of belonging to the True Church in order to gain eternal salvation. Others finally belittle the reasonable character of the credibility of Christian faith.

This was widely seen, in the United States, as a vindication of Father Leonard Feeney, who had been suspended and silenced in 1949, ostensibly for his refusal to give up the chaplaincy at Harvard University, but in reality for his preaching of No Salvation Outside the Church—which had resulted in a rash of conversions of well-to-do WASP (white Anglo-Saxon-Protestant) students; both of these being a great embarrassment for the university and the archdiocese of Boston. In the end, Feeney was refused the heresy trial he asked for, and his case was recast as a disciplinary one.

By the end of his pontificate, Pius apparently despaired of the future of orthodoxy, being quoted in his Life magazine obituary as saying that he would be "the last" pope to hold the entirety of the Catholic Faith. (Certainly, the average Catholic will recognize the condemned propositions in many a sermon and theology book available today.)

Pius also had a great deal of interest in the liturgy. The Liturgical Movement, started by Dom Gueranger in the nineteenth century to restore liturgical rites to their pre-eighteenth-century purity, had grown tremendously since his time. Missals in Latin and the vernacular were in the hands of the Faithful, and the Mass, in its "dead" language, was completely accessible to anyone who could read. In accordance with this spirit, Pius decided to revise the rites of Holy Week. Gueranger himself had advocated the return of the Maundy Thursday and Holy Saturday rituals to their original time in the evening. Pius commissioned Annibale Bugnini to revise them further. Bugnini took the opportunity to inject into them a bit of the vernacular. In addition, he removed at last from the Missal the prayers for the emperor, which had been retained in hopes that they would one day again be needed—even after their last use in Austria in 1918. In 1952, Pius removed most of the octaves—eight-day peri-

ods succeeding major feasts, such as the Epiphany and the Nativity of St. John the Baptist (this had the unexpected effect of downgrading these feasts in the popular mind). There were behind many of the liturgical theorists a definite (and non-Catholic) agenda. In 1947, Pius issued an encyclical on the liturgical movement, warning of possible abuses. Among these, he admonished the following:

> 62. Assuredly it is a wise and most laudable thing to return in spirit and affection to the sources of the sacred liturgy. For research in this field of study, by tracing it back to its origins, contributes valuable assistance towards a more thorough and careful investigation of the significance of feast-days, and of the meaning of the texts and sacred ceremonies employed on their occasion. But it is neither wise nor laudable to reduce everything to antiquity by every possible device. Thus, to cite some instances, one would be straying from the straight path were he to wish the altar restored to its primitive table form; were he to want black excluded as a color for the liturgical vestments; were he to forbid the use of sacred images and statues in Churches; were he to order the crucifix so designed that the divine Redeemer's body shows no trace of His cruel sufferings; and lastly were he to disdain and reject polyphonic music or singing in parts, even where it conforms to regulations issued by the Holy See.
>
> 63. Clearly no sincere Catholic can refuse to accept the formulation of Christian doctrine more recently elaborated and proclaimed as dogmas by the Church, under the inspiration and guidance of the Holy Spirit with abundant fruit for souls, because it pleases him to hark back to the old formulas. No more can any Catholic in his right senses repudiate existing legislation of the Church to revert to prescriptions based on the earliest sources of canon law. Just as obviously unwise and mistaken is the zeal of one who in matters liturgical would go back to the rites and usage of antiquity, discarding the new patterns introduced by disposition of divine Providence to meet the changes of circumstances and situation.

Observant readers will notice that what Pius condemned became standard liturgical practice in most Catholic churches within a quarter century. Nevertheless, his reasoning remains worthy of consideration.

The most important act of his pontificate was surely the definition of the Assumption of the Virgin Mary—that is, that at the end of her life, the Mother of God was assumed body and soul into heaven. Many Eastern Orthodox theologians condemned the teaching at this point, although its liturgical com-

memoration had come to the Latins from the East, and many of the greatest Orthodox churches (such as the cathedral in Moscow) were named after it.

Pius observed neutrality in the rigged 1946 plebiscite that ended the Italian monarchy. Many churchmen, of course, were happy with the end of the House of Savoy, although the deposed king, Umberto II, had been very pious (unlike his father). The next year, Pius told the Roman nobility that the privileges of their state in life were a thing of the past and that they must simply work for the common good in the new egalitarian order. Four years later, he issued a decree forbidding bishops to use whatever titles of nobility they may have been born with, and ordered them to remove all such heraldic trappings (like coronets) from their coats of arms. The pope realized that the new face of power in trans-Atlantic society was no longer hereditary, but corporate. From his pontificate on, bishops would shed all remains of feudal ceremony and take on the role of CEOs. In a European sense, he was definitely a liberal.

But his ghostly, remote image fixed itself in the minds of a generation as the archetypal pope. (It may be assumed that when most middle-aged people think of the word *pope*, it is Pius's face that appears in their mind's eye.)

## Bl. John XXIII
### (October 28, 1958–June 3, 1963)

Angelo Roncalli was born on November 25, 1881, at Sotto il Monte, southwest of Bergamo. Fourth of the thirteen sons and daughters of Batiste Roncalli and Marianna Mazzola, he was christened that same day in the Church of Santa Maria. The Roncallis were a modest family of sharecroppers in poor circumstances. But in common with many similar clans, they were very pious, praying together every day and attending Mass every Sunday and Holy Day. In 1892 at age eleven, Angelo entered the minor seminary of Bergamo for high school. This was made possible for the poor boy by the generosity of both the parish priest, Father Francisco Rebuzzini, and the owner of the land cultivated by the Roncallis, don Morlani. It was here that Angelo began his Journal of a Soul in 1895. But it was also his experiences up to this point—his family's poverty and piety, on the one hand, and don Morlani's assistance on the other, that led to his social vision which so many on both Left and Right have found incomprehensible.

Thanks to his intellectual and moral abilities, in 1901 Angelo was sent to

Rome to continue his studies. He graduated in Sacred Theology in 1904, and he was ordained on August 10. The next year Angelo was made secretary to the bishop of Bergamo, Giacomo Radini Tedesco. One year later he was put in charge of history and patristics in the seminary. From 1915 to 1918 he did military service as a reserve hospital chaplain in Bergamo. The soldiers became very fond of him, and he brought many back to their religion.

In 1921 Father Roncalli was called to Rome to run the Papal Missionaries in Italy; here he grew to love the foreign missions. In this he was influenced by meeting with the general of the Papal Institute of Foreign Missions (PIME), one of the greatest supporters of the missionary cause in the twentieth century. In 1925, Monsignor Roncalli entered the diplomatic service of the Holy See, and on March 19 he was consecrated bishop. Named apostolic visitor to Bulgaria, Bishop Roncalli suffered from the difficult social, political, and religious situation of this country. But his qualities of sympathy, good humor, and simplicity soon made him a favorite in the country. His time there also gave the bishop a lifelong interest in reunion with Orthodoxy.

In 1934, he was transferred to the apostolic delegation of Turkey and named apostolic administrator of the Latins of Istanbul. Here Bishop Roncalli, taking advantage of his prerogatives as papal delegate and of his good relationships with the diplomatic corps and the papal representatives of the Danube countries, succeeded in helping the Jewish communities persecuted by the Nazis. Interestingly, the money he was able to give to Jewish refugees came from Hitler's ambassador to Turkey, the much-maligned Franz von Papen. Von Papen gave money to the apostolic delegate that was earmarked to bribe the Turks to side with Germany.

In December 1944 Pius XII named Bishop Roncalli as apostolic nuncio to Paris, where he presented his credentials on January 1, 1945. In France the situation was very difficult: Many bishops had been loyal to Marshal Petain, and so could be accused of having collaborated with the Germans; at the same time, the later disastrous but at the time promising experiment with the "Worker-Priests" was being undertaken. Here too, Roncalli's mixture of shrewdness and openness succeeded in resolving the problems and winning the sympathies of the French.

On January 12, 1953, the nuncio to Paris was created cardinal by Pius XII and named patriarch of Venice. His pastoral program, expressed in a homily in St. Mark's Cathedral, exemplifies the way he wanted to be seen. Cardinal Roncalli said: "I want to be your brother—amiable, approachable, understanding." The new patriarch did not acquire either a patriarchal gondola or a motorboat, as had his predecessors. Instead he used the public ones to move about the lagoon.

The death of Pius XII left the cardinals very divided between so-called progressives and traditionalists. It was presumed that, because of his age, Roncalli would provide a quiet stopgap leadership for a few years, while the factions

strove to build up their positions and clarify the issues. On October 28, 1958, at seventy-seven years, to the surprise of many outside the conclave because of his advanced age, Roncalli was elected pope and assumed the name of his father and of the patron of his home country—John. He immediately began to distinguish his papal behavior from that of his predecessors. Two months following his election he visited sick children in the Roman hospital of the Bambino Gesu, and the following day he went to the prisoners in the jail of Regina Coeli.

Three months following his election, on January 25, 1959, in the Basilica of St. Paul, John announced the convocation of Vatican II and of the first Synod of the Diocese of Rome, and a revision of the Code of Canon Law. During his pontificate, John named thirty-seven new cardinals—among whom were a Tanzanian, a Japanese, a Filipino, and a Mexican—thus beginning an expansion of the college into the Third World. He was the first pope, after 1870, who directly exercised his ministry of Bishop of Rome by going personally to visit the parishes. On May 15, 1961, he issued Mater et magistra, a groundbreaking encyclical on the Church's social teaching. The pope used his moral influence for peace in 1961 when Cold War tensions developed over Berlin, in 1962 during the Algerian revolt from France, and later the same year in the Cuban missile crisis. On October 4, 1962, John joined pilgrims on the train to Loreto and Assisi to pray for the coming council. It was the first departure of a pope from Latium since the annexation of Rome to Italy in 1870.

In October 1962 Pope John inaugurated Vatican II in St. Peter's. He indicated a precise guideline of the scope of the Council: it was not to define new truth or to condemn errors, but to renew the Church in order to make her more holy and therefore more suited to proclaim the Gospel to the contemporary world; to seek for the reunion of the Christian Churches; and to find ties for the Church with the contemporary culture, opening a new phase of dialogue with the modern world, trying "that which joins instead of which divide." Earlier in 1962 John had entered into an agreement with Moscow. By this agreement, in order for the Russian Orthodox to be present at Vatican II, no condemnation of communism was to be allowed there.

On March 7, 1963, John received personally the representative of Nikita Kruschev, Alexei Adjubei, with his wife. Of this opening the pope said to his secretary, "It can be a disappointment, or a mysterious thread of Providence that I do not have the right to break off."

At the beginning of 1963 Pope John issued the encyclical Pacem in terris, the first document of this kind addressed not to the Catholics only, but "to all men of good will." Therein he attempted to write of the situation of the contemporary world, and of ways for establishing hope of peace and solidarity for all mankind. It was installed in the arches of the United Nations building in

New York. As result, on May 10, 1963, the international Balzan Prize for Peace was awarded to John.

Thirteen days later, it was announced that the pope was gravely ill, and on June 3, 1963, after four years, six months, and six days on the Chair of St. Peter, John XXIII died, invoking the name of Jesus. Later that year, he was posthumously awarded the U.S. Presidential Medal of Freedom.

Soon after his death, the cause for his canonization was opened. Two miraculous cures (then necessary for beatification) were found. One, in the Naples area occurred in 1966 and concerned a nun who had multiple stomach ulcers and other grave intestinal maladies. Another, in Sicily, took place in 1967 and concerned the healing of a woman who suffered from tubercular peritonitis and a heart problem. (On September 3, 2000, John XXIII was beatified by John Paul II.) His feast day is October 11, the opening day of Vatican II.

Such was the life of John XXIII. But was he a "conservative," or a "liberal?" On the face of it, the answer to this question would seem obvious. From his own time to this, liberal Catholics have claimed him and conservatives scorned him for opening up Vatican II, for introducing alterations in the liturgy (small but symbolically important changes in the Mass, and purging such rites from the Pontificale as the Coronation of a King and the making of a knight—little used ceremonies, to be sure, but whose prayers were indicative of traditional Catholic teaching on war and government); for appearing to orient the Church toward a more leftist political position; and for initiating ties with the Soviet Union. His fun-loving, "open-minded" manner overjoyed progressives and made traditionalists cringe. Moreover, his critique of pure capitalism led no less than William F. Buckley Jr., doyen of the American conservative movement at the time, to reject John's social teaching in a celebrated article entitled "Mater, si; Magistra, no." There was a particularly schmaltzy cartoon widespread after President John Kennedy's assassination, showing the murdered president from behind, walking beside the pope toward an apparent paradise. The caption read, "There was a man sent from God, called John." To this day, any institution with "John XXIII" in it will usually be a liberal enterprise.

This is an excessively simple reading of an extremely complex man and pontificate, because he apparently shared certain illusions common among intellectuals of that time: (a) communism would endure, and might triumph; (b) technology would infallibly make life better; (c) the experiences of the World Wars and the Atomic Age would inevitably draw men of good will together; and (d) most people would accept truth, if only it were presented to them correctly. His actions make complete sense in light of this. But his underlying beliefs must be examined in greater detail than most on either side are willing to give them.

In April of 1959, John forbade Catholics to vote for parties supporting communism. The much-attacked Mater et magistra condemned socialism openly, even while it critiqued capitalism for much the same reasons Leo XIII and Pius XI had. Even Pacem in terris, although startling in the universality of its intended audience, declared that belief in God and His truth was the essential cornerstone of real peace—a point ignored by both John's critics and his lauders.

On June 30, 1960, John issued an Apostolic Letter, On Promoting Devotion to the Most Precious Blood of Our Lord Jesus Christ. Concern with this particular devotion (which led to John's including "Blessed Be the Precious Blood of Jesus" among the invocations at the Divine Praises said at Benediction) and with others does much to dispel the notion of a Pope John who cared only about social advancement.

But it is the area of liturgy where he is most ignored. On the one hand, his changes to the Missal, while apparently small, were many and offered precedent to those who wished to tinker with the hitherto sacrosanct Mass (although Pius XII's new rites of Holy Week had also tended in that direction). But in Veterum sapientia, an Apostolic Constitution regarding the preservation of Latin, issued on February 22, 1962 we read:

> And We also, impelled by the weightiest of reasons—the same as those which prompted Our Predecessors and provincial synods (13)—are fully determined to restore this language to its position of honor, and to do all We can to promote its study and use. The employment of Latin has recently been contested in many quarters, and many are asking what the mind of the Apostolic See is in this matter. We have therefore decided to issue the timely directives contained in this document, so as to ensure that the ancient and uninterrupted use of Latin be maintained and, where necessary, restored. We believe that We made Our own views on this subject sufficiently clear when We said to a number of eminent Latin scholars: "It is a matter of regret that so many people, unaccountably dazzled by the marvelous progress of science, are taking it upon themselves to oust or restrict the study of Latin and other kindred subjects. . . . Yet, in spite of the urgent need for science, Our own view is that the very contrary policy should be followed. The greatest impression is made on the mind by those things which correspond more closely to man's nature and dignity. And therefore the greatest zeal should be shown in the acquisition of whatever educates and ennobles the mind. Otherwise poor mortal creatures may well become like the machines they build—cold, hard, and devoid of love.

This constitution was entirely ignored in succeeding pontificates and remains the only one of John's major writings that the Daughters of St. Paul (the religious order which keeps papal documents in English in print) refuse to reproduce. But this document is typical of John's methodology; attempting to safeguard what is essential in Catholicism by adapting to current needs what is not, based upon contemporary conditions. He perhaps misread the signs of the time completely, but, for a pope to be a saint does not require that he be perfect in his policy judgments, nor that one agree with them—so long as they be not based upon dogma. (Thus Dante put St. Celestine V, who is seen fleeing his office for the life of a hermit, in hell.) Both the miracles that earned Bl. John XXIII's beatification and the complexity of his writings and work should prevent conservatives and liberals alike from claiming or rejecting him glibly.

## Paul VI

### (June 21, 1963–August 6, 1978)

Born Giovanni Battista Montini at Concesio, Lombardy, on September 26, 1897, his father, Giorgio, was a wealthy bourgeois landowner; his mother came of the minor nobility. Giorgio had been an editor of a Catholic paper, as well as active in the Popolari and various Catholic social organizations. Studying under the Jesuits and at the Brescia diocesan seminary, Giovanni was ordained in 1920, studied at the College of Noble Ecclesiastics, and entered the secretariat of state in 1924, the same year he became a university chaplain at Rome. These two fields—diplomacy and student work—would characterize his career until he became pope. With student collaborators, he founded an anti-Fascist student newspaper in 1927. In 1931, because of Fascist legislation, he and his partners had to meet in private, but from the quiet meetings they held emerged the leadership of the postwar Christian Democratic party, successor to the Popolari. It was during this period that Giovanni's political and social beliefs crystallized. An avid foe of totalitarianism, he became convinced that liberal democracy (albeit with the Church acting as its conscience) ought to be the preferred form of the state. Alongside these activities, he pursued various diplomatic missions assigned him. During World War II, he became Pius XII's main liaison with the Americans, whom he admired tremendously. Giovanni also worked with various relief agencies and helped co-

ordinate the escape of Jews from the Nazis. In all of these experiences, he became convinced that men of good will, regardless of religion, could settle their differences and work for the common good.

In 1954, he was made archbishop of Milan. He dialogued there a great deal with the Communists, declaring that though their solutions were incorrect their critique of industrial society often was not. Giovanni organized a great deal of social work, going into factories, building villages for the poor and the like, as well as reconstructing many churches and other buildings damaged in the war. Created a cardinal by John XXIII in 1958, he was consulted heavily by the pope in setting up Vatican II. Thus, there was little surprise when he was elected in John's place.

Taking the name Paul, after the Apostle to the Gentiles (who was "all things to all men"), the new pontiff was crowned on June 30. This coronation was in itself indicative of the course of his pontificate; instead of the traditional tiara, he was crowned with one of modernistic design, which aroused much unfavorable comment from art critics. Afterward, he sold it and gave the money to charity. But zealous American Catholics bought it and donated it to the National Shrine of the Immaculate Conception in Washington, D.C., where it remains.

Paul's experiences had, as we observed, given him a desire to be "modern," to "streamline" the Church. He felt this was necessary if she was to attract modern men into her fold. He shared his predecessor's optimism about men accepting the truth, if only they could understand. Experience, alas, was to show (as it almost always does) that such hopes were doomed to disappointment.

His first interest was to continue the work of Vatican II. The sorts of new theologians Pius XII had warned about in Humani generis, such as Karl Rahner, were extremely influential at the Council—both as theological experts or periti for various influential bishops and as drafters of the Council documents themselves (which often show a studied ambiguity, as opposed to those of councils past)—they worked to put their own agenda across. This was to create an entirely new identity for the Church. Rather than being the divinely ordained means of salvation from hell for all humanity, she was to assist Mankind in being more fully itself, whatever that meant. Thus, for Rahner and his ilk, the concept of "anonymous Christianity," whereby everyone is already a member of the Church by virtue of his or her birth, was the animating concept of their ecclesiology. This was made palatable for the more conservative among the bishops through the quasi-traditional sounding notion of "implicit baptism of desire," which held that all those of good will are—by virtue of their own goodness—recipients of the graces of baptism. That these two ideas are virtually identical is hotly denied by many of a more traditional bent, but the practical results have been the same.

In pursuit of these ideals, all that separated Catholics from non-Catholics

and non-Christians—whether doctrinally, liturgically, or anywise else—must be broken down. The notion that Catholicism is the one true Faith necessary for Salvation, as spelled out in the Creeds, was to be dismissed as "triumphalism." Though this mind-set is merely implicit in the Council documents, it would become ever more explicit in post-Conciliar documents, until the point would come that the average Catholic would be hard put to say what the Faith really taught upon any given subject. To be sure, this was not the intention of Paul, or even most of the Council Fathers. But it happened anyway, and the pope himself was perhaps too much concerned with his own vision to notice.

The new pope opened the second session of the Council on September 29, 1963, with an allocution, in which he set four goals for Vatican II. First, these were to set forth more clearly the nature of the Church, particularly as regarded the role of bishops. From this came the oft-talked-about idea of collegiality, which emphasized the equality of the prelate with the pope (one prelate, however, remarked that the only biblical justification he could find for it was the action of the Apostles in the Garden of Olives: "And they all fled"). A second goal of the Council was to renew the Church; although what this meant was never really spelled out, the implication was that it was stale at that moment. A third goal was to restore unity among all Christians, though how this was to be done was a mystery. Finally, the Council's goal was to dialogue with the contemporary world—though to what end, and with which elements, was yet another mystery.

The Constitution on the Sacred Liturgy declared that although the vernacular should be given a bigger role, Latin was to be retained and all parishes should be able to sing simple Gregorian chant. (Subsequently this would go by the board; as an official U.S. Bishops' Conference text put it, the Constitution was "superseded by subsequent practice.") The Church's traditional teaching on Church and state relationships, non-Catholic religions, and much else was set aside or obscured by an enormous flood of conciliar and post-conciliar documents. The confusing nature of all of this was exacerbated by Paul's declaration, after closing the Council in 1965, that all of its acts had to be interpreted in the light of prior tradition; anything that appeared contradictory thereto was to be set aside. Moreover, he emphasized that its documents were not infallible. (What the layman in the pew was supposed to make of all this is unknown.) But other, less pious elements knew it was time to strike; hence the Italian government's legalizing of divorce, in defiance of the Lateran Treaty, in 1970.

What clerics great and small made of it, however, is a matter of record: it was the signal for bishop, priest, and nun, too, to do as they pleased—so long as what they pleased had never been heard of in Catholic circles before. In 1966, Latin was removed in most places; the Last Gospel and the Prayers at the Foot of the Altar had been excised two years previously. What came in?

Guitars! Dance! Clowns! It seemed that all was new and all would be remade. As one wag put it, Vatican II was the only example known to man of the spirit killing the letter. At last, in 1970, Paul issued his new Mass, which had so many variations it is hard to pin down. The Mass had come to resemble a Protestant service enough that the Lutheran Church of France took it for its own liturgy.

Now, none of this will seem too important to non-Catholics, perhaps. But the Mass is and was the central point of Catholic life; it shapes how they believe. Gone were the genuflections that had marked Catholic treatment of the Blessed Sacrament and reflected belief in Transubstantiation. On their own, priests began giving Communion in the hand, in emulation of the Protestants. Numerous complaints of this practice found their way to Paul, who in response issued a decree in 1968, Memoriale Domini. In the first part of this document, the pope explained eloquently the superiority of the traditional method over the innovation; he then went on to establish a mechanism for said innovation's adoption in places where "it had become the custom." Because it was not done at all before 1966, this meant that two years established a custom. The signal was clear: violate the law, and the violation becomes the law. But in any case, the change had the same effect it had when adopted by Cramner in England—twenty years after Communion in the hand became legal in the United States in 1977, less than 30 percent of American Catholics polled by Gallup believed in the Real Presence. This was particularly ironic, owing to Paul's decree permitting Communion in the hand only in those areas where it would increase devotion to the Blessed Sacrament!

From that time forward, a sort of anarchy appeared to descend upon the Church at all levels outside of the Vatican. Whether one spoke of liturgical or doctrinal abuses, anything went, and no one seemed responsible. If a bishop wanted to do something forbidden by Rome at the time (altar girls, lay preachers, etc.), he said he had to because the people demanded it. If it was something the people did not want (abolition of Latin, liturgical dancers, and so forth), well then it had to be done because Rome had ordered it. Either way, somehow, the poor bishop was never really in charge, if one believed his rhetoric. In reality, what was happening was the dissolution of papal power over the dioceses (partly, but not entirely, with the help of the pope himself). Even Paul spoke, toward the end of his life, of the auto-demolition of the Church. Meanwhile, seminaries, monasteries, convents, and, above all, pews emptied.

But Paul had other fish to fry. Among these were a total overhaul of the papal household, and an abolition of everything smacking of "triumphalism" and the temporal power. After his coronation, he gave away his custom-made tiara and would not wear it again. Paul informed the Roman nobility that he would no longer give them their annual audience, and in 1968 he issued Pontificalis Domus, which completely reorganized the papal household by

abolishing most of the lay positions therein. In 1970, he abolished the Noble Guards and the Palatine Guards of Honor, and he stripped the Black Nobility of their Vatican citizenship—a dubious reward for ancestral loyalty. There was scarcely a ceremony, be it ordination of priests or confirmation of youths, that he did not alter.

As with liturgy, so with architecture—statues, altars, and altar rails were torn out with a gleeful, childlike fury not seen since the Reformation (and so they still are). It was claimed that all this was mandated either by Vatican II or the New Mass itself, but not only are such activities not mentioned in the documents of the former, but the Latin rubrics of the latter command the priest to turn round and face the audience at the Orate fratres—which, unless he is to spin like a top, implies that the altar is in its traditional position. New structures were built to resemble modern banks, washing machine agitators, or space ships. The Nervi, the new audience hall at the Vatican built by order of Paul himself, was just plain ugly. All was justified by the pope as being in accord with "the times." Doubtless it was, although cultural critics might well wonder if the 1960s were indeed the best time to anchor the Church's ethos to. Whether or not, the result was that after forty years, Catholic things do not bear the outdated mark of Palestrina, but rather that of the Ventures.

Paul found other occupations, however. He traveled to the Holy Land, where he embraced the Patriarch of Constantinople on the Mount of Olives. There they lifted the mutual excommunications that were the legal mark of schism. In addition, he traveled to India, where he saw for himself the squalid conditions of the poor and met with Indian Orthodox leaders. Finally, Paul went to New York, where he addressed the United Nations. There, before the representatives of almost all of the world's governments, most of which were for various reasons antipathetic to the Church, he avoided saying anything substantive other than that war was a bad thing.

But for all his accommodation with what, all things considered, was the spirit of an exceedingly short-lived age, Paul did make some important contributions. His rapprochement with Athenagoras II of Constantinople was certainly a great step forward, although his encouragement of what appeared to be in the eyes of many Eastern Orthodox wholesale abandonment of Catholic tradition justified (in their minds) continued schism. (In 1965, when the position of the patriarchate at Istanbul appeared menaced by the Turkish government—angry over Cyprus—the pope returned the Turkish banners captured at Lepanto, in hopes of assuaging the threat.) So, too, with his overtures to the Armenian, Syrian, Coptic, and Assyrian churches. Paul's relationship with the Anglicans indicated he was on good terms with the Anglo-Catholic archbishop of Canterbury, Michael Ramsey, but the protean nature of Anglicanism (and of the various other kinds of Protestantism) negated his attempts to dialogue. The opposite numbers could and did often agree with the Catholic side, but their agreements bound no one save themselves. His attempts to open talks with non-Christian and non-believing elements were bound to founder upon the reef of Christ. Critics of these efforts believed that Christ called upon His Church to preach and baptize, not to dialogue.

In what he considered important, Paul could be firm. Perhaps the largest external non-political problem facing the Church in his pontificate was the wild alteration of sexual mores in the West. Seemingly overnight, all that centuries of Western culture had upheld in relations between men and women were overthrown. As a first step, the ever-widening influence of the contraceptive pill (legalized throughout the United States by 1964) challenged the whole concept of chastity, which, for many was merely a means of avoiding pregnancy rather than a virtue. "Let it all hang out" was the motto of many of the youth (and not so youthful) of the time. In 1967, the pope issued a letter reaffirming priestly celibacy. In those heady times, the reaction of many priests, who had apparently expected even clerical polygamy to be permissible in the near future, was hysterical. Many left the priesthood—so, too, did more thoughtful ones whose faith had been shaken by so many changes.

A greater storm awaited the hapless pontiff. The legalization of contraception in the United States, coupled with the pope's appointment of a commission to "look into" the Church's teaching on the matter, raised expectations that the Church would follow along with the teaching of the world. Instead, on July 25, 1968, Paul issued the encyclical Humanae vitae. In so doing, he annoyed many—to put it mildly. But his reasoning in that little read but much condemned document remains sound. Rather than trying as Pius XI did to put the case for the Church's teaching in its own terms, Paul argued primarily from naturalistic principles, in keeping with his idea that men of good will would respond to truth they could understand. Particularly chilling was his prediction regarding the consequences of artificial contraception:

> 17. Responsible men can become more deeply convinced of the truth of the doctrine laid down by the Church on this issue if they reflect on the consequences of methods and plans for artificial birth control. Let them first consider how easily this course of action could open wide the way for marital infidelity and a general lowering of moral standards. Not much experience is needed to be fully aware of human weakness and to understand that human beings—and especially the young, who are so exposed to temptation—need incentives to keep the moral law, and it is an evil thing to make it easy for them to break that law. Another effect that gives cause for alarm is that a man who grows accustomed to the use of contraceptive methods may forget the reverence due to a woman, and, disregarding her physical and emotional equilibrium, reduce her to being a mere instrument for the satisfaction of his own desires, no

> longer considering her as his partner whom he should surround with care and affection.
>
> Finally, careful consideration should be given to the danger of this power passing into the hands of those public authorities who care little for the precepts of the moral law. Who will blame a government which in its attempt to resolve the problems affecting an entire country resorts to the same measures as are regarded as lawful by married people in the solution of a particular family difficulty? Who will prevent public authorities from favoring those contraceptive methods which they consider more effective? Should they regard this as necessary, they may even impose their use on everyone. It could well happen, therefore, that when people, either individually or in family or social life, experience the inherent difficulties of the divine law and are determined to avoid them, they may give into the hands of public authorities the power to intervene in the most personal and intimate responsibility of husband and wife.

(Of course, from our vantage point in 2003, we can see how true his warning was—at least, if we are young enough to know what current dating practices are like, and honest enough to admit them for what they are.) Paul was not unaware either that there would be resistance to his teaching:

> It is to be anticipated that perhaps not everyone will easily accept this particular teaching. There is too much clamorous outcry against the voice of the Church, and this is intensified by modern means of communication. But it comes as no surprise to the Church that she, no less than her divine Founder, is destined to be a "sign of contradiction." She does not, because of this, evade the duty imposed on her of proclaiming humbly but firmly the entire moral law, both natural and evangelical.
>
> Since the Church did not make either of these laws, she cannot be their arbiter—only their guardian and interpreter. It could never be right for her to declare lawful what is in fact unlawful, since that, by its very nature, is always opposed to the true good of man.

What shocked the pontiff was not the opposition from the usual suspects in the secular world, but that from many so many Catholics—including such national episcopates as Belgium and Canada. Yet the situation was such that Paul could not or would not discipline clerical dissenters. Neither did he move in such cases as that of Canada when the hierarchy there supinely permitted Pierre Trudeau to introduce abortion in the country—despite his as-

serting that he would not if they objected. Again, one's sense of horror in these things is dulled, but in Catholic teaching abortion is murder, pure and simple. To expect Catholics not to oppose it is on the order of expecting them not to oppose the liquidation of the disabled and retarded (both of which oppositions, incidentally, brought the German episcopate into conflict with Hitler. Then as now, of course, any number of individual Catholics were willing to collaborate). From 1968 on, Paul VI did not really assert his authority against dissent within the Church, and he allowed each national conference of bishops to do as they pleased.

There was one exception to this rule: he dealt rather violently with the opposition to his liturgical changes. Most famous of these was the celebrated case of Archbishop Marcel Lefebvre. Lefebvre, former archbishop of Dakar and superior of the Holy Ghost Fathers, had founded, with Paul's approval, the Society of St. Pius X for the preservation of the traditional liturgical rites of the Church. In 1976, it became apparent that the archbishop would not use the new rites at all, so he was ordered by the local bishop (in Switzerland) to disband the SSPX. He was then told by the Vatican that if he ordained the current class he would be suspended. Lefebvre appealed to the Apostolic Signatura, the highest court in the Church, but Cardinal Villot, the secretary of state, forbade the Signatura to hear the case. This was a violation of canon law. The archbishop ordained the men, he and they were suspended, and Paul VI showed that he was able to act authoritatively in at least one instance.

That is the true tragedy of Paul's pontificate. For all practical purposes, he abdicated control of most of the local hierarchies. This would bear strange fruit, indeed. One hopes, for the sake of his reputation, that future Church historians will remember Humanae vitae rather than his other actions.

## John Paul I
### (August 26–September 28, 1978)

Albino Luciani was born on October 17, 1912, at Forno di Canale (renamed Canale d'Agordo in 1964) in Veneto. Ordained in 1935, he was first a parish priest and then diocesan seminary instructor at Belluno. Consecrated bishop of Vittorio Veneto in 1958, he was named patriarch of Venice by Paul VI eleven years later. In keeping with the then-current clerical fad for dispensing with traditional ceremonies, he refused the customary official en-

trance to Venice in a patriarchal gondola. Created cardinal in 1973, he was not one of the frontrunners at Paul's death. Paul had (naturally) revised the rules for election of the pope: He excluded all cardinals over age eighty from voting, and he ordered the conclave to meet in the hideous Nervi. But the cardinals themselves balked, opting for the traditional Sistine Chapel—they did not lift the age barrier. Albino was a compromise candidate, having spent his career in pastoral rather than diplomatic posts, the first such since St. Pius X.

He took the name John Paul I to show that he would continue the policies of his two predecessors. Although Paul's new regulations called for a coronation, John Paul dispensed with the ceremony, apologizing for doing so but claiming that the difficulty of his new post was too burdensome to go through with it. The new pope also initially did away with the sedia gestatoria (the papal chair, carried by a number of men called "bussolanti"), but owing to his short height was forced to bring it back for outside ceremonies.

There were many questions as to where he would lead the Church. These came to an end the night of his death. Conspiracy theories abounded: conservatives claimed he was killed because he intended to restore the Latin Mass, liberals that he was liquidated because he would end the ban on birth control. The official story was that he in fact died of a heart attack.

## John Paul II *

### (October 16, 1978– )

Karol Wojtyla was born May 18, 1920, in Watowice, Poland, the son of a former soldier in the Austrian army. In his youth, he worked in a factory and attended, during the German occupation, secret classes at the Jagiellonian University. Karol's interests were religion, theater, and poetry. He attended classes in the secret seminary run by Adam Cardinal Sapieha, archbishop of Cracow, and was ordained in 1946. He continued his studies thereafter in Rome and Cracow, specializing in phenomenology, a rather obscure philosophy popularized by Martin Heidegger and Max Scheler (Karol's personal favorite). Made an auxiliary bishop in 1958, Karol became archbishop of Cracow in 1964. Three years later he was created a cardinal. Always interested in young people, he combined a subjective philosophy with an emotional attachment to Catholic tradition. Karol figured as a moderate liberal (alongside

such as Josef Ratzinger) at Vatican II. Personal friendships and the experience of World War II made him particularly friendly to the Jewish people; moreover, his dealings with the Nazis and the Communists made him put personal intellectual freedom over most considerations. Like Paul VI, he was particularly loath to discipline erring brethren, much preferring persuasion to force. Eyebrows were raised when he allowed Billy Graham to preach in one of his churches.

His election came as a surprise to the Catholic world. As the first non-Italian since Adrian VI and a native of a Communist-occupied country, he was very much an unknown. It was, perhaps, a foregone conclusion that he would take the name John Paul. Not so foregone was his likewise refusing a coronation, although he assured the faithful that the ceremony was not abolished, but would return.

This strange duality, perhaps attributable to his philosophical background, would dominate his pontificate. On the one hand, he would insist on traditional moral teaching as far as abortion, contraception, homosexuality, pre- and extra-marital sex, women's ordination, and economics were concerned. At the same time, he refused to discipline even bishops and cardinals who openly dissented from Church teaching. Even so, from the beginning the Western media, although appreciating his enormous personal charm and PR ability, spoke pityingly of him as an Eastern European deprived of the wonderful influences of the enlightened Atlantic culture.

What was not at issue was his immediately destabilizing effect on the Soviet Bloc. Although no one could foresee it at the time, he would play an enormous part in bringing down that empire, which, at his accession, many inside and outside the Church sincerely thought would triumph. He condemned one product of such thought, Liberation Theology, which in essence reduced the salvation brought by Christ and His Church to the struggle called for by Karl Marx against oppressive structures. Its adherents, particularly in Latin America, were quite happy to collaborate with Communists for revolution. But in the face of a pope who knew firsthand where such collaboration would end, and with the fall of the Soviet Union, Liberation Theology imploded.

There were other problems, however. The whole neo-Modernist movement went from strength to strength. In 1980, John Paul wrote an apology to the Catholic people in Dominicae cenae, a letter on the worship of the Eucharist:

> I would like to ask forgiveness—in my own name and in the name of all of you, venerable and dear brothers in the episcopate, for everything which, for whatever reason, through whatever human weakness, impatience or negligence, and also through the at times partial, one-sided and erroneous application of the directives of the

> Second Vatican Council, may have caused scandal and disturbance concerning the interpretation of the doctrine and the veneration due to this great sacrament. And I pray the Lord Jesus that in the future we may avoid in our manner of dealing with this sacred mystery anything which could weaken or disorient in any way the sense of reverence and love that exists in our faithful people.

This was heartening, to say the least. In his own acts the pope would abide by this sense; for example, when he refused communion in the hand to the wife of the French president. This translated to nothing at all on the local level. On March 31, 1988, for example, Roger Cardinal Mahony, archbishop of Los Angeles, wrote in his letter on the Blessed Sacrament, The Day on Which We Gather, "In the simple acts of presenting, blessing and breaking bread and sharing the cup, Christ is present in memory and in hope." Mahony was far from the worst offender, either in word or deed. Similarly, in his early pontificate, John Paul was a sturdy opponent of altar girls, not least because allowing female servers would at once provide the illusion that one day the priesthood would open to them—it would also drive boys away from service at the altar. In tandem with Cardinal Mahony's letter, the pope had the Congregation for Worship issue an instruction, Inaestimabile donum, which declared: "There are, of course, various roles that women can perform in the liturgical assembly: these include reading the Word of God and proclaiming the intentions of the Prayer of the Faithful. Women are not, however, permitted to act as altar servers." But the German and American bishops (to name a few) generally permitted the practice and in 1994, after more than a decade of struggle, the Holy See conceded. The Pontifical Council for the Interpretation of Legislative Texts (the fact that such an organization existed showed how ambiguous Church legislation had become) issued a circular, with papal approval, that declared that in reality the law not only permitted the practice, but always had. Those with a grasp of language felt trapped in George Orwell's 1984.

Much of this seeming passivity might be attributed to a physical cause. On May 13, 1981, John Paul was shot in St. Peter's Square by a young Turkish man. Evidence appeared to show that he had done so at the behest of the Bulgarian secret service, at command, presumably, of the KGB. Whether or not that was the case, in 2002, while visiting the country, the pope formally absolved the Bulgarian people of any role in the crime. At any rate, subsequent to this event, John Paul seemed to lack a great deal of the zeal he had evinced for correcting abuses earlier.

One way in which the pontiff appeared to deal with the problem of disobedience on the part of national hierarchies was to favor various international movements such as the Opus Dei, Focolare, Miles Jesu, Communion and Liberation, and Schoenstatt. Though differing enormously from one another, they shared one major thing in common: Declaring complete loyalty to John Paul II, they lived their lives to all intents and purposes outside diocesan structures, carrying on their missions without either disapproving of Episcopal actions or appearing bound by them. What generally united them was a stated mission of bringing the Faith to bear in every aspect of life as it is lived, rather than leaving it to be a Sunday occupation coupled with abstract intellectual principles. In contrast to the rapidly emptying ranks of diocesan seminaries, these groups all shared growing numbers as well.

Occasionally, such figures as Fathers Charles Curran or Hans Kueng were lightly disciplined. Although these measures would inevitably generate screams of outrage from the ranks of the left, the ongoing persecution of innumerable conservative and traditionalist clerics and religious by bishops and superiors went on unabated.

On the Ecumenical front, another strange dichotomy appeared. On the one hand, in certain of his writings, and at the several Assisi inter-faith pow-wows, John Paul appeared to endorse salvation outside the Church and the equality of all religions. Yet, at other times he appeared to endorse the traditional teaching. In 2000, the Holy See issued Dominus Jesus, a document that lightly reminded the world of the Church's claim to be the sole means of Salvation, while quickly reminding non-Catholics that, in the view of modern Church leaders, they can be saved. Though a far cry from Eugene IV's Cantate domino, it roused a great deal of controversy in a world more used to an ecumenism of sheer equality.

Even so, the pope continued ecumenical conversations with the Anglican Churches despite their ordination of women and recognition of non-Apostolic Lutheran orders as valid. This was all the more ironic as Catholic bishops in English-speaking countries attempted to limit mass conversions from Anglican bodies and to ignore the "continuing" Anglican movement, which rejected the changes in Anglicanism while not yet seeing their paths to Rome.

More hopeful was the pope's work with the Eastern churches. Despite much hostility on the part of some Orthodox hierarchs, John Paul became quite friendly with the two patriarchs of Constantinople with whom he had to deal—Demetrios and Bartholomew. Apart from theological dialogue, he turned over to Orthodox use two churches in Rome and Ravenna, and John Paul followed Paul VI's lead in being the only foreign ruler to attempt to shore up the patriarchate's position vis-à-vis an ever-hostile Turkish government. In Romania, Georgia, Ukraine, and Bulgaria, he interacted with populace and clerics alike; in Greece, popular acclaim forced the local Orthodox bishops to deal with him. A series of mutual recognitions between Rome and the Assyrians, Armenians, Copts, and Syrians was another feature of the pontificate.

But could ecumenism not begin at home, with those favoring restoration

of the traditional liturgy of the Church? The pope apparently thought so, because in 1985 he issued an indult permitting its use. Predictably, many bishops, theologians, and others whined that Vatican II was being revoked (presumably they had never read its documents). In 1988, John Paul came close to an accord with Archbishop Lefebvre and the Society of St. Pius X. At the eleventh hour this failed when the archbishop, who had been promised bishops for his order at some future date, decided that Rome could not be trusted to deliver on its part of the agreement, and consecrated bishops on his own. The Holy See declared that the archbishop and his consecrands had incurred excommunication by this action, although the pope refrained from actually levying an anathema. Indeed, the case was made that, by the regulations of the pope's own 1983 Code of Canon Law, no such excommunication really applied, validly.

However that might be, in an attempt to avoid driving traditionalists around the world into the arms of the SSPX, John Paul formed the Pontifical Commission Ecclesia Dei, to "facilitate communion" with such folk. As a result, the indult permitting use of the Tridentine Mass was far more widely applied (although a papally appointed commission of cardinals determined that the traditional Latin Mass had never been validly outlawed—something not visible in the draconian measures of Paul VI and various bishops' conferences against it). Latin Mass parishes around the world sprung up under the papal aegis, as did a number of religious orders and houses. Certain small dioceses also became refuges for such folk, and, not surprisingly, their pews and seminaries filled. Alongside these developments, groups seeking "a reform of the reform" also emerged, urging that the New Mass be celebrated in accordance with its own rubrics. Even so, the vast majority of Catholics across the globe remained without access to such things.

The same could not be said of the pope himself. The most traveled of the pontiffs, he has visited nearly every major nation (save China and Russia—which he would like to visit) and scores of minor ones. His patented trademark has been to kiss the ground of each country he has visited. Many of these jaunts have been taken in connection with the beatification or canonization of local figures—more of whom John Paul has raised to the altars than any other pope.

The Third World held an ever-greater proportion of the world's Catholics, yet here, too, was a strange paradox. In many areas of Latin America, Africa, and Asia, doctrinal orthodoxy existed side by side with liturgical bizarreness, in some cases amounting to re-paganization. But with the virtual abolition of a universal liturgical mode, how could this be avoided, considering the Europeans and Americans had been allowed to transform their own liturgies into celebrations of bourgeois 1960s culture? In Latin America, evangelistic Protestant sects, often funded by North American sources, happily moved into a

spiritual climate often emptied of its local devotional practices by liberal clerics. This penetration has been likened to a second Reformation; alongside it have ridden the mores, such as they are, of the "developed" world.

In Europe and America, the pope faced a culture that, although having triumphed over communism, had an identical view of man. Both the United States (where "Merry Christmas" has been tacitly banished from stores and "under God" may be excised from the Pledge of Allegiance) and Europe (whose countries are removing every aspect of Christianity from public life) were rejecting the Faith on an official plane. Given the history of the latter continent, this was especially painful to the pope, who constantly reminded its leaders both of the origins of Continental culture and of the European Union itself, whose major founders had been devout. The continuing institutionalization of abortion, gay marriage, euthanasia, and more recently, cell research and cloning boded poorly for the Faith's future in these regions. Of course, the declining birthrates there boded poorly for any future at all. At any rate, the increasingly intolerant official stance toward those who oppose such developments may well lead some to wonder if, eventually, persecution—bloody or otherwise—might not be in store. Given the generally quiet acquiescence of the Church to these developments, such as the Vatican's happy signing of the accord ending Italian Catholicism's official status in 1984, little else might be expected.

The same spirit dominated much of the Church herself, as earlier noticed. The ongoing cry by well-to-do Euro-Americans for priestesses was addressed at last by John Paul in 1994:

> Although the teaching that priestly ordination is to be reserved to men alone has been preserved by the constant and universal Tradition of the Church and firmly taught by the Magisterium in its more recent documents, at the present time in some places it is nonetheless considered still open to debate, or the Church's judgment that women are not to be admitted to ordination is considered to have a merely disciplinary force.
>
> Wherefore, in order that all doubt may be removed regarding a matter of great importance, a matter which pertains to the Church's divine constitution itself, in virtue of my ministry of confirming the brethren (cf. Lk 22:32) I declare that the Church has no authority whatsoever to confer priestly ordination on women and that this judgment is to be definitively held by all the Church's faithful.

Because John Paul would not employ traditional language to define this decision, it was derisively laughed off as non-infallible; women's ordination adherents continued to hope and to call the Church's teaching "unjust," as though the pope had any authority to alter doctrine as he pleases. In any case,

dissenters—even among bishops—were not disciplined. This was the case across the board. In 1997, when the Congregation for Worship issued an instruction severely restricting the use of Extraordinary Ministers of the Eucharist, Roger Cardinal Mahony, for one, dismissed it with an airy "It doesn't apply to Los Angeles."

One great joy for the pope was the Jubilee Year of 2000. Millions of pilgrims descended on Rome and shrines all over the world. For many, such practices as confession and Corpus Christi processions were rediscovered. Even in Protestant northern Europe, shrines neglected since the Reformation were refurbished and primarily non-Catholic crowds prayed at such places as the shrines of Saints Mungo at Glasgow, Elizabeth at Marburg, Olaf at Trondheim, and Knud at Odense. (The author himself attended a papal Mass on the feast of SS. Peter and Paul, June 29, that year. Present were the patriarch of Constantinople, and various archbishops, including the new prelates of Westminster and New York, received the pallium. For a few moments, one had a dizzying vision of Catholic unity.)

But great as the benefits were for individuals, when the incense cleared things remained as they had been. Rome made some attempt to rein in abuses, to be sure. In March of 2001, the Congregation for Divine Worship issued the document Liturgicam authenticam, which required an exact translation of the Latin liturgy into the vernacular, rather than the free and easy ones prevalent since the 1960s. Predictably, national bishops' conferences dug in their heels. In July 2001, Archbishop Rembert Weakland of Milawaukee defied a direct command from the Holy See not to rip up his cathedral's interior. But no punitive measures followed. This sort of thing was not restricted to the United States: German bishops cheerfully rejected a papal command not to engage in the abortion referral trade. The declaration of John Paul II in 2002 that Catholic lawyers the world over ought not to assist in divorce cases brought sneering rejection from many of that "respectable" trade. Of course, the pope did not follow up his suggestion with excommunication.

The Vatican has no more control over most of the national churches than she does over the Anglicans or Lutherans. The pope, for all practical purposes, has precisely the amount of authority over a given diocese that the local bishop chooses to give him, and no more. The generality of prelates in the developed countries are "titularists," giving the pope a primacy of honor, but nothing more. This anomalous situation has subsisted for several decades, and there is a good reason why it has—money. On the one hand, if the pope took effective measures to end abuses and reassert papal control (apart from the fact that such action would be personally repugnant to him, flying in the face of both his philosophy and his personality), it would be the end of Peter's Pence. With that would also end the enormous amount of good the Holy See is still able to do, especially in the former Soviet Bloc and the Third World. By

the same token, if the bishops erupted into open schism and thereby had to remove the pope's picture from their fund-raising propaganda, the contributions of the faithful would dry up. So the bishops pretend that they are obedient, and the pope pretends that they obey.

What has been the result? Well, there have been many, but the most obvious to the outside observer is the sex abuse scandal. It is perhaps telling that Archbishop Weakland was forced to retire slightly early when his former male lover surfaced, having been paid off handsomely, and hungry for more. What were revealed by this were a priesthood unsupervised, an episcopate uncaring, and all equally independent of Rome. What was amusing to the informed witness was that many (particularly non-Catholic) voices were raised, demanding various solutions to the problem—a married priesthood and more lay control. Apart from the obvious reply to the former cure—since most molesters are married men, perhaps celibacy would do them some good—it is the latter that requires some attention. Perhaps what is necessary is more actual papal control—something none of the pundits call for.

One thing should be apparent from all the papal lives reviewed in this book: In some ways the pontificate of John Paul II is completely unprecedented; in others, for good or ill, it is typical.

* See Publisher's Note for update.

# AFTERWORD

AND SO, WE HAVE come at last to the end of our story. All too much has had to be left out, but a full treatment would cover many volumes and include every aspect of the history of every modern nation, as well as some no longer with us. Considering the increasingly enfeebled physical condition of John Paul II, we shall probably have a new conclave in the not too distant future. Fragmented as the cardinals are, none can say what will result. A compromise candidate? A schism? Who knows. Judging from past experience, anything is possible.

What may be gleaned from the past, however, given the pope's role as conservator, is that the next pontiff would do well to meditate on his mission as keeper of the keys. Popes who have too rapidly accepted the then-contemporary set of circumstances as permanent, or who have looked to the spirit of their own age—be it the 1960s, the Renaissance, or the Pornocracy—for guidance, have always come a cropper.

Certainly, as far as temporal affairs go, we are perhaps at the moment closer to conditions in the Apostolic age than at any time since that of Constantine. The Church has no temporal protector—save Liechtenstein and to a degree, Malta, there are no integrally Catholic governments. The vast majority of nations are more or less opposed to the Catholic ethos, and may well become violently so. Future popes shall have to deal with this.

Moreover, the neo-Catholicism of such as Rahner is dominant in much of the Catholic world, and would like nothing so much as to be able to join with the mainstream Protestant sects in baptizing whatever the Zeitgeist demands. Although this sect does not have much in the way of popular roots, they do control a lot of power and money. The next pontiff, if he is not allied to such, will no doubt either have to break with them or forcibly reintegrate them into the Faith. A superhuman task, either way.

Another problem lies in the continuance of both the Eastern schism and the Protestant revolt. The latter seems to be dissolving into a bland Unitarianism on the one hand, and a sort of neo-Pietism on the other. A third wing, however, does seem to be seeking sacramentality and authority. Reconciling the last (and, one hopes the second) faction, and healing the rift with the East for good, would appear to also be top items on the agenda.

Above all, future popes must recall, both for themselves and for their flock (if the institution is to regain its moral authority any time soon), that they exist to assist the individual Catholic to escape the gates of hell; these, although the Church believes they will not prevail against her, nevertheless lie in wait for us all—or so Catholics believe.

But one thing should also be certain from reading one's history. If these three challenges are met and defeated, new—perhaps at the moment inconceivable—ones will replace them to bedevil future generations. The popes of those times will have to deal with them, and succeed or not, as have their predecessors.

Clearly, history rolls on. It is not something to be put away between the covers of books, but enfolds each of us as we move on toward the grave, and the world toward its end. From Rome's basilicas, to the newest churches in Africa, to the Missions of California, to the devastated gothic abbeys of northern Europe, this fact is manifest. In that sense, the history of the popes can never truly be finished, until humanity and the Church end.

# *Appendix: Important Papal Documents*

## Coronation Oath of the Pope

I Vow:

To change nothing of the received tradition, and nothing thereof, I have found before me guarded by my God-pleasing predecessors, to encroach, to alter, or to permit any innovation therein;

To the contrary: with glowing affection as Her truly faithful student and successor, to reverently safeguard the passed on good, with my whole strength and utmost effort;

To cleanse all that is in contradiction with canonical order that may surface;

To guard the holy canons and decrees of our Popes likewise as Divine Ordinances of Heaven, because I am conscious of Thee, Whose place I take through the grace of God, Whose Vicarship I possess with Thy support, being subject to severest accounting before Thy divine tribunal over all that I confess.

If I should undertake to act in anything of contrary sense, or should permit that it will be executed, Thou willst not be merciful to me on the dreadful day of Divine Justice.

Accordingly, without exclusion, we subject to severest excommunication anyone—be it ourself or be it another—who would dare to undertake anything new in contradiction to this constituted evangelic tradition and the purity of the Orthodox Faith and the Christian Religion, or would seek to change anything by his opposing efforts, or would concur with those who undertake such blasphemous venture.

(Liber Diurnus Romanorum Pontificum, P. L105, S.54.) (German translation by Dr. Werner Henzellek) (Translated from German into English by Josef Eldracher from the paperback book "Vatican II, Reform Council or Constitution of a New Church," by Anton Holzer, page 343.)

## Pope Benedict XV's Peace Proposal

(On August 1, 1917, Pope Benedict XV, issued this peace proposal. It was generally ignored by the warring governments.)

To the Heads of the Belligerent Peoples:

From the beginning of Our Pontificate, amidst the horrors of the terrible war unleashed upon Europe, We have kept before Our attention three things above all: to preserve complete impartiality in relation to all the belligerents, as is appropriate to him who is the common father and who loves all his children with equal affection; to endeavor constantly to do all the most possible good, without personal exceptions and without national or religious distinctions, a duty which the universal law of charity, as well as the supreme spiritual charge entrusted to Us by Christ, dictates to Us; finally, as Our peacemaking mission equally demands, to leave nothing undone within Our power, which could assist in hastening the end of this calamity, by trying to lead the peoples and their heads to more moderate frames of mind and to the calm deliberations of peace, of a "just and lasting" peace.

Whoever has followed Our work during the three unhappy years which have just elapsed, has been able to recognize with ease that We have always remained faithful to Our resolution of absolute impartiality and to Our practical policy of well-doing. We have never ceased to urge the belligerent peoples and Governments to become brothers once more, even although publicity has not been given to all which We have done to attain this most noble end . . .

First of all, the fundamental point should be that for the material force of arms should be substituted the moral force of law; hence a just agreement by all for the simultaneous and reciprocal reduction of armaments, according to rules and guarantees to be established to the degree necessary and sufficient for the maintenance of public order in each State; then, instead of armies, the institution of arbitration, with its lofty peacemaking function, according to the standards to be agreed upon and with sanctions to be decided against the State which might refuse to submit international questions to arbitration or to accept its decisions.

Once the supremacy of law has been established, let every obstacle to the ways of communication between the peoples be removed, by ensuring through rules to be fixed in similar fashion, the true freedom and common use of the seas. This would, on the one hand, remove many reasons for conflict and, on the other, would open new sources of prosperity and progress to all . . .

With regard to territorial questions, such as those disputed between Italy and Austria, and between Germany and France, there is ground for hope that in consideration of the immense advantages of a lasting peace with disarmament, the conflicting parties will examine them in a conciliatory frame of mind, taking into account so far as it is just and practicable, as We have said previously, the aspirations of the peoples and co-ordinating, according to circumstances, particular interests with the general good of the great human society.

The same spirit of equity and justice should direct the examination of other territorial and political questions, notably those relating to Armenia, the Balkan States, and the territories composing the ancient Kingdom of Poland, for which especially its noble historical traditions and the sufferings which it has undergone, particularly during the present war, ought rightly to enlist the sympathies of the nations. Such are the principal foundations upon which We believe the future reorganization of peoples should rest. They are of a kind which would make impossible the recurrence of such conflicts and would pave the way for a solution of the economic question, so important for the future and the material welfare of all the belligerent States . . .

## *Lamentabili Sane*
## Syllabus of St. Pius X Condemning the Errors of the Modernists

With truly lamentable results, our age, casting aside all restraint in its search for the ultimate causes of things, frequently pursues novelties so ardently that it rejects the legacy of the human race. Thus it falls into very serious errors, which are even more serious when they concern sacred authority, the interpretation of Sacred Scripture, and the principal mysteries of Faith. The fact that many Catholic writers also go beyond the limits determined by the Fathers and the Church herself is extremely regrettable. In the name of higher knowledge and historical research (they say), they are looking for that progress of dogmas which is, in reality, nothing but the corruption of dogmas.

These errors are being daily spread among the faithful. Lest they captivate the faithful's minds and corrupt the purity of their faith, His Holiness, Pius X, by Divine Providence, Pope, has decided that the chief errors should be noted and condemned by the Office of this Holy Roman and Universal Inquisition.

Therefore, after a very diligent investigation and consultation with the Reverend Consultors, the Most Eminent and Reverend Lord Cardinals, the General Inquisitors in matters of faith and morals have judged the following propositions to be condemned and proscribed. In fact, by this general decree, they are condemned and proscribed.

1. The ecclesiastical law which prescribes that books concerning the Divine Scriptures are subject to previous examination does not apply

to critical scholars and students of scientific exegesis of the Old and New Testament.

2. The Church's interpretation of the Sacred Books is by no means to be rejected; nevertheless, it is subject to the more accurate judgment and correction of the exegetes.
3. From the ecclesiastical judgments and censures passed against free and more scientific exegesis, one can conclude that the Faith the Church proposes contradicts history and that Catholic teaching cannot really be reconciled with the true origins of the Christian religion.
4. Even by dogmatic definitions the Church's magisterium cannot determine the genuine sense of the Sacred Scriptures.
5. Since the deposit of Faith contains only revealed truths, the Church has no right to pass judgment on the assertions of the human sciences.
6. The "Church learning" and the "Church teaching" collaborate in such a way in defining truths that it only remains for the "Church teaching" to sanction the opinions of the "Church learning."
7. In proscribing errors, the Church cannot demand any internal assent from the faithful by which the judgments she issues are to be embraced.
8. They are free from all blame who treat lightly the condemnations passed by the Sacred Congregation of the Index or by the Roman Congregations.
9. They display excessive simplicity or ignorance who believe that God is really the author of the Sacred Scriptures.
10. The inspiration of the books of the Old Testament consists in this: The Israelite writers handed down religious doctrines under a peculiar aspect which was either little or not at all known to the Gentiles.
11. Divine inspiration does not extend to all of Sacred Scriptures so that it renders its parts, each and every one, free from every error.
12. If he wishes to apply himself usefully to Biblical studies, the exegete must first put aside all preconceived opinions about the supernatural origin of Sacred Scripture and interpret it the same as any other merely human document.
13. The Evangelists themselves, as well as the Christians of the second and third generation, artificially arranged the evangelical parables. In such a way they explained the scanty fruit of the preaching of Christ among the Jews.
14. In many narrations the Evangelists recorded, not so much things that are true, as things which, even though false, they judged to be more profitable for their readers.
15. Until the time the canon was defined and constituted, the Gospels were increased by additions and corrections. Therefore there remained in them only a faint and uncertain trace of the doctrine of Christ.
16. The narrations of John are not properly history, but a mystical contemplation of the Gospel. The discourses contained in his Gospel are theological meditations, lacking historical truth concerning the mystery of salvation.
17. The fourth Gospel exaggerated miracles not only in order that the

extraordinary might stand out but also in order that it might become more suitable for showing forth the work and glory of the Word Incarnate.

18. John claims for himself the quality of witness concerning Christ. In reality, however, he is only a distinguished witness of the Christian life, or of the life of Christ in the Church at the close of the first century.
19. Heterodox exegetes have expressed the true sense of the Scriptures more faithfully than Catholic exegetes.
20. Revelation could be nothing else than the consciousness man acquired of his revelation to God.
21. Revelation, constituting the object of the Catholic faith, was not completed with the Apostles.
22. The dogmas the Church holds out as revealed are not truths which have fallen from heaven. They are an interpretation of religious facts which the human mind has acquired by laborious effort.
23. Opposition may, and actually does, exist between the facts narrated in Sacred Scripture and the Church's dogmas which rest on them. Thus the critic may reject as false facts the Church holds as most certain.
24. The exegete who constructs premises from which it follows that dogmas are historically false or doubtful is not to be reproved as long as he does not directly deny the dogmas themselves.
25. The assent of faith ultimately rests on a mass of probabilities.
26. The dogmas of the Faith are to be held only according to their practical sense; that is to say, as preceptive norms of conduct and not as norms of believing.
27. The divinity of Jesus Christ is not proved from the Gospels. It is a dogma which the Christian conscience has derived from the notion of the Messias.
28. While He was exercising His ministry, Jesus did not speak with the object of teaching He was the Messias, nor did His miracles tend to prove it.
29. It is permissible to grant that the Christ of history is far inferior to the Christ Who is the object of faith.
30. In all the evangelical texts the name "Son of God" is equivalent only to that of "Messias." It does not in the least way signify that Christ is the true and natural Son of God.
31. The doctrine concerning Christ taught by Paul, John, and the Councils of Nicea, Ephesus and Chalcedon is not that which Jesus taught but that which the Christian conscience conceived concerning Jesus.
32. It is impossible to reconcile the natural sense of the Gospel texts with the sense taught by our theologians concerning the conscience and the infallible knowledge of Jesus Christ.
33. Everyone who is not led by preconceived opinions can readily see that either Jesus professed an error concerning the immediate Messianic coming or the greater part of His doctrine as contained in the Gospels is destitute of authenticity.
34. The critics can ascribe to Christ a knowledge without limits only on a hypothesis which cannot be historically conceived and which is repugnant to the moral sense. That hypothesis is that Christ as man

possessed the knowledge of God and yet was unwilling to communicate the knowledge of a great many things to His disciples and posterity.

35. Christ did not always possess the consciousness of His Messianic dignity.
36. The Resurrection of the Savior is not properly a fact of the historical order. It is a fact of merely the supernatural order (neither demonstrated nor demonstrable) which the Christian conscience gradually derived from other facts.
37. In the beginning, faith in the Resurrection of Christ was not so much in the fact itself of the Resurrection as in the immortal life of Christ with God.
38. The doctrine of the expiatory death of Christ is Pauline and not evangelical.
39. The opinions concerning the origin of the Sacraments which the Fathers of Trent held and which certainly influenced their dogmatic canons are very different from those which now rightly exist among historians who examine Christianity.
40. The Sacraments have their origin in the fact that the Apostles and their successors, swayed and moved by circumstances and events, interpreted some idea and intention of Christ.
41. The Sacraments are intended merely to recall to man's mind the ever-beneficent presence of the Creator.
42. The Christian community imposed the necessity of Baptism, adopted it as a necessary rite, and added to it the obligation of the Christian profession.
43. The practice of administering Baptism to infants was a disciplinary evolution, which became one of the causes why the Sacrament was divided into two, namely, Baptism and Penance.
44. There is nothing to prove that the rite of the Sacrament of Confirmation was employed by the Apostles. The formal distinction of the two Sacraments of Baptism and Confirmation does not pertain to the history of primitive Christianity.
45. Not everything which Paul narrates concerning the institution of the Eucharist (I Cor. 11:23–25) is to be taken historically.
46. In the primitive Church the concept of the Christian sinner reconciled by the authority of the Church did not exist. Only very slowly did the Church accustom herself to this concept. As a matter of fact, even after Penance was recognized as an institution of the Church, it was not called a Sacrament since it would be held as a disgraceful Sacrament.
47. The words of the Lord, "Receive the Holy Spirit; whose sins you shall forgive, they are forgiven them; and whose sins you shall retain, they are retained" (John 20:22–23), in no way refer to the Sacrament of Penance, in spite of what it pleased the Fathers of Trent to say.
48. In his Epistle (Ch. 5:14–15) James did not intend to promulgate a Sacrament of Christ but only commend a pious custom. If in this custom he happens to distinguish a means of grace, it is not in that rigorous manner in which it was taken by the theologians who laid down the notion and number of the Sacraments.

49. When the Christian supper gradually assumed the nature of a liturgical action those who customarily presided over the supper acquired the sacerdotal character.
50. The elders who fulfilled the office of watching over the gatherings of the faithful were instituted by the Apostles as priests or bishops to provide for the necessary ordering of the increasing communities and not properly for the perpetuation of the Apostolic mission and power.
51. It is impossible that Matrimony could have become a Sacrament of the new law until later in the Church since it was necessary that a full theological explication of the doctrine of grace and the Sacraments should first take place before Matrimony should be held as a Sacrament.
52. It was far from the mind of Christ to found a Church as a society which would continue on earth for a long course of centuries. On the contrary, in the mind of Christ the kingdom of heaven together with the end of the world was about to come immediately.
53. The organic constitution of the Church is not immutable. Like human society, Christian society is subject to a perpetual evolution.
54. Dogmas, Sacraments and hierarchy, both their notion and reality, are only interpretations and evolutions of the Christian intelligence which have increased and perfected by an external series of additions the little germ latent in the Gospel.
55. Simon Peter never even suspected that Christ entrusted the primacy in the Church to him.
56. The Roman Church became the head of all the churches, not through the ordinance of Divine Providence, but merely through political conditions.
57. The Church has shown that she is hostile to the progress of the natural and theological sciences.
58. Truth is no more immutable than man himself, since it evolved with him, in him, and through him.
59. Christ did not teach a determined body of doctrine applicable to all times and all men, but rather inaugurated a religious movement adapted or to be adapted to different times and places.
60. Christian Doctrine was originally Judaic. Through successive evolutions it became first Pauline, then Joannine, finally Hellenic and universal.
61. It may be said without paradox that there is no chapter of Scripture, from the first of Genesis to the last of the Apocalypse, which contains a doctrine absolutely identical with that which the Church teaches on the same matter. For the same reason, therefore, no chapter of Scripture has the same sense for the critic and the theologian.
62. The chief articles of the Apostles' Creed did not have the same sense for the Christians of the first ages as they have for the Christians of our time.
63. The Church shows that she is incapable of effectively maintaining evangelical ethics since she obstinately clings to immutable doctrines which cannot be reconciled with modern progress.
64. Scientific progress demands that the concepts of Christian doctrine

concerning God, creation, revelation, the Person of the Incarnate Word, and Redemption be re-adjusted.

65. Modern Catholicism can be reconciled with true science only if it is transformed into a non-dogmatic Christianity; that is to say, into a broad and liberal Protestantism.

The following Thursday, the fourth day of the same month and year, all these matters were accurately reported to our Most Holy Lord, Pope Pius X. His Holiness approved and confirmed the decree of the Most Eminent Fathers and ordered that each and every one of the above-listed propositions be held by all as condemned and proscribed.

PETER PALOMBELLI, Notary of the Holy Roman and Universal Inquisition

## The Oath Against Modernism: *Sacrorum Antistitum*

Given by His Holiness St. Pius X September 1, 1910.

To be sworn to by all clergy, pastors, confessors, preachers, religious superiors, and professors in philosophical-theological seminaries.

I . . . firmly embrace and accept each and every definition that has been set forth and declared by the unerring teaching authority of the Church, especially those principal truths which are directly opposed to the errors of this day.

And first of all, I profess that God, the origin and end of all things, can be known with certainty by the natural light of reason from the created world (see Rom. 1:90), that is, from the visible works of creation, as a cause from its effects, and that, therefore, his existence can also be demonstrated.

Secondly, I accept and acknowledge the external proofs of revelation, that is, divine acts and especially miracles and prophecies as the surest signs of the divine origin of the Christian religion and I hold that these same proofs are well adapted to the understanding of all eras and all men, even of this time.

Thirdly, I believe with equally firm faith that the Church, the guardian and teacher of the revealed word, was personally instituted by the real and historical Christ when he lived among us, and that the Church was built upon Peter, the prince of the apostolic hierarchy, and his successors for the duration of time.

Fourthly, I sincerely hold that the doctrine of faith was handed down to us from the apostles through the orthodox Fathers in exactly the same meaning and always in the same purport. Therefore, I entirely reject the heretical misrepresentation that dogmas evolve and change from one meaning to another different from the one which the Church held previously. I also

condemn every error according to which, in place of the divine deposit which has been given to the spouse of Christ to be carefully guarded by her, there is put a philosophical figment or product of a human conscience that has gradually been developed by human effort and will continue to develop indefinitely.

Fifthly, I hold with certainty and sincerely confess that faith is not a blind sentiment of religion welling up from the depths of the subconscious under the impulse of the heart and the motion of a will trained to morality; but faith is a genuine assent of the intellect to truth received by hearing from an external source. By this assent, because of the authority of the supremely truthful God, we believe to be true that which has been revealed and attested to by a personal God, our creator and Lord.

Furthermore, with due reverence, I submit and adhere with my whole heart to the condemnations, declarations, and all the prescripts contained in the encyclical Pascendi and in the decree Lamentabili, especially those concerning what is known as the history of dogmas.

I also reject the error of those who say that the faith held by the Church can contradict history, and that Catholic dogmas, in the sense in which they are now understood, are irreconcilable with a more realistic view of the origins of the Christian religion.

I also condemn and reject the opinion of those who say that a well-educated Christian assumes a dual personality—that of a believer and at the same time of a historian, as if it were permissible for a historian to hold things that contradict the faith of the believer, or to establish premises which, provided there be no direct denial of dogmas, would lead to the conclusion that dogmas are either false or doubtful.

Likewise, I reject that method of judging and interpreting Sacred Scripture which, departing from the tradition of the Church, the analogy of faith, and the norms of the Apostolic See, embraces the misrepresentations of the rationalists and with no prudence or restraint adopts textual criticism as the one and supreme norm.

Furthermore, I reject the opinion of those who hold that a professor lecturing or writing on a historico-theological subject should first put aside any preconceived opinion about the supernatural origin of Catholic tradition or about the divine promise of help to preserve all revealed truth forever; and that they should then interpret the writings of each of the Fathers solely by scientific principles, excluding all sacred authority, and with the same liberty of judgment that is common in the investigation of all ordinary historical documents.

Finally, I declare that I am completely opposed to the error of the modernists who hold that there is nothing divine in sacred tradition; or what is far worse, say that there is, but in a pantheistic sense, with the result that there would remain nothing but this plain simple fact—one to be put on a par with the ordinary facts of history—the fact, namely, that a group of men by their own labor, skill, and talent have continued through subsequent ages a school begun by Christ and his apostles.

I promise that I shall keep all these articles faithfully, entirely, and sincerely, and guard them inviolate, in no way deviating from them in teaching or in any way in word or in writing. Thus I promise, this I swear, so help me God, and these holy Gospels of God which I touch with my hand.

## *Unam sanctam*
## Boniface VIII

Urged by faith, we are obliged to believe and to maintain that the Church is one, holy, catholic, and also apostolic. We believe in her firmly and we confess with simplicity that outside of her there is neither salvation nor the remission of sins, as the Spouse in the Canticles [Sgs 6:8] proclaims: 'One is my dove, my perfect one. She is the only one, the chosen of her who bore her,' and she represents one sole mystical body whose Head is Christ and the head of Christ is God [1 Cor 11:3]. In her then is one Lord, one faith, one baptism [Eph 4:5]. There had been at the time of the deluge only one ark of Noah, prefiguring the one Church, which ark, having been finished to a single cubit, had only one pilot and guide, i.e., Noah, and we read that, outside of this ark, all that subsisted on the earth was destroyed.

We venerate this Church as one, the Lord having said by the mouth of the prophet: 'Deliver, O God, my soul from the sword and my only one from the hand of the dog.' [Ps 21:20] He has prayed for his soul, that is for himself, heart and body; and this body, that is to say, the Church, He has called one because of the unity of the Spouse, of the faith, of the sacraments, and of the charity of the Church. This is the tunic of the Lord, the seamless tunic, which was not rent but which was cast by lot [Jn 19:23–24]. Therefore, of the one and only Church there is one body and one head, not two heads like a monster; that is, Christ and the Vicar of Christ, Peter and the successor of Peter, since the Lord speaking to Peter Himself said: 'Feed My sheep' [Jn 21:17], meaning, My sheep in general, not these, nor those in particular, whence we understand that He entrusted all to him [Peter]. Therefore, if the Greeks or others should say that they are not confided to Peter and to his successors, they must confess not being the sheep of Christ, since Our Lord says in John 'there is one sheepfold and one shepherd.' We are informed by the texts of the gospels that in this Church and in its power are two swords; namely, the spiritual and the temporal. For when the Apostles say: 'Behold, here are two swords' [Lk 22:38] that is to say, in the Church, since the Apostles were speaking, the Lord did not reply that there were too many, but sufficient. Certainly the one who denies that the temporal sword is in the power of Peter has not listened well to the word of the Lord commanding: 'Put up thy sword into thy scabbard' [Mt 26:52]. Both, therefore, are in the power of the Church, that is to say, the spiritual and the material sword, but the former is to be administered for the Church but the latter by the Church; the former in the hands of the priest; the latter by the hands of kings and soldiers, but at the will and sufferance of the priest.

However, one sword ought to be subordinated to the other and tem-

poral authority, subjected to spiritual power. For since the Apostle said: 'There is no power except from God and the things that are, are ordained of God' [Rom 13:1–2], but they would not be ordained if one sword were not subordinated to the other and if the inferior one, as it were, were not led upwards by the other.

For, according to the Blessed Dionysius, it is a law of the divinity that the lowest things reach the highest place by intermediaries. Then, according to the order of the universe, all things are not led back to order equally and immediately, but the lowest by the intermediary, and the inferior by the superior. Hence we must recognize the more clearly that spiritual power surpasses in dignity and in nobility any temporal power whatever, as spiritual things surpass the temporal.

This we see very clearly also by the payment, benediction, and consecration of the tithes, but the acceptance of power itself and by the government even of things. For with truth as our witness, it belongs to spiritual power to establish the terrestrial power and to pass judgement if it has not been good. Thus is accomplished the prophecy of Jeremias concerning the Church and the ecclesiastical power: 'Behold today I have placed you over nations, and over kingdoms' and the rest. Therefore, if the terrestrial power err, it will be judged by the spiritual power; but if a minor spiritual power err, it will be judged by a superior spiritual power; but if the highest power of all err, it can be judged only by God, and not by man, according to the testimony of the Apostle: 'The spiritual man judgeth of all things and he himself is judged by no man' [1 Cor 2:15]. This authority, however (though it has been given to man and is exercised by man), is not human but rather divine, granted to Peter by a divine word and reaffirmed to him (Peter) and his successors by the One Whom Peter confessed, the Lord saying to Peter himself, 'Whatsoever you shall bind on earth, shall be bound also in Heaven' etc., [Mt 16:19]. Therefore whoever resists this power thus ordained by God, resists the ordinance of God [Rom 13:2], unless he invent like Manicheus two beginnings, which is false and judged by us heretical, since according to the testimony of Moses, it is not in the beginnings but in the beginning that God created Heaven and earth [Gen 1:1]. Furthermore, we declare, we proclaim, we define that it is absolutely necessary for salvation that every human creature be subject to the Roman Pontiff.

## Creed of Pius IV (Tridentine Creed)

994. I, N., with firm faith believe and profess all and everything which is contained in the creed of faith, which the holy Roman Church uses, namely: I believe * in one God the Father Almighty, creator of heaven and earth, of all things visible and invisible; and in one Lord Jesus Christ, the only-begotten Son of God, and born of the Father before all ages, God of God, light of light, true God of true God, begotten not made, consubstantial with the Father, by whom all things were made; who for us men and for our salvation descended from heaven, and became incarnate by the Holy Spirit of the Virgin Mary, and was made man; he was also cruci-

fied for us under Pontius Pilate, suffered and was buried; and he rose on the third day according to the Scriptures, and ascended into heaven; he sitteth at the right hand of the Father, and will come again with glory to judge the living and the dead, of whose kingdom there shall be no end; and in the Holy Spirit, the Lord and giver of life, who proceeds from the Father and the Son; who together with the Father and the Son is adored and glorified; who spoke through the prophets; and in one holy Catholic and apostolic Church. I confess one baptism for the remission of sins, and I await the resurrection of the dead, and the life of the world to come. Amen.

995. The apostolic and ecclesiastical traditions and all other observances and constitutions of that same Church I most firmly admit and embrace. I likewise accept Holy Scripture according to that sense which our holy Mother Church has held and does hold, whose [office] it is to judge of the true meaning and interpretation of the Sacred Scriptures; I shall never accept nor interpret it otherwise than in accordance with the unanimous consent of the Fathers.

996. I also profess that there are truly and properly seven sacraments of the New Law instituted by Jesus Christ our Lord, and necessary for the salvation of mankind, although not all are necessary for each individual; these sacraments are baptism, confirmation, the Eucharist, penance, extreme unction, order, and matrimony; and [I profess] that they confer grace, and that of these baptism, confirmation, and order cannot be repeated without sacrilege. I also receive and admit the accepted and approved rites of the Catholic Church in the solemn administration of all the aforesaid sacraments. I embrace and accept each and everything that has been defined and declared by the holy Synod of Trent concerning original sin and justification.

997. I also profess that in the Mass there is offered to God a true, proper sacrifice of propitiation for the living and the dead, and that in the most holy sacrament of the Eucharist there is truly, really, and substantially present the body and blood together with the soul and the divinity of our Lord Jesus Christ, and that there takes place a conversion of the whole substance of bread into the body, and of the whole substance of the wine into the blood; and this conversion the Catholic Church calls transubstantiation. I also acknowledge that under one species alone the whole and entire Christ and the true sacrament are taken.

998. I steadfastly hold that a purgatory exists, and that the souls there detained are aided by the prayers of the faithful; likewise that the saints reigning together with Christ should be venerated and invoked, and that they offer prayers to God for us, and that their relics should be venerated. I firmly assert that the images of Christ and of the Mother of God ever Virgin, and also of the other saints should be kept and retained, and that due honor and veneration should be paid to them; I also affirm that the power of indulgences has been left in the Church by Christ, and that the use of them is especially salutary for the Christian people.

999. I acknowledge the holy Catholic and apostolic Roman Church as the mother and teacher of all churches; and to the Roman Pontiff, the successor of the blessed Peter, chief of the Apostles and vicar of Jesus Christ, I promise and swear true obedience.

1000. Also all other things taught, defined, and declared by the sacred canons and ecumenical Councils, and especially by the sacred and holy Synod of Trent (and by the ecumenical Council of the Vatican,*particularly concerning the primacy of the Roman Pontiff and his infallible teaching), I without hesitation accept and profess; and at the same time all things contrary thereto, and whatever heresies have been condemned, and rejected, and anathematized by the Church, I likewise condemn, reject, and anathematize. This true Catholic faith, outside of which no one can be saved, (and) which of my own accord I now profess and truly hold, I, N., do promise, vow, and swear that I will, with the help of God, most faithfully retain and profess the same to the last breath of life as pure and inviolable, and that I will take care as far as lies in my power that it be held, taught, and preached by my subjects or by those over whom by virtue of my office I have charge, so help me God, and these holy Gospels of God.

## Syllabus of Modern Errors

A Condemnation of Modernist, Liberal Errors
Encyclical Letter of His Holiness
Venerable Pope Pius IX
December 8, 1864

The following propositions have been condemned and anathematized:

I. Pantheism, Naturalism and Absolute Rationalism

1. There exists no Supreme, all-wise, all-provident Divine Being, distinct from the universe, and God is identical with the nature of things, and is, therefore, subject to changes. In effect, God is produced in man and in the world, and all things are God and have the very substance of God, and God is one and the same thing with the world, and, therefore, spirit with matter, necessity with liberty, good with evil, justice with injustice.—Allocution "Maxima quidem," June 9, 1862.

2. All action of God upon man and the world is to be denied.—Ibid.

3. Human reason, without any reference whatsoever to God, is the sole arbiter of truth and falsehood, and of good and evil; it is law to itself, and suffices, by its natural force, to secure the welfare of men and of nations.—Ibid.

4. All the truths of religion proceed from the innate strength of human reason; hence reason is the ultimate standard by which man can and ought to arrive at the knowledge of all truths of every kind.—Ibid. and Encyclical "Qui pluribus," Nov. 9, 1846, etc.

5. Divine revelation is imperfect, and therefore subject to a continual

and indefinite progress, corresponding with the advancement of human reason.—Ibid.

6. The faith of Christ is in opposition to human reason and divine revelation not only is not useful, but is even hurtful to the perfection of man.—Ibid.

7. The prophecies and miracles set forth and recorded in the Sacred Scriptures are the fiction of poets, and the mysteries of the Christian faith the result of philosophical investigations. In the books of the Old and the New Testament there are contained mythical inventions, and Jesus Christ is Himself a myth.

II. Moderate Rationalism

8. As human reason is placed on a level with religion itself, so theological must be treated in the same manner as philosophical sciences.—Allocution "Singulari quadam," Dec. 9, 1854.

9. All the dogmas of the Christian religion are indiscriminately the object of natural science or philosophy, and human reason, enlightened solely in an historical way, is able, by its own natural strength and principles, to attain to the true science of even the most abstruse dogmas; provided only that such dogmas be proposed to reason itself as its object. —Letters to the Archbishop of Munich, "Gravissimas inter," Dec. 11, 1862, and "Tuas libenter," Dec. 21, 1863.

10. As the philosopher is one thing, and philosophy another, so it is the right and duty of the philosopher to subject himself to the authority which he shall have proved to be true; but philosophy neither can nor ought to submit to any such authority.—Ibid., Dec. 11, 1862.

11. The Church not only ought never to pass judgment on philosophy, but ought to tolerate the errors of philosophy, leaving it to correct itself.—Ibid., Dec. 21, 1863.

12. The decrees of the Apostolic See and of the Roman congregations impede the true progress of science.—Ibid.

13. The method and principles by which the old scholastic doctors cultivated theology are no longer suitable to the demands of our times and to the progress of the sciences.—Ibid.

14. Philosophy is to be treated without taking any account of supernatural revelation.—Ibid.

III. Indifferentism, Latitudinarianism

15. Every man is free to embrace and profess that religion which, guided by the light of reason, he shall consider true.—Allocution "Maxima quidem," June 9, 1862; Damnatio "Multiplices inter," June 10, 1851.

16. Man may, in the observance of any religion whatever, find the way of eternal salvation, and arrive at eternal salvation.—Encyclical "Qui pluribus," Nov. 9, 1846.

17. Good hope at least is to be entertained of the eternal salvation of all those who are not at all in the true Church of Christ.—Encyclical "Quanto conficiamur," Aug. 10, 1863, etc.

18. Protestantism is nothing more than another form of the same true

Christian religion, in which form it is given to please God equally as in the Catholic Church.—Encyclical "Noscitis," Dec. 8, 1849.

IV. Socialism, Communism, Secret Societies, Biblical Societies, Clerico-Liberal Societies

Pests of this kind are frequently reprobated in the severest terms in the Encyclical "Qui pluribus," Nov. 9, 1846, Allocution "Quibus quantisque," April 20, 1849, Encyclical "Noscitis et nobiscum," Dec. 8, 1849, Allocution "Singulari quadam," Dec. 9, 1854, Encyclical "Quanto conficiamur," Aug. 10, 1863.

V. Errors Concerning the Church and Her Rights

19. The Church is not a true and perfect society, entirely free—nor is she endowed with proper and perpetual rights of her own, conferred upon her by her Divine Founder; but it appertains to the civil power to define what are the rights of the Church, and the limits within which she may exercise those rights.—Allocution "Singulari quadam," Dec. 9, 1854, etc.

20. The ecclesiastical power ought not to exercise its authority without the permission and assent of the civil government.—Allocution "Meminit unusquisque," Sept. 30, 1861.

21. The Church has not the power of defining dogmatically that the religion of the Catholic Church is the only true religion.—Damnatio "Multiplices inter," June 10, 1851.

22. The obligation by which Catholic teachers and authors are strictly bound is confined to those things only which are proposed to universal belief as dogmas of faith by the infallible judgment of the Church.—Letter to the Archbishop of Munich, "Tuas libenter," Dec. 21, 1863.

23. Roman pontiffs and ecumenical councils have wandered outside the limits of their powers, have usurped the rights of princes, and have even erred in defining matters of faith and morals.—Damnatio "Multiplices inter," June 10, 1851.

24. The Church has not the power of using force, nor has she any temporal power, direct or indirect.—Apostolic Letter "Ad Apostolicae," Aug. 22, 1851.

25. Besides the power inherent in the episcopate, other temporal power has been attributed to it by the civil authority granted either explicitly or tacitly, which on that account is revocable by the civil authority whenever it thinks fit.—Ibid.

26. The Church has no innate and legitimate right of acquiring and possessing property.—Allocution "Nunquam fore," Dec. 15, 1856; Encyclical "Incredibili," Sept. 7, 1863.

27. The sacred ministers of the Church and the Roman pontiff are to be absolutely excluded from every charge and dominion over temporal affairs.—Allocution "Maxima quidem," June 9, 1862.

28. It is not lawful for bishops to publish even letters Apostolic without the permission of Government.—Allocution "Nunquam fore," Dec. 15, 1856.

29. Favors granted by the Roman pontiff ought to be considered

null, unless they have been sought for through the civil government. —Ibid.

30. The immunity of the Church and of ecclesiastical persons derived its origin from civil law.—Damnatio "Multiplices inter," June 10, 1851.

31. The ecclesiastical forum or tribunal for the temporal causes, whether civil or criminal, of clerics, ought by all means to be abolished, even without consulting and against the protest of the Holy See.—Allocution "Nunquam fore," Dec. 15, 1856; Allocution "Acerbissimum," Sept. 27, 1852.

32. The personal immunity by which clerics are exonerated from military conscription and service in the army may be abolished without violation either of natural right or equity. Its abolition is called for by civil progress, especially in a society framed on the model of a liberal government.—Letter to the Bishop of Monreale "Singularis nobisque," Sept. 29, 1864.

33. It does not appertain exclusively to the power of ecclesiastical jurisdiction by right, proper and innate, to direct the teaching of theological questions.—Letter to the Archbishop of Munich, "Tuas libenter," Dec. 21, 1863.

34. The teaching of those who compare the Sovereign Pontiff to a prince, free and acting in the universal Church, is a doctrine which prevailed in the Middle Ages.—Apostolic Letter "Ad Apostolicae," Aug. 22, 1851.

35. There is nothing to prevent the decree of a general council, or the act of all peoples, from transferring the supreme pontificate from the bishop and city of Rome to another bishop and another city.—Ibid.

36. The definition of a national council does not admit of any subsequent discussion, and the civil authority can assume this principle as the basis of its acts.—Ibid.

37. National churches, withdrawn from the authority of the Roman pontiff and altogether separated, can be established.—Allocution "Multis gravibusque," Dec. 17, 1860.

38. The Roman pontiffs have, by their too arbitrary conduct, contributed to the division of the Church into Eastern and Western.—Apostolic Letter "Ad Apostolicae," Aug. 22, 1851.

VI. Errors About Civil Society, Considered Both in Itself and in Its Relation to the Church

39. The State, as being the origin and source of all rights, is endowed with a certain right not circumscribed by any limits.—Allocution "Maxima quidem," June 9, 1862.

40. The teaching of the Catholic Church is hostile to the well-being and interests of society.—Encyclical "Qui pluribus," Nov. 9, 1846; Allocution "Quibus quantisque," April 20, 1849.

41. The civil government, even when in the hands of an infidel sovereign, has a right to an indirect negative power over religious affairs. It therefore possesses not only the right called that of "exsequatur," but also that of appeal, called "appellatio ab abusu."—Apostolic Letter "Ad Apostolicae," Aug. 22, 1851.

42. In the case of conflicting laws enacted by the two powers, the civil law prevails.—Ibid.

43. The secular Power has authority to rescind, declare and render null, solemn conventions, commonly called concordats, entered into with the Apostolic See, regarding the use of rights appertaining to ecclesiastical immunity, without the consent of the Apostolic See, and even in spite of its protest.—Allocution "Multis gravibusque," Dec.17, 1860; Allocution "In consistoriali," Nov. 1, 1850.

44. The civil authority may interfere in matters relating to religion, morality and spiritual government: hence, it can pass judgment on the instructions issued for the guidance of consciences, conformably with their mission, by the pastors of the Church. Further, it has the right to make enactments regarding the administration of the divine sacraments, and the dispositions necessary for receiving them.—Allocutions "In consistoriali," Nov. 1, 1850, and "Maxima quidem," June 9, 1862.

45. The entire government of public schools in which the youth—of a Christian state is educated, except (to a certain extent) in the case of episcopal seminaries, may and ought to appertain to the civil power, and belong to it so far that no other authority whatsoever shall be recognized as having any right to interfere in the discipline of the schools, the arrangement of the studies, the conferring of degrees, in the choice or approval of the teachers.—Allocutions "Quibus luctuosissimis," Sept. 5, 1851, and "In consistoriali," Nov. 1, 1850.

46. Moreover, even in ecclesiastical seminaries, the method of studies to be adopted is subject to the civil authority.—Allocution "Nunquam fore," Dec.15, 1856.

47. The best theory of civil society requires that popular schools open to children of every class of the people, and, generally, all public institutes intended for instruction in letters and philosophical sciences and for carrying on the education of youth, should be freed from all ecclesiastical authority, control and interference, and should be fully subjected to the civil and political power at the pleasure of the rulers, and according to the standard of the prevalent opinions of the age.—Epistle to the Archbishop of Freiburg, "Cum non sine," July 14, 1864.

48. Catholics may approve of the system of educating youth unconnected with Catholic faith and the power of the Church, and which regards the knowledge of merely natural things, and only, or at least primarily, the ends of earthly social life.—Ibid.

49. The civil power may prevent the prelates of the Church and the faithful from communicating freely and mutually with the Roman pontiff.—Allocution "Maxima quidem," June 9, 1862.

50. Lay authority possesses of itself the right of presenting bishops, and may require of them to undertake the administration of the diocese before they receive canonical institution, and the Letters Apostolic from the Holy See.—Allocution "Nunquam fore," Dec. 15, 1856.

51. And, further, the lay government has the right of deposing bishops from their pastoral functions, and is not bound to obey the Roman pontiff in those things which relate to the institution of bishoprics and the appointment of bishops.—Allocution "Acerbissimum," Sept. 27, 1852, Damnatio "Multiplices inter," June 10, 1851.

52. Government can, by its own right, alter the age prescribed by the Church for the religious profession of women and men; and may require of all religious orders to admit no person to take solemn vows without its permission.—Allocution "Nunquam fore," Dec. 15, 1856.

53. The laws enacted for the protection of religious orders and regarding their rights and duties ought to be abolished; nay, more, civil Government may lend its assistance to all who desire to renounce the obligation which they have undertaken of a religious life, and to break their vows. Government may also suppress the said religious orders, as likewise collegiate churches and simple benefices, even those of advowson and subject their property and revenues to the administration and pleasure of the civil power.—Allocutions "Acerbissimum," Sept. 27, 1852; "Probe memineritis," Jan. 22, 1855; "Cum saepe," July 26, 1855.

54. Kings and princes are not only exempt from the jurisdiction of the Church, but are superior to the Church in deciding questions of jurisdiction.—Damnatio "Multiplices inter," June 10, 1851.

55. The Church ought to be separated from the State, and the State from the Church.—Allocution "Acerbissimum," Sept. 27, 1852.

VII. Errors Concerning Natural and Christian Ethics

56. Moral laws do not stand in need of the divine sanction, and it is not at all necessary that human laws should be made conformable to the laws of nature and receive their power of binding from God.—Allocution "Maxima quidem," June 9, 1862.

57. The science of philosophical things and morals and also civil laws may and ought to keep aloof from divine and ecclesiastical authority.—Ibid.

58. No other forces are to be recognized except those which reside in matter, and all the rectitude and excellence of morality ought to be placed in the accumulation and increase of riches by every possible means, and the gratification of pleasure.—Ibid.; Encyclical "Quanto conficiamur," Aug. 10, 1863.

59. Right consists in the material fact. All human duties are an empty word, and all human facts have the force of right.—Allocution "Maxima quidem," June 9, 1862.

60. Authority is nothing else but numbers and the sum total of material forces.—Ibid.

61. The injustice of an act when successful inflicts no injury on the sanctity of right.—Allocution "Jamdudum cernimus," March 18, 1861.

62. The principle of non-intervention, as it is called, ought to be proclaimed and observed.—Allocution "Novos et ante," Sept. 28, 1860.

63. It is lawful to refuse obedience to legitimate princes, and even to rebel against them.—Encyclical "Qui pluribus," Nov. 9, 1864; Allocution "Quibusque vestrum," Oct. 4, 1847; "Noscitis et Nobiscum," Dec. 8, 1849; Apostolic Letter "Cum Catholica."

64. The violation of any solemn oath, as well as any wicked and flagitious action repugnant to the eternal law, is not only not blamable but is

altogether lawful and worthy of the highest praise when done through love of country.—Allocution "Quibus quantisque," April 20, 1849.

VIII. Errors Concerning Christian Marriage

65. The doctrine that Christ has raised marriage to the dignity of a sacrament cannot be at all tolerated.—Apostolic Letter "Ad Apostolicae," Aug. 22, 1851.

66. The Sacrament of Marriage is only a something accessory to the contract and separate from it, and the sacrament itself consists in the nuptial benediction alone—Ibid.

67. By the law of nature, the marriage tie is not indissoluble, and in many cases divorce properly so called may be decreed by the civil authority.—Ibid.; Allocution "Acerbissimum," Sept. 27, 1852.

68. The Church has not the power of establishing diriment impediments of marriage, but such a power belongs to the civil authority by which existing impediments are to be removed.—Damnatio "Multiplices inter," June 10, 1851.

69. In the dark ages the Church began to establish diriment impediments, not by her own right, but by using a power borrowed from the State.—Apostolic Letter "Ad Apostolicae," Aug. 22, 1851.

70. The canons of the Council of Trent, which anathematize those who dare to deny to the Church the right of establishing diriment impediments, either are not dogmatic or must be understood as referring to such borrowed power.—Ibid.

71. The form of solemnizing marriage prescribed by the Council of Trent, under pain of nullity, does not bind in cases where the civil law lays down another form, and declares that when this new form is used the marriage shall be valid.—Ibid.

72. Boniface VIII was the first who declared that the vow of chastity taken at ordination renders marriage void.—Ibid.

73. In force of a merely civil contract there may exist between Christians a real marriage, and it is false to say either that the marriage contract between Christians is always a sacrament, or that there is no contract if the sacrament be excluded.—Ibid.; Letter to the King of Sardinia, Sept. 9, 1852; Allocutions "Acerbissimum," Sept. 27, 1852, "Multis gravibusque," Dec. 17, 1860.

74. Matrimonial causes and espousals belong by their nature to civil tribunals.—Encyclical "Qui pluribus," Nov. 9, 1846; Damnatio "Multiplices inter," June 10, 1851, "Ad Apostolicae," Aug. 22, 1851; Allocution "Acerbissimum," Sept. 27, 1852.

IX. Errors Regarding the Civil Power of the Sovereign Pontiff

75. The children of the Christian and Catholic Church are divided amongst themselves about the compatibility of the temporal with the spiritual power.—"Ad Apostolicae," Aug. 22, 1851.

76. The abolition of the temporal power of which the Apostolic See is possessed would contribute in the greatest degree to the liberty and pros-

perity of the Church.—Allocutions "Quibus quantisque," April 20, 1849, "Si semper antea," May 20, 1850.

X. Errors Having Reference to Modern Liberalism

77. In the present day it is no longer expedient that the Catholic religion should be held as the only religion of the State, to the exclusion of all other forms of worship.—Allocution "Nemo vestrum," July 26, 1855.

78. Hence it has been wisely decided by law, in some Catholic countries, that persons coming to reside therein shall enjoy the public exercise of their own peculiar worship.—Allocution "Acerbissimum," Sept. 27, 1852.

79. Moreover, it is false that the civil liberty of every form of worship, and the full power, given to all, of overtly and publicly manifesting any opinions whatsoever and thoughts, conduce more easily to corrupt the morals and minds of the people, and to propagate the pest of indifferentism.—Allocution "Nunquam fore," Dec. 15, 1856.

80. The Roman Pontiff can, and ought to, reconcile himself, and come to terms with progress, liberalism and modern civilization.—Allocution "Jamdudum cernimus," March 18, 1861.

The Faith teaches us and human reason demonstrates that a double order of things exists, and that we must therefore distinguish between the two earthly powers, the one of natural origin which provides for secular affairs and the tranquillity of human society, the other of supernatural origin, which presides over the City of God, that is to say the Church of Christ, which has been divinely instituted for the sake of souls and of eternal salvation . . .

The duties of this twofold power are most wisely ordered in such a way that to God is given what is God's (Matt. 22:21), and because of God to Caesar what is Caesar's, who is great because he is smaller than heaven. Certainly the Church has never disobeyed this divine command, the Church which always and everywhere instructs the faithful to show the respect which they should inviolably have for the supreme authority and its secular rights . . .

. . . Venerable Brethren, you see clearly enough how sad and full of perils is the condition of Catholics in the regions of Europe which We have mentioned. Nor are things any better or circumstances calmer in America, where some regions are so hostile to Catholics that their governments seem to deny by their actions the Catholic faith they claim to profess. In fact, there, for the last few years, a ferocious war on the Church, its institutions and the rights of the Apostolic See has been raging . . .

Venerable Brothers, it is surprising that in our time such a great war is being waged against the Catholic Church. But anyone who knows the nature, desires and intentions of the sects, whether they be called masonic or bear another name, and compares them with the nature, the systems and the vastness of the obstacles by which the Church has been assailed almost everywhere, cannot doubt that the present misfortune must mainly be imputed to the frauds and machinations of these sects. It is from them that the synagogue of Satan, which gathers its troops against the Church of

Christ, takes its strength. In the past Our predecessors, vigilant even from the beginning in Israel, had already denounced them to the kings and the nations, and had condemned them time and time again, and even We have not failed in this duty. If those who would have been able to avert such a deadly scourge had only had more faith in the supreme Pastors of the Church! But this scourge, winding through sinuous caverns . . . deceiving many with astute frauds, finally has arrived at the point where it comes forth impetuously from its hiding places and triumphs as a powerful master. Since the throng of its propagandists has grown enormously, these wicked groups think that they have already become masters of the world and that they have almost reached their pre-established goal. Having sometimes obtained what they desired, and that is power, in several countries, they boldly turn the help of powers and authorities which they have secured to trying to submit the Church of God to the most cruel servitude, to undermine the foundations on which it rests, to contaminate its splendid qualities; and, moreover, to strike it with frequent blows, to shake it, to overthrow it, and, if possible, to make it disappear completely from the earth. Things being thus, Venerable Brothers, make every effort to defend the faithful which are entrusted to you against the insidious contagion of these sects and to save from perdition those who unfortunately have inscribed themselves in such sects. Make known and attack those who, whether suffering from, or planning, deception, are not afraid to affirm that these shady congregations aim only at the profit of society, at progress and mutual benefit. Explain to them often and impress deeply on their souls the Papal constitutions on this subject and teach them that the masonic associations are anathematized by them not only in Europe but also in America and wherever they may be in the whole world.

# *Glossary*

**acolyte:** A cleric, formerly the highest of the four minor orders of the Western Church. Among his duties are lighting altar candles and carrying candles in processions, during the singing of the Gospel, and at other times. He also prepares the water and wine for the priest's use at Mass and wields incense. In the Traditional Roman Rite, at his ordination the bishop hands him an unlit candle and an empty cruet, symbolic of these. For many centuries laymen and boys have been deputed to carry out the acolyte's tasks—these are the famed altar boys. In recent years girls have been admitted to this role, which has led to a precipitate drop in the number of males involved. Thus a fertile source of priestly vocations has dried up.

**advocate, devil's:** Slang name for the "Promoter of the Faith," an official of the Congregation of Rites (renamed the Congregation for the Causes of Saints by Paul VI in 1969), who, prior to the change in the canonization process put through by John Paul II in 1983, worked to disprove the sanctity of all candidates for sainthood. He would inquire into both their miracles and virtue in an attempt to find anything bogus about them. If the individual was canonized, he would do penance at the new saint's altar. Since the change, the promoter's job is now more purely one of evaluating all the evidence impartially.

**Agnus Dei:** Latin phrase meaning "Lamb of God." It has three general meanings:

1. A prayer recited by the priest and sung by the choir before the Communion at Mass. The words are taken from those of St. John the Baptist spoken to Christ in the Gospel of St. John.
2. A wax disc stamped with an image of a lamb, representing Christ as sacrifice for humanity's sins. They are solemnly blessed by the pope on

Wednesday in Holy Week the first and every seventh year of his pontificate. They are used to guard against fire, flood, storm, and miscarriage, and often are worn around the neck. Queen Elizabeth I forbade them to be imported into England or even owned by any of her subjects.

3. The image of a lamb with a halo and carrying either a cross or a pennon, and used as a symbol of the Blessed Sacrament. In England, this symbol (called the "lamb and flag") is often seen on ancient pubs owned by churches before the Reformation.

**allocution, papal:** An address given to the cardinals in a consistory. It often deals with questions regarding relations with secular powers.

**altar, Gregorian:** An altar that has been given the same privilege as the altar of St. Gregory in the church of that name on the Caelian Hill in Rome; a Mass celebrated there for a soul in purgatory gives a plenary indulgence. No new ones have been authorized since 1912, and, owing to the erection of table-altars in front of them, where they survive they are generally not used. A good example is the one in the church of St. Mary, St. Mary's, Pennsylvania.

**American college at Rome:** A pontifical college in Rome founded by Pius IX for seminarians from the United States. It was opened in 1859 at the urging of archbishops Kenrick of Baltimore and Hughes of New York.

**Ampulla, Sacred:** The vessel containing the sacred chrism with which the kings of France were crowned at Rheims. At the prayer of St. Remigius vessel and chrism came down from heaven in time for the crowning of Clovis as king of the Franks on Christmas Day, 496. It was used for almost every French coronation down to that of Charles X in 1825. In 1793, a mob smashed it at the cathedral of Rheims, but part of the contents was saved by a quick-thinking priest. The premier symbol of legitimacy in the country, the chrism remains today at the cathedral, awaiting its next use.

**anathema:** Originally a curse, it came to mean the most solemn form of excommunication. It is used in this sense in the Church councils, which, when defining doctrinal points say, "If anyone deny this and such, let him be anathema."

**apocrisarius:** Early term for papal representatives (today called legates and nuncios), but particularly for the pope's envoy to the imperial court at Constantinople.

**apostolic king:** Title granted the kings of Hungary by Sylvester II in 1000 to St. Stephen of Hungary. First used by the Habsburgs in the sixteenth century by Emperor-King Leopold I, it was officially granted to Maria Theresia by Clement XIII in 1758.

**apostolic letters:** A particular kind of document issued by the Roman Curia. One may be *simplex*, written in the pope's name; a *chirographum* (signed by the pope); a *motu proprio*; or an encyclical.

**assistant at the pontifical throne:** One of the group of patriarchs, archbishops, and bishops whom the pope has made an honorary member of the papal chapel. Their place in Church precedence is immediately after that of the cardinals, and are assigned a privileged place around the papal throne during ceremonies. In origin, this body was the papal court when the pope lived at the Lateran Palace. Until changed by Paul VI, each received the title "Count of the Apostolic Palace and Court of the Lateran."

**audience, papal:** A meeting with the pope. Private audiences are granted to individuals of note, but public audiences are given to large groups. The addresses given to such groups are often used by the pope to speak to the larger world.

**auditor:** An official who reports on a case in a Church court to his superior. An auditor of the Rota is a judge in that court.

**basilica, major:** Five large churches in Rome, also called "patriarchal" basilicas, because each has been assigned to the use of one of the five patriarchs: St. John Lateran to the pope, the patriarch of the West; St. Peter's to the patriarch of Constantinople; St. Paul's Outside the Walls, for the patriarch of Antioch; St. Mary Major, for the patriarch of Alexandria; and St. Lawrence Outside the Walls, for the patriarch of Jerusalem. In former centuries, each had an adjoining palace for the use of their respective patriarchs. As a further honor, the Holy Roman emperor and the king of France were titular canons of St. John Lateran, the king of Spain of St. Mary Major, and the king of England was an honorary monk of St. Paul's (which is in the care of the Benedictines)—in return, the abbot there was the chaplain for the Order of the Garter. Today, each of these has a papal altar that may not be used without papal permission. The churches of St. Francis and Our Lady of the Angels at Assisi are also called such and have papal altars and thrones.

**basilica, minor:** A title given to eleven churches in Rome, and a great and expanding number of others throughout the world. They are generally chosen for their historical significance, and boast somewhere within a yellow and red umbrella tokening their status as papal churches. Their clergy have certain rights of precedence.

**beatification:** The process by which inquiry is made into the sanctity of an individual. This proved, permission for his or her public veneration is given, generally on a local basis (that is, to a specific church, diocese, or religious order). This is often the last step before canonization as a saint. After this process, the person (now called a "beatus") is referred to as "The Blessed So-and-so," abbreviated "Bl."

**benediction, apostolic:** A solemn public blessing to which a plenary indulgence is attached, which was given by the popes before 1870 from the balcony of St. John Lateran on Pentecost or Ascension Day; from St. Peter's on the feasts of SS. Peter and Paul, Maundy Thursday, and Easter Sunday;

and from St. Mary Major on the Assumption. Twice a year bishops and other prelates are allowed to give it, and all priests do so for a dying person.

**biblical commission:** The Pontifical Commission for Biblical Studies, founded by Leo XIII in 1902, to look into Scriptural questions. Its findings are not infallible, and may in fact be reversed.

**biblical institute, pontifical:** A college for Scripture students founded by St. Pius X, it is capable of granting degrees.

**Black Nobility:** That portion of the Roman nobility that from 1870 to 1929 refused to accept the seizure of the Papal States by Italy and remained loyal to the pope as their temporal sovereign. Among the principal houses were the Colonna, Orsini, Ruspoli, Saccheti, Lancelotti, Massimo, Aldobrandini, Giustiani-Bandini, and Chigi-Albani. Until 1929 they provided all the members of the Noble Guard; the Lateran Treaty gave them dual citizenship, and they held the hereditary lay postions until most of these and their citizenship were abolished by Paul VI.

**briefs to princes, secretariate of:** A Vatican secretariate founded by Bl. Innocent XI in 1678 to deal with letters to kings and other important folk. Paul VI renamed it the Section for the Relations with States and folded it into the Secretariate of State, where it functions like most nations' foreign ministries.

**canon:** A priest who lives in community with other priests according to one or another form of the rule of St. Augustine. The highest category of these is members of a cathedral chapter of canons. Each are appointed by the bishop with the advice of the rest of the chapter. Their "canonries" include a stall in the cathedral choir (from which they chant the offices of the liturgy of the hours), a voice in the chapter (which helps the bishop administer the diocese), and a share of the chapter revenues (if any) called the "prebend." The chapter may run the diocese during vacancies and some have the right to nominate the next bishop. There are no such chapters in the United States (one skirmish between the American bishops and Leo XIII was that pope's insistence that such be created—in this he was defeated).

Churches in Europe and elsewhere, called "collegiate" churches, also served by chapters of canons, but these have no part in governing the diocese. Their role is purely that of singing the hours in choir, living in community, and fulfilling normal clerical duties at their respective churches. Both cathedral and collegiate canons are referred to as "secular."

Canons "regular" are members of various orders, such as the Norbertines, who also follow the rule of St. Augustine. Like their secular brethren, public recitation or chanting of the hours is key to their work, in addition to the specific vocation of their order (usually either or both education or missionary).

The Anglican and Lutheran state churches that retained bishops after the Reformation usually continue to have cathedral chapters also.

**Catharism:** A generic name for various dualistic sects powerful in Europe for about four centuries, starting at the end of the eleventh. The most notable were the Albigensians in the West and the Bogomils in the East. Claiming either that matter had been created by an evil god equal to the good one, or else a created being who had rebelled, the Cathars believed that procreation was the worst of all sins, for it involved capturing yet another soul in the prison of the flesh—analogous to the Scientologist belief in "Thetans" today. Given modern attitudes, they have been reinvented as heroes in current popular literature and scholarship, even as they were rehabilitated by the "Reformers" of the Protestant revolt.

**chrism:** Olive oil that has been mixed with a little balsam. The balsam represents Christ's Divine nature; mixing it with oil in turn symbolizes His dual being. Chrism is mixed and blessed by each bishop in the Western Church on Maundy Thursday. In the East, each patriarch prepares it for the bishops under him, as a sign of authority. Its recipe is also far more elaborate, often counting as many as fifty other ingredients such as ginger, pepper, rose-water, and wine. Chrism is used in blessing the baptismal font, at Baptism and Confirmation, and the consecration of bishops, bells, churches, altars, patens, and chalices. Although most kings and queens were anointed at their coronations with the oil of catechumens, by special papal permission the kings of France, England, Scotland, Jerusalem, and Sicily received chrism.

**consistory:** An assembly of the cardinals summoned by the pope. At these gatherings, the pope may promulgate new laws, deliver an address (called an "allocution") on some public matter in which he is interested, name new cardinals, present them with their red hats, and announce beatifications and canonizations.

**datary:** An official in charge of examining candidates for offices in the Curia.

**deacon:** The lowest of the three hierarchical orders (the other two are priest and bishop). The creation of the office is recorded in the Acts of the Apostles, where seven were appointed to look after the temporalities of the Church, and to administer charity. In the West, archdeacons came to lead the deaconate in each diocese, and to administer Church property—such tasks being deemed unworthy of the priesthood. Often the archdeacon became quite powerful, as readers of *The Hunchback of Notre Dame* will remember. The Council of Trent reduced the office to a ceremonial or titular one. In the West, the office became almost entirely a stepping-stone to the priesthood, although retaining such duties as singing the Gospel at High Mass, administering communion, and baptizing. Paul VI revived the permanent deaconate. In the East, permanent deacons still act as assistants in many parishes.

**diptychs:** Two tablets connected by a hinge, one side bearing the names of the living for whom the Mass was offered, and on the other the dead. On the side of the living, the names of the pope, patriarch, bishop, emperor,

and any benefactors were found. To remove one of these from the diptychs was the equivalent of excommunication. Although the practice ended in the West in the twelfth century and in the East in the fifteenth, it was the origin of the bidding prayers in the different rites.

**doctor of the Church:** A writer on theological matters, noted for both learning and holiness, whose feast day has been extended to the whole of the Latin Church. Although not as highly regarded as the Church Fathers, their writings are prized far above those of other theologians.

**exorcist:** Formerly the second of the minor orders, this office's duty was to cast out devils, to warn catechumens to depart, and to pour out the water at Mass. As time went on, exorcisms were done exclusively by priests with permission of the bishop, and so the Order of Exorcists became purely a step on the route to priestly ordination.

**Filioque:** Latin for "and the Son," used in the Athanasian Creed and added to the Nicene Creed in the West, to describe the belief that the Holy Spirit proceeds from Christ as well as the Father. Although employed as early as the 300s in the West, it was not disputed at the time by the East. Its addition to the Nicene Creed was one of the things Photius complained about in the seventh century, and disbelief in the "double procession" of the Holy Spirit has become a hallmark of anti-Romanism among the Orthodox. Similarly, pro-Roman circles have adopted the phrase "proceeds from the Father *through* the Son," which formulation has been accepted by various popes, as well as the Council of Florence. Catholics of the Eastern Rites are not obligated to use the phrase, so long as they believe the doctrine. Although it may seem an obscure point, in reality the double procession of the Holy Spirit, as Vladimir Soloviev pointed out, has all sorts of repercussions.

**Gloria in Excelsis Deo:** The angelic hymn used at all solemn Masses. A hymn of praise to the Trinity, it is taken from Luke 14:2, with additions from the Greek. Originally only used at Christmas.

**hypostatic union:** The Greek word *Hypostasis* means person or individual. This union is the union of the two separate natures of God and Man in Christ. It means that although Christ is of one substance with God according to His Divine nature, and with us according to His Human, these two natures are united perfectly in one person—neither diminishing the other. So it is that He has two wills, each perfectly Human or Divine.

**Iconoclasm:** The heresy that teaches that the veneration of images is evil. It was first inflicted on Christendom by an edict of Emperor Leo VI in 726.

**indult:** Permission granted by the pope to deviate from the common law of the Church (although never the moral law) in a given instance—performing certain liturgical ceremonies at sea, for example.

**interdict:** An ecclesiastical punishment that, although less grave than excommunication, and not depriving the person or place so punished of Church

membership, nevertheless deprives them of participation at certain ceremonies or reception of certain sacraments, depending upon the given offense.

**Knights Hospitallers:** A powerful military order of knights, founded in 1092 to defend a pilgrim's hospital dedicated to St. John (hence the name "Knights Hospitallers of St. John of Jerusalem") following a version of the rule of St. Augustine. Following the fall of the Holy Land in 1291, they took over Rhodes in 1309, from whence the Turks expelled them in 1532. Charles V gave them Malta in 1530, from which hold they fought the Barbary pirates until expelled by the French revolutionaries in 1798. As the Sovereign Military Order of Malta, they exist today as an independent nation, albeit with members from all over the world, and no real territorial base. There are also recognized Protestant branches stemming from commanderies that were taken over by local kings at the Reformation.

**Knights Templars:** Founded as the Poor Knights of the Temple in 1118, their headquarters in Jerusalem gave them their name. Like the Hospitallers, they received properties all over Europe to help them fight the Turks in the Holy Land. Suppressed in 1312, the Portuguese and Aragon branches of the Templars survived as the Orders of Christ and Montesa, which still exist.

**Lateran:** Palace in Rome, donated by Constantine to the papacy, and the major residence of the popes for centuries. It gave its name to the neighboring basilica of Our Saviour, which took the title "St. John Lateran."

**lector:** Latin for Reader, formerly the third of the Minor Orders. The position allowed its holder to read the Epistle at Mass and to bless bread and fruit. Since Vatican, laymen have been deputed to serve as lectors. In recent years, lectoresses have become popular as well, and together with altar girls, these ensure a primarily female population in the sanctuary.

**major orders:** Traditionally, the three orders of sub-deacon, deacon, and priest.

**Manicheans:** Doctrine proposed by Mani, a third-century Persian teacher. Dualistic in nature, it taught the usual notion of matter-as-evil, and so forth.

**metropolitan:** The chief bishop of an ecclesiastical province. Although all metropolitans in the West are archbishops, not all archbishops have dioceses subject (or suffragan) to them. In the East, any archbishop may be called a metropolitan, although they often no longer have any suffragan dioceses.

**minor orders:** Traditionally the lower ranks of the clergy through which all who wished to be ordained to the priesthood had to pass.

**Monophysitism:** A heresy first taught by the Archimandrite Eutyches around 448 and condemned by the Council of Chalcedon. Its major tenet was that the Divine nature of Christ absorbed His human nature entirely, leaving him with one nature alone. It became dominant in Syria, Egypt, Armenia, and Ethiopia, although the surviving bodies usually called Monophysite today are no longer.

**Monothelitism:** A seventh-century heresy endorsed by the emperor Zeno in his *Henoticon*, which aimed to reunite the Monophysites with the Church by allowing that Christ has two natures, Human and Divine, but only one will. Pope Honorius was condemned for tolerating it.

**Nestorianism:** A heresy first taught by Archbishop Nestorius of Constantinople in 451, which claimed that there are two persons, Human and Divine, in Christ. Mary, then, would be mother of Christ, but not mother of God.

**oratory:** A small private chapel.

**Origenism:** A series of heresies, taught by followers of Origen, who ascribed them to him (although erroneously). These included the idea that all would be saved eventually (including Satan), that souls exist before conception, and so on.

**pallium:** A band of white wool worn around his shoulders by the pope, representing the fullness of papal power. Similar ones are presented by him to the archbishops to show their participation in his authority and communion with him.

**Patriciate:** The body of Patricians, a rank of nobility peculiar to Rome and certain other Italian cities.

**Pelagianism:** Heresy taught by Pelagius (Latin for Morgan) a Briton priest, about 400. Its basic beliefs are denial of Original Sin, of the necessity of Baptism for Salvation, and the claim that human good will alone is sufficient to be saved. It is extremely widespread today, despite having been condemned as early as 416.

**penitentiary, grand:** cardinal-priest in charge of the Apostolic Penitentiaria, the court of the Church that deals solely with cases in the "internal forum"—that is, with private conscience. Charging no fees and acting in secrecy, its decisions cannot be revealed in public, but are intended solely for the comfort (or otherwise) of the plaintiff.

**porter:** Also called doorkeeper or "ostiarius," it is traditionally the lowest of the minor orders. Charged with opening the door and sanctuary for the priest, as well as the missal, and ringing the bell, it suffered the same decline as the other minor orders.

**priest:** The highest of the major order, the offerer of the Sacrifice of the Mass. The priesthood is of Divine institution, and its fullness is held only by bishops.

**primate:** The chief bishop in a given country, such as the archbishop of Esztergom in Hungary, or formerly, the archbishop of Canterbury in England. Although no longer given any powers under canon law, the title is still attached to certain archdiocese and carries with it many honors.

**protonotary:** Originally a chief notary, originating with the office of notary as ordered by St. Clement I in the first century. Until 1968 there were four

types; in that year, Paul VI reduced them to two. Although today primarily an honorary rank in the Church (the highest monsignors are protonotaries apostolic), the title retains both honor and substance in certain secular court systems—as in Canada, Australia, India, and the states of Pennsylvania, Maryland, Virginia, and Delaware, where this official functions both as clerk of the court and supervisor of the local notaries public.

**rota:** Founded in the thirteenth century and refounded by St. Pius X, the rota is a court of appeal in Rome. It is best known for its work in dealing with annulment cases. Most are quashed by the rota if one party appeals.

**Sacraments:** An outward sign of an inner bestowal of grace by Jesus Christ; the actual means by which we participate in His Divinity and His saving sacrifice. The Catholic and Orthodox churches, as well as the "lesser" churches of the East and the Anglo-Catholics, teach that there are seven: Baptism, Confirmation, Confession, Communion, Matrimony, Ordination, and Extreme Unction, all instituted by Christ Himself. To be valid, a Sacrament must have the right form (i.e., words said); matter (thing used); and intention (to do what the Church means to do by the rite).

**sanctus:** The phrase from Isaias, "Holy, holy, holy Lord, God of Hosts . . ." to which is added the Benedictus from the Gospel of St. Matthew (23:9). It is said by the priest or sung by the choir before the canon of the Mass.

**simony:** The sin of selling ecclesiastical offices or privileges. So called from Simon Magus, who attempted to buy priestly power from the Apostles.

**subdeacon:** Traditionally, in the Western Church, the lowest of the three major orders until the changes by Paul VI. The subdeacon's duties were wholly liturgical—singing the Epistle at Mass, bringing the sacred vessels to the altar, holding the paten during the canon, and giving the kiss of peace to the choir. But ordination to the subdeaconate meant perpetual celibacy. Both the Holy Roman emperor and the king of France had the privilege of acting as subdeacon at papal Masses.

**suffragan:** A diocesan bishop within a province, nominally subject to the metropolitan. Today this relationship is primarily honorary, although the archdiocesan tribunals still function as a court of appeal to those of the suffragan bishops.

**synod:** Originally, any ecclesiastical council, whether ecumenical, national, provincial, or diocesan. Today it is usually restricted to the last named.

**Three Chapters:** Three Nestorian documents by as many writers, condemned in 544 by the emperor Justinian and the Eastern patriarchs in an attempt to reconcile the Monophysites. The bishops of Africa, northern Italy, and Dalmatia objected to this condemnation on the grounds that although parts of the Chapters were heretical, their condemnation would have the effect of weakening the Council of Chalcedon. In 554 Pope Vigilius was at last pushed into condemning them by the emperor, while

confirming Chalcedon, but the resulting schism was not snuffed out until 700. The entire thing was not a question of Faith but of political expedience.

**Viaticum:** Holy Communion given to those in danger of death; often given just before the Last Anointing.

# *Bibliography*

Although the listing of the following books does not imply approval of all opinions they contain, they all were extremely helpful in preparing this book.


Attwater, Donald. *A Catholic Dictionary.* New York: Macmillan, 1958.

Bogle, Joanna and James. *A Heart for Europe.* Leominster, Herefordshire: Gracewing, 1999.

Bunson, Matthew. *The Pope Encyclopedia: An A to Z of the Holy See.* New York: Crown, 1995.

Butler, Rev. Alban. *The Lives of the Saints.* 2 vols. Sarto Books, 1982.

Cabrol, Rt. Rev. Fernand, O.S.B. *Liturgical Prayer: Its History and Spirit.* London: Burns, Oates, and Washbourne, 1922.

*Catholic Encyclopedia, The.* 15 vols., 3 supplementary vols. New York: Robert Appleton, 1907–12.

Chamberlin, E. R. *The Bad Popes.* New York: Barnes and Noble, 1989.

Clayton, Joseph. *Pope Innocent III and His Times.* Milwaukee: Bruce Publishing, 1941.

Corvo, Frederick Baron. *A History of the Borgias.* New York: Carlton House.

Denzinger, Henry. *Enchiridion Symbolorum, The Sources of Catholic Dogma.* St. Louis: B. Herder Book Co., 1957.

Duffy, Eamon. *Saints and Sinners: A History of the Popes.* New Haven: Yale University Press, 1997.

*Encyclopaedia Britannica, The.* Eleventh Edition, 29 volumes. Cambridge and New York, 1910.

*Encyclopaedia Britannica, The.* Fifteenth Edition, 30 volumes. Chicago, 1980.

Fiedler, Maureen and Rabben, Linda, editors. *Rome Has Spoken.* New York: Crossroad Publishing, 1998.

Gueranger, Abbot Prosper, O.S.B. *The Liturgical Year.* 14 volumes. Fitzwilliam, N.H.: Loreto Publications, 2000.

Hardon, John A., S.J. *Modern Catholic Dictionary.* Garden City, N.Y.: Doubleday, 1980.

Holweck, Rt. Rev. F. G. *A Biographical Dictionary of the Saints.* St. Louis and London: B. Herder, 1924.

*Holy Bible.* New York: P. J. Kennedy and Sons, 1914.

Katrij, Rev. Julian J., O.S.B.M. *A Byzantine Rite Liturgical Year.* Toronto and New York: Basilian Fathers Publications, 1992.

Luff, S.G.A. *The Christian's Guide to Rome.* Royal Tunbridge Wells, Kent: Burns and Oates, 1990.

Menczer, Bela. *Catholic Political Thought 1789–1848.* Westminster, Md.: The Newman Press, 1952.

Mourret, Rev. Fernand, S.S. *A History of the Catholic Church.* 8 vols. St. Louis and London: B. Herder, 1931.

*New Catholic Encyclopedia.* 5 vols. New York: McGraw-Hill, 1967.

Nicholas, Aidan, O.P. *Christendom Awake.* Grand Rapids, Mich.: William B. Eerdmans Publishing, 1999.

Noonan, James-Charles, Jr. *The Church Visible: The Ceremonial Life and Protocol of the Roman Catholic Church.* New York: Viking, 1996.

Packard, Jerrold M. *Peter's Kingdom: Inside the Papal City.* New York: Charles Scribner's Sons, 1985.

Parsons, Rev. Reuben. *Studies in Church History.* 6 vols. New York and Cincinnati: Fr. Pustet and Co., 1901.

Poulet, Dom Charles, O.S.B. *A History of the Catholic Church.* 2 vols. St. Louis and London: B. Herder, 1934.

Soloviev, Vladimir. *Russia and the Universal Church.* New York: Soloviev Foundation, 1992.

Summers, Rev. Montague. *The History of Witchcraft and Demonology.* New Hyde Park, N.Y.: University Books, 1956.

Walsh, Michael. *Dictionary of Catholic Devotions.* San Francisco: Harper San Francisco, 1993.

Walsh, William S. *Curiosities of Popular Customs.* Philadelphia: J. B. Lippincott, 1914.

# *Index*